HOT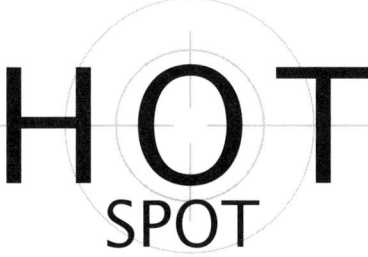
SPOT

LATIN AMERICA

HOT SPOT
SPOT

LATIN AMERICA

David W. Dent

Hot Spot Histories

GREENWOOD PRESS
Westport, Connecticut • London

Library of Congress Cataloging-in-Publication Data

Dent, David W.
  Hot spot. Latin America / David W. Dent.
     p. cm. — (Hot spot histories)
  Includes bibliographical references and index.
  ISBN-13: 978-0-313-33661-4 (alk. paper)
  1. Hot spots (Political science)—Latin America. 2. Latin America—Politics and government. I. Title. II. Title: Latin America.
  F1410.D46 2008
  980.04—dc22   2007039198

British Library Cataloguing in Publication Data is available.

Copyright © 2008 by David W. Dent

All rights reserved. No portion of this book may be reproduced, by any process or technique, without the express written consent of the publisher.

Library of Congress Catalog Card Number: 2007039198
ISBN-13: 978-0-313-33661-4
ISSN: 1934-631X

First published in 2008

Greenwood Press, 88 Post Road West, Westport, CT 06881
An imprint of Greenwood Publishing Group, Inc.
www.greenwood.com

Printed in the United States of America

The paper used in this book complies with the
Permanent Paper Standard issued by the National
Information Standards Organization (Z39.48-1984).

10 9 8 7 6 5 4 3 2 1

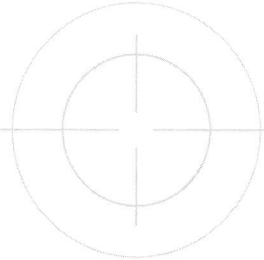

Contents

Preface — vii
Timeline — xi

Introduction: The Meaning of Hot Spot Terminology — 1

Chapter 1: Mexico — 55
   Border Crime and Drug Wars — 60
   Governance and Corruption — 64
   Guerrilla Conflict in Guerrero — 67
   Immigration — 68
   Oaxaca Protest Movement — 74
   Zapatista Rebellion in Chiapas — 76

Chapter 2: Central America — 81
   Darién Gap Controversy — 83
   Drug Wars, Youth Gangs, and Terrorism — 85
   Governance and Corruption — 90
   Panama's Canal: Is the Waterway at Risk? — 92
   Poverty and Human Development — 97

Chapter 3: Andean South America — 101
   Bolivia's *Salida al Mar* Controversy — 104

Border Conflicts and Ungoverned Spaces ... 106
Colombia's Civil War ... 108
Drug Wars and Terrorism ... 112
Governance and Corruption ... 116
Magdalena Medio (Colombia) ... 122
Morales and the Multinationals ... 122
PetroPolitics and Pipeline Wars ... 129
Shining Path and Tupac Amaru Movements ... 135
Venezuela: Chávez's Bolivarian Revolution ... 138

Chapter 4: The Southern Cone and Brazil ... 157

Amazon Powder Keg ... 159
Beagle Channel Dispute ... 161
Falklands/Malvinas Fracas ... 162
Governance and Corruption ... 165
Mapuche Power? ... 170
Tri-Border Area Terrorism ... 172

Chapter 5: The Caribbean: Cuba and Haiti ... 177

Cuba's Long-Distance Civil War ... 178
Drug Trafficking and Terrorism ... 185
Governance: Political Instability and Corruption ... 187
Guantánamo Bay: Is the U.S. Naval Base at Risk? ... 187
Haiti as a Failed State ... 191

Chapter 6: Non-Iberian South America: ... 195
Guyana and Suriname

Border Conflicts ... 196
Governance: Political Instability and Corruption ... 197
Caribbean–South American Terrorism ... 198

Chapter 7: Conclusion ... 201

Notes ... 207
Select Bibliography ... 235
Index ... 253

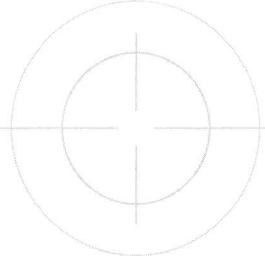

Preface

This volume in the series *Hot Spot Histories* focuses on Mexico, Central America, South America, and the Caribbean. It is designed to serve as a background guide for understanding current regional and global conflicts. It contains information from the current debate over potential security threats that have become part of the global war on terrorism that deals with security challenges in the wake of the terrorist attacks on New York City and Washington, D.C., on September 11, 2001. Although U.S. media attention to Latin America declined precipitously after it was discovered that none of the skyjackers were from Latin America and none crossed the border from Mexico to execute their plot, only a few Latin American hot spots—most of which have been in existence for decades—have achieved the level of security concern that has contributed to U.S. military intervention in Afghanistan, Iraq, and Iran. The U.S. intelligence and diplomatic community continue to target Colombia and Peru, both with decades-old insurgencies associated with drug trafficking and arms smuggling; however, there are many other conflicts that have the potential to affect security in the region. The rise to power of President Hugo Chávez in Venezuela has raised a variety of security concerns in Washington, particularly energy and weapons.

The United States considers Colombia a major Latin American hot spot because of a long-time armed conflict between the Colombian government and leftist guerrillas and right-wing paramilitaries. It is also one of the key areas in South America where U.S. authorities, and private military contractors, work with the government to control ungoverned spaces along the Colombia-Ecuador-Peru borders. Under Plan Colombia, the U.S.-backed war on leftist guerrillas and drug cartels has cost the United States $4–5 billion since 2000. Several of the hot spots, or trouble spots, in Latin America are designated as such as part of an effort to demonize leaders who oppose the Latin American policy of the United States and the way it goes about promoting democracy and freedom. This would include Fidel Castro, Evo Morales, Hugo Chávez, Daniel Ortega, and Rafael Correa, leaders who offer little in the way of security threats to the United States.

This reference book contains a detailed introduction devoted to hot spot terminology and six chapters divided by geographical region: Mexico, Central America, Andean South America, the Southern Cone and Brazil, the Caribbean (Cuba and Haiti), and non-Iberian South America including Guyana and Suriname. Within each of these geographical regions of Latin America a series of security-based hot spots are analyzed. Overall, thirty-five hot spots are included in this book. No attempt was made to measure them in terms of hot spot severity (or "temperature"); however, each one of the hot spots studied clearly varies in its background and the degree of threat to the United States, the nation itself, or its regional neighbors. After close examination of how hot spot threats are defined by government officials, it is obvious from the documentation in this study that many hot spots do not amount to security threats at all but are often treated as such for domestic political reasons. Despite Latin America's history of U.S. intervention, guerrilla insurgencies, revolutions, and economic difficulties, there are fewer terrorist incidents in the Latin American and Caribbean region than in other world regions, particularly South Asia and the Middle East. The Cold War prism through which the United States viewed the world for over 40 years has been replaced by a new prism, one that is far broader in defining security threats in the more globalized world of the twentieth century. Terrorism is now the shibboleth instead of Communism and radical revolutions with links to Cuba, China, or the Soviet Union.

In my effort to understand hot spot terminology, I found a number of basic flaws in the U.S. policymaking process and the way in which propaganda helps to start and continue foreign policies devoted to dealing with security-based hot spots. Although national security and crisis decision making are often not well understood by either the American public or the mainstream media, it becomes increasingly clear in an age of global communication that core challenges of the twenty-first century must not be left to partisan ideologues who feel they know what's best, often ignoring the Constitution, belittling international law in pursuit of some higher value or goal, or paying scant attention to history and culture. If this volume—and others that make up the series—provides a better understanding of hot spot terminology and regional and global conflicts, it will have achieved its primary purpose at a time when security threats are inflated for personal or domestic political gain.

Preface

The richness and accuracy of this volume would not have been possible without the assistance of Charles F. Andrain, Thomas W. Mullen, and Larman Wilson. They provided valuable assistance with editing, hard-to-find documents, and critical commentary. The journey toward a better understanding of hot spots in Latin America and the Caribbean would not have been possible without their insights and commitment to accuracy.

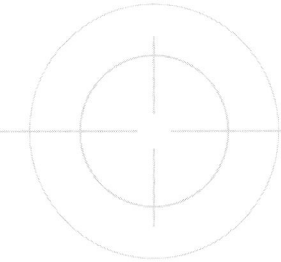

Timeline

1879–1884	Bolivia becomes landlocked after losing its mineral-rich, coastal territory to Chile in the War of the Pacific.
1899–1903	Colombian civil war between Liberals and Conservatives contributes to the loss of 120,000 people in what came to be known as the War of the Thousand Days.
1932–1935	Bolivia loses territory to Paraguay in the Chaco War.
1946	Juan D. Perón wins elections for the presidency of Argentina; his wife, Eva Perón, is put in charge of labor relations.
1948	Period of violence kills 250,000–300,000 in Colombian civil war between Liberals and Conservatives.
1952	Bolivian revolution brings social and economic reforms, including universal suffrage, nationalization of tin mines, land redistribution, and improvements in education and the status of indigenous peoples.
1953	Cuban revolution begins with Fidel Castro's failed attack on the Moncada Army Barracks in Santiago, Cuba on July 26, 1953.
1955	Argentina's President Perón is overthrown by the military, sending him into exile. Political instability follows for decades.

1959	Cuban rebels succeed in overthrowing dictator Fulgencio Batista. Castro gradually takes the helm and years later aligns Cuba with the Soviet Union as leverage against the United States.
1961, April	CIA-backed invasion of Cuba to remove Fidel Castro fails, producing one of the major foreign policy fiascos of the Cold War.
1965	National Liberation Army (ELN) and Maoist People's Liberation Army (EPL) in Colombia founded.
1966	Revolutionary Armed Forces of Colombia (FARC) is founded, later to be Colombia's largest guerrilla group.
1967	Ché Guevara is captured and executed in Bolivia for trying to lead a peasant uprising against the government. U.S. government is involved in the hunt, capture, and death of the Argentine-Cuban revolutionary.
1971	Colombian left-wing M-19 guerrilla group is formed.
1973	Juan D. Perón returns to Argentina from exile in Spain to become president for second time.
1973	Venezuela benefits from oil boom; oil and steel industries are nationalized.
1974	Argentina's President Perón dies and is succeeded by his wife, Isabel.
1976	Argentina's armed forces overthrow government and install Jorge Videla as president. Military suppresses left-wing opposition groups, and over the next six years between 6,000 and 15,000 people "disappeared" in the "dirty war" that followed the coup.
1978	Colombian president Julio Turbay begins battle against drug traffickers.
1979	Sandinista revolution in Nicaragua succeeds in removing Anastasio Somoza from power, ending more than three decades of dictatorial rule.
1980	Contra war begins as counter-revolutionaries begin secret attacks against Nicaragua from neighboring Honduras.
1981	Reagan administration initiates U.S. support for the Contras.

1982	Falkland Islands/Islas Malvinas war between Argentina and Great Britain. Argentina is defeated by the British, helping to put an end to military rule.
1983	Argentina returns to civilian rule, begins process of investigating military officials who carried out the "dirty war."
1983	U.S. invades Grenada to protect U.S. citizens, restore order, and divert media attention from foreign policy failures in the Middle East.
1986	Colombian right-wing paramilitary groups begin murder campaign against Patriotic Union Party (UP) politicians.
1986	Over 20,000 Bolivian miners lose their jobs following the collapse of the tin market.
1989	Carlos Andrés Pérez (AD) is elected president of Venezuela; economic depression necessitates an austerity program and IMF loan that lead to social and political upheaval.
1989	U.S. military aid/advising for drug eradication expands in Colombia, Bolivia, and Peru.
1989	U.S. invades Panama to capture and arrest General Manuel Antonio Noriega, once a staunch ally of the United States.
1990	Full diplomatic relations are restored between Argentina and the United Kingdom; Britain retains sovereignty over Falklands Islands.
1990	Some 4 million acres of Bolivian rain forest are allocated to indigenous communities.
1990	Full diplomatic relations with UK are restored, although Argentina continues to claim the Falklands/Malvinas Islands.
1992	Two attempted coups—first led by future-president Colonel Hugo Chávez, and the second by his supporters—in Venezuela contribute to the deaths of 120 people. Chávez is jailed for two years before being pardoned.
1993	Pablo Escobar, Medellín drug-cartel leader, is killed while trying to evade arrest.
1994	Zapatista rebellion begins in the Mexican State of Chiapas.
1998	Hugo Chávez is elected president of Venezuela.

1998	Colombian president Andrés Pastrana begins peace talks with guerrillas. To advance peace talks, Pastrana grants guerrillas a safe haven the size of Switzerland.
1999	Plan Colombia is established to end drug trafficking and defeat guerrilla movements.
2000	Plan Colombia provides almost $1 billion in U.S. military aid to fight drug trafficking and guerrillas who profit from and protect the trade.
2000	Venezuelan President Hugo Chávez becomes the first foreign head of state to visit Saddam Hussein since 1991 Gulf War.
2001, September 11	Terrorist attacks on New York and Washington, D.C., change focus of U.S. foreign policy to deal with elimination of terrorist threats, including pre-emptive strikes if necessary, with or without the support of the international community.
2001	Bolivian farmers reject a government offer of $900 each a year in exchange for the eradication of coca.
2001–2002	Peace talks in Colombia fail after two years of tortuous efforts to bring peace.
2002	Independent candidate Álvaro Uribe wins Colombian presidency promising to crack down on rebel groups.
2002	Venezuelan military removes President Chávez from power, claiming he had resigned; Chávez returns two days later after the collapse of interim government led by Pedro Carmona.
2002	Former president Jimmy Carter visits Havana and calls for more openness in Cuban society and a change in U.S. policy.
2003	Protests in Bolivia, triggered by government plans to export natural gas via Chile, result in 80 deaths and hundreds of injured. President Sánchez de Lozada resigns and is succeeded by Carlos Mesa.
2003	Colombian right-wing paramilitary groups begin to disarm; peace talks begin and continue into 2005.
2004	Energy protests in Bolivia continue as protesters demand greater state involvement in the gas industry.
2004	Venezuelan President Hugo Chávez wins referendum with 59 percent of vote.

Timeline

2005	Press reports in Cuba and Argentina reveal that 400–500 U.S. troops landed in Paraguay to set up a military base in order to monitor gas deposits in Southern Bolivia and the Tri-Border Area (TBA). U.S. embassies in the region deny any plans to establish a military base.
2005	President Chávez begins land reform program to assist rural poor.
2005	Venezuela and 13 Caribbean states launch Petro-Caribe, a cooperative agreement in which cheap oil is exchanged for increases in diplomatic influence.
2005	Bolivia experiences large-scale antigovernment protests and blockades over rising fuel prices.
2005	Bolivians elect socialist leader Evo Morales, the first indigenous Bolivian to win the presidency.
2006	Elections in Chile, Ecuador, and Peru bring more center-left presidents to South America.
2006	Colombian President Uribe wins a second term.
2006, July	Felipe Calderón elected president of Mexico, shifting the political process to the right. Losing candidate López Obrador contests the results for the next two months.
2006, August	Fidel Castro hospitalized for intestinal disorder with contrasting responses in Washington, Havana, and Miami; Raúl Castro takes the helm while his brother begins a long recovery and more operations that last into 2007.
2006, November	Daniel Ortega elected president of Nicaragua despite U.S. efforts to thwart his candidacy.
2006, November	Conflict continues in Oaxaca over efforts by indigenous groups to oust the PRI governor of the state.
2006, December	Hugo Chávez re-elected president of Venezuela.
2006, December	Former Chilean dictator Augusto Pinochet dies at age 91 after suffering a heart attack. Because of age and infirmity he never had to face criminal charges pending against him.
2007, January	President Chávez inaugurated with promises to bring more socialism to Venezuela through less press freedom and pledges to nationalize companies in telecommunications and electricity industries; increases his anti-American rhetoric.

2007	Fidel Castro recovers from illness, brother Raúl Castro vows to continue with his brother's achievements.
2007	Ecuadoran president Rafael Correa says he will not renew the lease on the U.S. base on the coastal town of Manta when it expires in 2009.
2007	Petroleum analysts worry that Hugo Chávez poses a much greater threat to America's energy than once believed.
2007, February	President Bush asks Congress to extend Plan Colombia for another five years with 76 percent of the funding ($446 million per year) going to military and police aid.
2007, May	President Chávez shuts down Radio Caracas Televisión (RCTV) by refusing to renew its license. The crackdown is seen as a threat in Washington and parts of Latin America.
2007, May	Violent protests against Peru's coca eradication program lead to government vows to increase force to prevent a Colombia-style marriage between drug trafficking and guerrillas. Signs of a Shining Path guerrilla revival are noted by U.S. authorities.
2007, June	Attack plot by individuals with connections to Guyana and Trinidad on John F. Kennedy airport in New York City is foiled by U.S. authorities. Plotters had links to Jamaat al-Muslimeen (JAM), a Sunni group in Trinidad with connections in Guyana and Iran.
2007, June	U.S. federal appeals court rejects President Bush's use of "unlawful enemy combatants," a term designed to allow suspected terrorists—whether captured abroad or in the United States—to be held indefinitely in military detention.
2007, August	Former Panamanian dictator and CIA asset Manuel Antonio Noriega becomes eligible for release from prison in Miami, but a U.S. federal judge rejects his request to return to Panama. Judge's decision paves the way for the ex-general to face money laundering charges in France.
2007, August	Rise of hot spot posts abroad makes it difficult for the U.S. Department of State to recruit people to serve in Colombia, Haiti, Peru, and Venezuela.

INTRODUCTION

The Meaning of Hot Spot Terminology

We must redouble efforts to remove every possible trouble spot which might draw us into conflict. . . . We must not have anymore Vietnams.

President Richard M. Nixon's handwritten notes at the close of a May 1972 summit meeting with Soviet premier Leonid Brezhnev. Quoted in Tim Weiner, "Quagmire Fatigue: Cozying Up to the Enemy's Friend, In Hope of Ending a Frustrating War."

New York Times (December 24, 2006)

The Soviet Union underlies all the unrest that is going on. If they weren't engaged in this game of dominoes, there wouldn't be any hotspots in the world.

Ronald W. Reagan during the 1980 presidential campaign

Hot spot terminology reflects a particular kind of threat perception based on the certainty that sources of conflict within states have the potential to flare up and, in doing so, become a much more serious threat or crisis that requires some kind of international involvement or intervention, usually military. Hot spots are usually considered a threat to national security because they have the capacity to "breed," spreading the danger regionally and globally. In remarks at the North-South Center in 2003, the head of the Southern Command, General James Hill, remarked that the terrorist threat in Latin America is often "a weed that is planted in the fertile ground of ungoverned spaces such as coast lines, rivers, and unpopulated border areas." The danger or threat, according to Hill, occurs when the "weed" is watered with money from drugs, illegal arms sales, and human trafficking, and it spreads, domino fashion, without respect for either geographical or moral boundaries.[1] Hot spots, or international trouble spots, also have the power to draw imperial powers such as the United States into strategic blunders or quagmires such as Cuba, Vietnam, Chile, Nicaragua, El Salvador, Panama, and Iraq. Part of this decision-making process can be the result of faulty intelligence, distorted perceptions of security threats, and the tendency of policymakers to rely on information that supports what they already know (often quite limited) about an existing hot spot. It is somewhat of a fantasy for American presidents to believe, as President Nixon's thinking reveals, that if "every possible trouble spot" could be eliminated, then the United States would not have any more Vietnams and peace, stability, and global respect would follow.

Believing he could carry out a low-cost conventional war against the Soviets, President Reagan called for aid to all anti-Communist insurgents fighting Soviet-backed Marxist regimes in Asia, Africa, and Latin America. President Reagan's Latin American policy eventually led to the Iran-Contra scandal and a negative ruling by the International Court of Justice.[2] The remarkable parallels between Presidents Nixon and Reagan, shown by the quotations at the beginning of this chapter, suggest that hot spot terminology is a major part of the rhetoric of threat assessment in the United States. The history of the United States' recognition of hot spots shows that many of Washington's foreign policies in the past 50 years are rooted in a misunderstanding of Third World countries, leaders, and cultural values. When misplaced analogies and flawed metaphors are used by the intelligence and national security communities to eliminate hot spots, in the name of national security and regional hegemony, foreign policy mistakes and military quagmires are a likely consequence. The media also play an important role in threat inflation, often acting as an enabler of government ambitions. According to Edward S. Herman, "Critical analyses of the reality of the 'threat' are [often] minimal, and the gullibility quotient of the media escalates in view of the alleged seriousness of the threat and need for everybody to be 'on the team.'"[3] Another feature of the threat inflation process is the tendency of the media to deny that the United States poses any threat to any imminent victim other than the specific target of intervention, occupation, or regime change. For example, the media ignored the fact that the United States posed a threat to the Panamanian people as a whole rather than to the Noriega regime only. There is also a "blowback" factor when unintended consequences from foreign policies create security threats because the American public is often ignorant of, or kept in the dark, concerning what the United States actually does abroad.⁴

The use of hot spot terminology has contributed to different interpretations of what constitutes a security threat and a new rationale for expanding the role of the region's security forces, including increased U.S. military/police aid to Latin American governments and secret intelligence operations aimed at finding terrorist cells in the region. However, Latin American governments involved in public security and police reform in the aftermath of recent democratization efforts have found that Latin American citizens are demanding "strong-man" rule after surges in violent crime, believing that this type of leadership will offer them more security than democratic pluralism.⁵ For political leaders concerned with public security, hot spot metaphors can serve as an important tool of political communication and persuasion, particularly when the party in power is inclined to use confrontation or force to deal with pending threats.⁶ It is important to keep in mind that the use of "national security" in defining threats may have less to do with the nation as a whole than with Washington officials and corporate interests with ties to those who control the levers of political power. This may also explain why security-based hot spots are of greater interest to public officials who worry about the decline in U.S. influence when elections produce a decisive shift to the left in Latin America. Despite the opposition to Venezuelan President Hugo Chávez by the Bush administration and the mainstream media, and despite Chávez's inflammatory rhetoric, the American public may be sympathetic to the social-welfare aspirations contained in his "Bolivarian Revolution," particularly improvements in health care and education, food and fuel subsidies, low-interest loans for small businesses, and the conversion of massive ranches and sugar plantations into worker-owned cooperatives.⁷ However, if these government-based initiatives are identified as socialism, or the targeted leaders are demonized because of their allies or alleged psychological defects, the level of support often drops because of the way political ideologies influence political beliefs and behavior in the United States.

With the loss of U.S. military bases in Panama beginning in the 1990s, the United States has created a network of smaller bases spread throughout the Western Hemisphere (discussed later in the section "The United States as a Hegemonic State"). These often work in tandem with the armed forces of Latin American countries, although this requires that the host government receive a waiver to the American Service-members' Protection Act (ASPA) if it has signed the Rome Statute, which established the International Criminal Court (ICC), under which U.S. troops could be prosecuted on charges arising from joint operations. The Washington Office on Latin America (WOLA), which has followed recent trends in U.S. military programs with Latin America, in its reports expresses concern about the tendency of the U.S. government to see "emerging" threats—gangs, drugs, epidemics, organized crime, illegal immigration, and natural disasters—as solely the responsibility of U.S. and Latin American militaries. In fact, the so-called "emerging threats" may be the result of the lack of institutional trust, corruption, and gross social and economic inequalities and other factors that rarely lend themselves to military/police solutions. The gap in military-to-military relations caused by the passage of ASPA was followed by Chinese military advances in Latin America; over time the anxieties caused by China's growing military influence in Latin America and the Caribbean led the Bush administration to issue waivers in order to *rebuild* military alliances and strengthen its influence in the Western Hemisphere.

In a speech at Georgetown University in January 2006, Secretary of State Condoleezza Rice announced a major overhaul of the diplomatic corps that would shift hundreds of Foreign Service positions to dangerous areas (hot spots) of the world where the United States is battling transnational threats of terrorism, crime, drug trafficking, and diseases.[8] By increasing America's engagement and dialogue with the world, Rice hopes to use "transformational diplomacy" as a more active way of promoting the growth of democratic states worldwide. According to Secretary Rice, the "greatest threats" are located within states rather than between them, and this represents a new form of threat-based thinking designed to put more diplomats in the Middle East and Asia and fewer in Europe and Latin America. According to foreign-policy elites in Washington, the best antidote for emerging hot spots is democracy and pro-market reforms; however, the tendency to ignore the competing and often antagonistic definitions of these concepts can render them useless as a guide to American foreign policy.

A tendency to ignore the transnational dimensions of terrorism by putting less emphasis on Latin America would be unfortunate, since Hezbollah and other terrorist organizations have roots in the Arab Muslim communities in South America and serve as a fund raising and recruitment organization with links to Lebanon and Iran (see Chapters 4 and 6). Moreover, Hezbollah's success in Lebanon in 2006 and the conflict in Iraq have contributed to the ideological alignment between the Latin American left and radical Islam based on anti-imperialism, racism, and opposition to U.S. hegemony around the globe. Spain's socialist Prime Minister José Luis Rodríguez Zapatero and Venezuela's President Chávez have both reached out to Muslims and have good relations with Iran's mercurial leader Mahmoud Ahmadinejad. Where Latin American leftists meet

Islamic radicals—Venezuela, Cuba, Ecuador, Bolivia, and elsewhere—Washington finds itself the victim of new anti-American coalitions.[9]

Threat Perception inside the Executive Branch of Government

Inside the White House threat perceptions are based on information gathered by the National Intelligence Office, the Central Intelligence Agency (CIA), and other agencies within the executive office of the president. Threat-based information is then communicated to the vice president and president on a daily basis. In a January 2005 face-to-face interview on "Imus in the Morning," Vice President Dick Cheney described how the process of security briefings and threat assessments were carried out in the executive branch of government.[10] Every day at 7 a.m. at home the vice president would meet with a briefer from the CIA, who hand-delivered a copy of the President's Daily Brief, or PDB. This would include a top secret, 10- to 12-page document with what the CIA considered the most important national security information from the previous day, including terrorist threats against the United States. One hour later the vice president would meet in the Oval Office with the president, who would have seen his own copy of the same brief, presented by another briefer and the director of central intelligence. Later, the vice president would sit in on a briefing from the FBI director about domestic threats. After that, "it's whatever's hot," according to Cheney, and often these threat-based discussions would take place within a National Security Council meeting with other members of the intelligence and policy-planning elite.[11] From this point on in the decision-making process, the president might issue a National Security Presidential Directive (NSPD) setting forth a target and rationale for dealing with a particular hot spot, a general foreign policy review, or some aspect of existing government operations. During his first term in office, President George W. Bush issued four NSPDs aimed at Latin America: NSPD 18, "Supporting Democracy in Colombia,"; NSPD 25 (which "directs U.S. government agencies to attack the vulnerabilities of drug trafficking organizations"); NSPD 29, "Transition to Democracy in Cuba"; and NSPD 32, "Latin American Policy."[12] The use of the PDB does not preclude the White House from formulating its communications so as to make sure that the president's views are supported regardless of the accuracy of the intelligence provided to the president and vice president. The information sharing that goes on within the National Intelligence Office is designed to encourage divergent views in order to avoid the "groupthink" blamed for past policy mistakes that led to the terrorist attacks of 9/11 and the invasion and occupation of Iraq in 2003. In May 2007 President Bush appointed Lt. General Douglas Lute to a new position designed to oversee the fighting in Iraq and Afghanistan as a war czar. It is too early to tell whether Bush's new war coordinator will help in spotting and dealing with hot spots around the globe.

One of the hubs within the new office is the National Counterterrorism Center, where analysts write reports on terrorist threats to the United States and then pass them on to the director. The director of National Intelligence (the head of the National Intelligence Office) is also required to brief the president each morning while at the same time overseeing the disparate agencies involved in the complex bureaucratic intelligence process.[13] Since Vice President Cheney's previously cited interview, the task of briefing the president and vice president on intelligence matters has now become the responsibility of the director of National Intelligence—not the director of Central Intelligence, the head of the CIA. This means that the Central Intelligence Agency is no longer relied on to produce the strategic intelligence—the power to know the United States' enemies' intentions—for which it was famous during the Cold War. The national security system is now dominated by the Pentagon and the National Intelligence Office, while the CIA is left with only small pieces of the bureaucratic intelligence puzzle on which Washington policymakers must depend to respond to security threats. In many ways this does not augur well for the strategic intelligence needed to protect the security interests of the United States. President Bush's national security adviser, Stephen Hadley, is also responsible for monitoring hot spots around the world, although little is known about the specific methodology for locating and responding to these security threats.

The use of threat-based hot spot terminology is often clouded by the diverse and sometimes loose meanings of the term used by U.S. government officials, advertisers, and the media to refer to a wide range of areas that have attracted special concern. Depending on who is speaking, a hot spot may be a fabulous surfing beach, a restaurant, an area in danger of ecological extinction, a popular nightclub, an upwelling of volcanic magma, or a bargain travel spot that is rapidly attracting large numbers of international visitors. For purposes of this study, hot spots are security threats (not physical locations) within nations that carry the potential to jeopardize the vital interests—regional stability, economic expansion, military cooperation and security, homeland security, hegemony, and access to raw materials—of the United States and the other states of the Western Hemisphere.

In a special issue of *The Defense Monitor*, "World at War," the Center for Defense Information (CDI) examined 15 ongoing significant conflicts (1,000 or more deaths) and another 23 "hot spots"—conflicts that have the capacity to "slide into or revert to war."[14] The CDI report examined only three hot spots in Latin America: two armed conflicts in Colombia and a low-level conflict in Peru between the government and the Sendero Luminoso. As of 2007, there were no government-versus-government armed hostilities in the world, including Latin America. Hot spots often form a "watch list" in the Pentagon because they involve the potential for becoming an armed conflict. There is still considerable potential for major conflict in Latin America—particularly in the Andean region and Amazon Basin—but there are far fewer wars and insurgencies today than was the case in Latin America in the 1980s (see Table I.1). The Andean region is arguably the most politically volatile area in the Western Hemisphere, plagued with pandemic violence, weak political parties, strong-man governments, drug trafficking, and networks of criminal and terrorist organizations. In any case, according to the CDI report, Latin America is one of the least conflictive regions of the world in the first decade of the twenty-first century, with far fewer hot spots than are found in Africa, Asia, and the Middle East. Is this observation the result of more sophisticated methods of conflict resolution, the role of inter-American organizations devoted to peace, or the way in which hot spots are defined and treated in Latin America?

The problems facing Latin America today are complex, multifaceted, and overwhelmingly the result of underlying economic and social inequities, particularly poverty and the unequal distribution of wealth and social services. In many cases the problems that some refer to as threat-based hot spots are aggravated by poor governance—corruption, inefficiency, poor leadership, perverted social priorities—issues chronically unresponsive to popular grievances. One of the priorities of the World Bank is to finance anticorruption programs through the promotion of good governance, freedom of the press, and administrative transparency. In Latin America the most corrupt institutions are political parties, legislatures, and police and court systems. In virtually all the cases of interrupted presidencies in Latin America over the past several decades, widespread allegations of corruption have existed. This pattern of institutional weakness often coincides with the emergence of failed states and trouble spots that concern those in the national security bureaucracy. The flaws in the use of security-based hot spot terminology will be examined throughout this book in an effort to understand how governments can best respond to emerging threats, existing conflicts, and their peaceful resolution.

The current use of security-based hot spot terminology often serves as a tool for arousing interest, stimulating concern or fear, and selling a particular foreign policy, even if the security threat is inaccurately perceived or grossly exaggerated. In *Overblown*, John Mueller finds that there is a tradition in American history of overreaction to overblown domestic and international threats.[15] Every American president since Franklin D. Roosevelt has used carefully crafted rhetoric to justify a variety of responses to objective or subjective threats to national security.

Table I.1 Armed Conflicts in Latin America, 1959–2005

Country	Reason for Conflict	Opposition Organization	Year of Conflict	Intensity Level of Conflict
Argentina	Government	Military faction	1963	Minor
			1973–1974	Minor
			1975	Internal war
			1976–1977	Intermediate
Argentina–UK	Territory	Malvinas-Falkland Islands	1982	External war
Bolivia	Government	ELN (National Liberation Army)	1967	Minor
		MAS (Movement Toward Socialism)	2003	Minor
			2005	Minor
Chile	Government	Military faction	1973	Intermediate
Colombia	Government	FARC; ELN; EPL; M-19; AUC	1965–1979	Minor
			1980–1988	Intermediate
			1989–1990	Internal war
			1991	Intermediate
			1992–1993	Internal war
			1994–1997	Intermediate
			1998–2001	Internal war
Cuba	Government	M-26-7	1958–1959	Internal war
Dominican Republic	Government	Military faction	1965	Minor
Ecuador-Peru	Territory	Armed combat	1995	Minor
El Salvador	Government	Military faction	1972	Minor
		ERP; FMLN; PRTC	1979–1980	Minor
			1981–1990	Internal war
			1991	Intermediate
El Salvador–Honduras	Territory	Armed combat	1969	Internal war
Guatemala	Government	MR-13; FAR; EGP; PGT; ORPA	1965–1967	Minor
			1968	Intermediate
			1969–1987	Internal war
			1988–1991	Intermediate
			1992	Internal war
			1993–1995	Intermediate
Haiti	Government	Tonton Macoute, Military faction	1991	Minor
			2001	
			2004	
Mexico	Government	EZLN	1994	Minor
Nicaragua	Government	FSLN	1978–1979	Internal war
		Contras	1981–1982	Minor
			1983–1988	Internal war
			1989	Intermediate

Table I.1 *(continued)*

Country	Reason for Conflict	Opposition Organization	Year of Conflict	Intensity Level of Conflict
Panama	Government	Military faction	1989	Minor
Panama–US	Government	U.S. invasion	1989	Intermediate
Paraguay	Government	Military faction	1989	Minor
Peru	Government	MIR; Tupac Amaru; ELN; SL; Sendero Rojo; MRTA	1965	Minor
			1980	Minor
			1981–1985	Internal war
			1986–1987	Intermediate
			1988–1992	Internal war
			1993–1999	Intermediate
Suriname	Government	SLA	1986–1988	Minor
Trinidad and Tobago	Government	Jamaat al-Muslimeen	1990	Minor
Uruguay	Government	MLN	1972	Minor
Venezuela	Government	Military faction	1962	Minor
		Military faction	1992	Minor
		Military faction	2004	Minor

Source: Andrés Solimano, "Political Violence and Economic Development in Latin America: Issues and Evidence," (Santiago, Chile: Economic Commission for Latin America and the Caribbean, 2004).

The parallels between Iraq and the numerous U.S. military interventions in Latin America are striking in the way preinvasion propaganda characterized the magnitude of the threat. Eldon Kenworthy analyzes how the Reagan administration used threat-based rhetoric to sell its policy toward Nicaragua in the 1980s. In his book *America/Américas: Myth in the Making of U.S. Policy Toward Latin America*, Kenworthy argues that a threat is far more credible if it "comes from international networks of 'communists' and 'terrorists' rather than from the [failures of] government of a small underdeveloped country." Nicaragua, for example, was described as a threat to the United States because it could serve as a "beachhead" for the Soviet Union, not because of its revolution, socialist policies, and anti-American ideology. Reagan sold his policy of supporting the Nicaraguan Contras by evoking powerful, culturally shared emotions "that play on the public's fear of terrorism, drugs, and illegal immigrants."[16] During the Cold War, the Soviet Union had little capability to project conventional military power into Latin America, according to William M. LeoGrande, since "its only opportunity to gain a foothold was to be invited in by ideologically sympathetic governments" such as those of Cuba, Grenada, and Nicaragua.[17] These traditional security concerns no longer exist in Latin America. No major power, with the possible exception of China, has the capability or motivation to project military power into the Western Hemisphere. With the end of the Cold War, traditional security concerns have been replaced by a host of "nontraditional" security issues: criminal activity and the resulting lack of public safety; narcotics trafficking; terrorism; health and environmental risks; proliferation of weapons of mass destruction; and poverty and social exclusion or marginalization. Issues traditionally conceived as political, economic, and social problems have been reconceptualized as "security threats" when they may not pose any danger to the vital interests of the United States.[18] China has targeted Latin America as a source of trade and resources, particularly petroleum and natural gas, but is not considered a threat to the vital interests of the United States, except among those, mostly conservatives, who worry about China's increasing power worldwide as demonstrated by Chinese port operations in Panama, increased military-to-military relations, and investment elsewhere in the region. Panama today is more of a "cold spot" than a security hot spot in the Americas.

Mexico has lost thousands of jobs to China in the past five years and worries about the flood of Chinese imports that compete with Mexican manufactured goods, but the Mexican government does not consider China a threat to its national security.[19] The same could be said of Chile, where the national economy is tied to growing imports from China. The value of Chinese imports to Latin America is growing rapidly, often at the expense of small and large manufacturing concerns throughout the region. It remains to be seen whether Washington policymakers will invoke the Monroe Doctrine in an effort to expel the Chinese from Latin American hot spots. Broadcaster Pat Robertson once told his television audience that the Monroe Doctrine could also serve as a justification for assassination and regime change in Venezuela to get rid of the threat posed by President Chávez.[20]

Threat-based hot spot terminology also assumes the existence of a "domino" effect in which trouble from a hot spot, if ignored, can spread like a wildfire or invasive weed, eventually endangering the security of the United States. "The domino metaphor said nothing about how to stop the dominoes from falling; its major value was to heighten the nature of the strategic threat and emphasize the consequences [and fear] of failing to intervene to stop other dominoes from falling."[21] When applied to Latin American hot spots, the domino theory has distinct advantages for Washington policymakers looking for a readily acceptable concept that will make it easier to militarize the problem and obtain the support of the media and the American public. In his effort to sort out the complex universe of politics, Murray Edelman argues that "political conflicts in American history centering around alleged threats" involve a process in which a particular threat becomes closely associated with the psychological and political necessity of emphasizing both the magnitude of the threat and the role of those in high-level administrative positions in protecting against the threat.[22] In fact, administrative personnel and organizations may exaggerate security threats to polarize the ideological differences within the general population. In other words, the scarier the intelligence reports of a particular hot spot, the easier it is to choose to exercise force rather than diplomacy. The problem for foreign-policy elites is not whether a threat is empirically verifiable but their ability to use a subjective threat to obtain specific policy objectives.[23] The United States has never been attacked militarily by a Latin American country. By any objective measure the security threat today to the U.S. government from the Western Hemisphere is minuscule and, in many parts of the region, nonexistent. Despite the fear of terrorism lurking behind the debate over border security and immigration, not one actual terrorist has been apprehended while trying to cross into the United States from Mexico. However, this has not stopped Washington—the only hemispheric power to possess nuclear weapons and the largest military power in the world—from raising the specter of a variety of subjective threats inside Latin America and the Caribbean. The "posture statements" written by Pentagon officials for congressional hearings are often designed to influence members of Congress to pass legislation providing more funds for a new program or strategy rather than to explore a broader range of policy options designed to mitigate a potential threat or conflict.

During the George W. Bush administration the intelligence community was pressured to provide scarier threat assessments that would justify a more confrontational approach to governments considered evil or enemy regimes: Cuba, Iran, Iraq, North Korea, and Venezuela. Newt Gingrich, former House speaker, complained that "The intelligence community is dedicated to predicting the least dangerous world possible"—as if security threats, and wars, were ideologically malleable in the hands of those who are more interested in intelligence that suits their political ideology than in accurate assessments of threats around the globe.[24] Media management is a critical part of persuading the public and Congress that an imminent threat exists and that an invasion may be needed to bring security and stability to a nation or region. The purpose of unleashing American military power around the globe, whether to remove a dictator or eliminate dangerous weapons, does not always rest on a purported danger or threat to U.S. security; U.S. intervention abroad is often designed to advertise the folly of defying the power of the United States.[25]

The way in which the United States responds to threats in Latin America also forms part of a set of beliefs among Washington policymakers that Latin Americans are inferior or immature and their governments—corrupt, greedy, inefficient, autocratic, and lacking sufficient resources—cannot deal adequately with threats and attacks by hostile states or nonstate actors.[26] Therefore, Washington policymakers easily convince the American public about the need for a U.S. response if a perceived threat appears as a "hot spot" with the capability of breeding more serious threats to the United States. Moreover, the use of threat-based rhetoric serves as a powerful tool of public persuasion and a rationale for dealing forcefully with enemy foreign powers, Communists, terrorists, "Islamists," "Islamic fascists," drug lords, radical populists, and violent local criminal gangs.

A preference for or indifference to authoritarian regimes in Latin America that will apply "iron fist" policies to eliminate a particular threat means the sacrifice of liberties and rights in the search for order and stability. In the 2004 Latinobarómetro study, more than 75 percent of the respondents in Paraguay, El Salvador, Guatemala, Costa Rica, Honduras, and Chile believed that harsh rule is sometimes necessary.[27] Even in the United States, 60 percent of respondents in a 2002 *Washington Post*—ABC News poll said it was okay to give up some personal privacy and liberties in order to combat terrorism. In Latin America, the penchant for strong-man rule dovetails with anti-democratic sentiments during periods of domestic turmoil and chaos. Unfortunately, political repression has often been seen as a "vaccine" against dissidents and opponents of the regime in power rather than a violation of human rights.

Partisanship and Threat Perceptions

In Washington, Republicans and Democrats generally differ in how threats are perceived and evaluated in Latin America. For example, Republicans tend to put more emphasis than Democrats on foreign policy goals such as free trade and privatization, antiterrorism, anti-immigration, anti-Communism, and political stability. When it comes to legislating reforms in current U.S. immigration policy, conservative Republicans are the most hostile toward immigration because they represent the part of the Republican Party that is culturally conservative and angry about illegal immigrants from Latin America, whom it perceives as disrespectful to U.S. law, abusive of tax-supported government programs, and disruptive to the economy. In general, Republicans have historically favored military aid and training, covert operations, tighter control over the border with Mexico, support for "friendly" dictators, use of force or confrontation over diplomacy, and private investment instead of financial contributions to international organizations. Democrats, however, are associated with policies that emphasize diplomacy and negotiations, economic aid over military aid, human rights protections and the avoidance of torture, and the utility of multilateral peace-keeping institutions such as the Organization of American States and the United Nations. American voters assume that the Republican Party can better keep the nation safe than the Democratic Party can, although the margin of difference has narrowed considerably since 2003. Thus, threat perception plays a key role in explaining the partisan differences between American administrations.[28] For example, Presidents Carter and Reagan brought different perceptions of the nature and intensity of the threat posed by the Sandinista revolution in Nicaragua in the late 1970s and 1980s. According to Robert Pastor, President Reagan viewed the Sandinistas as "an immediate, grave, Soviet-inspired threat that was testing the will and jeopardizing the interests of the United States [in Central America]. . . . To Carter, the Sandinistas represented a Central American revolution; the United States should try to help it and contain it simultaneously."[29] The partisan wrangling over the "Nicaraguan threat" illustrated how the Cold War influenced the policymaking process in Washington and the ease with which power shifts based on presidential elections can dramatically alter the meaning of hot spots, the severity of threats, and the appropriate response in constructing a Latin American policy. The fear of Communism continues to resonate in right-wing circles, who insist that Communism is alive in Latin America and no less dangerous, and perhaps much more, than it was when Fidel Castro was sponsoring revolutions and advocating anti-imperialism throughout the Americas.[30] Anti-immigration conservatives such as Colorado Congressman Tom Tancredo believe that immigration should be severely restricted and those who come to the United States from Latin America and are in the country illegally should be returned to their home countries.[31] Former presidential candidate and conservative commentator Patrick J. Buchanan believes a moratorium on immigration at the southern border is the only way to stop what he calls "the invasion" from Mexico. He claims that Mexican immigrants to the United States have no interest in assimilating and that some eventually want a reconquest of the southwestern United States—territory taken from Mexico after the Mexican-American War.[32]

In the presidential transition from Jimmy Carter to Ronald Reagan, diplomats in Central America discovered their jobs were in jeopardy if they viewed the hot spots in El Salvador and Nicaragua differently than the anti-Communist appointees about to set up shop in Washington. For example, shortly after Ronald Reagan's inauguration as president in 1981, Secretary of State Alexander Haig recalled Robert White, U.S. ambassador in El Salvador, to discuss the political instability and violence there. After failing to convince Haig that a peaceful solution to El Salvador's problems was clearly possible, White concluded that "the Reagan conservatives wanted to demonstrate an ability to crush revolutions. They wanted to say in El Salvador, this is what we could have done in Vietnam, had we not been saddled by reporters, columnists—all those liberals."[33] Ambassador White and many others were "purged" from the State Department during the early years of the Reagan administration because they were judged to be lacking in their anti-Communist ideology. The internal war in El

Salvador dragged on for another eight years, killing over 80,000 people (mostly civilians) over the span of the entire decade.

Despite the Bush administration's efforts to make "democracy building" a centerpiece of its foreign policy, policymakers in charge of U.S. policy in Haiti worked behind the scenes to undermine the U.S. ambassador and his reconciliation efforts while helping armed rebels remove Jean-Bertrand Aristide because his governing style and leftist ideology were seen as a political threat to the United States. Brian Dean Curran, American ambassador in Haiti until August 2003, was replaced after he complained that what the United States was doing in Haiti was antithetical to American interests in the Western Hemisphere and policy legitimacy in Haiti.[34]

Current Risk Assessment Theory

Recent risk assessment theory has shifted to include the threats posed by nations considered unstable rather than ones once considered to be the "declared enemies" of the United States. This change in emphasis is now the basis for the recent "unstable nations" listed by the Pentagon as potential targets for military intervention. Pentagon analysts believe that countries with the greatest instability and risk pose a greater threat to the United States than declared enemies or rogue states. According to the U.S. military planners, America's security is more likely to be threatened by failed or failing states than the dangers from "traditional challenges" or "irregular threats." Other vulnerabilities include countries considered inconsistent in their support of American foreign policy and those that resent U.S. influence and hegemony in world affairs. Nondemocratic states are sometimes considered more dangerous than other forms of government because they are more likely to be a breeding ground for threats from radicals, dissidents, and others opposed to the regime in power. This is a dramatic change from the Cold War, when the security concerns of the United States focused on the "Soviet threat" in Latin America and supported right-wing dictatorships that demonstrated their anti-Communism in alignment with Washington.

In diagnosing the problem of threats to American security, policy officials have shifted attention from powerful states such as the former Soviet Union to weak states, ones that have failed or are failing such as Haiti, Colombia, Peru, and Ecuador. From Washington's perspective, the security concern associated with failed states is what they can export to the rest of the world: international terrorists, drug traffickers, criminal gangs, or dangerous weapons.[35] The number of states at risk of failure varies from 20 to 50, depending on how one goes about measuring state failure. In 2006, the Fund for Peace and *Foreign Policy* conducted a study of 148 states using twelve social, economic, and military indicators in order to assess their vulnerability to violent internal conflict. According to the "failed states index" (FSI), most of the failed states are in Africa and Asia. Among the nineteen Latin American countries in the study, Haiti scored highest as a failed state, followed by Colombia, the Dominican Republic, Guatemala, Bolivia, and Nicaragua in the top six. The most successful states (nonfailed states) include Chile, Argentina, Uruguay, Costa Rica, and Panama (see Table I.2). Of interest in Table I.2 is that of the six

Table I.2 Failed State Index (FSI), Latin America, 2006

Country	Total Score, FSI	Rank Order ($N = 148$)	Severity of State Failure	Major Source of Conflict*
Haiti	104.6	8	High Alert	10, 12
Colombia	91.8	27	High Alert	2, 8, 9
Dominican Republic	85	48	Warning	4, 5
Guatemala	84.3	51	Warning	1, 5
Bolivia	82.9	56	Warning	5, 9
Nicaragua	82.4	59	Warning	5, 6
Cuba	81.9	62	Warning	7, 8, 9
Ecuador	81.2	63	Warning	5, 7
Venezuela	81.2	64	Warning	5
Peru	79.2	64	Warning	8
Honduras	76.7	69	Warning	1, 5
El Salvador	76.1	77	Warning	1, 8
Mexico	73.1	86	Warning	1, 5
Paraguay	72	87	Warning	7, 9
Brazil	63.1	101	Warning	5
Panama	59.6	107	Monitoring	5
Costa Rica	49.6	114	Monitoring	1, 5
Uruguay	41.2	120	Monitoring	4
Argentina	40.8	122	Monitoring	5
United States	34.5	128	Monitoring	2
Chile	32	132	Monitoring	9

*Failed State indicators: *Social indicators:* (1) mounting demographic pressures; (2) massive movement of refugees or internally displaced persons creating complex humanitarian emergencies; (3) legacy of vengeance-seeking group grievance or group paranoia; (4) chronic and sustained human flight. *Economic indicators:* (5) uneven economic development along group lines; (6) sharp and/or severe economic decline. *Political indicators:* (7) criminalization and/or delegitimization of the state; (8) progressive deterioration of public services; (9) suspension or arbitrary application of the rule of law and widespread violation of human rights; (10) security apparatus operating as a "state within a state" [death squads]; (11) rise of factionalized elites; (12) intervention of other states or external political actors.
Source: The Fund for Peace, "Failed State Index, 2006" (Washington, D.C., 2006; http://www.fundforpeace.org/programs/fsi/fsiindex).

countries that scored highest on the FSI, the most common source of conflict was indicator 5: "uneven economic development along group lines." Of the twelve indicators, uneven development and criminalization or delegitimation of the state emerged as the two best indicators of a failing state. These two factors are closely associated with corrupt, illegal, or ineffective political conditions. Under these conditions people shift their allegiances to other leaders, including opposition parties, drug mafias, warlords, ethnic nationalists, populist politicians, radical members of the clergy, or various kinds of rebel forces. The social and political consequence of the violence associated with failing states is the growth of fear and distrust. This, in turn, leads to the gradual disintegration of the social fabric and is closely tied to poverty, inequality, exclusion, and the erosion of legitimate governance. Those countries that rank high on the failed states index are more likely to contain security-based hot spots that threaten Latin America's democratic regimes. However, Colombia's failing state and the violence associated with armed actors there have not in themselves destroyed Colombian democracy. Despite concerns that members of Colombia's Congress have collaborated with right-wing death squads to exert political control along Colombia's Caribbean coast, the Bush administration considers Colombia a stabilizing force in the region and a Latin American success story. Colombian President Álvaro Uribe is considered a model for how to deal with terrorists and guerrilla forces in Latin America, despite human rights violations, government corruption, and a death-squad scandal involving a secret pact between national legislators and paramilitary warlords.[36]

Latin American countries that rank high on the failed state index become hot spots because of the way that weak states manifest severe political problems: corruption, greed, lack of due process, administrative inefficiency, politicized judiciary, mass demonstrations, and violent insurgencies, often connected to the drug trade. According to *The Economist*, "The chief reason why the world should worry about state failure is that it is contagious," capable of infecting neighbors and regions. Fear of Communism during the Cold War was also based on disease metaphors, suggesting that the ideology of Communism could easily spread like a cancer if not stopped in one fashion or another. Despite neoconservative optimism of the ease of spreading democracy and freedom, fixing a failed state is a complicated, costly, and time-consuming venture. However, United Nations peacekeepers in such places as Haiti, Guatemala, and El Salvador have had some success in pacification and improving governance.[37] The recent study by Logan and Preble argues that "failed states most often do not represent security threats" and attempts at fixing failed states through nation building or democracy building have been failures.[38] The connection between failed or failing states and Latin American hot spots will continue as Washington policymakers debate the accuracy and saliency of threats to national security.[39] Carleton University in Canada publishes Country Indicators for Foreign Policy (CIFP) that identifies countries at risk of violent armed conflict. The purpose of its "watch list" is to provide an early warning device in order for an appropriate third-party intervention—United Nations, World Bank, Organization of American States—to be developed in time to avert greater conflict and social disintegration. In its report for Spring/Summer 2004, CIFP listed Bolivia, Guyana, and Venezuela as three of ten countries considered to be conflict-prone and susceptible to outside intervention because of nine indicators: the potential for state failure; increasing gross human rights violations; increasing militarization; regional conflict developments; refugee flows and instability; a history of armed conflict; increased economic or environmental stress; health epidemics; and globalization. Guyana is listed as the most conflict prone on the watch list because of deep ethnic divisions, a history of disputed elections, civil unrest, violent local criminal gangs, environmental degradation, porous borders that provide an attractive route for South American cocaine, and poverty and economic stagnation.[40]

The CIFP list is another way of locating security-based hot spots that threaten local, regional, and global stability. According to the authors of the CIFP report, "The value of a watch list is that documenting such information and putting a country on a public list can itself bring about positive changes in behavior both by external and internal actors."[41] In what author Ron Suskind calls the "One Percent Doctrine," Vice President Cheney has defined threats in such a way that if the risk of a terrorist attack on the United States is "one percent," it would be treated as if it were a 100 percent certainty. In this form of risk assessment, there is also a 99 percent likelihood that a terrorist attack will not happen. With only a 1 percent chance of a threat to U.S. security—regardless of supporting evidence—the United States should respond with force to handle the threat.[42] In the current administration, described by some as an "evidence-free environment," the president is given wide latitude in assessing threats and taking confrontational action in the pursuit of national security. According to Jeffrey Kluger, "Critics of [Bush] Administration policy argue that a 1% possibility was never properly balanced against the 100% certainty of the tens of thousands of casualties that would accompany a war."[43] Many of the neoconservatives—Richard Perle, Kenneth Adelman, David Frum—who once strongly backed the Bush administration's invasion of Iraq on grounds of superpower prerogatives, "toughness," and "morality" now feel that the unfolding catastrophe in Iraq is the result of the "devastating dysfunction within the Bush administration." In other words, they believe that the fiasco in Iraq was caused by the incompetence of the Bush administration, not by the way the threat from Saddam's tyranny was defined or by the core beliefs of elite neoconservatives.[44] The quagmire in Iraq and the impending defeat almost certainly spell the end of neoconservative dreams of regime change, democratic governance, and the end of evil in the Middle East and elsewhere.

American Perceptions of Critical Threats to Vital U.S. Interests

The terrorist attacks of September 11, 2001, produced a heightened sense of threat and vulnerability among the American public, especially threats from international terrorism and unfriendly countries with weapons of mass destruction. As the world's attention focused almost exclusively on terrorism, wars in Afghanistan and Iraq, and the nuclear ambitions of Iran and North Korea, the United States soon dismissed Latin America as a lost continent. Washington—diplomats, generals, investors, and journalists—paid little attention to Latin America and the Caribbean, a region without nuclear weapons, of declining economic importance, and with only a nonthreatening level of anti-Americanism.[45] In an effort to find out what the public considers "critical threats" to the vital interests of the United States, the Chicago Council on Foreign Relations conducted a national poll in mid-2002 in order to measure these perceptions and then followed up two years later after the United States had taken substantial international actions against perceived threats around the globe. The 2002 poll found the following: (1) Latin America, as a world region, was considered to pose little threat to the United States; (2) the five most "critical threats" mentioned by the public included international terrorism, chemical and biological weapons, Iraq developing weapons of mass destruction, possibility of unfriendly countries becoming nuclear powers, and epidemics such as AIDS or the Ebola virus; (3) 60 percent of the public said that immigration and refugees were a critical threat, while only 14 percent of the elite sample considered immigrants and refugees a threat to the vital interests of the United States; (4) critical threats that carry the possibility of becoming hot spots in the world are mainly considered to be those associated with terrorism, military power, and destructive weaponry. None of the respondents mentioned a Latin American country as a threat to the United States in 2002, despite the war on drugs and terrorism, illegal immigration, growing xenophobia, and hostility toward Cuba, Venezuela, Bolivia, and other Latin American countries. Even Colombia, the third largest recipient of U.S. military and economic aid in the world, did not register as a threat to the United States (see Table I.3).

Table I.3 Critical Threats to U.S. Interests As Perceived by the U.S. Public, 2004

Critical Threat	% of Public Concerned (% Change Since 2002)	Relevance in Latin America
International terrorism	75 (–10)	Minor
Chemical and biological weapons	66 (–16)	No
Unfriendly countries becoming nuclear powers	64 (–19)	No
AIDS, Ebola virus, and other potential epidemics	58 (–13)	Yes
Large numbers of immigrants and refugees coming to United States	52 (–9)	Yes
Military conflict between Israel and Arab neighbors	39 (–24)	No
Islamic fundamentalism	38 (–23)	Minor
Global warming	37 (–9)	Yes
Economic competition from low-wage countries	35 (+4)	Yes
China as a world power	33 (–16)	Yes
World population growth	30 (–)	Yes
Tensions between India and Pakistan	18 (–27)	No
Economic competition from Europe	14 (+6)	No

Source: Chicago Council on Foreign Relations, "World Views 2004" (www.ccfr.org/globalviews2004).

In 2004 the high levels of concern about critical threats declined dramatically, while the most critical threats remained the same: international terrorism, chemical and biological weapons, and unfriendly countries becoming nuclear powers.[46] While a majority of the public mentioned immigration and refugees as a critical threat to U.S. interests in 2002 and 2004, many of the threats had little to do with Latin American trouble spots such as Haiti, Venezuela, Cuba, Colombia, and Mexico. With declines in virtually all the threats, perhaps the American public feels more secure after several years without another direct attack on American soil. The decline in the severity of critical threats may also stem from becoming more adjusted to living with threats portrayed by the media and political leaders. Despite the perception that a variety of security threats still loom large in the public's mind, the American public wants lower spending on defense and homeland security, gives less support for building U.S. military bases abroad, and strongly endorses the traditional constraints on the use of force by individual states. According to the findings in the Global Views 2004 report, "Majorities of the public and leaders do not support states taking unilateral action to prevent other states from acquiring weapons of mass destruction, but do support action if it has UN Security Council approval."[47]

In most of the countries in Latin America where security-based threats exist, there is a huge gap between the rich and poor and chronic problems trying to legitimize authority.[48] The Latin American countries listed as the states most likely to fail are also the most corrupt countries with the least support for democracy. Problems of legitimizing authority have become chronic, even after democratic elections and large electoral majorities. In the past the military often intervened in the electoral process by overturning the will of voters. Some voters believed that the military were less corrupt than civilians and accorded them significant authority to respond to internal conflicts. In his inventory of military coups in Latin America between 1900 and 2000, Peter H. Smith found a total of 147 successful overthrows of established governments in 19 countries. The virtual absence of military control in 2000 suggests to Smith that the decline in military coups beginning in the 1980s results from a reduction in major threats to national security and the prior responses by the armed forces for saving *la patria* (fatherland) from subversive and antipatriotic enemies.[49] After the collapse of the Soviet Union and the end of the Cold War, there were fewer plausible threats requiring military intervention. Despite major human rights abuses, many give credit to Latin America's armed forces. Today, most of the military institutions in Latin America let civilian governments handle the thorny issues of stimulating economic growth and reducing poverty and inequality as well as the painful process of downsizing the role of the state. In the absence of Communist subversion, the armed forces have found new missions such as "the war against drugs" and remain remarkably resilient to full subordination to civilian authorities.[50] In the case of Ecuador, a poor country dominated by international petroleum companies, the armed forces are obligated by government contracts to provide military security to California-based Occidental Petroleum. This strange arrangement includes counterintelligence operations to prevent hot spots from interfering with the "normal development of hydrocarbon activities."[51] Where democracy is the strongest in Latin America, the armed forces are weakest and less likely to consider reentering the political arena. As shown in Table I.4, the greater the press freedom and the lesser the corruption, the more democracy in Latin America.

Corruption, State Failure, and Latin American Hot Spots

There are clearly competing views of which sectors of society in Latin America are most corrupt and how to eradicate corruption in the name of good governance. According to Transparency International's (TI)

Table I.4 Latin American Democracy Ranking, 2006

Country	Democracy Rank	Press Freedom Rank	Corruption Rank
Chile	19	32	17
Uruguay	23	36	23
Costa Rica	29	15	45
Panama	40	59	71
El Salvador	46	59	47
Brazil	51	52	57
Peru	51	52	57
Bolivia	51	44	90
Dominican Republic	55	49	84
Mexico	62	68	57
Argentina	64	65	78
Ecuador	65	57	120
Nicaragua	65	62	96
Colombia	68	92	49
Honduras	72	76	105
Paraguay	75	83	96
Guatemala	103	86	96
Venezuela	123	119	120
Haiti	126	114	145
Cuba	128	146	46

Source: http://www.worldaudit.org/democracy.htm.

2004 Corruption Perceptions Index, Haiti, Paraguay, Guatemala, Bolivia, Venezuela, Honduras, Ecuador, Argentina, Nicaragua, and the Dominican Republic are the top ten most corrupt countries in Latin America. State failure largely derives from high levels of corruption and the absence of good governance, both of which impede the ability to reduce domestic conflict and provide stability for the nation. TI's methodology is not flawless, because corruption has many different strains and is subject to expert bias, but its Corruption Perception Index is used by the World Bank, Washington's lending policies, and international entrepreneurs.[52] According to Robert I. Rotberg, "Unless the developing world becomes much more stable, intercommunal (ethnic, linguistic, and religious) conflict is reduced or ceases altogether, corruption vanishes, good governance becomes common, or the war on terror is won conclusively, the propensity of nation-states to fail will be high and the policy consequences of that failure will correspondingly be serious and many."[53] In Latin America and the rest of the developing world, resources are scarce and the state has been weakened by neoliberal models of economic development. During the Cold War, state failures were attributed to Communist subversion, and policymakers worried about a "domino" effect in which one state after another would "fall" and land in the Communist orbit dominated by the Soviet Union. Today, security threats are less visible and the United States seems prepared to intervene in low-risk places considered unstable and opposed to U.S. policy.

In Latin America a nation's degree of corruption also affects attitudes toward democracy and government institutions. Charles F. Andrain and James T. Smith found in their fifteen-nation study that the most corrupt nations "display the weakest enthusiasm for political democracy" and the least amount of institutional trust. They also found an important link between corruption—the abuse of public office for private gain—and government policies: "Widespread corruption prevails in poorer, inegalitarian countries that spend low shares of the GDP for pensions, education and health care."[54] The least corruption prevails in wealthy societies that pay fairly high wages to public and private employees, who have fewer incentives to engage in extensive corruption. The problem in Latin America is that cohesive political institutions are lacking and, with a relatively closed policymaking process, it is more difficult to monitor the behavior of political-economic entrepreneurs. Without a competent, professional bureaucracy, it is difficult for government officials to differentiate the public from the private sphere, and officials therefore tend to use their public authority to secure private gain for family and friends and exercise other forms of extralegal favoritism. As Andrain and Smith point out, "In nations with low corruption, governments administer justice, reduce crime, provide social services, and raise taxes without incurring high transaction costs that hinder efficiency, growth, income equality, and political democracy."[55] The dilemmas associated with corruption in Latin America help us explain the attitudes toward democracy, trust, and social justice. Neoliberal assumptions about the positive relationship between capitalism and political democracy have been undermined by extensive income inequality, government corruption, and negative economic outcomes such as high unemployment, soaring prices of basic commodities, and widening gaps in income. For citizens to believe in the value of political democracy, government officials committed to a neoliberal agenda need to allow for the existence of widespread voluntary political participation. Many of Latin America's hot spots that pose threats of one kind or another are associated with high levels of corruption, lack of institutional trust, and severe income inequality, none of which is likely to be responsive to military/police action of one kind or another. The weakness in government institutions throughout the Andes often leads to a common situation in which political support and legitimacy must rely on patronage, political bosses, and wealth rather than the procedures and processes of democracy.

In an effort to explain confidence and support of government institutions, Andrain and Smith discovered that distrust in government institutions correlates with "low satisfaction with national political leaders, high perception of national corruption, low political involvement, weak national pride, and a wide gap between an individual's left-wing ideological identification and the more rightist ideologies of the parties governing the nation."[56] These characteristics exist throughout Latin America and illustrate how difficult it is for wealthy nations to spread democracy and institutional trust in government institutions. It is also important to keep in mind that democracy and American security interests do not always coincide, particularly when elections produce winners labeled "terrorists" or "radical populists," or candidates who simply oppose U.S. policies for a variety of reasons. The findings in Andrain and Smith's comparative study offer important lessons for assessing and responding to threat-based hot spots in Latin America and elsewhere in the world. In opinion polls and at the ballot box, disgruntled citizens in Latin America have been expressing their disgust with corrupt and incompetent government and electing left-populist politicians, who blame neoliberal economic policies and poor governance for slow economic growth, the perpetuation of poverty, and sparse investment in human capital through health and education policies.[57] Why would this political trajectory in South America pose a security threat to the United States?

New Ways of Dealing with Security Threats

A growing consensus in Washington holds that major states have a responsibility to intervene around the globe to prevent other states from harboring terrorists, acquiring weapons of mass destruction, protecting their own citizens from mass killings or genocide, preventing the spread of dangerous diseases, and preventing the destruction of key biospheres. To head off these internal developments after the 9/11 attacks, President Bush initiated a doctrine of preemption to reshape the global order. However, as one journalist put it, the philosophy of preemption requires a new standard of state responsibility based on "conditional sovereignty," armed intervention by the United States, and the necessity of building and spreading democracy.[58] In March 2005 the Pentagon published a major document with modifications in the preemptive-war doctrine that formed a new basis of dealing with security threats. In "The National Defense Strategy of the United States of America," the new strategy suggests the possibility of military intervention in places that do not visibly constitute a threat to the security of the United States, including twenty-five countries considered unstable and, thus, targets of military intervention. U.S. intelligence experts now believe that America's security is threatened less by declared enemies or "rogue states" than by failed or failing ones. Among the twenty-five "unstable nations" on the "watch list" are Venezuela under President Chávez, Haiti, Peru, Bolivia, and Ecuador. Most of these oppose the prevailing neoliberal agenda and Washington's emphasis on free markets and democracy.[59]

Several problems face the new security strategy initiated by Washington. First, the United States is losing credibility in the world because of its inept handling of the war in Iraq and lopsided support for Israel. The use of preemptive intervention and occupation may only arouse fears of imperial agendas.[60] Given the present state of the U.S. military, it is unlikely that signs of a failed state in the Andes or the death of Fidel Castro would result in a U.S. invasion, regardless of the level of state failure, political instability, or hot spot risks. The ease with which the White House carried out regime change in Latin America during the Cold War has been altered by globalization and by the assertion of democracy promotion as a universal goal. Second, efforts to globalize democracy to make the world safer and eliminate non-democratic states because they breed threats are far more difficult than most policymakers realize. "The Latin American experience would suggest that democracies only take root from within, and in some cases will never emerge regardless of foreign policy rhetoric that assumes there is a seed of democracy inside every society waiting to be released by an outside power protecting its own interests."[61] In the 2006 Latinobarómetro poll, Latin American attitudes toward support for democracy have increased slightly and there is more optimism about their economic growth. Overall, 58 percent of the respondents agreed that democracy is the best form of government; however, support for authoritarian government remains high in Guatemala and Paraguay, and support for democracy is below average in Mexico and Brazil. The string of election results in 2006 demonstrate less a shift to the ideological left than the growing importance of the social agenda along with the desire for governments that are both honest and effective.[62] The task of building effective democracies is not easy; however, the growing satisfaction with democracy in Latin America augurs well for the eventual decline in security-based hot spots in the region. Third, this kind of analysis targets "enemy" countries and security-based responses with propaganda designed to morally justify the necessity of intervention and tends to overlook the fact that the United States does not have a record of success in promoting democracy and human rights in Latin America. Those who conduct foreign policy and assess the risk of institutions' failing need to put more time into understanding the importance of sociopolitical conditions, values, and attitudes toward the political regime. Fourth, the United States is losing influence in Latin America, where democratically elected leaders are no longer willing to follow

Washington in lockstep. For example, at the 2005 meeting of the OAS General Assembly in Fort Lauderdale, Florida, the member states refused to back a U.S. proposal that the OAS should engage countries "where democracy is under threat" and to sanction intervention in order to bring good governance.[63] Obviously, the long history of U.S. intervention in Latin America serves as an impediment to using the OAS to sanction the use of force, regardless of the moral and political justification. The fact that many Latin Americans dislike George Bush and Hugo Chávez in equal measure suggests that voters are not driven to the polls by controversial political leaders, either in Washington or at home.

Europeans are not that different from the U.S. public in how they view the world around them: friends and allies, threats, attitudes toward the use of force, and the importance of international institutions. However, Europeans want the European Union to become a superpower like the United States in order to better counterbalance Washington and to inject a greater (and more accurate) strategic sensibility than what they have experienced during the George W. Bush administration. In world surveys of American and European attitudes of foreign affairs, Europeans are more favorable toward economic and political tools over military ones, multilateral approaches to conflicts rather than unilateral ones, and humanitarian missions instead of foreign policy initiatives based solely on national self interest. Europeans are not all the same, but their views of war and peace reflect a penchant for greater cooperation to ensure global peace and stability.[64] The global views on President Bush's foreign policy are overwhelmingly negative, with some of the strongest negative views of U.S. foreign policy expressed in Latin America.[65] This means that U.S.-defined hot spots around the world are not likely to be seen with the same degree of urgency by other nations.

Dilemmas of Threat Definition

The problems of threat identification and the ability to establish different levels of threats to national security have become a key part of the global political debates since the 9/11 attacks. The difficulty of threat definition and prioritization is examined in the Stockholm International Peace Research Institute's (SIPRI) 2003 Yearbook. First, SIPRI claims that governments cannot readily agree on the definition of terrorism and how to develop a counter-terrorism strategy. What happens when terrorist violence succeeds and leaders of terrorist organizations come to power through democratic elections? Are they seen as liberators of either their country or their population group, and are they seen as legitimate leaders by the world community? To what extent do terror tactics constitute the weapon of the powerless? May not "state terror" become equally destructive to democracy, institutional development, social trust, and freedom? Although most analysts agree that "terrorism" exists and constitutes a threat to national and international law, to human rights, and to national security, many question whether terrorism as a tactic constitutes a single, coherent threat to the world community.[66] The picture becomes more clouded when terror tactics, employed by actors with deep political roots in geographic and ethnic enclaves, are superimposed on groups or organizations with other motives and tactics. These would include drug mafias, urban criminal gangs, communities with ethnic and religious grievances, and other marginalized segments of society. Because there are so many different brands of terrorism, any effective counter-terrorism strategy will require careful attention to the origins, motivations, and tactics of individuals and organizations involved in these activities. In contrast, the concept of a "global war on terrorism," as announced by President Bush in the aftermath of the 9/11 attacks, is strategically vague, embraces unrealistic objectives, and may not be economically or politically sustainable over a long period of time. In fact, after several years of using the phrase "war on terror," the Bush administration has been trying new language to offset the public's increasing pessimism about the war in Iraq and its links to the ongoing fight against terrorism. In July 2005 Bush administration figures began speaking publicly about "a global struggle against the enemies of freedom" and the need for greater use of diplomacy in the war on terrorism.[67] It remains to be seen whether this revised terminology, with its emphasis on "freedom," will improve the chances of success in dealing with terrorism and the world's hot spots. Likewise, in April 2007 the British government stopped using the phrase "war on terror" on the grounds that it strengthens terrorists by making them feel part of a larger struggle. According to Hilary Benn, a key figure in the governing Labour Party, "We do not use the phrase "war on terror" because we can't win by military means alone, and because this isn't us against one organized enemy with a clear identity and a coherent set of objectives."[68] Francis Fukuyama, a former neoconservative theorist, argues that the morality of benevolent hegemony the United States has employed in Iraq has failed because of the "overestimation of the threat facing the United States from radical Islamism" and the incompetence within the American intelligence community.[69] Such a pattern of threat assessment is not new; it has been part of U.S. policy toward Latin America for over a century. Parts of Latin America clearly possess militant groups with a history of criminality and violence; however, few local criminal gangs have links to global terrorist organizations.

The second problem is the difficulty of assessing and countering the threat from the proliferation of mass destruction technologies: nuclear, chemical, and biological. According to SIPRI, "These weapons are properly the object of special fears and abhorrence because of their huge, indiscriminate and insidious destructive power and because of the way their use threatens to contaminate or disrupt the whole human environment."[70] Assessing the level of threat from nuclear, chemical and biological weapons may be easier than devising possible cures to reduce the threat. As SIPRI points out, "Unfortunately, the clearer the existence of mass-destruction capacities becomes and the more irresponsible their possessor is known to be, the harder it becomes to take resolute action to get rid of the capabilities without intolerable risk."[71] John Bolton, U.S. undersecretary of state for arms control, singled out Cuba in a speech before the Heritage Foundation in 2002 in which he claimed that Cuba not only possesses biological weapons but exports technology that helps other nations build such weapons. However, military and intelligence officials believe the evidence for such claims is shoddy and the claims exaggerated. The former head of the U.S. Southern Command (SOUTHCOM), General Charles Wilhelm, told National Public Radio that during his tenure as head of SOUTHCOM between 1997 and 2000 he never received evidence that Cuba was "developing, producing, or weaponizing biological or chemical weapons." The Bolton claim indicates the ease with which government officials can make an unfounded claim for domestic political purposes. Later, during Bolton's senate confirmation hearings, two former state department officials denied Bolton's claims and accused Bolton of bullying intelligence analysts, harassing colleagues, and exaggerating security threats around the world. To deal with the internal dissent, Bolton first tried to have the two experts on weapons of mass destruction fired; when this attempt failed, he reassigned them to different areas of responsibility. Bolton's ploy may have had more to do with discrediting former President Jimmy Carter's pending trip to Cuba than demonstrating, with evidence, that Fidel Castro posed a serious threat because of supplying bio-weapons to rogue nations.

The proliferation of weapons of mass destruction poses a global threat, yet Latin American leaders have declared the Latin American and Caribbean region a nuclear weapons–free zone. The nuclear weapon aspirations of Brazil and Argentina have been shelved by their recent ratification of the Treaty of Tlatelolco prohibiting nuclear weapons. On a visit to Pakistan and India in 2000, President Bill Clinton applauded Brazil and Argentina for terminating their nuclear programs. Because of these anti–nuclear weapons decisions by politicians in the Southern Cone, the region is considered less of a "hot spot" than world regions such as Asia and the Middle East, where weapons of mass destruction have already become a reality. In *The Atomic Bazaar*, William Langewiesche argues that a more realistic assessment of the spread of nuclear weapons to poor nations is needed because the fear of nuclearization can become more dangerous than the weapons themselves.[72]

The third problem of threat definition and prioritization is the shift from military and defense relationships to broader direct and indirect threats such as ethnic and religious conflict, democratic decay, the consequences of state failure, the results of environmental damage and climate change, interruption of vital supplies (fuel, food, water), diseases that afflict humans and animals, and major accidents and natural disasters. Climate change represents a challenge to international security that may be more threatening than the arms race between the Soviet Union and the United States during the Cold War. According to Thomas Homer-Dixon, director of the Trudeau Center for Peace and Conflict Studies at the University of Toronto, "Climate change will help produce the kind of military challenges that are difficult for today's conventional forces to handle: insurgencies, genocide, guerrilla attacks, gang warfare and global terrorism."[73]

The Organization of American States adopted a new multidimensional security concept to respond to the current threats facing the countries of the Western Hemisphere. It includes new nontraditional security threats such as political, economic, social, health, and environmental aspects. Reaching an agreement on threat perception is complicated because the United States and Latin America differ in what constitutes a serious security threat. For example, although both U.S. citizens and Mexicans see international terrorism and chemical and biological weapons as threats (as shown in Table I.5, for example, the foreign policy goals considered "very important" by the largest percentages of both elites and the general public in the United States are associated with combating international terrorism and preventing the worldwide spread of nuclear weapons), Mexicans show far more concern about drug trafficking, immigration, and world economic issues. Despite Washington's emphasis on spreading democracy and freedom as foreign policy goals, Americans and Mexicans regard bringing democracy to other countries as a low priority. Both also agree that the United States should not play the role of inter-American policeman. Many Latin Americans do not view U.S. influence in the world as a positive factor; this perception provides one of the pillars of growing anti-Americanism in the Americas and elsewhere.

Even within the United States there are wide gaps in foreign policy goals between elites and the general public over controlling and reducing illegal immigration, stopping illegal drugs from entering the United States, protecting the interests of American business abroad, and securing adequate supplies of energy abroad. Furthermore, even though the Bush administration considers democracy promotion a major objective of its foreign policy, neither a majority of elites nor a majority of the general public regards "bringing democracy to other nations" as important, necessary, or feasible.

Table I.5 Foreign Policy Goals Considered "Very Important" by Elites and Public in the United States, 2002

Foreign-Policy Goal	Percent of Elites	Percent of Public	Difference in Percentage of Elites and the Public
Controlling and reducing illegal immigration	22%	70%	48%
Stopping entry of illegal drugs into the United States	45%	81%	36%
Protecting interests of American business abroad	23%	49%	26%
Securing adequate supplies of energy abroad	51%	75%	24%
Improving the global environment	43%	66%	23%
Maintaining superior military power worldwide	52%	68%	16%
Protecting weaker nations against aggression	27%	41%	14%
Promoting market economies abroad	27%	36%	9%
Combating international terrorism	87%	91%	4%
Combating world hunger	59%	61%	2%
Defending our allies' security	55%	57%	2%
Preventing the spread of nuclear weapons	89%	90%	1%
Bringing democracy to other nations	33%	34%	1%
Promoting and defending human rights abroad	46%	47%	1%
Strengthening international law and institutions	49%	43%	–6%
Improving the standard of living in less developed nations	42%	30%	–12%

The Chicago Council on Foreign Relations and the German Marshall Fund of the United States, "World Views 2002" (October 2002).

A serious gap in agendas and priorities between the United States and Latin America now prevails. At the fourth Summit of the Americas held in Mar del Plata, Argentina, in November 2005, President Bush tried to convince Latin Americans that they should support the vaguely defined U.S.-supported "vision of hope" because it will avoid the possibilities of recurring financial shocks and the breakdown of democratic regimes. The Bush administration worries that Latin American governments may return to the authoritarianism of the past and that the voters will elect leaders such as Venezuela's Hugo Chávez or Bolivia's Evo Morales, who oppose U.S. policies in Latin America and see little hope in the vision offered by President Bush. His messy four-day trip did little to improve U.S.–Latin American relations. He confronted serious riots against himself and a rally of over 25,000 people led by President Chávez. The breach between the White House and the leaders of Latin America was too wide for the desired trade talks to succeed. President Bush ended his trip to South America with stops in Brazil and Panama, where his reception was more positive than in Argentina. According to *Time* magazine (November 4, 2005), "Far from being the *mejor amigo* he promised to be, Bush today is arguably more unpopular in Latin America than any U.S. president in history." The United States wants Latin American states to become reliable partners in the war on terrorism, to ensure more open markets for trade and foreign investment, and to oppose President Chávez. Latin Americans, on the other hand, want more liberal immigration laws, greater social investment and bigger development projects, and reduced agricultural subsidies. Some time may elapse before Latin America becomes the "reliable partner" desired by the Bush administration. As Latin America tilts further to the left, more and more Latin American countries are opposing U.S. policies and strengthening ties with China. In South America, many countries have refused to go along with Bush administration demands to exempt Americans from criminal prosecutions at the International Criminal Court (ICC), and none have sent soldiers to support the war in Iraq. Moreover, opinion surveys show President Bush with the lowest standing of any American president in Latin American history.[74]

The Organization of American States (OAS) adopted a new concept of hemispheric security in October 2003 that broadens the definition of security to include new "threats," one that has contributed to the use of Latin American armed forces in new and nontraditional missions.[75] The "new" threats include political, economic, social, health, and environmental problems, but the tendency to treat them as if they were security threats to the Americas raises problems of intervention, militarization, and the fallacy of viewing a broad range of regional problems through the lens of terrorism. The United States' policy toward Latin America is more fragmented and susceptible to competing domestic political constituencies than is the case in other regions of the world. This often means that policymaking is more ineffective and counterproductive, particularly in dealing with problems of trade liberalization, counter-narcotics measures, and regional peace and security matters. The failure to address Latin American sensibilities in security areas—arms sales, military bases, and the use of "non–NATO ally" status to reward some governments and punish others—tends to foster anxieties over existing regional conflicts and reinforces negative views of Washington's proposals for the region. The ongoing wars on drugs, crime, and terrorism have increased the militarization of Latin America, weakened democracy, and often made police forces part of the problem instead of the solution. The prevailing public security problems in Latin America have nothing to do with terrorism, and blurring the lines between proper police and military roles compounds the problem of achieving peace and stability.[76]

Threat Perception and Political Attitudes and Behavior

The United States' Latin American policymaking during the Cold War was often based on the manipulation of security threats and the creation of negative predispositions toward "enemy" nations. For instance, in 1970–1973, when the Nixon administration claimed that the Allende regime in Chile threatened hemispheric security, plans to prevent Allende from taking office emerged and later focused on the necessity of regime change. Refusing to accept the legitimacy of a democratically elected Chilean Marxist, Henry Kissinger denounced Allende's "peaceful road" to socialism—income redistribution, economic nationalization, and agrarian reform—and predicted that Allende would "soon be inciting anti-American policies, attacking hemispheric solidarity, making common cause with Cuba, and sooner or later establishing close relations with the Soviet Union."[77] There is a certain déjà vu quality to Kissinger's fear of the Chilean president and the recent statements by top officials in the Bush administration, who believe Hugo Chávez and Evo Morales represent a similar ideological threat to the United States and Latin America. The Church Committee, headed by Idaho senator Frank Church, investigated the role of the Nixon administration in Chile and declared that no objective threat existed. Nevertheless, the Nixon administration constructed a subjective threat based on their own negative assessments of the security conditions and general ideological orientations. According to Andrain and Smith, because right-wingers tend to take a less optimistic view of life, they may " perceive more threats that create social disorder, anarchy, and personal insecurity—especially threats that arise from dissidents, aliens, and unconventional individuals," while leftists tend to hold more optimistic orientations. Those who perceive social disorder as a major threat more likely support military governments and oppose peaceful multinational cooperation.[78] Leftists perceive different kinds of threats such as those arising from authoritarian governments, bureaucratic capitalist corporations, gross human rights violations, environmental polluters, and social inequality. Ideological orientations clearly become important in assessing threats, responding to Latin American hot spots, and advocating policy preferences. Andrain and Smith's findings are supported by the recent PIPA/Knowledge Networks poll that found Republicans far less concerned than Democrats about the Bush administration's fear-based justifications for war. The psychological dimensions of assessing threats and fears in the conduct of foreign policy will be examined in the entries that make up the major components of this book.

The media generate threat perceptions, general fears of other countries, and awareness of emerging of hot spots with security implications. Over time this process can create negative predispositions among the American public that make it easier to use force against a foreign power. In her examination of the relationship between threat perception, the media, and foreign policy opinion, Shana Kushner finds that people threatened by terrorism pick up cues from the media that impact on their political attitudes.[79] A security threat frequently promotes increased in-group solidarity, intolerance, ethnocentrism, stereotyping, and support for curtailing civil liberties. From 2000 to 2002 American attitudes shifted toward a more "hawkish" foreign policy that supported more defense spending, border security, covert action, and military intervention abroad. This shift made it easier to associate hot spots with serious security threats and greater U.S. military aid to Latin American governments. The shift in attitudes among the American public also made it easier to demonize foreign leaders, particularly those from small countries who use anti-American rhetoric and support policies that attempt to weaken U.S. influence abroad. The probability of acquiring more hawkish foreign-policy attitudes increased as people devoted more time to watching television. Kushner found the TV-threat variable one of the most significant factors in the formation of political attitudes toward security issues, particularly the use of force abroad. In contrast, newspaper reading *decreased* individual support for the war against Saddam Hussein. In sum, the broadcast media can heighten citizens' sense of threat and increase willingness to use armed force abroad. Kushner's study provides important implications for the responsibility of elites, the media, and citizens in the conduct of American foreign policy. Those in charge of the news need to recognize the objective content of threats, avoid sensationalist reporting that exaggerates the threats from terrorism, and more thoroughly examine the evidence presented by foreign-policy elites. If foreign-policy elites can exaggerate and reinforce threat perceptions to increase support for foreign-policy goals and objectives, then opinion manipulation threatens the ability of citizens to judge accurately the rationale for costly foreign policies. They cannot judge the degree of threats to national security if journalists succumb to the "rally" effect the White House gains from offering a heightened sense of subjective threat. Instead of continuing to favor official sources and relying on government framing of events, media personnel need to depend on those who can challenge the government with different threat assessments. Government officials often exaggerate threats for partisan political advantage, and the media's ideological and patriotic subservience to American leaders means that leaders are always "good" when responding to "threats" or "aggression." The use of "hot spot" terminology adds to the ability of government officials and the media to manipulate and exaggerate threats in world regions where Americans have little understanding of the severity of conflicts and the best course of action to minimize threats to the United States.

Threat Perception and Intervention in Latin America

The history of U.S. intervention and regime change in Latin America reflects a desire to prevent or preempt perceived threats to the capacity of the United States to project power in Latin America and beyond. Since the time of the Monroe Doctrine, Washington has worried about the ability of foreign adversaries to project power in the Western Hemisphere and the inability of weak Latin American governments to protect themselves and the United States' interests in them from a foreign presence. Unfortunately, the United States has not spent enough time worrying about the damages and negative consequences of over a century of regime change in Latin America. Many of these interventions were not just ruthless and costly—the majority were unnecessary.[80]

Military expansion and intervention often increase the threat of terrorism, both at home and abroad. Contrary to official rhetoric in Washington, U.S. interventions tend to produce undemocratic results as human rights violations escalate in the name of defending national security, fighting terrorism, and eliminating local insurgencies. With the establishment of a worldwide infrastructure the Pentagon calls "full spectrum dominance," the United States has shifted its military posture from defense to offense. As Latin America moves increasingly leftward in its domestic and foreign policies, the U.S. military command responsible for the region has become more involved in the internal affairs of Latin American governments in an effort to reassert U.S. hegemony in its "backyard." Pentagon threat perceptions now expand to locate and respond to "hot spots" before they spread, domino fashion, throughout the region.

Since the nineteenth century, Washington policymakers have learned that the use of extra-hemispheric threats can serve as powerful tools of public persuasion and forceful rationales for countering interference in the Americas. The Monroe Doctrine served as the perfect instrument to justify response to almost any kind of enemy or threat to the security of the Americas. The U.S. media have often contributed to the assessment of security threats by failing to question policy pronouncements and reporting the doomsayer arguments and claims of security threats verbatim without critical assessment. Many of the threats concocted by Washington policy makers during the Cold War proved false or grossly exaggerated, and in many cases the responses to them led to scandals and blunders that damaged the security of the United States. The logic of responding to external threats from the Monroe Doctrine forward has often been tied to a threat-based argument that great powers carry the burden of credibility and responsibility that smaller powers do not possess. In his speeches designed to convince the American people that Communist subversion in Central America posed the greatest threat to the United States, President Reagan gave many long and and alarming assessments of the Communist threat. After the launch of the war to remove Saddam Hussein in Iraq, hard-line Cuban Americans, magnifying the level of Cuba's threat to the United States, urged President Bush to carry out similar regime change on the island to get rid of Fidel Castro.

Unfortunately, threat perceptions too often emphasize a military response to a particular security threat when none is required. If, instead of focusing on "ungoverned spaces," "seams" in security structures, and "radical populists" as security threats to the Americas, U.S. officials spent more time closing the "seams" that persist between wealth and poverty, law and disorder, participation and isolation, and citizenship and neglect, Latin Americans would gain greater security. With the exception of Colombia and the small remnants of Peru's Shining Path insurgency, armed movements in Latin America do not constitute a terrorist threat to the United States.[81] Yet, according to Adam Isaacson, "In its worldwide search for terrorists and other 'new' transnational threats, Washington is once again encouraging Latin America and the Caribbean to arm, enlarge and reorient security forces to combat internal enemies."[82]

The emphasis on internal enemies reflects a Cold War focus on threat perceptions that Latin American governments have vowed to remove from security planning; however, U.S. military assistance is often tempting to governments that lack nonmilitary resources and technology to deal with security matters. The success of Hezbollah's style of warfare—a sophisticated national army with the lethal invisibility of a guerrilla army—is forcing the U.S. military to reassess how to respond to hybrid insurgencies that are difficult to track and target. In what some call "network warfare," Hezbollah's successes are increasingly seen as a threat to American national security, and military planners are struggling to find a counter-insurgency strategy to alleviate the threat.[83]

U.S. intervention in Latin America today is best understood as some form of political intervention aimed at supporting groups aligned with U.S. foreign policy, and suppressing popular groups advocating a more comprehensive democratization or change in the socioeconomic system. In the past ten years there have been three groups of Latin American countries that have become targets of U.S. political intervention: (1) countries defined as enemies and in need of regime change; (2) countries where popular classes and poor majorities threaten elite social orders; and (3) countries where neoliberal elites are in power but are considered institutionally weak and need some kind of strengthening.[84] The United States assumes a kind of moral authority to carry out its interventionist policies in Latin America in the name of democracy, although electoral intervention by foreign countries is illegal in the United States and would not be tolerated by Washington policymakers, regardless of the motives.

The United States as a Hegemonic State

The United States has a formidable global presence with undisputed military and economic power. The current emphasis on global hegemony as a basis for national security is expensive—particularly the militarization (and privatization) of foreign affairs—and may contribute to the

Human rights activists and torture survivors hold a 24-hour vigil in commemoration of the UN International Day in Support of Victims of Torture in Washington, D.C., on June 26, 2004. Protest followed revelations of torture and death of detainees at the hands of U.S. military personnel in Baghdad, Guantánamo Bay, and Afghanistan and included Sister Diana Ortiz, an American nun who was abducted, tortured, and raped by members of the Guatemalan security forces in 1989. (The Image Works)

way that hot spots are defined and assessed around the world.[85] In 2004 the United States spent as much on defense as the next twenty nations combined; the amount continues to escalate as it struggles to maintain foreign military bases and hundreds of thousands of U.S. forces in foreign lands. With over 730 U.S. military bases in 130 countries in 2006, the United States has military power on every continent with which to secure access to "vital national security interests" such as petroleum and other minerals. However, the United States no longer has the military presence in Latin America that prevailed during the Cold War, although it has established smaller bases in a number of areas with a variety of goals from counter-drug operations to civic assistance and anti-terrorism (see Table I.6). The growing hegemony of the United States in the world stimulates a growing debate over the proper role of the international system and the use of American power to achieve global power, security, and prosperity.

The asymmetries in power between the United States and Latin America mean that the United States is clearly the dominant economic, political, and military power in the Americas. For the past hundred years, the United States has experienced unrivaled hegemony in Latin America. As Cole Blasier points out, "No one should be surprised that the United States is a hegemonic state."[86] As the major hegemon in the Western Hemisphere, the United States assumed the right to impose its economic system, social and cultural values, and political institutions and values. Some area specialists maintain that interstate peace in Latin America is a direct consequence of U.S. hegemony.[87] This "hegemonic peace" hypothesis is rebutted by others who claim the several militarized conflicts were resolved without unilateral U.S. hegemonic management and the United States has been far more concerned about hot spots in Asia and the Middle East than throughout Latin America and the Caribbean.[88]

During the Cold War the overemphasis on security interests justified hegemonic behavior, including the use of armed mercenaries or regular forces in small Latin American countries such as Guatemala, Cuba, the Dominican Republic, Nicaragua, Grenada, and Panama. As long as foreign policy elites made the connection between security-based hot spots and international Communism, the American public was not bothered by military intervention, support for "friendly" tyrants, the use of torture, and economic injustice. A symbiotic relationship links the need to maintain hegemonic power with defense against a powerful enemy. "One needs an extrahemispheric threat to justify hegemonic control; and hegemonic control can be sustained only if extrahemispheric threats are beaten back."[89] The Bush administration's global war against terrorism is rooted in maintaining global hegemony through the claim that the

Table I.6 U.S. Military Bases in Latin America and the Caribbean: Size and Purpose (2005)

Base Location	Purpose of Military Base	Number of U.S. Troops
Guantánamo Bay, Cuba	Detainee center for foreign prisoners in the war on terrorism[a]	3,000
Soto Cano, Honduras	To enhance regional security, activities include military exercises, civic assistance, disaster relief, support for counter-drug operations, and de-mining activities	550
Manta, Ecuador	Forward Operating Location, with emphasis on counter-drug operations	Unknown
Aruba	Forward Operating Location, with emphasis on counter-drug operation	Unknown
Curaçao, Netherland Antilles	Forward Operating Location, with emphasis on counter-drug operations	200–230
Comalapa, El Salvador	Part of regional security activities in Central America	Unknown
Haiti	Part of international peace-keeping forces	13 (2003)
Paraguay	Anti-terrorism, drug smuggling, and threats from Bolivia	400–500
Colombia	Major activities include combating drug smuggling, combating left-wing insurgents, and de-mining training	800 U.S. military forces; 600 civilian contractors
Counter-Drug Radar Sites located in Peru and in mobile and secret locations[b]	Radar sites are located within host military bases to detect possible drug-smuggling flights	A typical detachment consists of 36 to 45 military personnel

Source: World Policy Institute (http://www.worldpolicy.org/projects/arms/reports/BasesMALA.html, accessed on December 15, 2005).

[a]Guantánamo Bay is the oldest military base outside of the continental United States and the only permanent overseas base where U.S. forces are stationed within a country the U.S. considers hostile.

[b]The known locations for the counter-drug radar sites include: Leticia (Colombia), Maranda (along border with Venezuela), Riohacha (Colombia), San Andrés Island (Colombia, east of Nicaragua), San Juan del Guaviare (Colombia), Tres Esquinas (southern border of Ecuador), Iquitos (Peru), Andoas (Peru), and Pucallpa (Peru). The rest of the radar sites are either mobile or secret.

United States is fighting terrorism in Iraq and Afghanistan in order to avoid fighting foreign terrorists on American soil and elsewhere around the globe. The chances of restraining the imperial ambitions of U.S. presidents is unlikely, according to Chalmers Johnson, "because the television and print media have by and large found it unprofitable to inform the public about the actions of the country's leaders."[90] With an uninformed public it is easier for Washington policymakers to absolve themselves from past actions and to claim falsely that hot spot threats have nothing to do with previous policies.

The United States had little difficulty dominating Latin America during the first three decades of the Cold War; however, this dominance started to wane under the presidency of Jimmy Carter, who altered the hegemony of the United States by focusing on human rights and nonintervention as well as on the new treaties with the Republic of Panama that eventually removed the U.S. military and political presence there beginning in 2000. President Ronald Reagan tried to revive U.S. hegemony through a doctrine of "peace through strength," a promise to rearm the United States and employ military power in support of foreign-policy objectives. The Reagan Doctrine focused on Central America, often exaggerating the security threat posed by the Soviet Union and Cuba in order to achieve his foreign policy goals. After the 9/11 attacks and the declaration of war against terrorism, Latin American and Caribbean leaders resisted U.S. efforts to reestablish hegemony in the region. The Latin American objections to the way Washington conducted the war against Saddam Hussein, as well as numerous foreign-policy failures in Latin America, contributed to a further decline in U.S. hegemony throughout Latin America. In election after election in Latin America, voters have chosen leaders who challenge the politics of elitism in favor of more participatory democracies that promise to benefit the poor and indigenous populations. According to Nadia Martínez, "The traditional conservative elites who were aligned with the United States were voted out, and replaced with socially minded, left-leaning leaders."[91] The exception to this trend is Mexico, where the leftist candidate, Andrés López Obrador, was narrowly defeated by Felipe Calderón, a candidate with strong ties to the traditional conservative elites.

The United States continues to exert a great deal of hegemony in Latin America through its economic and military power, yet the political drift to the left in Latin America shows the region's increasing rejection of Washington's lead. Washington policymakers worry about losing control in a region where they view security threats as growing and where they exert less control over events than in the past century. Despite the democratic trends in Latin America over the past twenty years, the hot spots of the twenty-first century will likely increase as states fail and unstable democratic regimes contribute to U.S. efforts to prevent security-based hot spots from spreading to other regions. It is impossible to explain the anger and distrust of the United States abroad, and the widespread incredulity that occurs when Washington policymakers claim they are interested in spreading democracy and freedom, without understanding the historical record of forcible regime changes by the United States and its allies over the past century.

U.S. Responses to Current Hot Spots

The United States has used a variety of means to respond to current "hot spots" and at the same time maintain an imperial presence in the Americas. For example, the George W. Bush administration has employed each of the following strategies, depending on the foreign policy goal and the way it defines and prioritizes a particular threat.

Military and Economic Aid

Military and economic aid have been used to consolidate U.S. efforts to maintain and protect U.S. interests in Latin America. The U.S. military presence in Latin America is designed to eliminate drug trafficking and terrorist networks. It includes the establishment of military bases, counterinsurgency and antidrug operations, and the use of private military contractors. The School of the Americas, renamed the Western Hemisphere Institute of Security Cooperation (WHINSEC) in 2001, has been in operation since 1946 and over a span of 50 years has trained over 65,000 Latin American military and police personnel in counterinsurgency tactics. U.S. military aid and bases, training, and arms sales to the Latin American region have all increased sharply since the war on terrorism was declared in 2001 (see Table I.7). In the last five years, U.S. military locations have proliferated in Latin America, although the United States has abandoned the old-style, full-fledged military base in favor of smaller Cooperative Security Locations (formerly known as Forward Operation Locations) and Ground Based Radar (GBR) sites. Joint exercises are common between U.S. and Latin American military forces; however, military-to-military relationships are banned if a country has signed on to the International Criminal Court and is not considered a major non-NATO ally. Countries without waivers are denied foreign military financing funds. Latin American governments that the United States judges to be insufficiently supportive of the war on terrorism are also denied economic and military aid.

Table I.7 Major Aid Recipients in Latin America, 2004 (millions of U.S. dollars)

Country	Military/Police	Economic/Social
Bolivia	60	102
Brazil	11	18
Colombia	551	150
Ecuador	44	38
El Salvador	6	38
Guatemala	3	43
Haiti	3	54
Honduras	4	41
Mexico	54	35
Nicaragua	1	43
Panama	11	12
Peru	76	102
Uruguay	2	0
Venezuela	4	3

Source: Bruce Finley, "High Noon in Latin America: U.S. Targets 'Lawless' Areas," *Denver Post* (December 5, 2005). Using U.S. government data and Washington Office on Latin America data, Finley shows that total U.S. military and police spending on Latin America increased from $400 million in 2001 to $866.6 million in 2004.

Currently, the only two old-style bases left are Guantánamo Bay, Cuba, which doubles as a detention center for illegal immigrants and "enemy combatants" suspected of terrorism (the 3,000 troops at Guantánamo constitute about half of the entire U.S. military presence in Latin America), and a base at Soto Cano, Honduras, that houses around 600 members of Joint Task Force Bravo. This post-Panama strategy is designed to minimize the U.S. military presence in the region while at the same time achieving Pentagon mission goals in the region.

Some of these strategies reflect the continuation of past policies; others reflect new threats and different perceptions of how to handle the danger to U.S. and regional security. Many analysts see Bolivia and Venezuela as test cases for how the United States handles the rising tide of leftist leaders in Latin America. More enlightened leadership in Washington should recognize that the Cold War paradigm of the past needs to be replaced by a greater respect for Latin America's sovereignty since the electoral mandates given to leaders by citizens contain solid repudiations of U.S. prescriptions for the ills confronting the region.[92] Although the United States has given millions of dollars in aid to the Bolivian government, Cuba and Venezuela have managed to undermine U.S. influence by providing development aid and services for programs that include money for rural clinics run by Cuban doctors and literacy classes taught by teachers from both countries.[93]

Intervention for Regime Change

The United States has resorted to intervention—regime change, democracy promotion, and military humanitarianism—to deal with hot spots in Latin America. Regime change in Latin America is less common and more difficult as a foreign-policy strategy than military aid and economic pressure; however, as the Pentagon and the White House have used regime change in Iraq and Afghanistan, they have also stood behind coup attempts to remove anti-U.S. leaders such as Hugo Chávez and Jean-Bertrand Aristide. Nevertheless, the Bush administration stresses winning "hearts and minds" as a necessary part of building a foundation for democratic rule as a bulwark against the emergence of dangerous hot spots. Using the National Endowment for Democracy (NED), the United States has funded efforts to promote "democratic" institutions and values in Latin America since the 1980s.[94] Although the NED is a quasi-public institution, it is often accused of meddling in Latin American elections. Nevertheless, it serves as a key instrument for the Bush administration's goals of bringing democracy and free markets to the rest of the world. The results of this effort are mixed, and Latin Americans have lost faith in the value of democracy, as the term is understood in the United States, as the best form of government. For example, from 1996 to 2005 the percentage of Latin Americans who regard democracy as the best form of government declined by 8 percent, except in Venezuela under President Chávez, where it increased by 14 percent. President Chávez is only one of many leaders who has expressed resentment at how the United States has tried to promote democracy. The global backlash is based on the view that what the United States does in the name of democracy is self-serving, coercive, and immoral.[95] The large amount of economic assistance the United States gives to opposition groups whose primary intent is to remove President Chávez has been a matter of diplomatic conflict between the United States and Venezuela. It seems obvious that the $26 million that U.S. AID has funneled to the opposition over the past five years is intended for regime change rather than democracy-building initiatives.

Economic Sanctions

U.S. leaders use economic sanctions as one of the coercive measures to change the leadership or policies of Latin American governments considered serious threats. The most common tool of this strategy—a punitive trade embargo—enables Washington policymakers to avoid or postpone policies that may require the use of armed force. In Latin America economic sanctions have been used in attempts to stop terrorism, remove a dictator, halt drug trafficking, improve a dismal human rights situation, or promote democracy. The United States has used economic sanctions against Fidel Castro's Cuba beginning with the last year of the Eisenhower administration without achieving the desired result of regime change on the island. After more than 40 years of failure, economic sanctions seem to some like a pathologic attempt to punish Castro for his defiance and humiliation of the United States.[96] Few Latin American governments, however, have escaped U.S. economic sanctions, often applied with the backing of multilateral institutions such as the Organization of American States or the United Nations. Nevertheless, whatever goals punitive economic sanctions attempt to achieve, they are rarely successful in changing the target government or eliminating a regional hot spot.[97]

Drug Certification

Drug certification helps U.S. anti-narcotics efforts to curtail threats to hemispheric security. When the U.S. Congress passed the Anti-Drug Abuse Act of 1986, it created a law that mandated annual reports to assess or certify anti-narcotics policies in the drug-producing and trafficking nations around the world, nineteen of which are located in Latin America and the Caribbean. If the United States judged that a Latin American government took insufficient steps to eradicate illicit drugs, the individual country risked decertification and drastic reductions in foreign aid from Washington. The certification process has not worked in reducing the number of drug-based hot spots in Latin America. Its application has led some critics in Congress to regard it as nothing more than a charade or a cover for providing more military assistance to justify the elimination of narco-guerrillas.

Private Military Contractors

The U.S. government has expanded the practice of relying on private military contractors to respond to hot spots around the world, particularly in Latin America and the Middle East. At the head of the pack of privatized warriors is Blackwater, a private army used by the Bush administration to fight its "global war on terror." As of 2007, Blackwater has more than 2,300 private soldiers deployed in nine countries, including nearly a thousand former Chilean commandos and Colombian forces for deployment in Iraq and Afghanistan. Your Solutions, a Chicago-based firm, started a secret training camp in Honduras to prepare Honduran soldiers to work for U.S. mercenary companies in Iraq in 2003. After it was announced that John Negroponte, former U.S. ambassador to Honduras, was to be the new U.S. Ambassador to Iraq, the Honduran government quickly pulled its troops out of Iraq and later imposed a $25,000 fine on Your Solutions for violating the country's labor laws.[98]

The decline of public support in the United States for the Iraq war and the growing doubts about how long an exhausted military can continue the endless campaign against global terrorism has increased opportunities for private security companies to fill the void. Civilian military contractors such as DynCorp, Blackwater, and Kellogg, Brown, and Root, form a major part of the military effort in Colombia, where anti-drug contracts amount to nearly $200 million annually. Although turning over some military jobs to civilians presumably saves the American taxpayers money, this outcome rarely occurs. Little accountability emerges when civilian contractors perform jobs once reserved for the military. "With the growing number of foreign soldiers, law enforcement agents, and intelligence operatives engaged in work formerly done by U.S. military forces and intelligence agents, many analysts worry about the consequences of outsourcing American foreign policy in the name of budgetary savings."[99] The lack of congressional oversight over private military contractors means that Latin American hot spots can be handled by the White House without the negative publicity of unpopular military forays, which often decrease poll numbers for the president. As American corporations expand into fractious and potentially hostile settings, particularly in areas that possess natural gas and petroleum, the possibility of relying on mercenary armies becomes more attractive, both for the U.S. government and the private mercenaries.[100] However, what happens when the interests of a large corporation, or of foreign governments hiring DynCorp or Blackwater, come into conflict with the interests of the U.S. government?

Free Trade and Promotion of Neoliberalism

Fifth, Latin America is the fastest growing region in the world for United States exports and free trade agreements have replaced generous programs of economic assistance that were popular during the Cold War. At the core of this shift in economic policy are "neoliberal" policies designed to stabilize and improve economies previously plagued by slow growth, high inflation, and statist involvement in chronic social and economic problems. "These [neo-liberal] programs stress the need for market competition, freer trade, expanded foreign investment, a deregulated economy, privatization, lower corporate income taxes, reduced taxes on the wealthy, decreased expenditures for social services, and more flexible labor markets with greater wage inequalities, part-time employment, and temporary contracts."[101] U.S. officials expected that pro-market policies would promote more prosperity and greater support for democracy,

On his three-country visit to Latin America in March 2002, President Bush joined four other Latin American leaders from the Andean Trade Preference Act. Along with President Bush (second from left), are, left to right, President Andrés Pastrana (Colombia), Alejandro Toledo (Peru), Jorge Quiroga (Bolivia), and Ecuador's Vice President Pedro Pinto. Although free-trade agreements have been one of the pillars of the Bush administration's efforts to eliminate hot spots in Latin America, many critics see market-based reforms and trade agreements as a reason for opposition to the United States and its economic policies. (The Image Works)

which in turn would reduce threats to national security while at the same time provide benefits to U.S. consumers by giving them access to cheaper goods. The United States approved the North American Free Trade Agreement with Canada and Mexico in the early 1990s and hopes to complete the Free Trade Area of the Americas (FTAA), a hemispheric trade zone, in the next few years. As of 2006, the United States has trade agreements with Chile, Central America and the Dominican Republic, Panama, and Peru. It also has bilateral investment treaties with Argentina, Bolivia, Ecuador, Grenada, Honduras, Panama, and Trinidad and Tobago.

At first these economic initiatives gained widespread government support in Latin America; however, beginning in the 1990s the failure of neoliberalism to satisfy popular demands brought about a reversal in support for free trade agreements, neoliberalism, and Washington-imposed solutions to Latin America's ills. The negative consequences of these neoliberal economic policies have generated opposition in the United States and Latin America, contributing to the election of a growing number of leftist political leaders who have built a base of support by opposing neoliberalism for its negative social impact. Venezuela's President Chávez has led the charge against the U.S. vision of free trade, arguing that U.S.-backed economic reforms unfairly benefit the United States but generate poverty in Latin America, not wealth. Differences between trade negotiators in the United States and Latin America have undermined the prospects for creating the FTAA. Some of the hot spots in Latin America are the direct result of the negative consequences of neoliberalism, particularly where Latin Americans have faced growing unemployment, greater economic inequality, and declining expenditures on social services. Recent studies of wealth inequality show a widening gap between the global haves and have-nots, with developed countries pulling ahead of the rest of the world. In Latin America, the obstacles to amassing wealth are rooted in vaguely defined property rights and land tenure systems and poorly developed financial markets. The uneven pursuit of neoliberal economic reforms in the Andes have failed to satisfy many hopes and rising expectations, and this often contributes to the emergence of hot spots in the region. Yet the Bush administration refuses to consider the possibility that radical free-market absolutism—accepting wealth accumulation by the few and gross inequalities—in Latin America is a threat to hemispheric security.[102] According to the United Nations, more than 200 million Latin Americans remain in poverty after decades of free-trade prescriptions and recent economic growth buoyed by high prices for commodities such as tin, copper, or oil. The connection between neoliberalism and hot spots will be examined in the chapters that follow.

Multilateral Security Arrangements

The United States has employed both multilateral and unilateral methods to deal with security threats. Collective systems of security and consultation such as the Rio Pact, the Organization of American States (OAS), and the United Nations were created in the 1940s to handle geopolitical security threats connected with the Soviet Union, Cuba, Nicaragua, Guatemala, and others.

When collective security systems failed or were considered antithetical to U.S. interests, however, Washington resorted to covert and overt military interventions, constructing rationalizations for these aggressive acts to make them appear to the U.S. public to be proper, legal, and necessary. Over the course of U.S. history presidents have exaggerated threats, particularly from alleged European designs on the Americas, sometimes as a smoke screen for their own expansionist desires.[103] This tendency did not end with the Cold War and the demise of the Monroe Doctrine; the global war on terrorism contains some of the same strategies and tactics found in an earlier era when the enemy was the Soviet Union with Cuba as its proxy.

Recent developments in the Americas have led to disagreements and strained relations among the members of the OAS. According to the Inter-American Dialogue, a Washington-based think tank, "The U.S. government views the OAS as a mechanism for building alliances with Latin American nations, gaining their support on critical issues, exerting leadership in hemispheric affairs. Latin Americans see the organization, in part, as a means to moderate and contain Washington's power and influence in the region."[104] This conflict makes it more difficult to assess Latin American hot spots and agree on appropriate courses of action. For example, one of the most difficult challenges for the OAS is in Venezuela, where some argue that President Chávez is pushing an authoritarian agenda. How does the OAS deal with Venezuela when the Inter-American Democratic Charter obligates the member states to respond collectively to threats to democratic governance?

Congress and Latin American Hot Spots

Security enhancement and democracy promotion are two of the Bush administration's major goals for the Western Hemisphere, along with helping to stimulate economic development and encouraging responsible governance.[105] The U.S. Congress has devoted little time to conflicts in Latin America, with the exception of Colombia and Venezuela, but is concerned with the emergence of "non-traditional threats" to U.S. interests and the possibility of democratic failures in Latin America. On September 28, 2005, the Subcommittee on the Western Hemisphere of the House Committee on International Relations held hearings on "Keeping Democracy on Track: Hotspots in Latin America." Several government officials and academics prepared written statements for the members of the Subcommittee that included insights on the meaning of "Latin American hot spots," the location of the greatest threats to democratic stability in the region, and actions by the United States to enhance the survival of democracy in the Americas. In his prepared statement, Michael Coppedge, a political science professor at the University of Notre Dame, defined a Latin American "hot spot" as a country that suffers from four types of political problems: (1) chronic state weaknesses such as corruption, a politicized judiciary, lack of due process, and administrative efficiency; (2) unstable democratic regimes and undemocratic regimes; (3) unstable governments based on severe conflicts between

Introduction 47

the executive and legislative branches of government that are "ineffectively mediated by a politicized judiciary"; and (4) governments hostile to the United States or likely to become so. In Coppedge's analysis, Latin American hot spots develop when potential threats affect the interests of the United States and the stability of Latin American democratic institutions. Table I.8 summarizes the four types of problems, with emphasis on where the potential threat to democracy is most acute and the most salient manifestations of the problem for the United States. Although Coppedge focuses mainly on the potential threat to democracies in Latin America, hot spots also include specific problems that threaten the security of the United States but do not involve the collapse of democratic states. Unfortunately, relations between the United States and Latin America have seriously deteriorated because of failures of leadership in Washington and dismal economic and social performance in Latin America. The United States is in an unusually weak position to improve its relationship with Latin America. According to Coppedge,

> Many Latin American citizens are looking for alternatives to the free-market policies of the Washington consensus; they question the need for the invasion of Iraq; they see only limited value in the free trade agreements the U.S. will agree to, when agreements are even possible; in many countries, although most citizens continue to value democracy in the abstract, large numbers are disillusioned with the actual parties, courts, legislatures, and presidents they have. U.S. support for democracy often rings hollow in the wake of the 2000 presidential election in the United States and the Bush administration's initial endorsement of the April 2002 coup attempt in Venezuela. There are plenty of Latin American leaders and activists who continue to share U.S. ideals and welcome U.S. assistance, but in this environment, open association with the United States is a liability for some of them. It would be more prudent if the United States respected the sensibilities of Latin Americans by taking a lower profile, working behind the scenes, multilaterally, using more aid and fewer threats and sanctions, offering more carrots and fewer [big] sticks."[106]

With an interest in maintaining hegemony in the Western Hemisphere, Washington often finds it difficult to respect the sovereignty of Latin American countries when potential threats enter the foreign policy "radar screen" of policymakers who consider Latin Americans inferior and see a domestic connection to the Latin American hot spot.

There is a growing backlash against "democracy promotion" in Latin America, which is rife with anti-Americanism and increasingly dominated by center-left governments. One of the most powerful critics of U.S. democracy-promotion programs is President Chávez, who regularly blasts these policies as a cover action for attempts to oust him from office. He

Table I.8 Latin American Hot Spots: Problems, Countries (2005)

Major Problem	Manifestations of Problem	Countries That Suffer from the Problem	U.S. Reaction to Potential Hot Spot Threats
1. Weak states	Corruption; politicized judiciary; lack of due process; administrative inefficiency; violent insurgencies; narcotrafficking; mass demonstrations	Colombia, Peru, Bolivia, Ecuador, Mexico, Paraguay, Guyana	Military aid; economic aid; private military contractors; military advisers; propaganda; work with Rio Group and OAS
2. Unstable democratic regimes and nondemocratic regimes	Lack of representative democracy; hostility toward the United States	Cuba, Venezuela, Haiti	Economic sanctions; propaganda; diplomatic isolation; regime change; political threats
3. Unstable governments	Severe conflict between executive and congressional branches of government, ineffectively mediated by a politicized judiciary	Brazil, Peru, Ecuador, Bolivia, Nicaragua, Honduras, Guatemala, Dominican Republic	Diplomatic pressure; propaganda; pressure through the OAS; economic (MCA) assistance
4. Governments hostile to the United States	Constant verbal criticism of the U.S. foreign policy; refusal to follow U.S. in OAS and UN voting	Cuba, Venezuela, Ecuador, Bolivia, Nicaragua, Mexico	Diplomatic pressure; propaganda; economic sanctions; political threats

Table I.8 *(continued)*

Major Problem	Manifestations of Problem	Countries That Suffer from the Problem	U.S. Reaction to Potential Hot Spot Threats
5. Non-Hot Spots	Strong states that demonstrate the ability to control borders, execute laws faithfully, adjudicate claims fairly, and maintain public order; low corruption and relatively high trust in key institutions	Chile, Costa Rica, Uruguay, Argentina	Diplomatic praise; favorable trade and investment; political neglect

Source: Michael Coppedge, Statement before the Subcommittee on the Western Hemisphere, House Committee on International Relations, United States Congress, hearings on "Keeping Democracy on Track: Hotspots in Latin America" (September 28, 2005).

accuses groups such as the NED of supporting the Venezuelan opposition in hopes of removing from office. In response, he has used his petrodollars to support anti-U.S. parties and candidates in Bolivia, Ecuador, Peru, and elsewhere in the Americas. The Bush administration has contributed to the skepticism of democracy promotion and its image in Latin America through its treatment of prisoners and detainees at U.S.-run facilities in Iraq, Afghanistan, and Guantánamo Bay; the rendition of foreign detainees; the establishment of a network of covert U.S.-run prisons overseas; the admitted practice of collecting information on telephone conversations without court warrants in the United States; so have the alleged manipulation of voting machines and disenfranchisement of black voters in Florida and Ohio in 2000 and 2004. According to Thomas Carothers, "Washington's use of the term 'democracy promotion' has come to be seen overseas not as the expression of a principled American aspiration but as a code word for 'regime change'—namely, the replacement of bothersome governments by military force or other means. Moreover, the Bush administration has caused the term to be closely associated with U.S. military intervention and occupation by adopting democracy promotion as the principal rationale for the invasion of Iraq."[107] The antidemocracy backlash will continue as long as the Bush administration does nothing to change the close association of democracy promotion with U.S. military intervention and occupation. The failure of democratization and nation building in Iraq and elsewhere may also be seen in Washington's concern for stability rather than democracy in a post-Castro Cuba, lest refugees begin pouring into the United States.

Hot Spot Rhetoric and Metaphors

The foreign policy elite and the media often use the terms "hot spot," "trouble spot," or "flash point" as a metaphor for local, national, or regional developments that may not immediately threaten the security (or some general interest) of the United States but have the potential to flare up into a major conflict. The existence of a hot spot can also lead to some form of U.S. intervention since it is often believed to carry a threat to national security. During the Cold War the Pentagon often referred to security threats in terms of "choke points" around the world where the Soviet Union and its allies could interrupt access to raw materials from Latin America and affect U.S. hegemony. The consequences of globalization have weakened the ability of "choke points" to instill fear in those who worry about national security. The domino theory served as a powerful metaphor to deal with communist enemies during the Cold War in the same way that hot spots have influenced those in the intelligence/security bureaucracy concerned with terrorist threats. The Panama Canal, political instability in Central America, and a foreign presence in the Caribbean Sea became important in geostrategic calculations, particularly in time of war. Today Panama is considered a potential threat to the security of the United States because of the growing presence of China, not because it lacks a strong state and is in danger of becoming an undemocratic country. Despite the importance of the Panama Canal to the United States and international shipping, it has never yet been attacked by terrorists, domestic or foreign. Nevertheless, those in the national security bureaucracy worry about Panama because of the proximity of the Canal to narcoterrorist conflict in neighboring Colombia and political turmoil in Venezuela. During the Cold War Washington policymakers used hot-spot type terminology—talk of Communization, Soviet beachheads, Cuban-inspired Marxist guerrillas, exporters of revolution—as alarming trends associated with Latin American countries "falling" into the hands of a foreign or domestic enemy. Today, Venezuela's strategic alliance with Iran and other Middle Eastern countries is designed to construct an alliance to reduce American influence in developing countries. The close relations with Iran and Cuba suggest to Washington that Venezuela has no interest in curbing terrorism and as such should be considered a threat and a primary target for intelligence operations dealing with terrorism and nonproliferation.[108]

Metaphors define policy responses and often involve alarmist rhetoric to "sell" the threat to the U.S. Congress and the American public. Since policy elites often incorrectly defined Latin America as located in the "backyard" of the United States, they can more easily magnify a security threat in the Americas than somewhere else in the world. For instance, the immigration debate is frequently framed in dualistic terms—pro-immigration vs. anti-immigration—and the "restrictionist" segment of the debate has grown with the fears associated with the war on terror.[109] The U.S. media has added fuel to the fire by publishing reports that resound with alarmist rhetoric about the threats of immigrants to national security, culture and economy. According to Barry, "The main message echoing through the media is that the combination of terrorism, mass immigration and unprotected borders constitute the country's utmost security threat."[110] In any case, the U.S. border with Mexico has become a "hot spot" because of the deepening sense of vulnerability experienced by many U.S. citizens, who see a connection between the increase in illegal immigrants crossing in high numbers and corporate downsizing, stagnant wages, and the continuing loss of medical and pension benefits. The anti-immigrant movement also gains support from the general public that has negative views of immigrants because of their inability (and suspected unwillingness) to speak fluent English, and perceived religious and cultural differences. President Bush would be less concerned with illegal immigration if the public felt indifferent toward the issue. The Republican Party for its part sees itself as competing for the growing power of the Hispanic voter in the United States, while the party's business base retains its interest in low labor costs.

Latin American "hot spots" with national security implications can also involve uncooperative governments and their leaders and allies, particularly those critical of Washington policymakers and their policies. The Bush administration began classifying rogue regimes that oppose the United States as evil in order to justify attempts to isolate and eliminate hostile powers.[111] In February 2005 Porter Goss, Director of the U.S. Central Intelligence Agency (CIA), classified Venezuela as a "potential area for instability" and one of several "flashpoints" for 2005. According to the CIA, today's Venezuela has become a hot spot because of the way President Chávez consolidated his power, treated his political opposition, and formed close ties with Cuba, Iran, Syria, China, and Hezbollah.[112] During the Cold War Chávez would have been called a "Marxist threat to the Americas" because of his ties to Cuba, with the potential to spread Communism to his South American neighbors. Goss named four other Latin American nations as areas of concern for 2005: Colombia, Haiti, Mexico, and Cuba. Even though President Chávez has been democratically elected twice and was victorious in a transparent recall referendum by a landslide in 2004, the Bush administration refers to the Venezuelan government as a "new breed of authoritarianism" and a "negative force" in the Western Hemisphere capable of spreading negative influence among its neighbors. Maximalist rhetoric about regional and strategic threats are used to justify intervention, war, hegemony, and occupation.[113] During his campaign for the presidency in 2007, Senator John McCain of Arizona claimed that President Chávez is "using his country's oil revenues to establish a dictatorship, bully his neighbors and succeed Castro as Latin America's leading antagonist of the United States."[114]

In major media outlets in the United States, Chávez is frequently portrayed as a brutal dictator who threatens the interests of the United States in Latin America. The *Miami Herald*, following the anti-Chávez line of the State Department, ran a front-page story on February 12, 2005, claiming that Chávez was arming Venezuelans for a "war with the U.S."[115] Several months later, religious broadcaster Pat Robertson joined the chorus of opposition to Chávez by claiming that Venezuela is becoming "a launching pad for communist infiltration and Muslim extremism." On this claim, Robertson added that the United States should get rid of him by using covert assassination teams because it would be "a whole lot cheaper than starting a war" to ensure *our* supply of oil.[116] Defense Secretary Donald H. Rumsfeld compared President Chávez to Adolf Hitler and expanded his efforts to define Chávez as a security threat because his government was working with Fidel Castro and Evo Morales.[117] The *Wall Street Journal*'s Mary Anastasia O'Grady claims that Argentine president Néstor Kirchner represents a security threat because he coddles Montonero and ERP guerrillas while condemning the military for its crimes during the "Dirty War" of the 1970s and 1980s. To make her point about the dangers lurking in Kirchner's Argentina, O'Grady asserts that "Argentina has a history of harboring the world's darkest figures, including Nazi fugitives after World War II. The Iranian and Syrian sponsored Hezbollah is widely suspected of orchestrating the Buenos Aires bombing of the Israeli Embassy in 1992 and the Jewish community center in 1994."[118] However, O'Grady fails to mention that the United States has a history of supporting right-wing dictators and ignoring the human rights abuses of state sponsors of terrorism because they opposed Communist regimes and left-wing dictators in Latin America. President Bush's repeated commitment to prevent any country from harboring international terrorists is undermined by the refusal of the White House to either prosecute or expel Luis Posada Carriles, former CIA anti-Castro agent and "one of the world's most unremitting purveyors of violence."[119]

In the world of political communication, language matters, because issues that are framed without adequate attention to metaphors and symbols will lack the emotional punch that politicians so desperately need to persuade their audience. Linguist George Lakoff believes that how a political issue is "framed" will determine its success in political communication. His "frame wars" involve choosing metaphors that link the terms of debate with the emotions of the audience in a favorable manner. For example, the use of World War II terminology—"Hitler," "holocaust," "fascist" (Islamic and otherwise), "world domination"—by Defense Secretary Donald Rumsfeld, Venezuelan President Chávez, and others may seem like hyperbole and nonsense, but they serve an important purpose by affecting the bedrock emotions of the audience and help to frame and win political debates. The Cuban countryside is dotted with large billboards of President George W. Bush made up to look like Hitler along with a message of defiance if Bush attempts to invade Cuba. The use of the term "hot spot" or "hot button issue" may seem like vacuous ways of framing the debate over national security policy; however, it serves an important communication function by touching the emotions of the audience that have been preconditioned to fear anything connected with terrorism, socialism, Islamists, and powerful weaponry. The mythology of World War II—a "good" war that the United States won by defeating evils abroad—still constitutes a part of defense strategy and American foreign policy, where hot spots demand a pre-emptive military response to violence and political instability in the Third World. When Tim Russert on *Meet the Press* on February 8, 2004, asked President Bush to respond to critics that he brought the nation to war under false pretenses, Bush justified his war decision by calling Saddam Hussein a "madman" who posed an imminent threat in a "new kind of war."[120] Unfortunately for American democracy, these assertions are rarely challenged directly by the mainstream media, leading to an endorsement of the use of force instead of diplomacy and negotiation.

Conclusion

The major security threats to the United States and Latin America vary by region, political ideology and partisanship, regime stability, and closeness to the United States. Hot spot terminology and rhetoric lack precision as a measure of critical threats and can easily change when perceptions of foreign policy elites and the public change. Threat perceptions based on security fears change over time and are often more subjective than objective in how they are used by Washington policymakers. The most commonly cited critical threats in the world include international terrorism, chemical and biological weapons, and unfriendly countries becoming nuclear powers. None of these are relevant to Latin America, although political ideology is a key variable for explaining the way Latin American hot spots are defined and treated by Washington policymakers. According to the Center for Defense Information, there are only three hot spots in two Latin American countries, each related to terrorist activities in Colombia and Peru. The use of hot spot or trouble spot terminology is often more ideological and subjective than an objective measure of a national security threat. Using a case-study approach, this book will examine seven regions (Mexico, Central America, Caribbean, English-speaking Caribbean, Andean South America, the Southern Cone and Brazil, and non-Iberian South America) using a threat-based hot spot approach to current conflicts. The hot spot metaphor is closely associated with the probability that an ongoing or incipient conflict can slide into a major conflict or war. The first region addressed is Mexico, where several hot spots considered security threats to both Mexico and the United States will be explored.

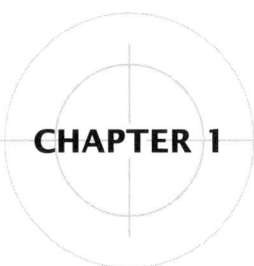

CHAPTER 1

Mexico

Mexico is the second most-populous country in Latin America after Portuguese-speaking Brazil and shares a 2,000-mile border with the United States. The Mexican economy is highly dependent on exports to the United States, particularly petroleum, cars, and electronic equipment. Mexico's economy depends on oil for a large part of its national income. As the world's fifth largest oil producer in 2003, its ninth largest oil exporter, and the third largest supplier of petroleum to the United States, Mexico is vital to the United States. With a population of 110 million, Mexico is a key player on the global political stage and of strategic importance to the United States because of border security and counterterrorism, trade and investment opportunities, antinarcotics cooperation, and environment and natural resources management. It represents one of the region's largest economies, and efforts to consolidate democracy since 2000 have given rise to a strong leftist trend, as evidenced by the power of the 2006 presidential candidate Andrés Manuel López Obrador (known in Mexico as AMLO) of the PRD (Partido Revolucionario Democrático). Although Felipe Calderón of the conservative PAN (Partido Acción Nacional) was declared the winner of the July 6, 2006, presidential election and was sworn in on December 1 of that year, for several months López Obrador refused to accept his narrow defeat, proclaimed himself the "legitimate" president, and named a "shadow government." The bitter aftermath of Mexico's presidential election raised serious doubts as to whether Calderón will be able to fulfill his campaign promises: to strengthen the rule of law and democratic institutions, promote job creation, and fight growing poverty and corruption. There are also growing demands in Mexico to engage in serious reform in the oil and gas industry, including efforts to allow private investment in order to expand as an oil exporter. Although Mexico is not a member of OPEC (Organization of Petroleum Exporting Countries), it has observer status and is a major player among the non-OPEC producers such as Norway and Great Britain. The environmental concerns that were incorporated into NAFTA (North American Free Trade Agreement) have added domestic pressures on PEMEX (Mexico's national oil company) to clean up its activities where oil spillage and pollution have been demonstrated to be damaging to Mexico's environment.

Since Mexico's economic woes in the 1980s, millions of Mexicans have migrated to the United States. With roughly 10 percent of Mexico's population of 110 million living in the United States, Mexico now has a social, economic, and political safety valve for its government, which is faced with political unrest, drug violence, border insecurity, and chronic unemployment, particularly in the southern states of Chiapas and Oaxaca. Mexicans make up 70 percent of all illegal immigrants in the United States and those who are workers send home $20 billion annually in remittances. This is a huge amount, greater than the total annual foreign aid budget of the United States and equal to Mexico's income from oil exports and tourism. In order to solve the sensitive issue of illegal immigration, the United States must face its dependency on Mexico. There is no doubt that political unrest on the U.S. southern border would cause even greater concern among Washington policymakers about border issues and overall security.

The anti-immigrant movement has grown by 600 percent between 2005 and 2007, comprising a national network of organizations working to restrict legal immigration and deport undocumented immigrants. The most influential anti-immigrant organizations are closely connected to mainstream conservative politics. Congressman Tom Tancredo (R-Colorado), a Republican candidate for U.S. president in 2008, warns in campaign speeches that immigrant terrorists "are coming to kill you and me and our families."[1] For those who oppose immigration from the south, what is happening along the U.S. border and elsewhere amounts to a twenty-first century "invasion" of the United States, with dire consequences if the influx is not stopped.

Although Mexico is clearly important to the United States in a variety of ways, there is not a serious military security threat from south of the border. From the time of the Mexican War (1846–1848) to the Mexican Revolution (1910–1917), the United States seized over half of Mexico's territory, intervened repeatedly to protect U.S. access to raw materials and maintain stability, and invested in a variety of economic activities, particularly petroleum and mining. After the revolution the United States developed a close relationship with the ruling party, which helped to protect U.S. security interests throughout the Cold War and beyond.

Since September 11, 2001, the United States and Mexico have drifted apart because of Washington's neglect of the Vicente Fox administration's concerns (2000–2006) as the former focused on the war on terrorism and the invasion and occupation of Iraq to remove Saddam Hussein. The bilateral security relationship has been complicated by Mexico's foreign-policy principles: revolutionary nationalism, anti-interventionism, and the protection of national sovereignty. The U.S. response to the 9/11 attacks put severe strains on U.S.-Mexican relations, as Mexico was forced to walk a fine line between adequate expressions of support for the people of the United States and its preference for diplomacy and negotiation over forceful military action.[2] In its 2004 survey of foreign-policy goals, the Chicago Council on Foreign Relations found that the American public was more concerned than "leaders" with two goals considered to be "very important": stopping the flow of illegal drugs into the United States and controlling and reducing illegal immigration (see Table I.5). Reducing illegal immigration means figuring out some way to address the issue of job creation and poverty reduction in Mexico. Mexico's new president, Felipe Calderón, took office in December 2006 pledging to root out corruption, eliminate criminal gangs and drug traffickers, and provide more cooperation with the Bush administration in reducing illegal immigration to the United States. Even if these goals were accomplished legislatively, grave consequences could result for Mexico and the United States if the billions of dollars in remittances were significantly reduced. U.S. congressional efforts to solve the immigration conundrum increased in 2007 by a series of legislative efforts aimed at allowing undocumented workers to become legal members of their communities.

In his assessment of Latin American hot spots, Michael Coppedge categorizes Mexico as a "weak state" because of corruption, border violence, narco-trafficking, a politicized judiciary, and the existence of small, but violent, insurgencies (see Table I.8). Mexico's verbal criticism of Washington for its unilateral foreign policy, and its refusal to vote along with the United States at the Organization of American States (OAS) or the United Nations, are further reasons why Mexico is regarded as one of the hot spots in Latin America. However, according to many in the Mexican officer corps, poverty is the most serious threat to national security, not drug traffickers, small-arms merchants, guerrillas, or terrorists. President George W. Bush, in a speech to the nation on September 17, 2002, stated, "Poverty does not make poor people into terrorists and murderers. Yet poverty weakens institutions and corruption can make weak states vulnerable to terrorist networks and drug cartels within their borders."[3] However, studies carried out by the National Bureau of Economic Research find that poverty (as measured by per-capita income) is a weak indicator of terrorism.[4] If poverty contributes to weak states, and weak states are associated with crime, terrorism, and drug trafficking, then why is Latin American poverty not more of a threat to U.S. security? Would a U.S.-backed war on poverty in Mexico help the United States deal with immigration, border crime, drug trafficking, guerrilla uprisings, and terrorism? Washington is less concerned with Mexico's status as a weak state than with the flow of immigrants into the United States and the growing number of trans-boundary problems: crime, air and water pollution, drug trafficking, human rights violations, labor exploitation, and the fear associated with members of Middle Eastern or other terrorist organizations infiltrating the United States from Mexico.[5]

The border between the United States and Mexico runs for 1,951 miles from the Gulf of Mexico in the east to the Pacific Ocean in the west. The boundary touches four large Sun Belt states in the United States and six states in Mexico. The U.S.-Mexican borderland is the fastest-growing industrial belt in Mexico and the busiest land crossing in the world. On March 1, 2003, responsibility for immigration and border-related matters was transferred to the Department of Homeland Security. U.S. security along the border is the responsibility of agents and inspectors who are part of the U.S. Citizenship and Immigration Services (USCIS), Drug Enforcement Agency (DEA), and Federal Bureau of Investigation (FBI). U.S. Customs and Border Protection (CBP) is responsible for protecting U.S. borders within the Department of Homeland Security. Still, the massive bureaucracy in charge of securing the border is often stymied by poor communication, inadequate language training, faulty intelligence, and a poor track record of working cooperatively on security matters. According to Katherine McIntire Peters, the bureaucracy responsible for border security constitutes an institutional threat to U.S. security:

> Lines of authority along the border are often chaotic, since no single agency is in charge of border management. The Immigration and Naturalization Service is responsible for tracking people; the Customs Service facilitates commerce while keeping out contraband; the Coast Guard secures the coastline and seaports. Other agencies are involved as well, although to a lesser extent: The Agriculture Department inspects plants and food for disease and contamination; the State Department issues visas to foreigners who want to enter the country; and the Commerce Department ensures that certain technologies aren't exported to nations that might use them to build weapons. While federal personnel work together cooperatively at many ports, the agencies maintain separate information data bases and have distinct missions, cultures and workforces.[6]

The new national strategy that went into effect on March 1, 2003, was designed to overcome the bureaucratic problems discussed by Peters;

however, the megabureacracy that now makes up the Department of Homeland Security has yet to demonstrate that additional spending, personnel, and programs have made America safer from terrorists. It is still too soon to assess whether this bureaucratic overhaul of the security bureaucracy will result in a safer and more secure nation. As the U.S. Border Patrol expands to stop illegal immigration, terrorist infiltration, and drug smuggling, cases of bribery and corruption among Border Patrol agents have developed into major worries for U.S. officials.[7] The size of the Border Patrol has increased threefold since 1995, and the Bush administration and Congress are spending billions of dollars to secure the border, including the construction of hundreds more miles of border barriers. It is interesting that the number of workplace arrests made by U.S. immigration authorities in 1997 was 17,554; however, by 2003 the number had plummeted to 445.[8] There are clearly partisan differences in these figures, particularly the prevailing ideologies of the Democrats versus those of the Republicans when it comes to government's role in enforcing its regulatory powers.

The scope of U.S.-Mexican relations extends far beyond high-level diplomatic and official contacts; there are nearly one million legal border crossings per day and more than 600,000 American citizens live in Mexico. There are more than 2,600 U.S. companies operating in Mexico, and U.S. investors count for 55 percent of foreign direct investment in Mexico. Total U.S. trade with Mexico, now the U.S.'s second-largest trading partner after Canada, has more than doubled since NAFTA went into effect in 1994. Although there are no universally recognized hot spots in Mexico, border crime and arms trafficking, illegal immigration, terrorism, and controlling the flow of illicit drugs into the United States are of major concern to the two governments. The Zapatista rebellion in Chiapas is still a thorn in the side of the Mexican government but does not constitute a security threat to either Mexico as a whole or the United States. The same could be said of the 2006 protest movement in Oaxaca, which lasted for several months and centered on the removal of a corrupt governor of the state. Lack of good governance and political corruption continue to plague Mexico, but it is not included in the Failed State Index (discussed in the Introduction) and does not rank in the top ten of the most corrupt countries in Latin America. However, when Americans are polled about the most important goals of American foreign policy, close to 60 percent of the American public mentioned "controlling and reducing illegal immigration" with Mexico. During his first month in office, President Felipe Calderón announced a new plan to root out corruption through anticorruption education programs, better disclosure of government activities, and a uniform system to revise spending in government departments.

Since the 9/11 attacks, the U.S. media has focused on the potential threats from loosely controlled borders because of the possibility of terrorists slipping into the United States from Mexico. Although often exaggerated for partisan political gain, the debate over illegal immigration is tied to the importance of security rather than the loss of jobs to American workers in the United States.[9] Anti-Mexican racism may also be detected in the polarized debate over immigration reform in the United States. Print coverage of Mexico in the United States does not provide an accurate picture of political and economic life with the bulk of the subjects focused on security-based hot spot terminology. Drugs, corruption, immigration, violence, and political instability tend to receive a lot of media attention, and this leads to coverage that is shallow, belated, and woefully inadequate to get an accurate picture of what is happening in Mexico and the rest of Latin America.[10] The following discussion centers on six hot spots: border crime and drug wars; governance and corruption; guerrilla conflict in Guerrero; immigration; Oaxaca protest movement; and the Zapatista rebellion in Chiapas.

BORDER CRIME AND DRUG WARS

The U.S. border with Mexico has become a threat-based security hot spot because of the possibility of terrorists crossing from Mexico into the United States, smuggling of illegal immigrants, drug trafficking, and an assortment of criminal activities close to the United States. Mexico faces similar problems on its southern borders with Belize and Guatemala, where illegal immigrants cross into Mexico from Central America. The relative lack of state control and supervision along the border also contributes to the heightened sense of security threats in the aftermath of the war on terrorism and the invasion of Iraq. The U.S. government claims to have apprehended record numbers of illegal immigrants since 2001, but the agencies involved in border security are often caught between political and economic necessity. Mexico has installed three checkpoints to prevent "terrorists" from entering the United States and claims that seven Iraqis were caught in 2005 trying to cross into the United States.[11] In a survey of 500 agents in 2004 by Peter D. Hart Research Associates, 90 percent said that stopping terrorists—not illegal immigrants—was a major part of their job; however, they also said that they had not been given the tools and training by the government to do this type of work successfully.[12] The undocumented population in the United States has doubled since 1996, but the large increase is dispersed throughout the United States. After the 9/11 attacks the U.S.-Mexico border became a site of crisis and insecurity in the popular imagery. Governors in Arizona and New Mexico declared states of emergency on their borders, and this was followed by the belief—driven home by the media and the anti-immigration movement—that any undocumented immigrant could be a national security threat.[13]

Latin American and Caribbean drug trafficking remains one of the major threats to the United States, and Washington spends approximately $500 million per year to combat the production, distribution, and transshipment of drugs through the Americas. U.S. government funding for antidrug efforts in Latin America increased more than 150 percent between 1990 and 2000. In this ten-year period the United States spent close to $20 billion to counter illicit drugs. Over this period the top recipients of antidrug funds have been Colombia, Mexico, Ecuador, Netherlands Antilles, Peru, Bolivia, Haiti, Venezuela, El Salvador, and the Bahamas. As a foreign-policy goal, stopping the flow of illegal drugs into the United States was far more important to the general public than among opinion leaders. For example, only 22 percent of elites said the goal was "very important," while 81 percent of the public felt the same way (see Table I.5).

Demand for illegal drugs in the United States has created powerful crime syndicates in Mexico, particularly since the interdiction along a well-known drug route through the Caribbean from Colombia has helped to shift the transshipment to Mexico. According to the United States government, in 2004 some 92 percent of cocaine entering the United States did so through Mexico. This means that with the failure of drug prohibition in the United States, Mexican criminal gangs now control eleven of the thirteen largest drug markets in the United States. Mexican reporting on drug-related violence is of questionable reliability because of the dangers to journalists who investigate drug trafficking and money laundering, but reporting on drug cartel gang activity indicates that more than 500 people died in drug-related violence in 2005.

Corruption and incompetence remain the hallmarks of Mexico's police, and during President's Fox's term in office, efforts to reform the police and criminal justice system stalled because of congressional opposition. This means that Mexico's capacity to deal with the threats from narcotics is limited because of structural constraints and corruption. There are four major cartels that supply the illicit drug market in the United States: the Tijuana cartel, the Gulf cartel, the Juárez cartel, and the Sinaloa cartel. All except the Sinaloa cartel are located along the border with the United States. In 2002 the Mexican government formed the Federal Agency of Investigation (AFI), an elite force of young, college-educated officers that is far more qualified and less corrupt than local police forces in dealing with the law enforcement efforts operating along the border. According to the *Economist*, "The sheer scale of the United States' illegal imports of drugs from Mexico has created some of the world's most powerful and dangerous organized criminal gangs."[14]

Central American gangs such as MS-13 and M-18 have expanded their operations in Mexico, where they have set up lucrative operations to bring people and drugs across the border with the United States. In the United States the gang problem is treated as a law enforcement issue to be solved through tough laws and long prison sentences, not through social initiatives that could possibly address the root causes of violence associated with gangs and turf wars. U.S. plans are under way to fund a law enforcement academy in El Salvador to train officials from across the region in antigang strategies. The U.S. involvement in fighting gangs in Central America is also connected with the growing influence of Venezuela and Cuba, two countries of security concern in the region.[15] Illicit arms trafficking is another area of concern in U.S.-Mexican relations, because drug traffickers and terrorists are major purchasers of these products. The United States has made numerous efforts to coerce Mexico to adopt more aggressive strategies to stem the flow of illicit drugs but has been less willing to do much about the illicit trade in guns because of domestic opposition from the gun lobby in the United States. While agreeing to clamp down more on illegal drugs, the Mexican government has called on the United States to do something about the illegal gun trade, which has allowed narco-traffickers to acquire better weapons than those employed by their own armed forces. Why should Latin America do something about drug trafficking if the United States is unwilling to take more aggressive steps to curb the sale of illicit arms in Latin America, the Mexicans ask.[16]

Washington's approach toward illicit narcotics—largely unilateral, punitive, and counterproductive—has been a serious irritant to Mexico and the rest of Latin America because the United States refuses to acknowledge adequately the huge demand and consumption of drugs in the United States. Disproportionate costs, financial and human, are also paid by Mexicans in their own struggle to combat drug cartels and related crime. For many years, the most offensive tool in combating drugs was the 1986 law the U.S. Congress passed, requiring certification that certain countries were cooperating with the United States in the drug war. The law was based on the assumption that the United States should not have to provide aid—financial, trade, military—to governments that are not willing to cooperate with the U.S. counter-narcotics effort. The annual certification process is based on an up-or-down judgment by the United States, and if a country is judged uncooperative, sanctions are applied to it. The president of the United States can issue waivers to the law, and presidents can grant a waiver based on national security interests. However, the certification process has come under criticism in recent years, provoking congressional hearings and demands from Latin American governments that the process of judging other countries on their level of assistance be terminated.

Congressman Lee Hamilton (D-Indiana) expressed his dissatisfaction with the drug certification statute during congressional hearings that took place on April 29, 1998, by making the following arguments. First, the decertification law does not foster cooperation. According to Hamilton, "Every single government in Latin America opposes the statute as an imposition and as an affront to their sovereignty."[17] Second, the law requires, every March 1, an impossible up-or-down judgment on whether each major drug-producing and drug-transiting country has "cooperated fully" with the United States. No country can meet this standard, and "the president puts our entire bilateral relationship with the country at risk" based on a single issue. Third, the law is applied unequally: some countries get the benefit of the doubt, while others do not. Fourth, the sanctions that are part of the law are applied unequally. For example, Colombia has been decertified four years in a row, while its assistance has been increased. Other Latin American countries have been certified fully and seen their assistance from the United States decreased. Fifth, sanctions under the decertification law have hurt U.S. businesses—through export credits and loans—more than the target country. The Washington Office on Latin America (WOLA) has been a critic of drug certification and has called the process an annual charade because it is bad foreign policy and often counterproductive. According to political scientist Michael Shifter, "Washington analysts from across the political spectrum have aptly characterized this process as a 'circus.'"[18] Under pressure from Latin American governments weary of the U.S. government passing unilateral judgment on how other countries are living up to U.S. standards of compliance, the certification process was amended by Congress in 2002, effective for one year. Certification is now based on countries' adherence to international agreements rather than their level of cooperation with the United States in the drug war.

The growing number of abuses committed by the Mexican police and legal system during and after drug arrests helped to pass legislation in May 2006 to decriminalize the possession of marijuana, cocaine, heroin, and other illegal drugs for personal consumption. The purpose of the legislation was to close loopholes in current law in which judges have sided with traffickers by claiming they were addicts. According to the *Los Angeles Times*, "Recreational drug users hailed it as one of the most progressive laws in the world."[19] The decree passed both houses of Congress, and President Vicente Fox indicated his approval of the legislation. Worried about the influx of drug tourists and the expansion of the domestic market for Mexican drug cartels, U.S. officials managed to convince the

Fox administration that such legislation would contribute to the perception that Mexico tolerates drug use and this perception would turn the country into a narcotics haven. Shortly after, the Mexican president reversed himself by returning the bill to Congress to "make the needed corrections so it is absolutely clear in our country the possession of drugs and their consumption are, and will continue to be, a criminal offense."[20] This legislative failure will not end the debate over how to halt the flow of drugs to the United States, or the possibility of legalization as one of the means to counter the growth of narcotics-related business activities in Mexico. Moreover, the current flap over drug legalization ignores the security threat to the United States from drug-related activities in Mexico, including high levels of corruption, crime and violence; economic distortions; human rights violations, and threats to the legitimacy of the state in dealing with narcotics matters.[21]

Low-key cocaine gangs in Mexico continue to dominate the movement that reportedly moves up to 5 tons of Colombian cocaine each month into the United States. Ricardo García Urquiza was captured in November 2005, accused of being responsible for as much as 20 percent of the illicit drugs that come into the United States from Mexico. Mexican drug lords tend to be more like businessmen who live in modest homes and drive ordinary vehicles than like the megacartel drug lords of the past. Gone are the days when Pablo Escobar and other members of the Medellín (Colombia's second largest city) drug cartel lived in luxurious splendor in Colombia. The "securitization" of social and political problems has been used to justify the expanded roles for the region's militaries in dealing with current or "emerging" threats such as gangs, drugs, organized crime, illegal immigration, and natural disasters. This means that any type of illicit cross-border activity is now considered a "potential" terrorist threat because of the possibility of smuggling terrorists, money to terrorists, or weapons.[22]

GOVERNANCE AND CORRUPTION

When Vicente Fox Quesada was inaugurated as president of Mexico on December 1, 2000, he brought with him a campaign promise that he would clean up graft and liberate the country from the scourge of corruption, improve the quality of governance, and work with the United States on a more humane policy to handle the immigration that brings millions of undocumented Mexicans to the United States to supply cheap labor. However, President Fox made little headway in solving these problems, and his successor, President Felipe Calderón, faces many of the same challenges as his predecessor. While political scandals often plague those in positions of political power, they do not detract from the ability of astute politicians to overcome political damage from even the most public forms of corruption and cronyism. Andrés Manuel López Obrador, arguably one of Latin America's most significant populists, campaigned in the 2006 presidential election by addressing the needs of the poor and underprivileged. His loss to Calderón by the narrowest margin in Mexican history served as a repudiation of Venezuelan President Hugo Chávez, since the latter was a strong backer of López Obrador and his populist approach to Mexico's political problems. In an effort to legitimize his government on taking office in December 2006, President Calderón adopted some of the proposals that formed the core of leftist demands articulated by López Obrador—including an anticorruption campaign and a jobs program—for change during the presidential campaign. Nevertheless, it is too soon to tell whether the leftist tide in Latin America has receded since the leftist victories that swept Latin America in 2005–2006.

What worries the United States is that candidates like López Obrador, and others on the left, have succeeded in challenging the model of development that has provided significant benefits to the rich instead of Mexico's poor. While acknowledging that globalization is a fact of life, López Obrador claimed that he could work to bring about change in what has become known as the Washington Consensus. In an interview with the *New York Times* before the July 2, 2006, election he stated, "This country is immensely rich. Its problems are problems of maladministration—above all, corruption."[23] By turning the election into a referendum on the Fox administration's free trade and probusiness policies, López Obrador's appeal rested on promises to eliminate corruption by making corporations and the rich pay more taxes. His opponents achieved some degree of success by undermining his credibility through personal attacks, claiming he was an authoritarian or leftist dictator in the making, and by claiming that his approaches to poverty, job creation, and wealth distribution would lead to financial ruin.[24] Dick Morris, a U.S. political consultant who worked for Fox in 2000 and Calderón in 2006, wrote "Menace in Mexico" for the *New York Post*, linking López Obrador with President Chávez and Cuba's Fidel Castro. According to Morris, "López Obrador could be the final piece in their (Chávez and Castro) grand plan to bring the United States to its knees before the newly resurgent Latin left" and "a harsh shift in U.S. immigration policies could fuel a leftist victory in Mexico."[25] By linking his opponent to President Chávez, Calderón was able to convey enough fear to cause voters to opt for a less threatening alternative in the July 2 election. Calderón spent millions on aggressive TV and radio ads portraying López Obrador as a shrill demagogue who would spend Mexico into ruin through lavish social welfare programs.[26] Despite his leftist orientation, López Obrador would have been foolish to push for a sharp departure from existing policies had he won the presidency in 2006. Mexico's proximity to the United States and the close ties between the two countries (especially through NAFTA) prevented an electoral victory for the left; however, it opened the door for a flood of criticism and alarmist rhetoric that an AMLO presidency would represent a dangerous shift to the left in Mexico and throughout Latin America. After the Federal Electoral Tribunal officially ruled that Calderón beat his leftist rival, López Obrador declared himself the "legitimate" president of Mexico and proceeded to set up a parallel government designed to undermine Calderón. This lasted until Calderón was formally inaugurated in a tumultuous transfer of power in early December 2006.

In the last ten years Mexico has made considerable progress in creating a less authoritarian state apparatus. Elections are monitored carefully, and the political process is far more open than when it was dominated by the Partido Revolucionario Institucional (PRI), Mexico's ruling party for more than seven decades. Under the PRI, Mexican elites created a corporatist system based on a dominant party and government-controlled organizations (particularly labor and peasant components). Once the authoritarian aspects of the corporatist system eroded in the 1990s, Mexico started to transform its political system into a more pluralist society.

In 2000 the PRI was defeated for the first time since it was established in 1929, and the incoming President Fox promised that he would provide the political change needed to fix Mexican democracy. By improving the quality of elections, curtailing government corruption, providing for broader group representation, making the party system more competitive, and striking a greater balance between presidential and other institutional bases of power, Mexico is more democratic than at any time in its modern history.[27] In 2005, Mexico ranked fifth out of twenty Latin American and Caribbean countries in the Fitzgibbon survey of the degree of democracy in Latin America. Of the fifteen indicators of democracy, Mexico ranked high in civilian supremacy over the military, political maturity, party organization, government funds, and government administration.[28] As the old system of rule begins to break down, Mexico has made serious strides to make elections more fair and competitive, even adopting some features of U.S. election campaigns. At the core of these electoral reforms is the creation of the Federal Election Institute (IFE), an independent institution that serves as a watchdog of voting procedures. IFE is also responsible for monitoring media coverage of elections for bias and mudslinging that undermines the integrity of the electoral process. Prior to the July 2006 election, IFE ruled that some television spots were too false to be on the air, that others were simply too rude, and that President Fox must not interfere with the campaign, even to help his party's candidate, Calderón.[29] The razor-thin margin separating the top two candidates in the election and the confusion following the preliminary announcement of the results have raised questions about how much actual progress Mexico has made in rooting out fraud and corruption from the electoral process.

Prior to his chaotic swearing-in ceremony, Calderón named military and security veterans as his top law enforcement aides and vowed to crack down on criminals who challenge the authority of the state. Mexico experienced a wave of drug-related violence in 2006 that has claimed more than 2,000 lives, many in execution-style killings, and more than a dozen people have died in Oaxaca in demonstrations calling for the resignation of Governor Ulises Ruíz. The swearing in ceremony for Calderón was brief and raucous, with opposition lawmakers determined to prevent a "fraudulent" winner from taking office. According to *New York Times* reporter James C. McKinley, Jr., "Never before in modern Mexican history has a president been sworn in under such chaotic and divisive conditions."[30] The legitimacy of the Calderón presidency will continue to be challenged until some measures are taken to satisfy some of the demands of the opposition. Mexico's governing apparatus has improved since the end of PRI rule in 2000; however, corruption, electoral fraud, and political legitimacy problems still contribute to its hot spot status, especially if the Mexican left gains in future elections.

GUERRILLA CONFLICT IN GUERRERO

Contemporary Mexico is the product of previous struggles by guerrilla leaders such as Emiliano Zapata, Francisco "Pancho" Villa, Rubén Jaramillo, Genero Vázquez, Lucio Cabañas, and others. Almost two dozen guerrilla groups have been identified as still operating in Mexico, but most are too small to constitute a serious threat to Mexican society. However, there are still two major guerrilla movements operating in Mexico: the Ejército Zapatista de Liberación Nacional (EZLN), which led the Chiapas rebellion in 1994, and the Ejército Revolucionario Popular (ERP) in the state of Guerrero. The ERP appears to be descended from the Party of the Poor (a Marxist-Leninist party founded in the early 1970s by Lucio Cabañas, with operations in Oaxaca, Guerrero, and Mexico City), with deep roots in Mexico's long history of armed peasant insurrection that reaches back to Zapata. While the EZLN is the largest guerrilla group, with approximately 2,000 followers in Chiapas, the ERP is much smaller, with an estimated membership of some 50–200 followers. Since its emergence in 1995, the ERP and its leftist guerrilla units have carried out armed skirmishes in more than six states, and there have been reports of ERP military action in the heart of Mexico City. While there has been an elusive search for peace with the EZLN, the Mexican government has tried to eliminate the ERP because it has a more revolutionary agenda and operates closer to the economic heart of Mexico.

The ERP has made numerous appeals throughout Mexico, but its program for change has drawn little support. In a 1996 manifesto the ERP called for the removal of the "illegitimate" Mexican government; the restoration of popular sovereignty; the implementation of major economic, social, and political change; the establishment of "fair" international relations; and the punishment of those guilty of "crimes against the people." The Mexican army and police consider the ERP a Marxist group of criminals and terrorists and continue their goal of using army patrols to weaken and eventually eliminate the guerrilla group on national security grounds.

The Mexican military is accused of carrying out a "genocide plan" of killing, torturing, and kidnapping hundreds of suspected subversives in the southern state of Guerrero during the administration of Luis Echeverría (1970–1976). In a secret report issued during the last year of the Fox administration, the Special Prosecutor's office said that the Mexican military destroyed entire villages that the government suspected of serving as base camps for Party of the Poor leader Lucio Cabañas. The report raised a number of concerns within the Fox administration, namely how to deal with the egregious abuses by the long-ruling PRI before 2000. The report puts most of the blame for the abuses on the military, not the rebel groups, and some critics are reticent to believe that the army conducted the operations alone, without civilian involvement. Unlike the militaries in Argentina and Chile, the Mexican military has not acknowledged the institution's leading role in the country's "dirty war," only that they operated out of a sense of duty to the wishes of state officials at the time.[31] The guerrilla conflict in the State of Guerrero has not been eliminated; however, it is not a major security threat to the current Mexican government.

IMMIGRATION

The migration of millions of Latin Americans, mostly to the United States, continues at an astonishing pace, creating problems for governments throughout the Americas. Of major concern is the loss of human capital, human rights violations, protection of national sovereignty, and terrorist threats stemming from illegal border crossings. Almost two-thirds of Latin American immigrants send remittances to their families south of the border, although the dollar amount of the transfers varies from country to country. The Inter-American Development Bank estimates that Latin Americans living in the United States sent $50 billion in

Undocumented worker on his way to the United States from Tapachula, Guatemala, one of millions who attempt to cross the Mexican and U.S. borders every year in search of employment, security, and a better life. (The Image Works)

the 2005–2006 period to friends and relatives south of the border. Mexico was the number one recipient, followed by Brazil, Colombia, Peru, Ecuador, Guatemala, El Salvador, the Dominican Republic, and Honduras. According to the United Nations Economic Commission for Latin America and the Caribbean (ECLAC), "in some countries [remittances] represented 10% of GDP and more than 30% of export." The importance of immigration as a domestic issue has been a major source of political tensions over how to handle the large influx of illegal immigrants from Mexico. If the U.S. border with Mexico is closed and tightly monitored for security reasons, the flow of remittances to families is likely to decline, contributing to serious social and economic problems.

There is no doubt that the influx of illegal immigrants from Mexico is changing the face of the United States. About 6–7 million illegal immigrants from Mexico live in the United States, and legal and illegal immigrants remit close to $1.7 billion each month to Mexico.[32] The driving force for undocumented immigrants from around the world is the opportunity for higher wages, eight to ten times the prevailing rate at home. Despite the advantages of using illegal immigrants to cut costs on producing goods and services, a 2006 *Time* poll found that 63 percent of Americans consider illegal immigration a problem in the United States, with 83 percent worried that providing social services for illegal immigrants costs taxpayers too much. Others worry about the increases in crime and reduced job opportunities because of illegal immigrants. And close to 75 percent of those polled in January 2006 said that the U.S. government is not doing enough to keep illegal immigrants out of the United States.[33] Efforts to tighten the borders in the aftermath of the 9/11 attacks have not stopped undocumented Mexicans from entering the United States. In fact, the tougher restrictions have made human smuggling more lucrative, with tenfold increases in what smugglers charge for the trip across the border.

President Bush stepped up his efforts to fight illegal immigration in November 2005 with trips to the border states, where he put more stress on keeping illegal immigrants out of the United States rather than on promises to businesses to create ways of employing illegals. "We are going to prevent people from coming here in the first place," Bush promised in answering questions in El Paso, Texas. Bush also wants a guest worker program granting illegal immigrants who are already in the United States a right to work legally north of the border for a specified number of years before having to return home. Many Republicans are opposed to the guest worker program, claiming it provides amnesty to lawbreakers, while others claim the program would be unworkable since few of the workers would agree to leave or sign up for the program in the first place. The efforts to sell immigration reform will no doubt emphasize border security and the war on terrorism. Before leaving office, President Fox offered to cooperate with immigration reform but also demanded an expansion of legal channels for Mexican immigrants seeking employment in the United States. Bush's policy has expanded the number of Border Patrol agents, has increased the capacity at migrant holding centers in border states and Florida, and is spending hundreds of millions to upgrade surveillance technology. Bush has also promised tougher enforcement against employers who hire illegal immigrants, but this will be a tough sell to U.S. businesses. In his 2006 State of the Union address, which focused on terrorism, freedom, and energy independence, President Bush left out the Western Hemisphere except to say that immigration reform is necessary to keep American competitive and safe: "Our nation needs orderly and secure borders. To meet this goal, we must have stronger immigration enforcement and border protection. And we must have a rational, humane guest-worker program that rejects amnesty, allows temporary jobs for people who seek them legally and reduces smuggling and crime at the border."[34] President Bush continues to argue for a "comprehensive" solution to be the basis for the immigration reform efforts of his party; however, many Republicans are opposed to his solutions and are willing to buck the president on one of his signature domestic/foreign policies.

If public opinion polls on Bush's immigration policy are representative of the nation, he will have a tough time succeeding with his initiatives. For example, in a CBS/*New York Times* Poll in January 2004, only one-third of Americans supported the president's guest worker/amnesty proposals. In a *Washington Post*/ABC News poll in the same month, only 34 percent of respondents supported the way Bush was handling immigration policy. More than three-quarters of Americans say they favor restricting immigration into the United States as a way to combat terrorism. In 2002 the Chicago Council of Foreign Relations found that opinions on immigration varied greatly between the public in general and opinion elites (see Table I.5). While 14 percent of the opinion elite said the current flow of immigrants and refugees is a "critical threat" to the United States, more than 60 percent of the public felt this way. This 46-percentage-point gap in attitudes is the largest between opinion leaders and the public and indicates that the public is far more concerned than is the nation's elite. In the same survey, 70 percent of the general public said "controlling and reducing illegal immigration" was "very important" as a foreign-policy goal, while only 22 percent of opinion elites felt it was "very important" as a foreign-policy goal. Despite the 9/11 attacks, carried out by foreign-born terrorists, America's opinion leaders are far less concerned about immigration than the public is. One of the main reasons that the public is more concerned about illegal immigration is the feeling that jobs are being threatened by immigrants from low-wage countries; elites, on the other hand, are more likely to be insulated from competition over jobs. In any case, the wide difference between elite and public opinion serves in part to explain the current difficulties the president and Congress face on the immigration issue. In the past quarter century, Washington policymakers have paid little attention to the opinions of most Americans, who desire reductions in both legal and illegal immigration to the United States.

In a study of recent trends in immigration, *Immigrants at Mid-Decade: A Snapshot of America's Foreign-Born Population in 2005,* the Center for Immigration Studies (CIS), an anti-immigrant policy institute, found that the nation's foreign-born population exceeds 35 million, a figure that represents 12.1 percent of U.S. residents who were born abroad. Using data from the U.S. Census Bureau, the CIS found that about 3.7 million of the 7.9 million immigrants who arrived in the United States after 2000 are in the country illegally. Mexico is the source of about a third of all immigrants, with an estimated 10.8 million Mexico-born people living in the United States. This accelerated growth of the undocumented population in the United States is the primary reason for the rise in "anti-illegal-immigrant" opinion in parts of the United States and for President Bush's decision to address the implications of this growth for public policy at the federal, state, and local levels. In his speeches on immigration reform it is clear that President Bush is trying to strike a middle ground between temporary legal status and deportations in an effort to assuage the clamor for tougher policies within his party and as an opportunity to strengthen his party's appeal to Hispanics, the fastest-growing segment of the U.S. population. Critics on both the left and the right believe the temporary-worker dimension of his plan is unworkable and will eventually prove to be fruitless in bringing greater security to the border. The symbolism associated with building "border walls" over greater distances worries those who recall the criticism of the Soviets dividing Germany and building the Berlin Wall to halt the flow of East Germans to the west. Mexico's conservative president, Vicente Fox, called the legislative efforts to solve the immigration dilemma with more fences a "shameless policy," but he was unable to make much headway on the issue before leaving office in 2006.

The battle in the United States over illegal immigration is creating friction between Republicans in favor of efforts to tighten control over the border and Catholics who feel compelled to assist illegal immigrants. After the Republican-controlled House of Representatives passed a tough border security bill in December 2005, the United States Conference of Catholic Bishops attacked the bill as extremely punitive and called for Church members to strongly oppose it. The rift between conservatives opposed to illegal immigration and the Catholic hierarchy rests on the domestic importance of the Catholic vote for Republicans in key states. Those who control the Republican Party worry that they may lose a critical voting bloc if Catholic voters return to the Democratic Party over immigration. Others in the Church dismiss the growing division over immigration, claiming that Republicans and the Catholic clergy have differed before on other issues, such as the war in Iraq and the death penalty, without having much effect on parishioners.[35]

In the 2006 presidential campaign in Mexico all three major candidates focused on the failures of the NAFTA years—falling incomes and rising joblessness—and the emigration issue, particularly the treatment of Mexican migrants in the United States. Immigration was one of the hottest topics in the 2006 presidential election.[36] Every attack against illegal Mexican workers in the United States got huge coverage in the Mexican press. Unlike his opponents, López Obrador spoke of emigration in negative tones, arguing that the flow northward is a "tragedy for Mexico" and something that Mexico is responsible for stopping. "If I am elected," he told David Rieff, "I will propose a conference on migration with the United States. Building a wall is not a viable solution. The only thing that will work is creating jobs in Mexico. Fox was not able to maintain good relations with Washington. But I can't see any reason why I can't succeed in doing so."[37] The fear in Washington that AMLO is a threat because of his association with President Chávez doesn't wash with most Mexicans; however, López Obrador has no quarrel with the United States, does not attack President Bush, and directs his scorn at the political and business elite of Mexico. Nevertheless, negative stories in the American press about the dangers lurking in a future AMLO administration—hostile to foreign investment and antagonistic toward the private sector—dominated the election. For López Obrador, the answer to Mexico's social and economic ills is a more efficient government that provides jobs for millions of Mexicans so that they will not have to migrate to the United States, destroying family life and depriving Mexico of its most resourceful and energetic citizens. Regardless of who is president of Mexico, finding the resources to fulfill the demand for jobs is a Herculean task.

Mexico's national government is far more democratic and the rule of law is more likely to apply to governance than it has in the past. The United States, fearful of another terrorist attack, would be far more secure by putting its energy into a good relationship with Mexico than in trying to ignore or disparage the next president of Mexico because of his "populism" and leftist political ideology. It is possible that popular expectations will far exceed the ability of President Calderón to fulfill his campaign promises of prosperity and security; however, he has six years to prove he is willing to work with Washington to improve life south of the border and possibly reduce the flow of migrants northward.

The elevation of immigration in the national debate over globalization and security helped to create a movement for social justice in the United States. In response to the Sensenbrenner bill, which was designed to criminalize the undocumented, angry Hispanics and their Spanish-language radio DJ leaders mobilized huge marches in hundreds of cities in favor of immigrant rights. Despite a backlash by those opposed to President Bush's immigration plan, the voices of a new movement have articulated a strategy that has merged traditional labor interests and civil rights tactics with more global organizing.[38]

In the aftermath of Hurricane Katrina in 2005, the Mexican government assisted with the recovery and handling of undocumented Mexican workers in the New Orleans area. The Department of Homeland Security also allowed contractors to hire undocumented workers without being penalized for hiring workers without proper documentation. These changes in labor laws, following President Bush's decision to lift the Davis-Bacon Act, which requires federal contractors to pay at least the minimum wage, re-ignited the immigration debate in the United States and underscored the need for major changes in immigration policy. The immigration debate will not be solved until existing laws against hiring illegal aliens are enforced with some degree of certainty and regularity; however, the cooperation following Katrina shows that there is still a reservoir of good will between the United States and Mexico when it comes to binational national emergencies.

OAXACA PROTEST MOVEMENT

The protest movement in the state of Oaxaca began in the summer of 2006 and lasted for 5 months before federal police took back the center of the capital city from protesters in October and returned control of Oaxaca to state law enforcement officials. The protest movement consisted of a loose coalition of groups determined to remove Governor Ulises Ruíz for engaging in heavy-handed tactics in breaking up a teachers' strike and ignoring the wishes of the people on economic and social issues. The conflict is a reflection of the inequalities in Mexican society, high levels of unemployment and crime, severe shortages of classrooms and teachers, increasing levels of corruption at the local and national levels, repressive responses to the struggle of indigenous communities for greater autonomy, and difficult efforts to remove Governor Ruíz, regarded as corrupt and illegitimate. In studies of indigenous and nonindigenous poverty, indigenous populations in Mexico and throughout Latin America are found to be much poorer than the nonindigenous, with disparities in educational attainment, income, and economic benefits from education similar to those in poverty. The existing data in Mexico shows that 90 percent of the indigenous population lives in poverty, while less than 50 percent of the nonindigenous population is poor.[39] The racial and ethnic disparities in Chiapas and Oaxaca contribute to the demands of organized groups for a greater share of Mexico's economic growth.

Oaxaca's conflict has energized a series of events that now threaten Mexico's stability and the ability of President Calderón to defuse what is rapidly becoming Mexico's newest hot spot. The magnitude of the "fire" in Oaxaca can be seen in what happened during the summer and fall of 2006: "70,000 public school teachers and approximately 350 organizations united in a new Asamblea Popular Pueblo Oaxaca (APPO) that occupied the center of the city, took over local radio and television stations, blocked the state's executive, judicial and legislative offices, built barricades across the metropolitan region, led massive marches of 800,000 people and demanded the removal of the governor, Ulises Ruíz."[40] What is being demanded in Oaxaca is the result of social, economic, and political changes taking place in Mexico's south. Farmers are leaving the land and emigrating to other parts of Mexico and to the United States; indigenous communities are being destroyed as ancestral lands suffer from pollution and widespread destruction of forests; the city of Oaxaca cannot keep up with the relentless and chaotic urbanization that has brought with it severe problems of water, sewage, transportation, public security, and air contamination; at every level classrooms and teachers are in short supply, contributing to poverty and unemployment; corruption in Oaxaca is pervasive as bribes and payoffs make the business of politics more profitable than drugs; and grass-roots organizations struggle to create a new form of democratic rule that is nonviolent, anticapitalist, and inclusive and that meets the needs of the majority of the people. The Oaxaca movement also illustrates the failure of neoliberal economic policies and NAFTA to address the inherent problems of globalization. The agents of change in Oaxaca have confronted a situation where Mexico's federal government has supported the status quo by applying repressive tactics to movement members and ignored the root causes of the conflict, particularly the extreme poverty and unjust government policies that benefit only a few.

People around the world have tuned in to the violence in Oaxaca and started activist networks to express their solidarity with the Mexican protesters. The resistance movement in Oaxaca represents the first challenge to a federal government with little credibility, elected amid charges of fraud in July 2006. Unless President Calderón has the political will to respond to Oaxaca's valid demands and begin talks that will lead to serious reforms, Mexico will face more violence and instability in the poverty-stricken south.[41]

During the final standoff in the colonial capital, at least thirteen people were killed, dozens injured, and many colonial landmarks defaced or burned. After Felipe Calderón assumed the presidency in December 2006, the Oaxaca protest leader, Flavio Sosa Villavicencio of the New Left movement, was arrested along with 130 protesters in an effort to take a firmer hand in dealing with civil unrest. By the end of 2006 calm had been restored to Oaxaca, but protesters say that they have not given up, while local authorities sent work crews to remove graffiti painted by APPO.[42] In the meantime, Mexico's federal police, dressed in full riot gear, continue to occupy key parts of the city, and Governor Ruíz proudly declares that he has won the battle through mass repression. In 2007 thousands of the original protesters celebrated the Oaxaca protest movement that began one year earlier.

Poverty by itself may be a weak predictor of terrorism; however, Mexico's poverty-stricken south is also plagued with weak institutions that contribute to corruption, violence, and security threats. The social, economic, and political problems in Mexico's south constitute a hot spot for the Mexican government, although it seems to be a low priority for the federal government with more emphasis on the north than the impoverished south.

ZAPATISTA REBELLION IN CHIAPAS

The Zapatista rebellion began on January 1, 1994, when a masked indigenous army seized a Mexican army base, the colonial tourist town of San Cristóbal de las Casas, and several small towns in the southern state of Chiapas. The Mexican government responded with considerable force and managed to regain control over the region within two weeks. The armed uprising occurred the same day NAFTA went into effect and shocked the Mexican government, which had been touting the potential benefits of the trade pact. Suddenly confronted with a potential "hot spot" on its southern flank, the United States increased military aid and training for Mexico's armed forces under the rubric of assistance for drug interdiction and antiterrorism. By supporting the government's counterinsurgency strategy in Chiapas, the United States has placed itself in the awkward position of being seen to support an unpopular regime at the expense of meaningful reforms. A United Nations Indian rights investigator has identified at least fourteen high-risk hot spots in Mexico where land disputes involve violence.

Zapatista rebel in Chiapas, Mexico, a member of the Zapatista Army of National Liberation (EZLN), during the revolt in Southern Mexico over the creation of NAFTA and the neglect of the region by the central government in Mexico City. (The Image Works)

The Zapatista Army of National Liberation (Ejército Zapatista de Liberación Nacional, EZLN) has a mere 500 to 1,000 fighters, backed by a lightly armed militia of a few thousand, hundreds of thousands of sympathizers in Chiapas, and numerous international peace and human rights groups. The current Zapatista leader, Subcomandante Marcos, claims he is fighting for the same causes that motivated Emiliano Zapata 100 years ago: land and liberty for rural farmers and indigenous communities, today hurt by globalization and NAFTA. The Zapatista rebels and the Mexican government agreed to the San Andrés Accords in 1996 in an effort to bring peace to the region, but conflicting claims of compliance undermined the negotiations over conflicting demands. The situation deteriorated further the following year when soldiers from the Mexican Army massacred 45 unarmed men, women, and children in the small village of Acteal in Chiapas state. The military was joined by numerous paramilitary groups in an effort to dismantle all civilian groups that support, or are suspected of supporting, the EZLN. In the various declarations of the Lacandón Jungle, the Zapatistas argue that the uprising grew out of the failure of the Mexican government to address the real needs of Mexico's large indigenous communities, particularly in the age of global capitalism and neoliberalism.

The 1994 uprising among indigenous groups in Chiapas continues as a standoff between the Mexican government and the Zapatistas, and other armed groups have been dormant, but the issues that lead to the conflicts involving Indian communities have the potential to flare up again. "Since the Zapatista uprising in 1994, more than a third of the state has been heavily militarized."[43] With between 25,000 and 30,000 soldiers permanently located in regions of Chiapas that are Zapatista strongholds, the army has taken over the state police forces. One of the solutions to the conflict in Chiapas and other indigenous zones is the implementation of the Accords on Indigenous Rights and Culture signed by the Mexican government in 1996. The accords recognized the existence of *pueblos indios* (Indian peoples) by recognizing the legitimacy of "self-determination" and "autonomy," using these explicit terms.

The Zapatista uprising and the Chiapas conflict is rooted in the growing disparity between the Mexico that is rich, urban, and technologically advanced and the Mexico that is poor, rural, and undeveloped technologically. Many of the indigenous communities in the state of Chiapas still lack electricity, running water, or telephones, and productive land is in scarce supply. The region is divided along religious, ethnic, and political lines, creating the potential for chronic flare-ups between contending groups. Chiapas remains a hot spot because of the devastation of agriculture (a result of trade liberalization), the lack of credit and government assistance, and repressive measures taken by state and federal authorities.

Mexico

The Zapatista struggle aims to embrace all the exploited and dispossessed of Mexico; they hope to build an anticapitalist program, a more democratic political process, and a new constitution that will take into account the basic needs of the Mexican people: land, housing, food, work, health care, and a more just and democratic political system. Marcos continues to campaign for a new left-wing movement that will eventually topple the current government without firing a shot and usher in a socialist form of government for Mexico. Although there have been no major battles since 1997, human rights observers continue to report paramilitary violence and intimidation in Chiapas. During the 2006 presidential campaign Marcos, dressed in his trademark ski mask, military fatigues, and pipe, crossed the country giving speeches to small crowds with little media attention. In contrast to the 2000 presidential race, the problems of indigenous communities and the popularity of armed revolutionaries are not issues that resonate with the Mexican electorate. Immigration and job creation are the two most salient issues in the 2006 campaign, with all three candidates promising to address these problems if elected. Although a gifted orator with a cultlike following, Marcos does not have the support he once had when he led an army out of the jungles of Chiapas. Most of the mainstream candidates in the 2006 race argued that times have changed since the early years of the Zapatista revolt. For example, candidate Calderón said, "What Mexico wants is to live in peace, to live a democratic life—that is to say, just the ideals that Marcos probably does not share."[44] The Zapatista revolt in the 1990s contributed to the protest in Oaxaca in 2006, described in the previous section.

CHAPTER 2

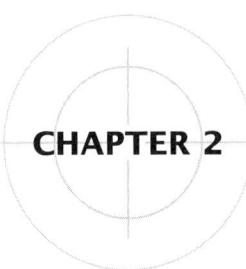

Central America

Central America is the southernmost region of North America, which connects North America with South America. Its geopolitical divisions have changed over time as a result of international conflicts, civil wars, and political changes related to independence struggles. Today, Central America comprises Belize (formerly British Honduras), Costa Rica, El Salvador, Guatemala, Honduras, Nicaragua, and Panama. International organizations vary according to which of these seven nations they consider to be part of this subregion of the Americas.[1] Although for hundreds of years Central America has been described by residents and travelers alike as a region of great beauty and potential, no such Eden has appeared. Even now, after years of revolutionary turmoil and attempts at democratic transition and economic reforms, Central America remains one of the most underdeveloped areas of the world, a land of poverty, violence, and instability, not of prosperity and political tranquility. The reasons for Central America's lack of development are complex, but geographical, historical, and political-economic explanations are at the core of most of the analysis.[2] During the Cold War, Central America became the focal point of U.S. security concerns and dominated the U.S. media for at least a decade. The perceived threat from Communism in Central America contributed to the use of hot spot terminology to justify military efforts to counter Soviet and Cuban influence in region. As Central America has gone from dictatorship to formal, political democracy—a painful process of violent conflict costing over 350,000 lives—and the Cold War has ended, the region has turned into a forgotten part of Latin America devoid of security threats of the magnitude perceived by Washington policymakers in the 1970s and 1980s.[3] Elliott Abrams, President Reagan's secretary of state for inter-American affairs (1985–1989), spent virtually all of his

The Panamanian dictator Manuel Antonio Noriega provided intelligence and logistical support for U.S. policies during the Reagan and George H. W. Bush administrations until the U.S. military invaded Panama and arrested him. After spending 15 years in a Miami jail, Noriega failed in his effort to return to Panama in August 2007. Instead, a federal judge ruled against his status as a prisoner of war, a decision that paved the way for Noriega's extradition to France, where he faces money laundering charges. Once the media revealed Noriega's involvement in drug trafficking, money laundering, and close ties to the Bush administration in 1989, Panama quickly became a Latin American "hot spot" with regime change a foregone conclusion. (The Image Works)

time dealing with Central America, mostly Nicaragua, denouncing the Sandinistas and aiding the Contras, an alliance of several Nicaraguan resistance groups waging war against the revolutionary government in Managua. In order to heighten the threat from revolutionary Nicaragua, Abrams gave false testimony to Congress and this in turn destroyed his credibility and weakened the Reagan administration's case for regime change to counter Soviet influence.[4] In the end, the Reagan Doctrine proved to be an unworthy strategy for promoting U.S. security interests south of the border. Poverty, violence, internal wars, and poor governance have contributed to the migration northward, mostly to the United States, for millions of Central Americans.

The hot spots discussed in this chapter are "cooler" than those in other parts of Latin America, but the ones examined are important for understanding security-based hot spot thinking and areas that carry the potential for security concerns. In any case, most of the ones treated in this chapter are rooted in the poverty and political flaws found in the region. At present, Central American hot spots include the following: the Darién Gap controversy; drug wars, terrorism, and youth gangs; governance and corruption; Panama's canal; and poverty and human development.

DARIÉN GAP CONTROVERSY

The Darién Gap is located between Panama and Colombia, a formidable natural barrier and the last missing link in the inter-American road connection between South and Central America. What is missing to bridge the two continents is the construction of an 80-mile long highway between the two segments of the Americas. The Darién Gap is important because of its potential as a future interoceanic route across the Mesoamerican isthmus, a major center of plant diversity in the Americas, the home of transboundary indigenous groups, and a growing center of drug trafficking. The Gap protects the Panama Canal from Colombia's territorial ambitions and provides a sanctuary for narcoguerrillas and other nefarious types. The Gap is also a positive thing for those concerned with the spread of agricultural pests and diseases, because it serves as a "fence" to protect agricultural interests in the United States and elsewhere. The greatest obstacle to the creation of an Interamerican Highway is the vast wetlands system that encompasses the Tumaradó swamp. The enduring presence of the Darién Gap is an indication of the complex forces involved in this strange piece of geography in Latin America. The future of the Darién Gap may rest on how the forces of globalization resolve the conflicting demands for world commerce and regional integration with the conservationists and the need for greater security.

Panamanian police patrol over the Darién Gap near La Palma, an ungoverned region along the Panama-Colombian border where the forests provide valuable cover for FARC rebels from Colombia. After the 1989 U.S. invasion, Panama dissolved its armed forces in favor of a civilian "Public Force" for defense and cooperation from the United States. (The Image Works)

The U.S. Congress passed a law in 1884 that included a plan to build an inter-American railroad system, but this dissolved with the creation of Panama and the construction of the Panama Canal beginning in 1903. The idea of an inter-American highway system emerged again at several inter-American conferences, but the Depression put the whole idea on hold. However, World War II reinforced the conviction that geopolitical integration was a strategic imperative for the United States, and between 1943 and 1963 $270 million was spent on the highway, with the U.S. government providing $170 million to build the highway from the U.S.-Mexican border to Panama. By the early 1970s it seemed that the opening of the Darién Gap was about to become a reality. The U.S. Congress earmarked $100 million for the construction of the Darién Gap highway; Panama and Colombia were set to contribute another $50 million. However, in 1975 a U.S. court ruled in favor of a legal suit brought by the Sierra Club, Friends of the Earth, and other environmental groups, arguing that closing the gap would have adverse effects on indigenous tribes and the fauna and flora of the region. The presence of hoof and mouth disease also posed a serious obstacle to completing the highway. The U.S.

Department of Transportation was prohibited from pursuing the project until a bona fide environmental impact statement was conducted. Colombia ignored the U.S. jurisdiction ruling and proceeded to expand the road. As of 2007, 145 kilometers of road remain to be built, and the chances of completing the project remain slim.

The search for alternate routes across the Central American isthmus brought renewed focus on the Darién region. The Darién Gap is one of the five major interoceanic routes in Central America that have been considered as alternatives to the Panama Canal. The growing number of regional trade blocs have increased the interest in the Darién Gap highway. However, over time the value of the Darién Gap as a "seal" remains to this day, largely because of the existence of agricultural diseases, uncontrolled migration of Colombian nationals, increased drug trafficking, and growing campesino settlements from both sides of the border, which often result in deforestation. Colombia's interest in developing the Pacific coast has reduced the need to push through development in the Darién region. With Panama's restored sovereignty over the Canal in 2000, there is a consensus that the Darién Gap problem can be addressed only through a binational effort aimed at the creation of a transboundary integration zone that recognizes the interests and rights of both Panama and Colombia and the indigenous settlements that inhabit the area. The significant issues at play in the future of the Darién Gap center on the argument "that if the road is not built it will fester as a breeding ground for guerrillas and drug producers."[5] If the Darién Gap is bridged with a road, on the other hand, there is also the possibility that the problems that exist in the Andes to the south will spread north and further undermine the security of Central America, Mexico, and the United States. The greater the security threats in South America, the less the chances for a completion of the highway linking Panama with Colombia.

DRUG WARS, YOUTH GANGS, AND TERRORISM

Although there are no terrorist organizations of any size in Central America that are capable of threatening the security of the United States, youth gangs operate throughout Central America and in the Mexican state of Chiapas and are often engaged in petty crime, extortion, turf battles, drug activity, and human smuggling.[6] Gang violence in Central America is linked to Central American communities in the United States and Canada. The thousands of gang members in Guatemala and Honduras have extended their sphere of influence to major cities in the United States, including Los Angeles; Washington, D.C.; Chicago; Denver; Houston; Durham, North Carolina; and Omaha, Nebraska.[7] Although the real size and level of organization of Central American

Former gang members' meeting of Men Against Violence, an organization devoted to preventing gang violence and rehabilitating former gang members. The meeting of former gang members in Managua, Nicaragua, in 2004 indicates that gangs can be eliminated, but it is a difficult and time-consuming process. (The Image Works)

gangs is not clear because little serious research has been done on the subject, there is little question that youth gangs are a serious problem. Recent estimates put the number of active gang members in Central America and Mexico at more than 100,000.[8] Central American governments have few resources to respond to gang violence; weak police forces and ineffective criminal justice systems add to the daily challenges of dealing with these problems.[9] Governments in the region have responded primarily with authoritarian policing practices, including neighborhood crime sweeps, arrests, and lengthy criminal sentences. With overcrowded jails and poorly trained police, there have been reports of extrajudicial killings of gang leaders suspected of involvement in gang-related riots and criminal activity.

The largest and most violent gangs in Latin America are located in Honduras, Guatemala, and El Salvador; many of these are transnational in character. This means that crime and gang violence in Central America are closely tied to similar activities in the United States. Many analysts who study this activity have found a connection between illicit gang activity and illegal immigration, drug smuggling, and trafficking in arms and persons to related gangs in Washington, D.C., suburban Maryland, and Los Angeles, California.[10]

During a meeting with six presidents of Central American and Caribbean nations in May 2005, Secretary of Defense Donald H. Rumsfeld and other senior officials at the Pentagon spoke of the connection between economic development and security in an effort to build support for the Central American Free Trade Agreement (CAFTA). According to Rumsfeld, "the threat to Central America and the Caribbean security comes from an anti-social combination of gangs, drug traffickers, smugglers, hostage takers and terrorists."[11] The defense secretary's concern was aimed at Central America and its serious crime problems; however, it failed to note the increasing contact between gang members in both regions and how gang violence may threaten political stability, foreign investment, and hamper social development. Rumsfeld also failed to mention that Central America's street gangs are largely the result of policy decisions made in Washington after the civil wars ended in the early 1990s. Between 1998 and 2004, the United States deported over 34,000 criminals to El Salvador, Guatemala and Honduras.

Salvadorans living illegally in the United States and deported to their homeland often brought Los Angeles gang culture with them. In a country with a deadly mix of poverty and armed violence, thousands of local teenagers were recruited into gangs that reignited local turf wars and started a reign of terror throughout the country. Central American governments claim they have no way of dealing with the thousands of gang members that contribute to the violent crime that plagues the region. According to Indira Lakshmanan, writing in the *Boston Globe*, the *Maras*, or youth street gangs, "have links to an estimated 8,000 to 10,000 members in more than 30 U.S. states" and "with their role in trafficking people, illicit drugs, and weapons into the United States, the Maras pose a transnational threat that sets them apart from other street gangs."[12] The *Rocky Mountain News* found over 100 different gangs in the Denver area with an estimated 12,741 members. Gangs in Colorado have expanded in numbers, become more sophisticated in their operations, and are increasingly violent in their activities.[13] Denver is prime "real estate" because it is located near major north–south and east–west interstates, which makes it ideal for trafficking guns, drugs, and humans. With a growing population and a higher-than-average percent of high school dropouts, Denver is also a prime area for gang recruitment. The threat from urban gangs is compounded by the growing connection between drug cartels in Mexico, as well as Russian organized crime and Asian criminal groups.[14] In the FBI's 2005 *National Gang Threat Assessment*, gangs are a far more serious threat to national security than terrorist groups, at least as defined by the federal government. "Despite their vigilance in looking for associations between gangs and international terrorist groups in the post-9/11 environment, few investigators have identified any associations in their jurisdictions, and those who have, describe the connections in terms of speculation supported by little evidence."[15]

The major gangs with ties to the United States are the "18th Street" gang and their main rival, the Mara Salvatrucha (MS-13). Both are the product of harsh immigrant life in the United States, particularly Los Angeles, where it was easy to recruit Salvadorans who fled the country's civil conflict. The FBI estimates that the MS-13 gang has an estimated 8,000 to 10,000 members nationwide, and it has been referred to as the most dangerous gang in America, with members in thirty-three states and the District of Columbia.[16] Perhaps the most dangerous urban gangs, however, are in Brazil, where *favela*-based drug gangs are heavily armed and occasionally challenge the authority of the state. The Maras that exist in Central America are much less powerful than those in Brazil and constitute a rather minor threat to national security, either in Central America or in the United States.

The Pentagon is convinced that street gangs are the greatest security threat in Central America and the Caribbean.[17] The FBI maintains there is no link between MS-13 and al Qaeda and other terrorist groups, but the gangs have become more involved in organized crime groups that traffic in guns and drugs. Over the past several years, the Bush administration has begun to redefine the meaning of threats from terrorism toward more traditional power politics in the region: containing left-leaning governments bent on curtailing Washington's influence in the region. There is no evidence that al-Qaeda is making inroads into criminal networks controlled by violent gangs. However, the growth of street gangs—largely the result of U.S. security and immigration policy—offers the Bush administration the opportunity to expand its influence in the region through economic initiatives and training programs. This would appear to be a regional strategy designed to block Venezuela's efforts to influence events in the region. The United States is aggressively pursuing the Maras by using racketeering statutes once employed against the mafia. After the United States decided to deport undocumented immigrants who had committed crimes or had a criminal record in the mid-1990s, governments in Central America have tried "get tough" laws, leading to overcrowded prisons and frequent prison riots, only to find that crime has increased on a yearly basis.

The young democracies of Central America have struggled to deal with high levels of crime, which have come in the wake of democratization efforts. Crime, drug addiction, and gang violence have given the region one of the highest murder rates in the world. "In 2004, the estimated murder rate per 100,000 people was 45.9 in Honduras, 41.2 in El Salvador, and 34.7 in Guatemala. In the United States, the corresponding figure was 5.7."[18] Although there is wide variation in homicides per 100,000 population, homicide rates in El Salvador and Honduras and Nicaragua are the highest, while those in Panama and Costa Rica are the lowest. With weak police, intelligence, and military institutions, the increase in violence has overwhelmed local law enforcement agencies. Efforts to thwart the growing impact of organized crime and gangs in Guatemala have been undermined by the government's inability to legislate tougher penalties or putting former soldiers in the streets to back up the police. Since 2003, Guatemala has been battered by street gangs and vigilante groups supported by the police, turning the country into one of the most violent in Latin America.

Corruption and poor governance compound this dilemma and constitute a serious threat to the security of Guatemala, Central America's largest country, with over 12 million people. The discovery of oil in neighboring Belize, at a time when the price of petroleum is high and government pressure for more revenues is growing, has reignited the long-festering territorial dispute with Guatemala that still relies on the slogan "Belize is ours" as a symbol of Guatemalan nationalism. The areas where oil has been discovered are close to Guatemala, and exploration is taking place or planned on land still claimed by Guatemala. Mayan migrants from Guatemala have crossed into Belize and have settled on land where some of the drilling is taking place. Efforts at resolving the border dispute are under way through negotiations among representatives of the two countries, but the stakes are much higher now.[19]

The issue is not whether these social problems exist in Central America, but how to forge an appropriate response and clarify the motives from each side. The Central American presidents wanted a subregional rapid response force to confront the street gangs which are considered a form of urban insurgency. By grafting the criminality of street gangs onto subregional security threats—terrorists, drug traffickers, arms traffickers—the United States has elevated the level of security threat. This means that one can understand the erosion of the legitimacy and effective sovereignty of nation-states by portraying urban gangs as part of the more dangerous transnational criminal organizations. In such a view, gang leaders are no different from warlords or drug barons and constitute the same kind of threat as the one from terrorists or insurgencies. According to Max Manwaring, professor of military strategy at the U.S. Army War College, the more advanced gangs "challenge the legitimate state monopoly on the exercise of control and use of violence within a given political territory."[20] Based on this assumption, Manwaring argues that the more advanced gangs in Latin America contribute to state failure and regional instability. The Maras that threaten Central America have not reached the level of threat postulated in the Manwaring theses, and their ability to network internationally is largely the result of U.S. deportation policy and draconian measures in El Salvador and Honduras to eliminate these gangs. This has had the effect of spreading violence throughout Central America, something that did not exist earlier.

Joint military exercises are taking place in Central America to combat drug trafficking, although the "war is asymmetrical" because the traffickers have far more resources to counter government efforts. DEA's Guatemala office indicates that as aircraft interdiction increases, the traffickers take to the sea. "After Guatemala's chief drug enforcement officer was arrested in Virginia in November on drug trafficking charges, President Oscar Berger publicly acknowledged that his law enforcement agencies and courts were so rife with corruption that he was working on a request for the United Nations to take over prosecutions of organized crime." All this is part of a U.S. effort to develop a rapid response network to deal with organized crime and drugs. Arms trafficking in Nicaragua has been linked to terrorist organizations in Colombia, particularly the United Self-Defense Forces of Colombia (AUC), a right-wing paramilitary group.

Since the closure of six military bases in the old Panama Canal Zone in 1999, the United States has changed its defense strategy from full-fledged military bases in favor of relatively small facilities called Cooperative Security Locations (CSL), initially named Forward Operating Locations (FOL), in host country bases. In some of these new facilities, U.S. military personnel are joined by private military contractors or mercenaries to reduce the impact of joint activities. From these small airbases, the United States engages in aerial surveillance of Andean drug-producing areas and a counterinsurgency function to assist in fighting the war on terrorism. Special forces engage in frequent joint training missions in counternarcotics, but they have also been involved in unacknowledged operational missions throughout the region.[21]

GOVERNANCE AND CORRUPTION

The democratic transition has not been easy in Central America; with economic policies that have increased unemployment, inequality, and urbanization and with stores of weapons and thousands of ex-combatants, governments are faced with a declining confidence in democracy. Public opinion polls show that the less secure the citizenry, the less support for democracy. In a 1999 United Nations survey, 55 percent of Salvadorans said they would support a military coup under conditions of high crime, although not high unemployment.[22] The problem of governance and corruption has plagued Nicaragua for decades and recently has contributed to the return to power of Daniel Ortega, the Sandinista former president during the 1980s who tried to carry out a revolution in the face of the United States' sponsorship of the Contra rebels. In a continuation of the Cold War, the Bush administration mounted a concerted effort to block the return of the left-wing Sandinista party to power prior to the November 2006 presidential election.[23] Despite a revival of Cold War reporting on candidate Ortega and the Sandinistas, Ortega won the presidential race with close to 40 percent of the national vote. President Ortega's electoral victory places him in a precarious position between Washington and his "leftist brothers" in Cuba and Venezuela and between the goals—the eradication of poverty and efforts to curb "savage capitalism"—of his Sandinista Party and opposition political parties in the National Assembly.[24] Nicaragua also contains thousands of former Contras, many angry at Ortega's return to power and fear that he will resume expropriating property, rationing food, and jailing dissenters.[25]

Poor governance in Guatemala is the result of a successful coup against the democratic socialist government of Jacobo Arbenz Guzmán in 1954. Backed by the Eisenhower administration, the new military dictatorship represented the interests of the local oligarchy and the Boston-based United Fruit Company. The regime change in Guatemala soon resulted in a genuinely Communist insurrection and a genocidal campaign of repression that cost the lives of more than 100,000 Maya Indians. The discovery of police documents in Guatemala City confirmed an earlier UN commission's finding that the National Police helped identify and kill leftists during its 1960–1996 civil war. The Guatemalan army was responsible for most of the killings during the war, working hand-in-hand with the National Police. An estimated 200,000 people were the victims of an ideological war against purported enemies of the regime.

Since 2000, however, Guatemala has suffered from a new plague in the form of the violent deaths of at least 1,000 women. Few of these grisly murders have been investigated, and only three killers are in prison. Although Guatemala has signed several international conventions protecting women, laws have not been enforced, and the police often attribute the deaths to being a gang member, prostitute, or a victim of an enraged husband or boyfriend. The lack of effective official response tends to give an official green light to the killers of innocent women.[26]

Latin America is known as a region where periods of democracy have alternated with periods of authoritarianism or dictatorship. Now there is a concern in policymaking circles that the present cycle of democracy building is coming to a close, and this poses serious problems for U.S. interests in the region. In his discussion of the "syndrome of authoritarian democracy," Donald E. Schulz details eight trends or tendencies that have subverted political institutions and undermined democratic rule.[27] Schulz places the blame on internal problems in Latin America—socioeconomic inequality, poverty, and antidemocratic political cultures—and U.S. policies, many rooted in Cold War anti-Communist doctrine that continues to strengthen the military—traditionally the greatest threat to human rights and democracy—while encouraging democratic practices. In response to the economic hardships and social dislocations caused by neoliberal economic policies, Latin American governments have adopted "authoritarian measures in order to maintain public order and national security. And so civilian presidents, allied with military forces, are creating limited and militarized forms of democracy as they carry out economic restructuring." The rise in violent crime and pervasive drug trafficking have undermined government institutions, increased public insecurity, and overwhelmed the abilities of police, courts, and other civilian institutions to operate under the rule of law. In his study of corruption and victimization, Mitchell A. Seligson found that corruption erodes legitimacy in government institutions, which in turn hampers the success of any process of democratization.[28] In the 2005 Fitzgibbon survey of scholarly images of Latin American democracy, Guatemala, Nicaragua, and Honduras are the least democratic of the Central American countries; Costa Rica, Panama, and El Salvador rank much higher. Costa Rica ranked first among the twenty Latin American countries in 2005 and held the number one position since 1965 (see also Table I.4).

PANAMA'S CANAL: IS THE WATERWAY AT RISK?

The Panama Canal is an important water passage, source of political pride for people in both the United States and Panama, and a worry to conservatives in Washington, who fear a threat to U.S. security because of China's investments in Panama and its interest in the Panama Canal. From 1903 until 1999 the United States controlled both the waterway and a ten-mile wide strip of territory known as the Panama Canal Zone as if they were U.S. territory. The treaties that provided U.S. hegemony over the Panama Canal were resented by Panamanians, and eventually riots and international diplomacy culminated in two new treaties in 1977 that specified that Panama would take control over the canal and all of its operations on December 31, 1999. As I have written elsewhere, "Panamanians objected to their second-class status, the privileges of U.S. citizens in the Canal Zone, the use of Panama for numerous military bases, and the general feeling that Panama was receiving inadequate compensation for the canal."[29] The two new treaties guarantee the permanent neutrality and security of the canal, allowing ships of all nations to use it even in times of war. Nevertheless, conservative political leaders such as

Miraflores Locks, Panama Canal. With a new motto—"Providing Passage into the Twenty-First Century"—Panama has undertaken a Third Set of Locks project that will allow the aging canal to be competitive beyond 2025. The expansion project is expected to cost $5.25 billion and take 7 to 8 years to complete. With China controlling port facilities, critics warn of future Chinese military bases and even a future missile threat to the Americas. (Author's photo)

Ronald Reagan opposed the treaties and accused President Carter of a "give-away" to a ruthless dictator, General Omar Torrijos.

At the time of transition another controversy erupted over the contracts signed with a Chinese company, Hutchison Whampoa, for a long-term lease on the Canal ports. The People's Republic of China (PRC) is an important factor in Latin America's current economic development, but it poses threats to U.S. foreign policy in the region and beyond. China's ascendance in Latin America has diminished the influence of Taiwan. Beijing would like to have observer status as a lender at the Inter-American Development Bank, and Chinese leaders have forged close ties with Hugo Chávez and Fidel Castro, political relationships with economic advantages. Furthermore, growing networks of trade and investment between China and Latin America suggest common interests that weaken the influence of the United States in the region. According to Perez-Stable, "By 2015, new Chinese investments in the region may add up to $100 billion."[30] As far as economic development strategy is concerned, however, China and Latin America are not in agreement on how to best manage

A young Chinese-Panamanian schoolgirl walks past Chinese script on a shop wall in Panama City, a sign of growing Chinese influence in Panama and beyond as the U.S. influence has declined. Critics of this trend feel that China has made Panama and the Canal another Latin American hot spot by its control of the main ports and the interests of the Chinese military in Latin America. (The Image Works)

economic choices: China holds steadfast to the benefits of economic liberalization; Latin America has become disenchanted with neoliberalism's unfilled promises and vacillates between capitalist and noncapitalist solutions. Current Chinese leaders believe that its economic reforms, rapid economic growth, and rising global power will eventually allow it to challenge the world's most powerful nations—including the United States—for control of the international system. China's global power continues to grow based on its being the world's most populous nation, the world's second largest economy, the world's second largest defense budget, a permanent member of the UN Security Council, one of the few nuclear weapons states, and the development of political relationships that tend to exploit the growing dissatisfaction with the United States, particularly in Latin America. Latin America and the Caribbean are important to China because of raw materials, particularly energy, and the political necessity of getting Latin American governments to shift their diplomatic recognition of Taiwan to the PRC. The six nations in Central America—Guatemala, El Salvador, Honduras, Nicaragua, Costa Rica and Panama—retain full diplomatic relations with Taiwan, but all South American states but one (Paraguay) have moved to recognize Beijing. Most of the Caribbean has switched allegiances to the PRC in the last few years. Nevertheless, there is solid regional commitment to Taiwan as a state separate from China in Central America and the Caribbean. If the PRC was able to engineer a switch among these countries in favor of Beijing, Taiwan's claims of legitimacy as an independent state would be seriously jeopardized.

With its rapidly growing economy, China is scouring the world for raw materials to bolster its legitimacy, dampen popular dissent, continue its military build-up, provide overseas aid, and to ensure a reliable flow of energy supplies. Petroleum is the primary resource that South America can offer the Chinese, particularly Venezuela, the world's fifth largest producer of petroleum. China has invested over $1 billion in petroleum projects in Venezuela as well as an additional $60 million in natural gas wells. China also has its eye on purchasing petroleum from Ecuador, Argentina, Colombia, and Mexico. Latin America is also important because of a variety of minerals (aluminum, copper, iron) and food items (soybeans). China's vast economic expansion has caused a sort of high-stakes competition to gain control of the world's oil supplies. China is now the number two nation among the leading consumers of petroleum, while its domestic production has stagnated. According to the Department of Energy, China is expected to need more than 12 million barrels per day in 2020, almost as much as the United States (16 million), and both will need to import more than two-thirds of their needs. China is now aggressively pursuing supplies in Angola, Canada, Indonesia, Iran, Kazakhstan, Nigeria, Saudi Arabia, Sudan, and Venezuela. China's quest for foreign oil is now seen as a national security matter, particularly the ties to countries that pose a threat to the United States; its efforts to secure supplies of these commodities in Latin America have raised suspicions that it is using its buying power to create a circle of friends willing to undermine American foreign-policy goals.

As a major exporter, China is also interested in access to good port facilities in the Caribbean and the Panama Canal. For the South American exporters of raw materials to China—Argentina, Brazil, Chile, and Peru—the trade relationship is advantageous. For other Latin American countries, economic ties to China are a mixed blessing, according to Claudio M. Loser, because Mexico, Central America, and the Caribbean "perceives a risk of losing its competitive advantage with the U.S. and other significant markets" when China is clearly a lower-cost, better educated producer.[31]

China's military and security interests in the Western Hemisphere also worry the United States because China is increasingly using diplomatic and military ties to gather information on the host country, a practice with which the United States is quite familiar. According to Peter T. R. Brookes, "In 2004, more than 100 military exchange programs took place, involving Chinese military leaders visiting more than 60 countries and senior officers from about 50 countries visiting China. Some exchange programs featured joint military exercises, security sessions involving military officers from multiple countries, combined seminars on defense and security, and field trips."[32] China's growing military ties in Latin America mean that Washington can no longer count on the intelligence and security domination it once had in the Western Hemisphere. China is making progress in its grand strategy to become a world power, perhaps gradually replacing the United States in the developing world. As China continues to make progress in improving its economy and spreading its political influence, the United States faces troubling challenges in the Western Hemisphere, where some national leaders such as Hugo Chávez welcome the arrival of another world power to offset the historical domination of the United States in the region.

What worries Washington is that China's desire to expand its influence around the globe will eventually diminish U.S. hegemony and power. The Pentagon believes that China is expanding its capacity to fight wars beyond its own territory, and this constitutes a challenge to global order. The debate over China's military power will be fueled by claims of China's exaggerated strength and the need to respond with greater U.S. military power.[33] Although Chinese military-to-military contacts and peacekeeping activity are growing along with growing economic ties, China does not at this time constitute a threat to U.S. interests in the region.[34]

On his return from the Summit of the Americas in November 2005, President Bush declared that "It's in our nation's interest that this canal be modernized" but gave no indication that the U.S. would pay for the widening, estimated to cost $7–8 billion. Talks leading to a United States-Panama free trade agreement have stalled, in large part because of Panama's concerns that American producers could undercut the price of pork, chicken, and rice by local producers. At a meeting of defense ministers in October 2006, Nicaraguan President Enrique Bolaños announced plans to build a rival to Panama's canal that would allow larger ships to traverse the Atlantic and Pacific Oceans. The project would cost an estimated $18 billion and take more than a decade to build. Panama's plans to upgrade its canal at a cost of $5.2 billion was put to a referendum on October 22, 2006, but there are serious concerns about whether such a project could be carried out without massive corruption and faulty construction. Despite these political concerns, Panamanians voted overwhelmingly to modernize the country's aging canal. Many Panamanians were convinced that the $5.25 billion project would generate jobs and keep the canal viable for future generations. The costly overhaul will double the canal's capacity by adding a third set of locks that are 40 percent longer and 60 percent wider that the current locks. The third lane project will be financed by loans and higher fees charged to shippers, mostly U.S., Chinese, and Japanese firms involved in global trade. Nicaragua's plans to build its own canal with public and private funding is now in doubt because of the Panamanian vote; however, the desire for a second canal still exists in Nicaragua. Nicaraguan officials insist their dream of having their own canal argue that there is sufficient growth in cargo shipping around the globe to sustain two waterways, and theirs would accommodate larger ships. The $18 billion project would have wider channel capacity and cut one day off shipments between California and New York. Chinese tankers could save as much as 36 days and $2 million on their round trips to the U.S. East Coast.[35] The vote in favor of Canal modernization and expansion has contributed to a construction boom in Panama City, with new high-rise buildings going up at a dramatic rate and waterfront property increasing in value. Panama's current political stability is also a factor in the economic investment that seems apparent in the wake of the decision to begin a third-lane project.

POVERTY AND HUMAN DEVELOPMENT

The revolutionary violence that plagued Central America in the 1970s and 1980s has all but disappeared, but the region still faces severe economic, social, and political problems. The Cold War threat posed by the Soviet Union and Cuba is no longer part of the threat assessment process; however, there are serious challenges in the consolidation of democracy, protection of human rights, and institutionalizing good governance and transparency. With peace accords in El Salvador, Guatemala, and Nicaragua, Central America began a series of economic and political reforms to erase the conflict and violence from previous decades. Poverty relief remains a pipe dream when neoliberal economic policies and poor governance result in huge social costs, particularly increased poverty and social inequality.

The economic and social conditions that fueled the armed conflicts of the past did not improve, leaving poverty reduction and the implementation of a more equitable development model for the new leaders of the region. One-half of the eight poorest countries in Latin America are in Central America, including Honduras, Guatemala, El Salvador, and Nicaragua. Within this group, Nicaragua (79 percent) and Honduras (67 percent) have the highest rates of poverty, according to the Economic Commission for Latin America and the Caribbean. Central America has made important advances in democratization and the protection of human rights since the 1970s, but much remains to be done to implement the peace accords fully and address the high levels of poverty and corruption and the lack of public security. The poorest sectors in Central America are concentrated in rural areas, where small farmers and the landless must struggle with land and income inequality, natural disasters, and poor agricultural production. Hurricane Mitch struck Central America in 1998, killed 26,000 people, and left a swath of destruction and losses of millions of dollars. This natural calamity set back the economic development of Nicaragua and Honduras by thirty years and pushed many from rural areas to migrate to the United States.

In the latest UN Human Development Index, five of the six Central American countries rate very poorly in life expectancy, literacy, and per capita income (see Table 2.1). Only Costa Rica (rank 41) is ranked by the UNDP as "high human development" of the 162 countries that make up the index. Panama is in position number 52, and El Salvador ranks number 95. Central American poverty, as measured by levels of literacy, per capita annual income, technological development, and life expectancy, contributes to the region's backwardness and feeds the problems that plague the governments of the region. This would include drug trafficking, youth gang violence, and terrorism.

Guatemala faces enormous challenges in fulfilling the UN goal of reducing extreme poverty and hunger by half. As of 2006, over half of all Guatemalans live in poverty, and over 2 million of 11 million Guatemalans live on less than one dollar a day. Social exclusion is one of the mainstays of Guatemala's history, based primarily on the concentration of agricultural land ownership and the exploitation of peasant and

Table 2.1 Human Development Index, Latin America, 2006

Country	HDI Ranking
Argentina	36
Chile	38
Uruguay	43
Costa Rica	48
Cuba	50
Mexico	53
Panama	58
Brazil	69
Colombia	70
Venezuela	72
Peru	82
Ecuador	83
Paraguay	91
Dominican Republic	94
El Salvador	101
Guyana	103
Nicaragua	112
Bolivia	115
Honduras	117
Guatemala	118
Haiti	154
United States	8

The Human Development Index (HDI) is designed to provide a broader definition of well-being than Gross Domestic Product (GDP). It provides a composite measure of three dimensions of human development: life expectancy; adult literacy and enrollment at the primary, secondary, and tertiary level; and purchasing power parity (PPP) income. Although it is by no means comprehensive, it does provide a composite measure to compare nations in terms of human progress and the complex relationship between income and well-being.

indigenous labor. These social and economic inequalities seriously limit the options and opportunities of the rural population, among whom the poverty rate rises to over 80 percent. The 1996 peace accords that put an end to armed conflict between Guatemala's army and the Guatemalan National Revolutionary Unity also mandated a national agenda to eradicate the causes that had led to such violence and conflict.

Guatemala's poverty contributes to the lack of support for political institutions and the fragility of the state apparatus. Its democratic system is fragile, and many of the promises of meaningful change go unresolved: unemployment, public safety, corruption, drug trafficking, organized crime, youth gangs, poor education and health services. One of the biggest obstacles to reducing poverty is the lack of participation of civil society in government decisions relevant to public policies. Without government efforts to improve the quality of life in the form of unemployment, social mobility, and development opportunities, the well-being of the disadvantaged sectors will make little progress toward a more prosperous and equitable society.

The current situation in El Salvador is depressing and poses numerous risks to U.S. security. Almost half of the population of six million lives in poverty, and at least 2 million have emigrated to the United States to escape a future of poverty. In 2004, El Salvador suffered from corruption scandals and a dramatic increase in violent crime. The cost of dealing with violence amounted to almost 12 percent of GDP, more than was spent on health and education combined. According to the United Nations Development Program (UNDP), 43 percent of the population are poor, and 19 percent live in absolute poverty. The levels of rural poverty are serious and chronic, but the government in El Salvador faces a stagnant economy, a high deficit, and a heavy debt burden. What is needed to improve the quality of life in El Salvador is a forceful effort to create jobs, reform the tax system, combat corruption, and significantly increase investment in health, education, and women's policies. The current government of President Antonio Saca is aware of these social dilemmas and has promised to revitalize the economy and reduce extreme poverty by between 7 and 8 percent; however, the spending has been insufficient. There is no doubt that the hot spots in Central America are rooted in the politics of poverty and inequality, conditions that can breed terrorism, violence, and U.S. intervention.

CHAPTER 3

Andean South America

The Andean states make up a large segment of South America and include Venezuela, Colombia, Ecuador, Peru, and Bolivia. The Andes mountains, the world's longest mountain range, run down the western side of South America; the geography of the Andes—tall mountain ranges that separate the coastal areas from the Amazon Basin—helps explain the lack of integration and the ethnic divisions that serve as obstacles to political and economic development. The region's major natural resources—copper, iron, tin, oil, and natural gas—have created a dependency on minerals that in turn has hindered the development of diversified economies and contributed to border disputes, political instability, strong-man rule, security-based hot spots, and domination by foreign powers. The Andean region is not only characterized by its wealth of energy resources; narco-terrorism and severe governance problems also plague the Andean countries. These conditions make it possible for foreign powers and international financial institutions to influence events in the Andean region. Venezuela, for example, holds 7 percent of the world's crude oil reserves and remains the fourth-largest supplier of the United States. President Hugo Chávez is a hawkish member of OPEC, where he feels it is in Venezuela's best interests to keep oil prices high and maintain Venezuela's close ties with the governments of Iran, Iraq, and Syria to bolster his nationalistic foreign policy. The value of coca in rural areas of the Andes, boosted by the voracious appetite for cocaine in the United States and elsewhere, has contributed to the political instability, foreign intervention, indigenous protest movements, corruption, and de-democratization. Until a concerted multilateral effort succeeds in effectively dealing with the conundrum of drug production and trafficking, the Andean region will continue to suffer its plethora of political and economic problems that provide the genesis of many security-based hot spots.

During the Cold War, each of the Andean countries suffered from periods of democratic breakdown in which governments were overthrown or displaced by U.S.-aligned military dictatorships. Revolutionary movements and right-wing military juntas dominated the region until a wave of democratization and economic liberalization began in the 1980s. As the military retreated to the barracks, democratic rule has spread, along with fair elections and civilian succession. The challenges to democratization—ethnic and regional cleavages, persistent poverty, and traditions of political violence—facing the Andean governments are closely associated with the war on drugs and guerrilla insurgencies. The authors of *Politics in the Andes* argue that, "Since the early 1990s, the Andean region of Latin America has been the most unstable and violent area in the hemisphere."[1] Andean governments have drifted to the left, with socialist leaders being elected in Venezuela, Ecuador, and Bolivia. Colombia and Peru, which elected more moderate political leaders who have espoused free-trade and market principles, have strengthened ties with the United States. The fact that democratically elected governments have not abandoned capitalist models of economic development is one reason that Washington and the international financial community remain supportive of nearly all these countries. The Andean nations have been plagued with political corruption, economic instability, and wide economic gaps between the rich and the poor. So far, no single economic model of development has emerged, and political shifts from one administration to another reflect less concern with ideology—left versus right—than with whether a government is competent and produces perceptible improvements. Political parties and legislative bodies tend to have little legitimacy in the Andean countries, and candidates who stress the importance of national sovereignty and are not afraid to challenge international economic organizations and international relations where the United States is clearly dominant often have electoral advantages over those who do not.

Indigenous peoples make up a majority of the population in Peru and Bolivia and are a significant ethnic element in Ecuador. Venezuela and Colombia are considered mestizo countries, meaning most of their population has mixed European and indigenous ancestry. However, up to a quarter of Colombia's population is of African descent, a figure that represents the largest black population in the Spanish-speaking world.

The Andean nations have had boundary disputes that have led to major military confrontations, particularly between Peru and Ecuador and between Peru, Bolivia, and Chile. Bolivia's struggle to regain an outlet to the sea is a consequence of losing the War of the Pacific to Chile in the latter half of the nineteenth century.

Many of the current political disputes in the Andean region are rooted in regional and class differences. After more than a year in power, Bolivia's president, Evo Morales, faces growing resistance from the conservative political and business elite of Santa Cruz who want more political autonomy. At the center of the dispute is control over the revenue from the extraction of natural resources such as natural gas, oil, iron ore, and tropical timber. President Morales's most popular policy, the nationalization of gas and oil, has angered foreign governments and financial investors, particularly in Brazil.

The Andes region is a complex and fascinating part of South America; however, sustaining dysfunctional democracies, rooting out corruption, battling drug traffickers, reducing violence, alleviating poverty, and providing security remain the core challenges for the twenty-first century. The U.S. intelligence community continues to worry about the emergence of radical populists such as Presidents Chávez and Morales who resist ties to the United States and attempt to reverse the trend toward more private control of national economies and free-market policies once popular in the 1990s. Many of those in the conservative media outlets in the United States report almost exclusively on the hot spots in the Andes related to narco-terrorists, leftist governments, and populist, strong-man, rulers. Three of the most powerful Latin American guerrilla movements formed in the Andes region: Peru's Sendero Luminoso (SL, Shining Path) and Colombia's duo of the Fuerzas Armadas Revolucionarias de Colombia (FARC) and the Ejército de Liberación Nacional (ELN). While SL was the most powerful and brutal of these three during the 1980s and early 1990s, it was rooted out by the Peruvian government in a series of security measures and no longer presents a security threat to the nation or its neighbors. There are now signs of a Sendero resurgence, but the number of followers and the capacity to engage in the kind of terrorism carried out in the past are extremely limited.

There are more hot spots in the Andean region than elsewhere in Latin America, each with its own characteristics and sense of urgency. Some of the following hot spots have existed for decades and are rooted in international controversies; others are fairly recent and are representative of trends that have taken place over the past ten years. This chapter begins with a festering controversy over Bolivia's lack of an access to the sea (*salida al mar*) and then covers nine additional hot spots in the Andean region: border conflicts, Colombia's civil war, drug wars and terrorism, government legitimation and corruption, violence in the Magdalena Medio region of Colombia, Bolivia's election of an indigenous president with a nationalization platform, petroleum politics and pipeline controversies, Peru's Shining Path and the Tupac Amaru, and Venezuela's Bolivarian Revolution.

BOLIVIA'S *SALIDA AL MAR* CONTROVERSY

The dispute between Bolivia and Chile over a Bolivian coastline is one of the major disputes in South America; the controversy is the result of Bolivia's loss in the War of the Pacific (1879–1884), which left the country landlocked and bitter over the treaties ending the war that gave Chile most of the disputed territory in the northern desert region, then rich in guano, a source of nitrates for fertilizer and explosives. Bolivian governments have struggled for more than a century to find a solution to the problem, both directly through negotiations with Chile and multilaterally through the Organization of American States (OAS) since 1979. Achieving a peaceful settlement is difficult, because there is an absence of diplomatic relations between the two nations, and nationalistic impulses detract from a diplomatic solution and the willingness of both parties to resolve their differences in a peaceful manner. Many of those living in northern Chile are from Bolivia and have family connections in both countries. Without a peaceful settlement between the two countries, the prospects for future violence and political instability will clearly increase as oil and gas gain value as state commodities and as nationalism and xenophobia grow. The maritime problem is a crucial issue for Bolivia because the current impasse obstructs trade with the rest of the world. President Morales has taken this delicate issue on, but he is caught in a predicament over relations with Chile because he espoused a hard-line anti-Chile position leading up to his electoral victory in December 2005. The answer to Bolivia's access to the Pacific Ocean may rest with how President Morales deals with Venezuela, since President Chávez has supported Bolivia's demands for access to the sea and is anxious to construct an energy alliance with him. Bolivian political leaders continue to use international organizations as a means to legitimize its claim and recover its loss as a maritime nation.[2] Chile opposes any such deal that would restore Bolivian sovereignty over territory Chile acquired over a century ago. The United States has little interest in trying to mediate between the two parties in the conflict.

The desire for a corridor to the Pacific is deeply rooted in Bolivia's national psyche: textbooks portray the 1879 war as a vengeful Chilean land grab; each May it celebrates a Day of the Sea; at the Lake Titicaca Naval Base, two miles above sea level, a monument depicts a Bolivian soldier thrusting his bayonet into the neck of a Chilean soldier beside the words "What once was ours, will be ours once more."[3] Nationalist rhetoric does not make the *salida al mar* controversy a significant hot spot;

however, it does have the capacity to generate international conflict and xenophobic tensions between the two nations.

The history of the boundary conflict is instructive for what it tells us about conflict resolution, border disputes, and Andean politics. After two U.S.-mediated peace treaties in 1883 and 1884, the War of the Pacific came to a formal close, but the rearrangement of Bolivia's borders to suit Chile left a residue of remorse and resentment among Bolivians who regard the diplomacy engineered by both Chile and the United States as unfair. Throughout the twentieth century a number of diplomatic efforts were made to resolve the Chilean/Bolivian conflict. In 1904 Chile and Bolivia signed a treaty acknowledging Chilean ownership of the Bolivian littoral in exchange for the construction of a railroad from Arica to La Paz by Chile. For the next twenty-five years the conflict continued; at one point Bolivia filed a complaint with the League of Nations claiming the 1904 treaty was forced upon it. In 1929, without consulting the Bolivians, Peru and Chile signed a U.S.-brokered free transit agreement in which Chile was granted Arica and the Peruvian/Chilean border was established between Tacna and Arica. By mid-century, oil (and natural gas) became an integral part of the controversy; to resolve the dispute Bolivia was granted the right to build an oil pipeline to Arica, but without complete control over the sale of petroleum. Protests increased in the 1960s as Chile made investments to improve the economic development of the region, but negotiations failed, and diplomatic relations between Bolivia and Chile were severed in 1962. Bolivia pursued several efforts to gain access to the sea during the Pinochet years in Chile, but little progress came from these efforts. The fact that Chile does not recognize Bolivia's claim that a small strip of land is of national interest due to trade in mineral exports makes a diplomatic solution difficult. In 2000 Bolivian, Argentine, and Chilean experts discussed maritime issues involving sovereignty over land and water. In these discussions Chile argued that giving up its sovereignty over land once held by Bolivia would jeopardize its national security, but that it would consider renting a piece of the land to Bolivia. The Chileans also argued that, since they have maritime issues with Argentina, it would be foolhardy to stir up problems on two borders in dispute.

At present, the maritime issue is dormant, and the global war on terrorism has left both parties reluctant to move because of security concerns over foreign threats. However, as the Bolivian gas market grows, exporting through a Pacific port becomes important for future economic development and national pride. In an effort to lower tensions over Bolivia's ocean access, then-President Carlos Mesa indicated in early 2004 that he was willing to conduct bilateral negotiations with Chile over border and immigration issues without mentioning the oceanic issue.[4] At the summit meeting of the Non-Aligned Movement of countries that met in Havana, Cuba, in September 2006, President Morales lobbied to regain a small part of Chile's coastline in what he calls a "gas for sea" policy. This would mean that Bolivia would supply gas to Chile or export it through Chilean ports in exchange for winning access to the sea. Without full diplomatic relations, appeals to the Organization of American States to help broker a solution, and support from President Chávez, Bolivian demands for a *salida al mar* are likely to fall on deaf ears. The *salida al mar* controversy will remain as a serious border conflict until a workable compromise is crafted. It does not rise to the level of South American hot spot for now, however.

The renewed border tensions between Chile and Bolivia and between Chile and Argentina carry the potential for governments to engage in xenophobic responses. In response to the growing sentiment in favor of Bolivia's historic demand for a sovereign outlet to the Pacific, Chile has staged massive military maneuvers near its northern borders. The tension from these episodes is compounded by Peruvian concern about Chile's rearmament efforts. On its eastern front, Chile has responded with nationalist indignation to allegations of Argentine spy networks operating inside Chile and a break-in by Chilean intelligence agents into the Argentine consulate at Punta Arenas.[5]

BORDER CONFLICTS AND UNGOVERNED SPACES

Despite recent efforts to portray the Latin American scene as one devoid of interstate conflict, there are numerous interstate irritants that constitute hot spots in the Andean region. What is interesting is that while interstate provocations have been multiplying, governments have been restrained from escalating these into major incidents. The most serious of these provocations centers on Colombia, with episodes of cross-border incursions with Venezuela. The Venezuelan military suffered casualties along the border with Colombian armed groups crossing into Venezuela and by Venezuelan national guardsmen crossing into Colombia. Colombian President Álvaro Uribe tried to play down these episodes, but the rise in anti-Venezuelan rancor among Colombian politicians and the media continues unabated. Bilateral commissions have been used by Venezuela and Colombia to address numerous issues, including resolution of the maritime boundary in the Gulf of Venezuela.

Tensions between Ecuador and Colombia arise from Bogotá's efforts to control its southern border, where serious guerrilla activity prevails. Ecuador, angry over Colombian accusations about Ecuadoran army-issue weapons found on members of the Colombian left-wing guerrilla movement FARC and the arrest of a top Colombian guerrilla leader in

Quito, realizes that it cannot avoid what is happening among its conflict-ridden neighbors. The borders that separate Colombia from its five neighbors—Ecuador, Peru, Brazil, Venezuela, and Panama—provide sources of conflict because they are largely uncontrolled and demands for regional cooperation have been unmet. Relations between Venezuela and Colombia have been strained due to the latter's tolerance of insurgents, many of whom operate freely on either side of the Venezuelan border. Brazil and Peru worry less about spillover because of forbidding geography, but growing crime and drug trafficking remain a constant issue.

It is impossible for Colombia's neighbors to ignore completely the bitter civil war that has been going on in Colombia for five decades. Although there have been no major incidents involving soldiers from neighboring countries, each government surrounding Colombia must deal with guerrilla sanctuaries along the borders, humanitarian headaches caused by large numbers of refugees seeking to escape the violence, expanding prison populations, security concerns tied to access to petroleum, drug trafficking, and the growing military involvement of the United States in the northern Andean region. Colombia's civil war has been felt most acutely in Ecuador, where its official neutrality clashes with cross-border attacks from FARC guerrillas using Ecuadoran territory and with the large number of Colombian criminals held in Ecuadoran prisons. Ecuador has responded to Colombian complaints by threatening to demand visas of all Colombians, and Colombia criticizes Ecuador's government for its refusal to treat the FARC guerrillas as terrorists and cooperate with the Bogotá government in its fight against them.

Relations between Colombia and Venezuela are influenced by how each government relates to Washington; Colombia's conservative government is a strong ally of the United States, and President Uribe remains on friendly terms with President Bush. Relations between Colombia and Venezuela were damaged in 2005 when the Uribe government paid bounty hunters to capture a leading FARC member in Venezuela and return him to Colombia without notifying Chávez's government about the capture. President Chávez is reluctant to join hands with Colombia in its fight against guerrillas because of his own war of words against Washington. Brazil is also wary of getting militarily involved in the Colombian conflict for its own political reasons, but it has played a mediating role when possible. Brazil's major concern is the fear of the cocaine trade spreading even more into its territory, and it has started joint air force exercises with Colombia to patrol their common border in search of drug-smuggling flights in the Amazonian region.

Peru and Bolivia, the world's next largest producers of coca after Colombia, have been accused of having close links with Colombia's FARC guerrillas, and the pressure on Colombia from Washington to reduce coca production has caused a "balloon effect" when drug production inevitably shifts from one country to another. There is evidence that FARC has established ties in Argentina, Chile, Peru, Bolivia, Ecuador, and Brazil. Many of the FARC connections are involved with other national insurgent groups linked to drug trafficking, gun running, and money laundering. Unless the Colombian military is successful in defeating FARC at home, there is a good possibility that it may export instability throughout the Andes region. U.S. military commanders are pressing proxy armed forces to target rebels along the Ecuadoran-Colombian-Peruvian border. Military officials worry that the violence and lawlessness in these ungoverned spaces could give criminals and anti-U.S. terrorists a foothold to destabilize governments and plot attacks against the United States and its allies in Latin America.[6] The Andean countries—Bolivia, Colombia, Ecuador, and Peru—are the largest recipients of military/police aid from the United States because of drugs and guerrillas. Despite the terrorist fears along the border areas in the Andes, U.S. officials have failed to provide hard evidence that terrorists in Latin America have the capacity to jeopardize U.S. interests in the Andes.

Border tensions are also the result of the large number of internally displaced Colombians and refugees seeking asylum in Ecuador and Venezuela. According to a BBC News report by James Painter, "The UNHCR estimates more than 30,000 people have sought asylum since 2000, most of them Colombians, and 10,000 have been recognized as refugees."[7] Uribe's crackdown on FARC guerrillas has driven some into the Darién Gap, and fears are growing that they will infiltrate Panama. Others have crossed the border into Ecuador, giving rise to added tensions in the region. Venezuela, Ecuador, and Panama each feel the effects of Colombia's internal conflict, not least because their border areas are poor and underdeveloped. Thus, the Colombian civil war is at the root of many security-based hot spots in the Andean region.

COLOMBIA'S CIVIL WAR

Colombia is a weak state and ranks a close second behind Haiti on the failed state index because of its inability to control more than two-thirds of its territory, the loss of authority to insurgent groups and drug traffickers across wide geographical areas, and the inability of the state to provide personal security in rural areas. Yet, in the areas over which it maintains control, the Colombian government is comparatively strong and well performing. Despite multiple insurgencies and high levels of violence, Colombia has not experienced a military coup in over fifty years, and executive and congressional elections are held on a regular basis.[8] According to Robert Rotberg, "Colombia is tense and disturbed.

Andean South America

Female FARC guerrilla leading a column of insurgents in the mountains of Cauca Department in Southern Colombia. At least 40 percent female, FARC continues to expand its numbers in an effort to overthrow the Colombian government, a form of civil war that has lasted for more than 40 years. (Photograph by Juan Reich, Archivolatino. Courtesy of Redux Pictures.)

It boasts the second highest annual per capita murder rate in the world. Its politicians and businessmen routinely wear armored vests and travel with well-armed guards, a clear inability of the state's ability to ensure personal security."[9] Colombia stands as a good example of a large number of nation-states that are at risk of failing because their governments are unable to deliver important political goods to most of their citizens and because of their failure to subdue long-standing insurgencies. More important to understanding the civil war in Colombia is the number of forces that benefit from the current standoff among the Colombian government, various guerrilla groups, the military, paramilitaries, and the United States with its current financial commitment to rooting out drugs and terrorists, no matter what the cost.

The United States considers Colombia a major hot spot because a long-time armed conflict pits the government against leftist guerrillas and right-wing paramilitaries. Along with the Tri-Border Area (TBA) of Brazil, Argentina, and Paraguay (discussed in Chapter 4) and the Darién Gap (discussed in Chapter 2), Colombia is one of the key areas in South America where the U.S. officials work with Latin American governments to control ungoverned spaces. In Colombia, the major opposition groups engaged in armed conflicts against the government include the Revolutionary Armed Forces of Colombia (FARC), the National Liberation Army (ELN), and the United Self-Defense Forces of Colombia (AUC). The leftist FARC and the ELN emerged in the 1960s and have continued to operate in rural Colombia, whereas the AUC is a right-wing organization of paramilitaries. Both Colombian insurgent groups are financed by drug trafficking and other criminal activities. The U.S. government has made Colombia a security priority, providing billions to assist the Colombian government across a broad range of programs to tackle the root causes of human rights abuses and democratic instability while providing protection assistance necessary to address the armed conflict. The U.S.-backed war on leftist guerrillas and drug cartels has cost the United States $4–5 billion since 2000. The ungoverned spaces in Colombia are located along the Colombia-Ecuador-Peru borders, where indigenous groups, petroleum companies, and drug traffickers clash with local militaries and U.S. forces determined to win what they now call a "war on terrorism." For those who live in these violent and economically depressed regions and who rely on income from coca fields, the concern is likely to be support for alternative crops and access to markets rather than military action aimed at eliminating threats.

The Colombian government has been involved in a peace deal with paramilitaries since 2003, when it announced that it began a program of gradually eliminating the outlawed AUC with promises of amnesty and benefits for disbanding. In one of its largest disarmament efforts, the Colombian government announced in December 2005 that in exchange for turning in weaponry, including rifles, grenades, rockets, and helicopter gunships, the central government would grant 3,000 members of the AUC amnesty and a monthly stipend of $180. President Uribe says he hopes to dissolve the AUC completely by the end of 2007. However, critics of Uribe's plan, including many human rights groups, complain that those responsible for various crimes, including massacres of civilians, will never be brought to justice for such acts. Some of the paramilitary leaders who have been given sharply reduced prison terms in exchange for demobilizing are on a 2004 U.S. government list of suspected drug traffickers. The peace deal also bothers those who argue that the amnesty is not only too soft on the paramilitaries for the crimes they committed but also does little to keep them from reorganizing. On Capitol Hill, lawmakers have voiced concern about the ability of demobilized paramilitaries to avoid justice in many criminal investigations of human rights atrocities against labor unionists and ill-gotten gains from crime and drug trafficking.[10]

Recent investigations reveal significant paramilitary control of the Colombian political system, producing a serious legitimacy crisis for the current Uribe administration. Colombia's "Para-politics" scandal alleges a serious penetration of Colombia's public institutions, despite efforts to disarm thousands of AUC members. This scandal raises questions about the effectiveness of the disarmament process when the level of infiltration has reached the government's intelligence agency. While the Colombian Supreme Court has stepped in to investigate the extent of links between paramilitaries and politicians, the threat to security derives from the fact that the paramilitaries control a significant portion of the international narcotics trade and a restructuring of AUC may be occurring in various regions of Colombia. The United States has a heavy stake in the outcome because of financial assistance for the demobilization process and the potential for regime collapse due to paramilitary crimes and corruption. Private military contractors, now heavily involved in security activities in Colombia, may also be affected by the outcome. The current AUC scandal is only part of the rationale for labeling Colombia a major hot spot in South America.

On the domestic front, Colombia's government has done little to prosecute crimes related to the killing of labor activists, a reflection of how serious labor union violence is in a country that wants a trade deal with the United States. This form of terrorism—Colombia leads the world in the murder of labor activists—has been attributed to paramilitary organizations with close ties to the Uribe administration. The lack of investigative efforts and the corruption among Colombian justice officials is a clear sign of how little is being done to eradicate right-wing terrorism against labor leaders at the same time the Bush administration is touting the benefits of free trade.

The political violence and massive numbers of displaced people in Colombia have contributed to a culture of insecurity that stimulates the conditions for unemployment, drug trafficking, distrust of the police, and youth gangs and other forms of violence. Democratic accountability and political stability are impossible to achieve without changes in the security environment. The objective of the Uribe administration is to establish security by using a military strategy to remove terrain from illegal armed groups, which include the FARC, ELN, paramilitaries, and organized crime, so that all Colombians can exercise their rights within a democratic framework. The conflict with the FARC, however, has been going on for over forty years with no sign of a solution to ending the conflict. Former M-19 guerrilla leader Antonio Navarro Wolff argues that the current strategy is not working and a new course is the only way the government can end the standoff. In a recent article, he argues that what is needed is a new rural development program with wide-ranging land reform, alternative development options, youth programs, an end to U.S.-backed fumigation efforts, and a strong state presence in vulnerable areas.[11]

Colombian rebels do not need much popular support since they have been successful in financing themselves through coca and marijuana profiteering. This explains why Colombia's civil war has dragged on for so many decades with little to show for the money spent.

Colombia's indigenous community is often caught in the middle of the conflict between guerrilla forces and the Colombian military. President Uribe worries about the claims of autonomy by indigenous communities, particularly when they conflict with his national security programs and emphasis on free trade agreements with the United States.[12] Nasa Indians in the Department of Cauca continue to feel threatened by right-wing paramilitaries, left-wing guerrillas, and state security forces. So far, the democratic security promised by the government has yet to reach the indigenous communities in northern Cauca Department.

DRUG WARS AND TERRORISM

As shown in Table 3.1, the largest, and oldest, terrorist organizations operate in Colombia. The fuel that drives terrorist groups in Latin America is money from the illicit drug trade, particularly the cocaine and heroin industry in Colombia, Peru, and Bolivia. For much of the late twentieth century, cocaine was transported by distribution rings in Colombia known as cartels, often centered on one family or extended family. At first the Medellín cartel dominated the smuggling of cocaine into the United States; it was eclipsed in the early 1990s by its archrival, the Cali cartel, led by two brothers: Gilberto Rodríguez Orejuela and Miguel Rodríguez Orejuela. According to U.S. law enforcement officials, the highly efficient Cali cartel was responsible for smuggling over 200,000 kilograms of cocaine into the United States between 1990 and 2002. After pleading guilty to drug trafficking charges in Miami in 2006, each brother was sentenced to 30 years in prison and agreed to forfeit $2.1 billion in assets linked to the drug trade. In its heyday, the Cali Cartel was estimated to make $5 to $7 billion a year, funds were used to buy politicians, a credit card company, a pharmaceutical firm, and a chain of 350 drug stores in Colombia. The guilty pleas signaled the end of the Cali cartel; other traffickers, including the drug cartels in Mexico, now control smuggling operations into the United States, and the Colombian cocaine trade is run by a more fractured and decentralized constellation of criminal organizations.[13] The decentralization of the drug trade means that anti-drug efforts require more law enforcement resources and the threat level from drug smuggling is far greater than when drug trafficking was controlled by only a few cartels.

In an effort to capture individuals in Colombia associated with cocaine trafficking, a federal grand jury in Washington indicted 50 commanders

Table 3.1 Terrorist Organizations in Latin America

Name of Organization	Location	Strength in Numbers
National Liberation Army (ELN)	Colombia	3,000–5,000
Revolutionary Armed Forces of Colombia (FARC)	Colombia	9,000–12,000
United Self-Defense Forces of Colombia (AUC)	Colombia	8,000–11,000
Tupac Amaru Revolutionary Movement	Peru	100
Sendero Luminoso (SL, Shining Path)	Peru	200
Lautaro Popular Rebel Forces	Chile	Unknown
Manuel Rodríguez Patriotic Front	Chile	50–100
Revolutionary Organization of the People in Arms (ORPA)	Guatemala	Unknown
Guerrilla Army of the Poor (EPG)	Guatemala	Unknown
Guatemalan National Revolutionary Union (URNG)	Guatemala	100–200
Guatemalan Worker's Party	Guatemala	Unknown
Hezbollah	Tri-Border Area	Unknown
Islamic Jihad	Tri-Border Area	Unknown
Ansar Allah (Followers of God)	Tri-border Area	Unknown
Jamaat al-Muslimeen	Trinidad, Guyana	1,100
Tupamaros	Uruguay, Venezuela	Unknown

Source: CRS Report to Congress, "Latin America: Terrorism Issues" (http://www.fas.org/sgp/crs/terror).

of the Revolutionary Armed Forces of Colombia (FARC), the richest and best equipped Marxist insurgency in Latin America. The indictment claims that the FARC is behind 50 percent of the world's cocaine trade and 60 percent of Colombia's cocaine exported to the United States.[14] There are both leftist and rightist groups involved in this activity, however, and the conflict shows no signs of abatement despite a major financial and military commitment by the United States and cooperative efforts by Latin American governments.

Colombia will continue to be a problem for the Bush administration throughout its second term. After six years of the administration's Plan

Colombia, Washington has spent close to $5 billion on combating narco-terrorism without defeating either drug traffickers, guerrillas, or paramilitaries. The latest coca cultivation estimates leave no doubt that overall Andean coca cultivation in 2006 may have reached its highest level in 20 years. The high cultivation levels, especially in Colombia, indicate that despite Plan Colombia's best efforts, the Andes region continues to produce robust cocaine supplies for the U.S. and European markets. It is a costly war with no end in sight, regardless of the amount of economic and military aid Washington is funneling into Colombia. According to Rodrigo Pardo, "Uribe aligned himself with Bush's controversial world view in exchange for continued funding for Plan Colombia and political support for his AUC demobilization process."[15] The price of joining President Bush's foreign policy was a deterioration of relations with Colombia's neighbors and some alienation from the new political trends in Latin America. If President Uribe wants to negotiate with guerrillas and reintegrate the AUC in his second term, he will need a more diversified foreign policy that separates him from U.S. Latin American policy.

Likewise, Peru's coca eradication program is facing stiff resistance from coca growers determined to expand production in the main growing areas. President Alan García (2006–2011) vows a tough line approach to continue coca eradication in hopes of maintaining good relations with Washington. Breaking the bonds between drug trafficking and guerrillas will not be easy, but such an approach proved to be successful under García's predecessor, Alberto Fujimori, now under house arrest in Peru after spending several years in exile living in Chile.

A growing alliance of leftist leaders in Latin America—Hugo Chávez in Venezuela, Rafael Correa in Ecuador, and Evo Morales in Bolivia—is challenging U.S. drug policy, accusing the United States of hypocrisy on the basis of its own consumption of illicit drugs, or of using the drug war to justify a military presence in Latin America. Ecuador's President Correa opposes the spraying of illegal Colombian crops on the Ecuadoran border because the herbicides destroy legal crops and endanger people's health on Ecuador's side of the border. Although Colombia insists the fumigation is safe, Ecuador has withdrawn its ambassador to Bogotá in protest of the policy. For a speech to the United Nations in September 2006, Bolivia's President Morales held up a small green coca leaf while denouncing "the colonization of the Andean countries" by the imposition of U.S. demands to criminalize coca leaves, a substance that "does no harm to human health." Quoting Morales's speech in a reflective article on the folly of U.S. anti-drug policy, John Tierney claims that "Drug prohibition in Bolivia and Afghanistan has done exactly what alcohol prohibition did in America: it has financed organized crime [and terrorism]."[16]

U.S. efforts to stop peasants from growing coca in the Andes have contributed to the deaths of U.S. soldiers and the expenditure of billions of dollars. This approach has not stopped the crops from flourishing, and the street price of cocaine has plummeted over the past two decades. In Tierney's view, U.S. anti-drug warriors put President Morales in power, enabling him to use international organizations to denounce the United States while at the same time gaining stature in Latin America.

Latin American governments are also angry at the way the drug war has been militarized through the use of small military bases used to launch airplane surveillance and fumigation efforts over Colombia, Peru, and Bolivia. President Correa has promised to refuse to extend the lease on a major U.S. counternarcotics operation in Manta, located on the north coast of Ecuador and the center of South American anti-drug activities.

In a war of words over drug policy, the U.S. ambassador in Caracas has charged that drug smuggling has soared in Venezuela due to President Chávez's refusal to cooperate with the U.S. Drug Enforcement Agency. Venezuela denies the charge that smuggling has increased, but the rhetorical assaults afford Chávez the opportunity to criticize the U.S.-backed drug war and remind Washington of the common Latin American view of the hypocrisy associated with a failed policy.[17]

The drug war in Latin America has also been criticized from the conservative or neoliberal point of view as having hindered the advancement of free markets and the rule of law. Álvaro Vargas Llosa, free market advocate and son of novelist Mario Vargas Llosa, argues that the U.S. drug war, which he calls "friendly fire from the United States," is "a policy that thrives on repression and the suffocation of supply by engaging underdeveloped countries in a forceful reallocation of resources, the commitment of political capital, and the cessation of civilian power to their military establishments, and it has been counterproductive, hurting individual rights and further weakening institutional safeguards against intrusive governments."[18] No doubt the thousands of employees of the Drug Enforcement Agency (DEA) in Washington would disagree with this assessment, but at the core of the drug wars may well be a spark for the hot spots that generate fears about security and the loss of freedom. This "danger" has nothing to do with terrorists from the Middle East operating in Latin America.

By trying to solve the problem of cocaine by getting rid of coca leaves, the United States makes it easier for Latin American leaders to rant about U.S. "imperialists" criminalizing a substance that, in its traditional form, has been used legally for centuries in the Andes as a mild stimulant and appetite suppressant. The eradication approach also reinforces the Latin American view that the United States is guilty of hypocrisy when it claims to fight a drug war while at the same time being a major source for the demand for drugs as well as a channel for money laundering through U.S. banks.

GOVERNANCE AND CORRUPTION

The Andean countries are plagued with institutional weaknesses that often put democratic institutions at grave risk. Extremely weak political institutions combined with deep ethnic and class divisions have made it hard to govern either Bolivia or Ecuador. Military coups are less frequent than during the Cold War, but they still happen, often inflamed by opposition demagogues, ousting elected presidents on the grounds of corruption, poor governance, runaway crime rates, faltering economic reforms, and social distress. Public outrage over these political weaknesses have spawned indigenous-military coups and military mutinies in hopes of improving the quality of governance. Ecuador, Bolivia, and Venezuela have each experienced these difficulties in which institutions are at risk of collapse—an outcome that would pose a serious threat to U.S. interests in the region—and Peru is not too far behind.[19] Quoting the Latinobarómetro studies, the *Latin American Newsletters* believe that "[b]eyond authoritarianism we shall prove that the threats to the region are rooted in poverty and severe inequalities." The overwhelming victory by indigenous leader Evo Morales in December 2005 has given him more legitimacy than any Bolivian president in the past 60 years and a platform to criticize counter-drug efforts in the Andes. However, after a year in power and the support of two-thirds of Bolivians, Morales struggles to consolidate his power and increase the political legitimacy of the presidency. According to *The Economist* magazine, "The inexperienced, often inept, government [of Bolivia] has achieved little beyond boosting ethnic and national pride, and gas royalties."[20]

In the 2006 presidential election in Ecuador, candidates from the left and right battled over ties to Venezuela, the government's foreign debt, ties with the United States, and nationalist economic proposals. Rafael Correa, a charismatic economist, campaigned against the Bush administration's policies in the region with promises for a "citizen's revolution" designed to address social programs, opposition to free trade agreements, and threats to reduce foreign debt payments and eliminate U.S. military bases on Ecuadoran soil. In the first round of elections, Álvaro Noboa, a conservative banking and banana magnate with close ties to Washington and Wall Street, beat Correa by 3 percent largely by calling him a "friend of terrorists, a friend of Chávez, and a friend of Cuba," forcing Correa to defend his ties to Hugo Chávez and admiration for the Venezuelan's "Bolivarian ideals."[21] The threats to reduce foreign debt payments upset Wall Street and prompted a series of op-ed articles in the *Wall Street*

Journal in which columnist Mary Anastasia O'Grady attacked Correa, calling him a power-hungry demagogue who will "trash the capitalists" and "make the U.S. an official enemy" if he won the presidency in a runoff with Noboa. In an effort to frighten Correa's supporters and heighten the fear of another leftist in South America, O'Grady called critics of neoliberal economic policies and U.S. military intervention members of the "Latin American axis of outcasts," including Venezuela, Cuba, Bolivia and Argentina.[22] Although both Ecuadoran candidates campaigned as populists, Noboa expressed his outright support of closer ties with the United States and made false accusations that Correa was a Communist because of his close ties with Chávez and Castro. Noboa promised to sever diplomatic relations with Cuba and Venezuela if elected in the runoff election against Correa.

In the 2006 campaign, Correa called for greater government control over the petroleum industry and for the removal of the United States military from a small airbase on the Pacific coast. It is possible that the *Wall Street Journal* attacks on Correa may have helped him win the presidency. Now that he is president, Correa's biggest challenge will be to bring political stability and government legitimacy to Ecuador, a country that has had eight presidents since 1996, including three who were driven from office by street protests. In a summary of Latin America in 2006, the Inter-American Dialogue expressed concern that Correa "has a messianic streak, institutions are dysfunctional and presidents there don't normally finish their terms. Correa may fall into the temptation of refashioning the political system in his own image."[23] Although a friend of President Chávez and Venezuela, Correa softened his leftist rhetoric during the runoff vote and made a deliberate effort to meet with representatives of the business community, as well as the U.S. ambassador, during the campaign. In contrast to the vocal criticisms heard from U.S. officials during Nicaragua's recent elections, the U.S. Embassy remained silent during Ecuador's 2006 presidential campaign and, once Correa's win was announced, called to congratulate him and offer its cooperation.

Venezuela is slightly more than twice the size of California and, with a population of approximately 25 million, the sixth-most populous country in Latin America. Until the middle of the twentieth century, Venezuela's history was marked by long periods of political instability, revolutionary violence, and dictatorial rule. After World War I the Venezuelan economy shifted from agricultural exports to an economy dominated by petroleum production and export. After the overthrow of General Marcos Pérez Jiménez in 1958, Venezuela experienced a period of civilian democratic rule and earned the reputation of a stable two-party system for more than 30 years. The relative stability came to an end in 1989, when deep popular dissatisfaction erupted in the form of riots and coup attempts. The recognition that the prevailing political system under President Carlos Andrés Pérez no longer served the interests of the Venezuelan people was based on resentment directed at the traditional political parties, huge income disparities, corruption, and neoliberal economic policies.[24] After two unsuccessful coup attempts in 1992, followed by the impeachment of President Pérez on corruption charges the following year, many Venezuelans became frustrated and willing to jettison the rules of the democratic game for serious reforms that were promised by the election of Hugo Chávez in 1998. Voters re-elected President Chávez in July 2000, but after strikes and massive demonstrations demanding Chávez's resignation in 2002, a brief military takeover removed him from office before military troops loyal to him restored him to power two days later. This constitutional crisis was a serious blow to the prevailing political system and contributed to numerous efforts to reconcile the differences between government and opposition. The United States has remained committed to regime change in Venezuela since the failed coup attempt in 2002, which the United States supported while maintaining that it was not a coup. By maintaining hostile relations with Iran, Cuba, Nicaragua, and Venezuela, the United States has lost considerable influence throughout Latin America.

With the help of the Organization of American States, the United Nations Development Program, the Carter Center, and a few Latin American and European governments, an agreement was signed that set the stage for a possible recall referendum, allowed under the 1999 Constitution, on May 29, 2003. After months of struggling to obtain the necessary signatures to allow the referendum, and a highly controversial signature verification process, a presidential recall referendum was held on August 15, 2004. Following the vote count, considered free of electoral fraud by international observers, President Chávez won with 59 percent of the vote. Despite widespread abstentions, President Chávez's supporters gained in both state governorships and legislative elections.

Regardless of size of government, weak states lack the mechanisms to fight corruption and the most corrupt nations are poor.[25] The more democracy in a political system, the less corruption that infects the political process; however, the road to democracy is difficult: "The transition to democracy tends to be a very corrupt period, during which shaky institutions, rapid privatizations and unclear rules contribute to the problem."[26] Peru's ex-spymaster, Vladimiro Montesinos, received an estimated $10 million in cash from the U.S. Central Intelligence Agency as part of an effort to gather intelligence on the drug war. In an agency-to-agency relationship, from 1990 until 2000 the CIA directed the cash payments to Peru's Narcotics Intelligence Division (DIN), but part of the funds went into Montesino's pockets. After facing trial on murder, arms and drug trafficking charges, Montesinos fled Peru but was later captured and imprisoned in the same prison he helped build for captured terrorists. The United States accumulated a great deal of evidence of corruption, human rights abuses, illegal arms deals, and drug trafficking by Montesinos, but it dismissed these reports because he was a CIA asset and a key to Washington's drug war in the Andes. Using his CIA-backed position, Montesinos arranged an arms deal with Colombia's FARC guerrillas, the main target of Washington's billion-dollar counter-narcotics aid package to Colombia. After ten years as a close aide to President Alberto Fujimori, Montesinos had at least $264 million secretly deposited in foreign bank accounts in Switzerland, the United States, and the Cayman Islands, among others.[27]

Andean governments often resort to a state of emergency to deal with protests that jeopardize national interests. In Ecuador, President Alfredo Palacio declared a state of emergency in March 2006 after more than a week of protests by thousands of indigenous communities against free trade talks with the United States. In an effort to quell the nationwide disturbances, Palacio deployed troops to highland communities in an effort to open blocked highways and the loss of millions of dollars of commerce. The major demands from the indigenous communities are to (1) put the possible free trade pact to a national referendum, (2) cancel oil concessions to multinational Occidental Petroleum, and (3) convene a constitutional assembly to rewrite Ecuador's constitution. Organized by the Confederation of Indigenous Nationalities of Ecuador, the protest movement made up of Indians and students marched through the streets of Quito, the capital, chanting "We don't want to be a North American colony," and "Get out, Occidental."[28] Nevertheless, protest leaders vowed to press on while the Ecuadoran president continued with final round discussions with the United States over trade talks.[29] With the ability of indigenous protesters to shut down the country's commerce by blocking roads and attracting attention at home and abroad, Andean presidents operate at disadvantage since these opposition efforts have resulted in the removal of presidents in Ecuador and Bolivia over the past ten years. With a treasury swollen by windfall petroleum revenues, the protests have focused more on extracting more spending from government than on virulent opposition to negotiations over a free-trade agreement with the United States.

Peru rejected Ollanta Humala in the runoff election in June 2006, opting for ex-President Alan García. Humala ran on a center-left platform that blamed big corporations and corrupt politicians for the poverty and lack of opportunity that prevails in Peru. He also had the support of Venezuelan President Hugo Chávez, which made García a "lesser-of-two-evils" candidate for those who remembered García's disastrous first term as president of Peru. A mestizo who spoke no Indian language, Humala represented Peru's provincial middle class; as an outsider without previous political experience and a coherent manifesto, he symbolized a threat to democracy and economic prosperity. According to *The Economist*, "His nationalism is that of the populist military *caudillo*" and the fact that he is loathed by most better-off Peruvians and the media signals a dose of authoritarianism for Peru if he is declared president.[30] Humala declared he would restructure government with a new constitution with a state apparatus that will reduce the role of the private sector, ban foreign companies from "strategic" businesses, and modify the tax breaks given to foreign mining companies to stimulate investment. For Washington, the danger centered on his leftist ideology and the support he garnered from Venezuela's Hugo Chávez. Some Peruvian analysts blamed his loss on the support he received from President Chávez and the fear of another President Morales. García's win centered on his success in convincing Peruvians that he was the lesser of the evils, that he was chastened and reformed after his disastrous presidency in the 1980s, and that he would improve the government while addressing poverty and needed social programs. The challenge to the García administration will be to demonstrate the ability to keep the Peruvian economy going while addressing antipoverty programs that meets the educational and health needs of the poor and underprivileged. If he is unable to display some economic competence, address the debilitating effects of corruption, and keep democracy on track, García may be overthrown by the military or by those in the countryside who are looking for good governance in Lima after the failed presidencies of Alberto Fujimori and Alejandro Toledo. Under the latter administration Peru's interior minister, Fernando Rospigliosi, was forced to resign after the country's Congress voted to censure him after he was accused of doing nothing about the indigenous uprising in southern Peru that led to the death of a mayor accused of corruption. Rospigliosi's untimely departure was a further blow to President Toledo, whose approval was less than 8 percent of the population at the time of the scandal.[31]

Weak states operate at a disadvantage when attempting to handle past human rights violations. This was rarely a problem when democracies were weak and the military exercised considerable power. However, once democracies began to emerge in the 1980s, the newly elected governments faced expectations from many sectors of society to hold responsible those accused of severe human rights violations such as torture, political murder, disappearances, and other crimes. In attempting to resolve the human rights violations of previous regimes, South American governments have had four major policy options to choose from: domestic prosecution, amnesty for violators, truth commission, and victim reparations. Each carries its own risks, and shaky governments have often tried truth commissions because they avoid the risk of provoking outrage over trials and outrage over amnesty. Truth commissions are designed to carry out an official investigation into human rights violations, but without holding those identified as perpetrators criminally responsible—both elected civilians and military officials. Truth commissions have been used in Argentina, Brazil, Chile, Peru, and Guatemala.[32] With the creation of the International Criminal Court (ICC) in 2002 to address the most heinous cases of genocide, war crimes, and crimes against humanity, international prosecution may become a more viable option for Latin American governments in the future.[33]

Bolivia faces an autonomy movement based in the four eastern provinces, where political leaders fear that President Morales may be able to use a constituent assembly to impose the values of the Andean-Indian communities on the entrepreneurial east. The sharp divide between the eastern provinces and the Andean-Indian communities has led to talk of secession and independence. As long as the army remains loyal to President Morales and his Movement to Socialism (MAS), the street protests, hunger strikes, and opposition demands may fail to dislodge him from power. President Morales has demonstrated that he can govern effectively despite the failure to produce a constitutional blueprint. He has signed agreements with foreign energy companies over the nationalization of oil and gas, pushed a land reform law through Congress, and largely played by the rules of the political game and the laws of economics. In a move to restore some degree of fiscal sanity, Morales plans to follow the example of Chile and establish a stabilization fund to save part of its gas windfall for leaner times.[34] The power of the armed forces in the Andean region is not what it used to be during the Cold War, but the role of the military often expands when weak political institutions and poor leadership prevail.

In response to Morales's electoral victory, the Bush administration decided to slash military aid to Bolivia by 96 percent, mostly for training Bolivian military officers at the Western Hemisphere Institute for Security Cooperation (WHINSEC, formerly the School of the Americas). This budgetary decision holds the potential to anger the Bolivian military, an institution that has a history of coups and counter-coups. If President Morales ends the eradication programs favored by the United States, farmers in Peru and other parts of the Andes will demand the same, leading to a flood of cheap cocaine into the U.S. and Europe. Nevertheless, the main reason for the budget slash is that Bolivia has failed to ratify a pledge not to extradite U.S. personnel to the International

Criminal Court (ICC), since the Bush administration does not recognize the ICC as legitimate. Under pressure, just over 100 countries have signed the agreement, but the Bush administration decided to issue waivers to eleven Latin American and Caribbean countries in October 2006 to blunt a leftward trend in the region that has cost the United States influence. President Bush's waiver will allow the United States to resume training the militaries, although the ban on giving countries weapons remains in effect. These security-based concessions are also designed to counter the gains made during the ban by China, which has exchanged senior military officials with Ecuador, Bolivia, Chile, and Cuba and provided military aid and training to Jamaica and Venezuela.[35] Training at WHINSEC has declined as presidents from Bolivia, Costa Rica, Nicaragua, Venezuela, Uruguay, and Argentina now refuse to send military personnel to the school for counterinsurgency training.

MAGDALENA MEDIO (COLOMBIA)

Located in the heart of Colombia, the Magdalena Medio region is one of the poorest and most violent regions of the country. According to the World Bank, "Magdalena Medio is a microcosm of the actors and issues underlying Colombia's armed conflict with guerrillas, right-wing paramilitaries, with the army battling for control while the civilian population struggles to survive."[36] With 70 percent of the population below the poverty line, efforts have been under way since 1995 to tackle the persistent poverty and violence in the region. The Program for Development and Peace in Magdalena Medio (PDPMM) started in 1995 with the assistance of the Catholic Diocese of Barrancabermeja, the Colombian government, and the World Bank. The project is designed to dovetail with the national government's strategy of supporting regional and local initiatives that build social capital and attack the root causes of violence. To support this process, the Colombian government obtained a $5 million Learning and Innovation Loan from the World Bank and $1.25 million from the national oil company to finance the project, which started in the fall of 1998. Hopes for peace in the Magdalena Medio region depend on programs designed to reduce poverty and improve the quality of life. It remains to be seen whether these programs will have any effect on Colombia's civil war, drug trafficking, and the strength of rural insurgencies.

MORALES AND THE MULTINATIONALS

After years of widespread indigenous protests aimed at international financial institutions and the United States, premature presidential resignations, a controversial war on drugs, and the failure of Washington

Bolivian President Evo Morales—first indigenous president in Latin America and a former coca farmer—and Venezuelan President Hugo Chávez at the balcony of the Presidential Palace in La Paz, Bolivia, January 22, 2006, after Morales is sworn in as president. The United States considers both of the leaders "radical populists" and a threat to U.S. security interests in the region. (The Image Works)

consensus-style politics, Bolivians elected Evo Morales president in December 2005. The Morales victory was historic for several reasons.[37] An Aymará, Morales is now the first indigenous president in Bolivia's 180-year history and the first president to win more than 50 percent of the popular vote—an overwhelming mandate drawn from broad segments of Bolivian society. According to Daphne Eviatar, "for the popular former leader of the coca growers' union to have won the presidency by an overwhelming and closely monitored vote suggests the vitality of Bolivian democracy and the evolution of a new Latin American consensus." Yet what appears to be a powerful mandate to carry out his promises to nationalize oil and natural gas reserves, to oppose the U.S.-imposed policy of "zero coca," and to alleviate poverty must be tempered by the serious challenges Morales faces in trying to move away from neoliberal economics in this cash-poor but resource-rich country.[38] Morales's success is another example of Latin America's recent democratic revolutions, in which frustration with Washington-backed economic prescriptions have put left-leaning leaders in power. He is the seventh Latin American leader to take power since 2000 from the center-left. Although he has toned down some of his more strident rhetoric and forged a more accommodating tone with U.S. officials, he remains untested as an executive in a country with serious political and economic weaknesses. Still, his landslide victory and his skills as a protest leader and orator offer the possibilities of meaningful change in Bolivia. The political trends in South America that Morales represents worry Washington as more and more Latin American countries are strengthening ties to China, which is investing heavily in the region, and are taking exception to the failed economic prescriptions imposed by Washington and by international financial institutions such as the International Monetary Fund (IMF). The rise in anti-U.S. sentiment is reflected in the refusal of South American countries to send soldiers in support of the war in Iraq or to accede to the Bush administration's demands to exclude U.S. personnel from criminal prosecutions before the International Criminal Court.

With the support of poor indigenous farmers and laborers, who make up the 40 percent of the population considered extremely poor by the World Bank, Morales will have to balance demands to solve poverty by nationalization of the energy sector and radical redistribution of land with the power of local business leaders engaged in energy production and agricultural exports. Moreover, if Morales tampers too much with the existing oil and natural gas contracts, he may suffer the wrath of the *transnationales* (foreign oil companies), who are prepared to threaten Bolivia with legal claims in international arbitration. How Morales resolves these conflicting demands will be the real test of his presidency and possibly the future of Bolivia. Morales knows that Bolivia, the most impoverished nation in South America, did not benefit from the economic policies of the 1980s, which administered "shock therapy" to bring down inflation by privatizing its oil, gas, water, electric, and other major industries. The privatization schemes did not bring prosperity as promised, but increased poverty and provoked a wave of anger against international financial institutions and Washington. Unlike Venezuela's Hugo Chávez, who enjoys a well-developed energy sector that allows him to reap the benefits from record oil prices, President Morales has no bargaining chip to offer other political leaders. Although President Morales is a long way from being a Chávez copy, the "democratic revolution" he promises that would transfer wealth and power from Bolivia's white and mestizo elite to the mainly Andean Indian poor is bound to anger the prosperous eastern provinces, which fear a Venezuelan path to a totalitarian regime.

There are deep fears in Washington about the results of a Morales presidency, not merely because he repeatedly called himself during the campaign "Washington's nightmare," but because he is an unpredictable leader with a revolutionary program and an electoral mandate. With close ties to Fidel Castro and Hugo Chávez, Morales brings solid anti-U.S. credentials to his presidency, which naturally makes it difficult for Washington to praise him for his programs and electoral accomplishments. Furthermore, by 2006 Morales was the sixth leader in South America to be elected with a left-of-center agenda, and despite his pledge to work with Washington, there are those who see him as a serious threat to the hemisphere and in need of containment.

It is also important to understand that the United States is responsible for both the Morales victory and his current governing predicament. Bolivians who voted for Morales see the United States as a symbol of foreign capital, the guiding hand of a failed war on drugs, bearing some responsibility for Bolivia's current poverty. Clearly, the left-leaning trend in South America has less to do with a Castro-Chávez cabal than with the frustration over economic policies that have worsened relations with the United States and exacerbated poverty and inequality.[39] Treating President Morales as a threat because of his association with Castro and Chávez may well become self-fulfilling. The Bush administration may find it beneficial to label Morales as a "leftist" threat to the hemisphere because of his economic policies and anti–drug war agenda; however, it would be far better to engage Morales and spend time devising alternative solutions to Bolivia's severe economic and political problems. Bolivia is still considered a security threat by the Pentagon because of its political instability, drug trafficking, money laundering, and opposition to the prevailing neoliberal agenda. The United States has no military bases in Bolivia, but the recent maneuvers in Paraguay suggest that Washington feels Bolivia is worth watching and has the capacity to flare up into a Latin American hot spot.

With a campaign based on Bolivia's reassertion of sovereignty over its natural resources, and polls showing over 75 percent of Bolivians in favor of nationalization, President Morales nationalized the energy sector on May 1, 2006. Although it is uncertain exactly what contractual changes may emerge, it seems that partnerships with the multinationals is the desired outcome, not confiscation of everything foreign in the economy. Nevertheless, the nationalizations will confirm Washington's worst fears about President Morales as a threat to Andean drug eradication efforts and foreign investment in the energy sector. Washington policymakers, and much of the right-wing media in the United States, are convinced that he is a danger to the United States and Latin America. Without supplying any evidence, some of those involved in the national security area, particularly the Pentagon, suspect that he is a terrorist aligned with Fidel Castro and Hugo Chávez. This kind of hysteria is common when Latin American leaders attempt to change contractual arrangements to reflect national needs and priorities more closely. Bolivia's reassertion of sovereignty in the energy sector poses problems for the governments that have invested heavily in Bolivia; however, it may be more prudent to negotiate new deals that open the door for state oil companies in Malaysia, China, and India.

It is too soon to assess the impact of President Morales's promises to transform Bolivia on the rest of South America. He has moderated his anti-U.S. tone and is mostly vague on details of how he plans to implement his "communal socialism" to solve Bolivia's economic troubles. Washington is worried about this pledge to "depenalize" the cultivation of coca, the prime ingredient for cocaine; efforts to squeeze more profits from the oil and natural gas industry; and other policies that run counter to U.S. interests. He has expressed an interest in "finding solutions" with the United States, the largest donor to Bolivia with interests in trade and a punitive drug policy. President Morales knows that he must maintain positive relations with his neighbors, particularly Brazil and Argentina, but he maintains he wants "partners, not bosses" in developing oil and gas reserves.

President Morales will also face challenges with Chile, even with the recent election of the socialist Michelle Bachelet as president, because of the *salida al mar* controversy discussed earlier in this chapter. The two countries have not had full diplomatic relations since the 1970s, and President Morales is sensitive to nationalist demands to open up talks on this troublesome issue. Before becoming president, Morales led a successful protest against a pipeline that would have sent Bolivian gas to Mexico and the United States through a Chilean port. President Morales wants the state to be a key force in economic development and recognizes that he must welcome trade with countries outside of South America. U.S. officials fear that President Morales could become more radical than President Chávez and move Bolivia to the brink of civil war. The United States hopes to dilute Morales's influence by encouraging Bolivia's neighbors to guide him in a more pragmatic direction, perhaps following in the footsteps of Luiz Lula da Silva of Brazil, a less nationalistic approach than the one in play in Venezuela under Chávez. Nevertheless, President Morales has a powerful mandate and the support of many governments in Latin America; however, he does not have the huge oil revenues that have enabled Chávez to fund social programs, and many of his radical supporters are anxious for him to deliver on social promises.[40]

Perhaps it is time to dispense with the use of "leftist" as an ideological concept to categorize Latin American governments. As Michael Shifter and Vinay Jawahar point out in their 2005 article on political trends in Latin America, "Whatever governments are in place in Latin American countries—and whoever is in charge—they must deliver concrete results for broad sectors of the population that have not seen much, if any, improvement in their well-being in recent years."[41] President Morales's nationalization is popular in Bolivia; even large segments of the business community support the move, where his "nationalization" amounts to only a limited takeover of three key companies involved in the energy sector. It worries Washington that Morales has promised to nationalize mining and forestry, and redistribute unused land to landless farmers, a strategy used by President Chávez in Venezuela.[42] This is also a concern among the Santa Cruz–based far right, made up of ranchers and industrialists who insist that true land reform could lead to civil war. Promising to rewrite the constitution in order to minimize checks on presidential power,[43] President Morales has sparked demands in Santa Cruz and other provincial capitals for greater political autonomy from the central government in La Paz. Hundreds of thousands of protestors marched in December 2006 to express their opposition to President Morales's efforts to rewrite the Constitution to allow changes based on a simple majority instead of a two-thirds vote, to increase the power of the indigenous population in the west. Bolivia's poor indigenous majority now have more power than at any time in Bolivia's history, and they believe that new laws are necessary to reflect the needs of the majority, not the laws of the past that have stemmed from the non-Indian elite, including the military, that have dominated the recent politics of Bolivia.[44]

After announcing that Bolivia would nationalize oil and gas fields on May 1, 2006, President Morales said that he would not compensate oil companies—British Gas, Total of France, Repsol of Spain, and Petrobras of Brazil—because they had already recovered their investments and earned a substantial profit from their operations in Bolivia. Morales also confirmed that his government would seize farmland and redistribute it to peasants. The most affected country is Brazil, whose oil giant, Petrobras, has investments in gas and oil, and whose farmers hold land in Bolivia. Bolivia's energy nationalizations are to be followed by a six-month phase in which energy contracts are renegotiated.[45] Joseph Stiglitz, winner of the Nobel Prize in Economics, said on a visit to Bolivia in May 2006 that Bolivia's nationalization of gas and petroleum was necessary because prior national legislation had a negative impact on the country. He called the current nationalization "recuperation of stolen goods" since the previous contracts were not legal.

After almost twenty years of neoliberalism and structural adjustment strategies, Bolivia remains the poorest country in South America. Foreign investment has increased over this span of time, largely in the form of multinational corporations taking control of privatized industries. However, economic prosperity has not followed in the wake of modest economic growth and the declining rates of inflation. Latin Americans no longer believe in the dictum that greater trade leads to greater general prosperity, the economic faith of liberal globalizers in the United States. Increased international trade and foreign investment by multinationals can be beneficial to poor countries such as Bolivia, but free markets are no guarantee that this will automatically happen. The popular backlash against the Washington consensus in Latin America clashes with the Bush administration's belief in the creation of a hemisphere-wide free trade zone known as the Free Trade Area of the Americas (FTAA), a sort of super-version of the North American Free Trade Agreement (NAFTA), a brainchild of the multinationals interested in opening new markets for U.S. firms and products. Often presented to Latin American leaders as a win-win deal, the acceptance of FTAA would be far easier if the United States were not perceived as hypocritical, shoving "free-trade doctrine down the throat of every country it meets while practicing, when it pleases, protectionism."[46] At a press conference prior to declaring war on Iraq, President Bush was asked about the different views around the world as to the seriousness of the threat from Saddam Hussein; however, his answer quickly moved to his thinking on free trade, telling the reporter that "free trade is good for both wealthy and impoverished nations."[47] This dogma of free trade does not resonate among Bolivians, who have taken the economic medicine offered by the World Bank and the International Monetary Fund only to sink further into the morass of poverty and despair.

The Morales victory in 2005 was helped by Bolivia's earlier battle against multinational energy giant Bechtel Corporation in 2000. Bolivians won their "water war" against Bechtel, an American multinational that had increased rates after taking over the waterworks in a privatization move that sparked similar efforts elsewhere in Latin America. However, Bolivians are still without water even though it is supplied by a community-run utility named Semapa. Semapa struggles with a lack of money because of its inability to secure international loans and obtain governmental support at home. According to journalist Juan Forero, "The water war experience shows that while a potent left has won many battles in Latin America in recent years, it still struggles to come up with practical, realistic solutions to resolve deep discontent that gave the movement force in the first place."[48] Bolivia's frustration with U.S.-backed privatization policies has been the source of Morales's growing political strength, based on the failure of international economic prescriptions that have not translated into sustained growth and poverty reduction.

Bolivia's close neighbor Argentina has bounced back from economic disaster by ignoring IMF and World Bank orthodoxy, and Latin American governments are bringing the state back in to run economic enterprises.

Market-oriented changes demanded by the IMF, World Bank, and Washington policymakers have fueled anger in the streets that has severely weakened governments and given rise to leftists like Morales and others.

A Morales presidency also worries the Bush administration because he has pledged to decriminalize the cultivation of coca—one of the reasons he won the presidency in 2005. In an interview with the *New York Times* prior to the election, Morales said he would eliminate all penalties for the cultivation of coca if elected president. Morales argued that most coca production goes for traditional use and that legalization is necessary; the U.S. maintains that most Bolivian coca winds up as cocaine and that efforts must be maintained to keep it illegal and fight for its eradication.

The military in the U.S. believes that Morales is a terrorist, a murderer, and possibly the "worst thing to happen in Latin America in a long time."[49] According to Michael Shifter, "There is this tremendous fear [in Washington] that Chavez is living out the Fidel Castro dream of exporting revolution throughout Latin America and destabilizing the region—something that wasn't done during the cold war and is now being financed by Venezuelan oil."[50]

PETROPOLITICS AND PIPELINE WARS

The dramatic increase in oil prices from 2000 to 2007 has brought about a change in the politics of energy in Bolivia, Brazil, Ecuador, Peru, and Venezuela. The data presented in Table 3.2 indicate that South American energy sector is dominated by Venezuela (oil), Argentina (natural gas), and Brazil (electricity). There is now a new security dimension to energy politics in Latin America, and energy security may now be more important than military power and democratic stability. In his study of "Petroleum Politics in Latin American," Genaro Arriagada points out that "Potential confrontations over oil and gas supplies and transportation networks have become geopolitical flashpoints."[51] Some form of nationalization is now under way in these countries, the result of failed privatization policies that came with low royalties and tax rates when the price of oil was $15 a barrel. Popular protests against foreign oil companies have driven presidents from power because the deals they struck with foreign companies left little for the majority of the population. For example, Bolivia's privatization plan in 1996 gave Bolivia only 18 percent of oil and gas profits.[52] The populist leaders in the Andes who have come to power since 2000 recognize the importance of changing these lopsided laws so that the high profits from oil and gas can be used to benefit the people. Of course, petroleum nationalization efforts are not new in Latin America and elsewhere in the world. What is different today is the growing importance of petroleum and gas, the regional influence of Venezuela,

Carrying a sign that reads "Texaco Never Again," Ecuadoran Secoya Indian elders join demonstrators in a march to the Superior Court of Justice in the Amazon town of Lago Agrio, at the start of a trial in which indigenous peoples are seeking to force Chevron-Texaco to clean up its environmental contamination from oil drilling. (The Image Works)

and the declining ability of the United States to control events without stoking further hostility and anti-U.S. sentiment. Past nationalizations that came in the wake of the Mexican, Guatemalan, Cuban, Chilean, and Nicaraguan revolutions were not welcomed by Washington and inevitably contributed to regime change through U.S.-backed coups and counterrevolutions. In contrast to prior nationalizations in Latin America, Bolivian President Evo Morales is demanding changes that are far less radical than what is being portrayed in the mainstream press in the United States: He wants the foreign oil companies to renegotiate their contracts so that Bolivians enjoy a larger share of the profits.

On May 1, 2006, President Morales announced that the Bolivian state was retaking Bolivia's gas fields in order to stop the "looting by foreign companies." What this means is that foreign companies must sell 51 percent of their holdings to the Bolivian government and renegotiate their contracts within a period of six months. Some suggested that Morales was simply following in the footsteps of President Chávez, who, two months earlier, had announced that he was converting thirty-two private oil fields into joint ventures with the Venezuelan government and doubling

Table 3.2 Energy Sector Production, South America

Country	GDP (PPP)[a] (2005, Estimated) (Billions of U.S. Dollars)	Oil Production (2005, Estimated) (Barrels Per Day)	Natural Gas Production (Billions of Cubic Meters)	Electricity Production (2003) (Billions of Kilowatt-hours)	Total Pipelines (kilometers)[b]
Argentina	537.2	745,000	37.15[c]	83.29	30,875
Bolivia	23.59	42,000	8.44[d]	4.25	7,364
Brazil	1,580	2,010,000	5.95[c]	359.20	16,536
Colombia	303.1	512,400	6.354[c]	47.14	10,494
Ecuador	52.66	493,200	0.16[c]	11.27	2,035
Peru	168.9	120,000	0.91[d]	22.68	1,945
Venezuela	161.7	3,081,000	29.4 (2003)	87.44	13,614

Source: CIA World Factbook, 2005.
[a]PPP = Purchasing Power Parity.
[b]Pipelines include lengths of pipelines for transporting natural gas, crude oil, or petroleum products.
[c]2001 figures.
[d]2004 figures.

the country's share of per-barrel profits. However, President Morales's power is limited by the fact that Bolivia's natural gas reserves are worth considerably less than Venezuela's oil and are more vulnerable to shifts in world markets.

Two weeks later, in a similar move against foreign energy producers, Ecuador began a process of taking over Occidental Petroleum's assets in the country after indigenous groups in the eastern oil region accused the company of exploiting natural resources with little benefit for Ecuadorans. The Ecuadoran government insisted that the tightening of state control over natural resources did not amount to a nationalization of the oil industry. Nevertheless, energy officials in Quito claimed that Ecuador will receive an extra $100 million a year in oil revenues because of the contract cancellation with Occidental. The Bush administration is caught between its support for U.S.-based multinationals, ongoing efforts to build more free-trade agreements with South American countries, and fears that President Chávez is gaining influence throughout Latin America.[53]

The Ecuadoran economy is highly dependent on its petroleum sector; except for Venezuela, no other South American country has such a high stake in oil. The most contentious oil issue in Ecuador has been with Occidental Petroleum over contracts and close ties between President Chávez and Ecuador's president, Rafael Correa. In the oil boomtown of Lago Agrio, U.S.-equipped Ecuadoran troops patrol the main street in groups of seven to reduce violence and protect the oil industry. According to the U.S. Southern Command, the threat stems from what insurgents are capable of doing in these areas: setting up military bases, exploiting the lack of government control, and using well-established drug routes to smuggle arms and terrorists into the United States. Although hard evidence of anti-U.S.-terrorists operating in Latin America is lacking, those in the U.S. military attached to the U.S. Embassy in Quito believe that weak government control in isolated areas means that military/police solutions may be necessary. However, Latin American defense ministers question these initiatives and see how increases in military assistance and the creation of a multinational armed force could be counterproductive. Farmers who struggle to earn livings in remote areas would much rather have fewer soldiers from the United States and more economic assistance to improve the quality of life.[54] Without comprehensive rural development programs and a stronger state presence, it will be a long time before the conflict with Colombian guerrillas is resolved.

President Chávez began offering cash-poor Caribbean countries affordable fuel, debt relief, and antipoverty funding. As of 2005, thirteen countries have signed on to PetroCaribe, a new energy trading project designed to ease the burden of high energy prices, demonstrate solidarity in the Caribbean region, and reverse the influence of the United States in the Caribbean. Oil is sold to member countries at unsubsidized market prices, but the international agreement provides long-term financing at special terms. PetroCaribe's benefits include financing at 1% over 25 years and a two-year deferral of loan payments. To further social development, Chávez has promised $50 million a year to fund subsidies for basic commodities and adult education classes. Because of PetroCaribe, Cuban medical personnel now staff medical clinics in Venezuela's urban slums. PetroCaribe creates a permanent organization that allows Venezuela to use oil aid as a political instrument since oil supplies are for domestic consumption only and cannot be resold. PetroCaribe is also tied to Chávez's Bolivarian Alternative for the Americas (ALBA), which involves financing social and economic development programs. Venezuela and Cuba have reached an agreement according to which Venezuela sells oil to Cuba at about two-thirds of market price; since Cubans do not need all the oil that Venezuela sells them, Cuba has the advantage of obtaining subsidized supplies for domestic use and for reselling a portion on the world market. In exchange for oil, Venezuela receives 30,000 to 50,000 skilled Cuban workers, mostly in the areas of medicine, education, and sports.[55] While this accord has tremendous benefits for Cuba, it makes it greatly dependent on Venezuela and could easily lead to a repeat of the economic calamity that Cuba faced when the Soviet Union collapsed and subsidies disappeared.

In late 2005 President Chávez offered to supply cut-rate natural gas to poor communities in the United States to offset the anticipated energy price increases. This form of petrodiplomacy worries Washington because it helps to export Chávez's South American populism to the United States. Citgo and its owner, Petróleos de Venezuela, S.A. (PDVSA), took out a full-page ad in the *New York Times* with the title "How Venezuela is Keeping the Home Fires Burning in Massachusetts." The ad explained how Citgo, working through Citizens Energy Corporation and Mass Energy, was providing cheap heating oil to low-income families and the institutions that serve them such as schools, hospitals, and nursing homes. The first installment of cut-rate Citgo heating oil was delivered to the Bronx, New York, to great fanfare by the residents of one of New York's poorest neighborhoods.

Venezuela is seeking more income and new markets for its petroleum by reviewing the thirty-three existing operating agreements with oil companies from the 1990s and exploring new agreements with Russia, China, and Iran. In an effort to get more lucrative deals while the price of petroleum is high, Venezuelans are trying to exert greater control over their resources and increase the number of buyers worldwide. However, concern is rising in the United States, where Venezuela exports about 1.2 million barrels of oil a day, or nearly 15 percent of American imports.[56] Although the United States is still Venezuela's principal market with over 50 percent of its total production, Venezuela claims it would not cut U.S. exports because of new markets in China. Nevertheless, the unpredictable situation has Washington worried because Venezuela indicated that it would allow China to expand production while the price of oil is high. With the largest reserves in Latin America, Venezuela's efforts to rewrite contracts and expand production could force energy executives in the United States to increase imports from presently more reliable suppliers in West Africa, the Middle East, or Central Asia. According to Noam Chomsky, Venezuela has the closest relations with China of any Latin America country, and the plan to sell oil to China is part of an effort to reduce its dependence on the openly hostile U.S. government.[57] In his effort to curb American influence in the world, President Chávez is also trying to strengthen Venezuela's relationships in the Middle East. While verbally sparring with Washington since 2002, President Chávez has turned Iran into Venezuela's closest ally and is a strong defender of its nuclear program. By reaching out to countries on the margins of American influence, Chávez hopes to counter American power by supporting Muslim countries, denouncing Israel, and pushing OPEC members to limit oil exports in order to maintain high prices.[58] In an effort to diversify Venezuela's energy exports away from the United States and toward countries as far away as China and as close as Brazil, President Chávez wants to build a 5,000-mile natural gas pipeline that stretches from Venezuela to the southern end of the continent.[59] The $20 billion gas pipeline would take a decade to build and possibly be the longest pipeline in the world. The project is not without its detractors—many who argue that it will damage the environment in the Brazilian Amazon and others who say that the "great gas pipeline" is more of a pipe dream than a project that is likely to be completed. During a brief visit to the pipeline project in December 2006, Chávez promised, "we'll build a great bloc of political, economic and social power to seek world equilibrium this century, where we don't have one policeman who wants to be the owner of the world."[60]

In Bolivia, three former presidents and eight former energy ministers were charged with violating the Constitution in signing dozens of contracts with foreign energy companies since 1995 without Congress's approval. The contracts with petroleum companies in Brazil, France, and Spain attracted billions of dollars in investments, but these only paved the way for the plundering of Bolivia's natural resources without adequate compensation for the country. After winning the 2005 presidential election, President Evo Morales began renegotiating contracts that will cost the petroleum companies considerably more in taxes and royalties. The charges by Attorney General Pedro Gareca were leveled against ex-presidents Carlos Mesa, Gonzalo Sánchez de Lozada, and Jorge Quiroga. If President Morales is able to successfully renegotiate these contracts, he will have accomplished a great deal in moving Bolivia toward a more just and equal society.

Sources of national income have an effect on the strength of political institutions and levels of corruption. Latin American countries that make their money from oil tend to be more corrupt than those countries that rely on non-oil international trade. This may explain why Chile is less corrupt than Venezuela and Mexico. As indicated in Table 3.2, the energy sector in the Andes region is quite robust, with Venezuela, Colombia, and Argentina as major oil producers and Argentina, Venezuela, and Bolivia major producers of natural gas. Although Brazil cannot compete with Venezuela and Mexico in terms of petroleum reserves, its mostly state-owned oil giant Petrobras is expanding oil production by drilling wells far from home. After Evo Morales nationalized Bolivia's energy sector in May 2006, Petrobras reduced investments in Bolivia and began investing in the Gulf of Mexico, new fields off the coast of Nigeria and Angola, and refineries in the United States, Europe, and Asia.[61]

SHINING PATH AND TUPAC AMARU MOVEMENTS

Peru's wars against subversion are part of a struggle against guerrilla groups that threatened the very existence of the state. The shock waves from the Cuban Revolution in 1959 and the subsequent explosion of more than thirty guerrilla movements throughout Latin America in the 1960s eventually led to military responses to handle the emerging threats. Civilian governments ran the risk of being overthrown by the military if they appeared to be ineffective in dealing with revolutionary movements. The morality of seizing power and fighting the war against subversion was based on the nature and magnitude of the threat from enemies of the regime. Embattled governments, with the support of the United States, responded by increasing the power and authority of the military. New laws were passed that increased military budgets, the size of the military, and the role of the armed forces in policymaking and administration. A "total war" against Communist ideology and guerrilla sabotage led to a new kind of warfare—counterinsurgency—that, in the name of national security and the survival of Western and Christian civilizations, restructured state and society in fundamental ways; the logic of war focused on enemies of the state and would inevitably require repressive tactics, particularly torture, "dirty" wars or state-sponsored terrorism (death squads), and intimidation.

Between 1968 and 1980 Peru experienced a period of reformist military rule based on the failures of civilians and political parties to provide

Terrorism school conducted by members of the Shining Path (Sendero Luminoso) guerrilla group at a training camp near Ayacucho, Peru, December 1987. (The Image Works)

national security and national development. While in power the military spoke of creating "a fully participatory social democracy which is neither capitalist nor communist but humanistic."[62] The period of military rule proved to be overambitious and authoritarian, eventually contributing to economic and political pressures to return to civilian rule. In 1978, Peru became a part of Operation Condor, a secret intelligence operation, inspired by a hemispheric security doctrine that targeted subversives with dangerous ideas that challenged the traditional order, and executed by South American military governments with the assistance of the United States government. According to McSherry, "The Condor apparatus was a secret component of a larger, U.S.-led counterinsurgency strategy to preempt or reverse social movements demanding political or socioeconomic change."[63]

The return to full civilian control in 1980 was met with the growing violence associated with a threat from Sendero Luminoso (SL, Shining Path), a revolutionary movement originating in the south-central Andean highlands in and around Ayacucho. Sendero Luminoso, under the leadership of professors and students from the local University of Huamanga, advocated a violent peasant-based revolution. Abimael Guzmán, a former university professor, formed the SL in the late 1960s, based on his own interpretations of Communist ideology. Sendero militants devised an Andean version of Marxist-Leninist ideology based on the principles of José Carlos Mariátegui as well as Mao Zedong. The goal of SL was to articulate indigenous demands through a Maoist class analysis of Peru's entrenched system of race and class discrimination, the source of the poverty and inequalities throughout Peru, particularly in the areas of greatest indigenous influence. In an effort to destroy Peru's existing institutions and replace them with a peasant revolutionary regime, Sendero engaged in particularly brutal forms of terrorism, including bombing campaigns, intimidation, kidnappings, and selective assassinations. To rid Peru of foreign influences, SL bombed diplomatic missions and foreign business operations. Sendero also committed several atrocities in the 1980s and 1990s. After fifteen years of preparations, the leadership proved dedicated and effective, eventually moving their operations from the countryside into the cities of Peru, including the shantytowns around Lima, the capital. Sendero launched its "people's war" at the time of the May 18, 1980, election that brought Fernando Belaúnde Terry to the presidency. The Belaúnde administration paid little attention to SL until late 1982, when it declared an emergency zone in the Ayacucho area and unleashed the military to deal with the growing threat. For the next three years, violence escalated and thousands perished, human rights violations skyrocketed, and billions in property damage occurred.[64] Over 6,000 Peruvians died during the Belaúnde administration (1980–1985). To complicate matters for the Peruvian government, a new guerrilla group appeared in 1984, the Lima-originated Tupac Amaru Revolutionary Movement (MRTA). José Gabriel Túpac Amaru was an eighteenth-century rebel leader who fought Spanish colonial control;[65] MRTA was founded on the anti-imperialist principles that led to the Cuban Revolution.

The Belaúnde administration's inability to stop the spreading violence and solve pressing economic difficulties contributed to his declining popular support and paved the way for the election of Alán García, a youthful candidate of the rejuvenated APRA party. Alán García's nationalistic leadership brought the Peruvian economy to its knees—the economy declined by 20 percent under his leadership—and political violence surged. By the end of the García administration in 1990, casualties from the civil war exceeded 20,000 and economic damage soared to $14 billion.[66] Surprisingly, the military remained in the barracks, committed to upholding civilian rule. Sendero continued to operate during the transition elections in 1989 and 1990, killing over 100 candidates and local officials and intimidating others to withdraw from the electoral competition. Expressing their frustration with the inability of political parties and the military to quell Sendero's political violence, voters elected Alberto Fujimori, a newcomer, to straighten out Peru's economic and political mess.

President Fujimori embarked on an aggressive and successful campaign against the SL and MRTA shortly after taking office, but to do so he resorted to dictatorial methods. With the support of the Peruvian military, Fujimori disbanded Peru's congress and courts, claiming they were inhibiting him from cracking down on terrorism. Within a few years Fujimori had captured most of the leaders of the rebel groups, including Abimael Guzmán in September 1992 and others in 1995. However, from prison Guzmán continues to guide the remnants of the SL through various front groups inside Peru. Despite Fujimori's arrest and detention in Chile until 2007, many poor Peruvians consider him a heroic figure who ended the SL insurgency, curtailed hyperinflation, and built schools and hospitals in remote areas neglected by previous governments.

Although the Fujimori regime (1990–2000) manipulated fears of a Shining Path "resurgence" to maintain its own political power, the root causes of the insurgency were never addressed, and the guerrilla group has managed to regroup and rebuild itself. Analysts in Peru believe the Shining Path is split into two factions: a pro-peace faction that follows the word of Guzmán to end violent actions until political conditions are again ripe for revolution, and a *"Proseguir"* ("continue the struggle") or *Sendero Rojo* (Red Path) faction that believes in the doctrine of popular revolutionary warfare.[67] There are now signs of a revival of Sendero, due to the political neglect of peasant communities and the fact that it is the only guerrilla group in Latin America that has not been invited to dialogue to discuss a political solution to the simmering armed struggle. These signs are enough to warrant a hot spot designation; however, SL clearly does not have the number of members and followers that it had in the 1980s.

VENEZUELA: CHÁVEZ'S BOLIVARIAN REVOLUTION

Hugo Chávez's Venezuela is Washington's number two hot spot (after the Tri-Border Area in the Southern Cone, discussed in Chapter 4) because of its hostility to U.S. interests and policies, a hostility that the Pentagon believes will tend to destabilize the region. Both Donald Rumsfeld, U.S. Defense Secretary (2001–2006), and John Negroponte, Director of National Intelligence until 2006, have been unrelenting in their attempts to portray Chávez as a threat to U.S. national security, and under Chávez Venezuela is quickly approaching an explosive situation. In an October 2005 U.S. Army publication, President Chávez and his Bolivarian Revolution were labeled the "largest threat since the Soviet Union and communism."[68]

President Chávez, speaking at the United Nations, attacked President George W. Bush, calling him "the devil" and later during a visit to a Harlem church in New York, "an alcoholic and sick man." Although many criticized his personal attack on President Bush, his anti-imperialist speech was well received at the UN and throughout Latin America. (The Image Works)

The mercurial president of Venezuela has put forth a revolutionary agenda in the name of Venezuela's liberator, Simón Bolívar. At the heart of this effort is the eradication of social inequities using a mild agrarian reform, subsidized food, microcredit, a mass literacy drive, and universal access to public health. This means that President Chávez has sharply deviated from the regionwide acceptance of market economics and pluralist democracy in an effort to help poor Venezuelans. He is critical of the United States for its imperialist designs in the world and its domination of Latin America. Despite his highly charged rhetoric, President Chávez does not fit the mold of someone who is pursuing a revolutionary or "leftist" path for Venezuela. For example, he has welcomed foreign investment in the petroleum sector, and land reform efforts have been half-hearted in application. President Chávez has been able to consolidate control and amass power, despite efforts to remove him from office from 2002 through 2004. His power has been enhanced by ample petroleum resources, the failure of previous governments, a weak opposition, and constant U.S. efforts to destabilize his administration and topple him. According to Michael Shifter, "Chávez's relentless attacks on the increasingly corrupt, unresponsive and insulated traditional order had great appeal and account for part of his support today."[69] The most vexing problem for the United States is how to reconcile the need for Venezuelan oil—Caracas provides about 15 percent of U.S. oil exports—with the security concerns tied to the erosion of democratic practices and safeguards within the country. According to Shifter and Jawahar, Washington has not been very astute in dealing with the Chávez government. "Its overly reactive posture has resulted in major, costly blunders, such as its initial support of the April 2002 coup against Chávez" and these mistakes have helped to fuel anti-U.S. sentiment throughout the region.[70] Since the bungled 2002 removal effort, the United States has spent millions trying to strengthen political parties and other antigovernment groups that want to remove Chávez from office.[71]

The major goal of the Bolivarian Revolution is to transform Venezuela from a capitalist, oligarchical nation into one that effectively represents the whole population.[72] In March 2006, Venezuela changed its coat of arms by reversing the direction of the original image of a galloping horse from right to left to reflect the aims of the Bolivarian Revolution with its social programs and international policies. The redesign came after President Chávez called the original image an "imperialist horse."[73] The Bolivarian Revolution with its emphasis on Constitutional revisions, reform programs, and strong opposition to U.S. policies in Latin America and elsewhere has led to increasing support for President Chávez. A majority of Venezuelans in a Latinobarómetro poll said that their country was governed for the benefit of all, rather than a few powerful groups.[74]

The Oil Basis of Venezuelan Power

The Chávez threat being fostered in the United States and elsewhere stems from his extravagant foreign policy initiatives and growing stature on the international stage, particularly among key members of the Organization of Petroleum Exporting Countries (OPEC). President Chávez's visits to OPEC members such as Iran, Libya, and Saddam Hussein's Iraq prior to the 2003 invasion have contributed to the view of him as an enemy of the United States.

The petroleum sector is extremely important to the Venezuelan economy because it supplies 85 percent of export earnings and about 50 percent of the central government's operating revenues. As the fourth-leading supplier of imported crude and refined petroleum products to the United States, Venezuela is of key concern to Washington. Between 1914 and 1929, four U.S. oil companies helped to transform Venezuela into one of the world's leading producers of petroleum. "By 1930, thanks to lucrative contracts from Juan Vicente Gomez, U.S. petroleum companies gained 99 percent control of Venezuelan oil production, investing relatively little while taking billion of dollars out of the country."[75] With friendly dictators opposed to Communism and willing to make generous oil concessions to American oil companies, Washington did not have to worry about instability, expropriation of U.S. property, or revolutionary upheavals.

Beginning in the 1930s, Venezuela's political system changed in response to nationalist demands that more oil revenue remain in Venezuela. At first there was little talk of outright expropriation of foreign petroleum interests, but soon taxes were raised on foreign oil profits in order to pursue public works projects and improve services to the poor. After the formation of the Organization of Petroleum Exporting Countries (OPEC) in 1960, Venezuela decided to nationalize its iron and oil industries in 1975 and 1976. By 1980, the huge profits that U.S. investors reaped from Venezuela's oil under the "friendly dictators" of the past had come to a close.

Almost 60 foreign companies representing 14 different countries now participate in some aspect of Venezuela's oil sector; however, new laws have been passed under President Chávez that mandate that all oil production and distribution activities are the domain of the Venezuelan state, with the exception of joint ventures involved in extra-heavy crude oil production. Because of petroleum exports, the United States is Venezuela's leading trade partner, with lopsided trade surpluses in Venezuela's favor. In turn, Venezuela is the United States' third largest export market in Latin America, and the U.S. government is concerned with promoting and protecting business interests that export there.

The United States feels threatened by President Chávez because he plans to triple petroleum exports to China over the next several years and desires a seat on the UN Security Council. With support from the Mercosur countries of the Southern Cone and most of the rest of Latin America plus China and Russia, he stands a good chance of acquiring the seat despite the displeasure of the United States. The increase in oil exports to China does not mean that he is planning on terminating oil exports to the United States; his plan is to diversify the Venezuelan economy.

The U.S. Department of Energy estimates that Venezuela has five times the Saudis' petroleum reserves, but oil has to sell above $30 a barrel to make the investment in extra-heavy crude worthwhile. As long as the price of oil remains high and President Chávez remains in power, Venezuela's Bolivarian Revolution will continue to use petroleum as a weapon to weaken the United States in Latin America and beyond.[76]

Venezuela as a Hot Spot

As a Latin American hot spot, Venezuela is of much less concern to the governments of Latin America than to Washington policymakers anxious over oil dependency, trade relations, political instability, and terrorism. The White House's March 2006 National Security Strategy report lists Venezuela as a "regional challenge" because "[i]n Venezuela, a demagogue awash in oil money is undermining democracy and seeking to destabilize the region." President Chávez is feared as a threat to the region and the United States for several reasons: his pursuit and consolidation of power, regarded as undemocratic; his use of Venezuela's oil revenues abroad to build support for the Bolivarian Revolution throughout Latin America and beyond; his efforts to form trade networks among Latin American countries to counter U.S. trade policies; his dealings in military equipment with Russia, Spain, and other countries; his alliance and friendship with Fidel Castro, regarded as a league to export "revolution" throughout Latin America, reminiscent of Che Guevara 40 years earlier; his solidarity with Iran, including its right to develop nuclear energy, and his own pursuit of that capability; and his suspected sympathy for both Islamic and narco-terrorists.

Chávez as Caudillo

What is most worrisome to Washington is Chávez's authoritarian tendencies, reflected in an unprecedented concentration of power with few checks and balances. It is hard to pin down the sources of President Chávez's political views, since he relies on ideas from so many thinkers, from Jesus and Marx to Trotsky, Simón Bolívar, and Peruvian José Carlos Mariátegui. He also admires Albert Einstein and Noam Chomsky, Muammar el-Qaddafi, and Che Guevara. Regardless of where the president gets his ideas, however, *chavismo* is strongly committed to the idea of the Latin American *caudillo*, or strongman, who can rule without restraints on his power.[77] The U.S. Department of State goes to great lengths to argue "that democracy in Venezuela is in grave peril" because

President Chávez has "embraced a repressive political agenda that has polarized the country, created political upheaval, marginalized the opposition, suffocated democratic debate, and resisted external efforts to support democratic political activity." In a separate box on "The State of Democracy in Venezuela," the State Department's Website offers several ways of attempting to correct what it calls the abandonment of the democratic tradition under Hugo Chávez.[78] The site, however, contains no mention of Chávez's high approval ratings in recent polls and policies initiated to alleviate the suffering of Venezuela's poor. President Chávez is getting stronger as a result of the slow demise of Fidel Castro in Cuba, the unintended consequences of the war in Iraq, and economic globalization.

Nevertheless, after winning his third presidential election in December 2006, President Chávez planned to consolidate his power further in order to prevent challenges to his rule from emerging. President Chávez stirred up additional fears with a plan to nationalize Venezuela's main telephone and electricity companies in January 2007. When Chávez closed down RCTV in May 2007, critics accused him of further deeds to undermine Venezuelan democracy and spread his authoritarianism to the rest of Latin America. Chávez's efforts to silence the media in 2006–2007 will clearly provide ammunition for those in the opposition who argue that the regime is creeping toward a more authoritarian state.

Petrodollar Largesse in the Americas

At the core of the of the Bolivarian Revolution, and of the concern in Washington with President Chávez, is his billion-dollar spending on development projects throughout the Western Hemisphere in order to build a bulwark against U.S. imperialism worldwide. With oil revenue rising at dramatic rates, President Chávez is spending billions on pet projects abroad to counter U.S. influence in the Americas.[79] According to Juan Forero, "The new spending has given more power to a leader who has been provocatively building a bulwark against what he has called American imperialistic aims in Latin America."[80] Using oil as a weapon, President Chávez has subsidized samba parades in Brazil, eye surgery for poor Mexicans, and heating fuel for poor families in the United States itself. At least thirty countries around the world have received some form of aid or preferential deals. In his efforts to establish his leftist government as a political counterpoint to the conservative Bush administration, President Chávez has spent more than $25 billion abroad since taking office in 1999. This means his annual spending amounts to close to $4 billion annually in subsidies designed to enhance his status throughout the hemisphere. Venezuela's spending now surpasses the $2 billion the United States allocates annually for economic and military aid programs throughout the Americas. With the lavish spending of his country's oil windfall, Washington fears that President Chávez is fast becoming the next Fidel Castro, a hero to Latin America's underclass with the intent of opposing the United States wherever possible, from the FTAA and counter-drug campaigns to covert efforts to militarize the region in search of terrorists and criminal gangs.[81]

Although it is not clear exactly how much the Venezuelan government has spent from its oil revenues, much of the spending involves generous bond purchases, selling oil at cut-rate prices to thirteen Caribbean countries, the purchase of Brazilian oil tankers, and investing in Uruguayan gas stations. In the case of Cuba, Chávez has supplied almost 100,000 barrels of cut-rate oil per day in exchange for volunteer Cuban doctors and medical experts who have staffed many of the new people's clinics and are training Venezuelan doctors, nurses, and medical technicians. By using Venezuelan oil revenues for health care missions in poor working class communities, Chávez is laying the foundation for a future free national health care system.

Chávez has his critics at home and abroad, mostly for the spending that many see as irresponsible efforts to burnish his image as the region's leading statesman rather than his successful efforts to embarrass the Bush administration. According to John Negroponte, the U.S. director of national intelligence, Hugo Chávez is "spending considerable sums involving himself in the political and economic life of other countries in Latin America and elsewhere, this despite the very real economic development and social needs of his own country."[82] The Bush administration and the corporate media insist that he is less interested in fighting poverty and inequality than in consolidating power at home and uniting as much of Latin America as possible against the United States.

Formation and Consolidation of Latin American Trade Ties

The fact that the United States is Venezuela's leading trade partner has not translated into harmony in foreign relations. President Chávez opposes the proposed Free Trade Area of the Americas (FTAA) and is in the process of becoming a member of the Mercosur trade bloc along with Brazil, Argentina, Paraguay, and Uruguay. One of the major foreign policy goals of the Chávez administration is to forge greater hemispheric cooperation and integration with its neighbors in South America. Through three initiatives—PetroCaribe petroleum initiative, South American Community of Nations, and the Bolivarian Alternative for the Americas (ALBA)—Chávez is seeking greater regional integration and a world that is dominated less by the United States.

The Chávez administration's proposed Bolivarian Alternative for the Americas (ALBA) is a trade agreement designed to counter the hegemony of U.S.-dominated trading blocs such as the FTAA. By opposing the FTAA and neoliberalism in Latin America, President Chávez hopes to extend the concept of Bolivarian social missions internationally in an effort to put an end to the tradition of U.S. intervention in Latin America and the belief that Latin America is incapable of independent and sovereign development. At a summit meeting of Mercosur in 2007, President Chávez told reporters that he wanted to "decontaminate Mercosur from neoliberalism" as a way to wean the region from U.S. influence.[83]

President Chávez also wants to provide an alternative source of credit for governments fed up with the control and conditionality mandated by the International Monetary Fund (IMF), World Bank, Inter-American Development Bank, and private lenders, thus reducing or eliminating their influence in Latin America. Venezuela's political ideology and anti-U.S. rhetoric are both part of the concern in Washington that President Chávez is a threat to American interests; however, what really seems to bother policymakers in Washington is the perception that what Chávez is doing with his Bolivarian Revolution is diminishing the power of the United States in Latin America and elsewhere.[84] Bolivia and Ecuador have moved in this direction and are borrowing from the Bank of the South in order to diminish their dependency on the United States.

Transactions in Military Resources

After the United States refused to sell Venezuela spare parts for its aging fleet of U.S.-made F-16 jet fighters in 2005, President Chávez angered the Bush administration by claiming he would simply give the planes to China or Cuba so that they could study the technology. The U.S. Department of State claimed that Venezuela is contractually forbidden to sell or give away the aircraft without the permission of the United States. In 2006, President Chávez added to the view of Venezuela as a security threat when he said he would purchase an unspecified number of Russian war planes to replace the F-16s, for which he then suggested that Iran could be a possible buyer.

In what has been perceived as an affront to the Bush administration, President Chávez signed a $2 billion arms deal with Spain to buy military equipment as well as similar efforts to buy combat aircraft from Brazil and 100,000 assault rifles from Russia. However, after objections by the U.S. government in October 2006, Spain cancelled the deal to sell military aircraft to Venezuela.[85] The deal would have created hundreds of jobs in Spain and fulfilled the benefits of free trade; however, Spain was not able to convince the United States that the deal involved transport planes, not attack aircraft, and posed no threat to Venezuela's neighbors.

Venezuela stopped sending military personnel to Ft. Benning for counterinsurgency training at WHINSEC, the former School of the Americas, in 2004. Although Venezuela has a small number of troops in the United States—one at a military base in Dayton, Ohio, and the other in Miami, Florida—the rapid deterioration of political relations will not be easy to reverse because of prior efforts at regime change by Washington.

The Castro Connection

President Chávez has developed close personal and policy ties with Cuba's Fidel Castro and Bolivia's Evo Morales, for which he has been called a closet Communist by his opponents. The Bush administration has relied on reactionary anti-Castro figures such as Otto Reich and Roger Noriega to assess security threats in Latin America. According to Reich, President Chávez is a threat to the security of the United States because of his alliance with Castro, defense of Iran's right to develop nuclear power, misappropriation of Venezuela's oil riches, anti-U.S. rhetoric, threats to cut off oil exports to the United States in order to sell oil to China, and involvement in Bolivia and Nicaragua.

In what amounts to a strategy of guilt by association, America's op-ed pages often highlight the Venezuelan president's friendship with Castro as a sign that the Cuban model is being copied in Venezuela. This is often followed by the charge that Chávez is "meddling" in the internal affairs of other Latin American countries—without much discussion of the frequent and blatant involvement of the United States in the internal politics of Latin American countries, particularly during the Cold War. The September 11, 1973, U.S.-backed coup against Salvador Allende in Chile and the treatment of political opposition groups in Latin America in the 1970s led to the formation of human rights advocacy groups such as the Washington Office on Latin America (WOLA).[86] The United States has done little to change the perception among a broad spectrum of Venezuelans that "democracy promotion" is nothing more than a propaganda tool to remove leaders who oppose U.S. objectives in Latin America and elsewhere in the world.[87] The Bush administration has on several occasions openly threatened to penalize the governments of Nicaragua, Bolivia, and El Salvador if their citizens elected candidates who opposed U.S. policies.

Nuclear Ambitions in Iran and Venezuela

As far as Washington is concerned, Venezuela's relationship with leftist leaders in Latin America is less troublesome than the growing Venezuela-Iran alliance. President Chávez has vocally supported Iran's right to build a nuclear program.[88] In April 2006 Chávez blamed the high oil prices on President Bush's threats against Iran, asserting that Iran has the right to develop nuclear energy for peaceful purposes.

In addition, in October 2005 President Chávez announced his intention to develop a peaceful nuclear program of his own, with the assistance of Brazil and Argentina. The United States is wary of these plans, which worry Washington because they come on top of the Venezuelan president's efforts to buy more military hardware and his rhetoric in support of Iran. South America is currently a nuclear free zone, and some analysts in the Pentagon consider President Chávez's gambit nothing more than a bluff; however, others fear that the mercurial president may be serious, and the last thing Washington wants is a Latin American country threatening to acquire a nuclear weapons program. Venezuela denies it will become a nuclear threat and says it has a right to explore these possibilities.

According to nuclear experts in South America, Argentina's program offers the best fit because it specializes in small reactors appropriate for medical research and generating power, and the system of safeguards and inspections. Although Argentina's nuclear power plants are still under construction, and unlikely to ever reach completion, decades of nuclear technology research, development, and implementation have provided Argentina and Brazil with two significant capabilities: uranium enrichment and a knowledgeable nuclear scientists.[89] Both Brazil and Argentina had nuclear arms programs during the time they were under military dictatorships in the late 1970s and early 1980s. Since then, civilian governments have halted these programs because of economic factors and other priorities. Still, the United States worries about a nuclear threat from Venezuela, not solely because of Chávez's nuclear ambitions but his antagonism toward the United States and his links to the Iranian government.

Suspected Terrorist Ties

As a "radical populist," President Chávez constitutes an emerging security threat because he is purported to have links to terrorist groups. To highlight his independence from U.S. control and hegemony, he has refused to cooperate with Plan Colombia (the U.S. effort to eliminate the cocaine supply and the guerrilla and criminal organizations that profit from it) next door and denied Venezuelan airspace to U.S. counternarcotics surveillance flights.

The U.S. Southern Command believes that militant Islamic groups are deeply involved in Latin America's "narco-terrorist networks." The U.S. military claims that Hamas, Hezbollah, al-Gamaat and others, operating out of Venezuela's Margarita Island, a vacation spot with a sizable Muslim population, are funneling millions of dollars to worldwide terrorist organizations.[90] *U.S. News and World Report* published "Terror Close to

Home" in 2003, claiming that Venezuela is a potential hub of terrorism in the Americas because its government is issuing ID cards to thousands of foreigners, including many from Syria, Pakistan, Egypt and Lebanon, a policy that could enable the cardholders to obtain passports and U.S. visas.

When the Inter-American Committee Against Terrorism, an agency of the Organization of American States (OAS), met in March 2006 to issue a declaration on hemispheric cooperation to fight terrorism, Venezuela alone opposed the resolution because of references to UN efforts to limit the proliferation of weapons of mass destruction. The United States is not worried about an angry Venezuelan response during an inter-American meeting, but President Chávez's larger aims are beginning to stir security concerns. His brash anti-U.S. rhetoric is bothersome to Washington policymakers; however, what really seems to concern the Bush administration is that Venezuela's economic policies and international relationships are seen as diminishing the power of the United States in Latin America and around the globe.[91]

The connection between President Chávez and Islamic terrorists is tenuous at best, but the fear in Washington is that the Venezuelan president's rhetoric will forge an anti-imperialist alliance—fueled by record oil prices—and weaken its interventionist efforts in the Middle East. There is no doubt that Hezbollah has a global reach, including South America. It is blamed for the attacks on Jewish and Israeli targets in Argentina in the early 1990s and possesses known cells throughout Latin America.[92] There is no evidence of a Venezuelan-Hezbollah alliance with the capacity to threaten U.S. interests in the region.

Following in the footsteps of his predecessors, President Chávez has offered government assistance to the on-again, off-again negotiations between Colombian guerrillas and the Colombian government. The Venezuelan opposition and right-wing commentators in the United States see this connection differently, claiming Chávez ignores the cross-border movements of the Colombian guerrillas and secretly offers financial and material assistance.

Although those in Washington worry that regional conflicts can become safe havens for terrorists because of poor governance, external aggression and internal revolt, the Bush administration's strategy for addressing regional conflicts—conflict prevention and resolution, conflict intervention, and postconflict stabilization and reconstruction—seem hardly a realistic solution to the challenge from Hugo Chávez.

Possible Weaknesses in the Bolivarian Revolution

Despite the popularity of his anti-imperialism at home and abroad, President Chávez has been less successful in devising long-term solutions to Venezuela's economic problems. Unemployment has remained constant and crime has increased in many part of Venezuela. *Latin American Newsletters* claims that the Bolivarian Revolution has yet to materialize despite heavy public spending and windfall oil earnings. Until recently, GDP growth has been sluggish and economic mismanagement remains a chronic problem for Venezuela. The Bolivarian Revolution provides the president with a powerful symbol of Venezuelan nationalism, but the economic model propelling Venezuela is best described as "protectionist capitalism" instead of radical socialism. A true revolution would have pursued a redistributionist agenda, but this has not happened.

Others doubt that Chávez's Bolivarian Revolution is sustainable, either for Venezuela or the rest of the region. According to Shifter, "Its approach is fundamentally clientelistic, perpetuating dependence on state patronage rather than promoting broad-based development. Random land-reform measures and occasional confiscations of private property have had less of an economic than a political and symbolic rationale. Crime, a dominant concern for Venezuelans, has gotten worse."[93] It is possible that support for the Bolivarian Revolution is beginning to slide, with more and more Venezuelans worried about the use of petrodollars to finance an expensive foreign policy while social and economic needs at home are ignored. In a 2006 Latinobarómetro poll a majority of Venezuelans showed a positive attitude toward democracy (although a slight decline since 2005) and little support for an authoritarian government. Crime, unemployment, and poverty topped the list of voters' concerns in the poll.[94] However, the rising crime and violence in Caracas did not prevent Chávez from winning the 2006 presidential race with over 62 percent of the national vote. To the surprise of many analysts in Venezuela, the spike in killings around the country occurred while Venezuela's economy boomed, with high oil prices and one of the fastest-growing economies in Latin America.[95]

Some officials in the Bush administration believe President Chávez's influence is waning because of elections in Peru, Colombia, and Mexico, where supporters of Venezuela's president lost to anti-Chávez candidates. This was especially evident in Mexico, where conservative Felipe Calderón got considerable political mileage out of linking his rival, Andrés Manuel López Obrador, to Chávez. On the other hand, Chávez ally Daniel Ortega, Sandinista leader and former bête noire of the United States, won the November 2006 election in Nicaragua, and Chávez himself won another six-year term on December 3. With his support for Iran, Cuba, and elsewhere, he will remain a thorn in the side of the United State for some time.[96]

Opponents of President Chávez—both at home and abroad—build their case against the Venezuelan leader on three pillars: imcompetence, corruption, and authoritarianism. Greg Grandin refutes each of these charges by pointing out that the Chávez administration is often judged through the prism of competing lessons drawn from the Cold War rather than on its own merits. Grandin concludes, "Chavismo has its shortcomings, but its achievements have been impressive."[97]

Chavismo As Seen Through U.S. Media

The U.S. media is also a factor in the demonization of President Chávez. In his study of the opinion pages of the twenty-five newspapers with the highest circulations in the United States during the first five months of 2005, Justin Delacour "found that 95 percent of the nearly 100 press commentaries that examined Venezuelan politics expressed clear hostility to the country's democratically elected president."[98] With approval ratings above 70 percent it is strange that U.S. columnists have insisted on negative portrayals of the Venezuelan leader. Unable to question the Venezuelan president's popular mandate, the *Miami Herald*, *Wall Street Journal*, *Washington Post*, and *Los Angeles Times* have uniformly referred to President Chávez as a "tyrant," "populist strongman," "authoritarian," and one of the world's worst dictators.

Wall Street Journal reporting on Venezuela continues to emphasize the dangerous, disruptive, and messianic impulses of the Venezuelan government. The *Journal's* Latin American correspondent, Mary Anastasia O'Grady, refers to President Chávez as the "Ugly Venezuelan" and "an apologist for terrorism." After he won the December 2006 election, her column described Chávez as a "menace" to the United States who is hiding inside a false democracy. "Venezuela is not a democracy," according to O'Grady, and President Chávez "is nothing but an old-fashioned authoritarian otherwise known in Latin America as a *caudillo*."[99]

The constant op-ed attacks on the Chávez government appear to stem more from threats to U.S. business interests than the lack of political openness or a genuine concern for democracy. The near-absence of alternative perspectives about Venezuela and its popular leader in the U.S. press serves to escalate the perception that President Chávez is a threat to the interests of all governments in the Western Hemisphere. By refusing to provide space for commentary that sympathizes with the Venezuelan government's popular support and policies of extending education, health care, subsidized food, and microcredit to the country's poor, U.S. newspapers contribute to the perception that Venezuela is a Latin American trouble spot and is fair game for biased media attention and pre-emptive U.S. government intervention.

In retaliation for the biased media coverage of Venezuela and in an effort to integrate Latin America, President Chávez joined with

Uruguay, Argentina, and Cuba in 2005 to form Telesur, a television project designed to break CNN's virtual monopoly on news about Latin America. Aram Aharonian, Telesur's director, calls the new network "the first anti-hegemony project on a mass scale in Latin America."[100] Richard Lugar, head of the Senate Foreign Relations Committee, called the network an "instrument of Chávez's authoritarian policies," and warned that such an instrument of communication presented a threat to Washington foreign policy goals. Al Jazeera, the Arabic news service, now has an office in Caracas and plans to work with Telesur to counter news favorable to the United States.[101]

Part of the problem of reporting on Latin American hot spots is a lack of understanding of Latin American history and the nature of inter-American organizations. When President Chávez uses his oil riches to buy fighter jets, Russian arms, and forges ties with Cuba, Iran and Syria, he is described as a pro-terrorist outlaw and a "regional menace." After the Pentagon announced in April 2006 that it will deploy a U.S. Navy carrier strike group to the Caribbean Sea, the *Wall Street Journal* seemed relieved that Chávez is finally being taken seriously and that the United States may be planning regime change in Caracas.

It is irresponsible for the U.S. media to exaggerate the Venezuelan threat by offering one story after another trying to link President Chávez with countries opposed to the United States and undermining Latin America's preferences for nonpermanent membership on the United Nations Security Council. According to O'Grady, "America's [UN] ambassador, John Bolton, has said that Venezuela is not acceptable, setting up a choice for Latin American governments between reassuring the U.S. or appeasing Chávez."[102]

The U.S. press coverage of Venezuela consistently puts President Chávez and the Bolivarian Revolution in a negative light as a threat to U.S. interests. What the U.S. media has embraced is a series of distortions that constitute an imperial mythology using the following assertions: Venezuela is undemocratic, run by a dictator who has muzzled dissent and the press; Venezuela is more corrupt under Chávez than under his predecessors; Venezuela is a violator of human rights, a hindrance to the war on drugs, and an obstacle to the war on terrorism; Venezuela has a mismanaged economy, leaving the poor worse off despite soaring oil revenues; Venezuela "meddles" in the internal political affairs of its neighbors.[103] When Defense Secretary Donald Rumsfeld asserts that "We've got Chávez in Venezuela with a lot of oil money. He's a person who was elected legally, just as Adolf Hitler was elected legally, and then consolidated power," his assertions go unchallenged in the U.S. press. If security-based hot spots can be manufactured by the major newspapers and magazines—*New York Times*, *Washington Post*, *Newsweek*, *New*

Republic, and the *Miami Herald*—by asserting that "would-be dictators" plague Latin America and undermine democracy, then misreporting on controversial political leaders in Latin America only contributes to a heightened sense of fear when none exists.[104]

The Washington-Caracas War of Words

President Chávez uses inflammatory rhetoric to criticize President Bush's Latin American policy, calling the president of the United States a "donkey," a "drunkard," "the devil," "Mr. Danger," and a "coward"—almost daring President Bush to invade Venezuela to rid the hemisphere of such an irritant. The Bush administration considers Venezuela a security-based hot spot because of the goals of the Bolivarian Revolution: the replacement of capitalism with socialism, opposition to the U.S. trade policies such as FTAA, and attacks on U.S. imperialism for crimes against humanity.[105] According to Joel Wendland, "The Bolivarian Revolution is sweeping Latin America" in an effort to lay the foundation for socialism in the twenty-first century.

President Chávez's defiance of Washington, and his efforts to increase his own power at the expense of the world's only superpower, makes it difficult to engage in diplomatic efforts to ease tensions and solve binational issues. U.S. officials are frustrated with Chávez, but Secretary of State Condoleezza Rice and Secretary of Defense Donald Rumsfeld have achieved little in their war of words against the Venezuelan president, likening him to Hitler and naming him a "dangerous" political leader and one of the "biggest problems" in the Western Hemisphere.[106]

Regime Change Fears and Attempts

Since 2001, President Chávez has claimed that the United States was planning to invade Venezuela or trying to assassinate him. In reaction, he has created a new reserve civil defense and declared that Venezuela's acquisition of weapons is purely defensive. The hostility has increased since Washington endorsed the April 2002 coup that briefly unseated the president and has grown with hostile rhetoric provided by the Bush's foreign policy team.

The Bush administration would like to remove Chávez or at least mollify his anti-U.S. rhetoric; however, the prospects for regime change are slim unless the United States is willing to carry out a military invasion followed by a long-term occupation of a South American country. This is not likely; in a 2003 Pew Research Center for The People and the Press poll on U.S. attitudes toward the use of military force to remove dictators of countries that may threaten, but have not attacked the United States, only 15 percent responded that it is "usually" the right thing to do.[107]

U.S. dependence on Venezuelan oil prevents Washington from carrying out efforts to destabilize the Chávez regime. President Chávez used the Fourth Summit of the Americas in November 2005 to denounce the United States as a "capitalist, imperialist model" of democracy that does not serve the needs of Latin America. He stated that he would continue to export petroleum to the United States but that, if Washington decided to attack Venezuela, his government would blow up its own oil fields in defiance of such a gesture.

In an effort to quell the growing hostility toward President Chávez, Venezuela's Foreign Minister Alí Rodríguez presented the Organization of American States with a request for an investigation into the possibility of a U.S. "attack" on Venezuela.[108] Citing statements from U.S. officials and noting the parallels to the political climate that preceded the April 2002 coup that briefly deposed Chávez, Rodríguez warned that an assassination attempt would have negative consequences for the United States, both in Latin America and throughout the world. Rodríguez insisted that Venezuela has no intention of exporting its model of government on anyone, the U.S. government denied it is planning an attack on Venezuela or is considering assassination as a solution to what Washington considers the threat of "radical populism." Several months later, during Secretary of Defense Donald Rumsfeld's trip to Latin America, a senior State Department official traveling with the defense secretary said of Chávez, "A guy who seemed like a comic figure a year ago is turning into a real strategic menace."[109]

The United States insists it has no plans for regime change in Venezuela, but Washington policymakers consider him an "unfriendly" leader with ambitions that undermine U.S. foreign policy objectives. Although sales of military equipment to Venezuela by U.S. companies have been banned since May 2006, President Chávez claimed an August 2006 shipment of military equipment contained in diplomatic baggage violated international law and was intended to foment further opposition to the his administration. Media reports in Venezuela called for an investigation and close attention to the incident, "asserting that the United States brought military equipment into Chile in diplomatic baggage before the coup that toppled Salvador Allende in 1973."[110]

The Fear of "Radical Populism"

The fear of "radical populism" among Washington policymakers is based on the belief that populists such as President Chávez and Evo Morales are anti-democratic, anti-American, and a threat to U.S. security interests. This fear-based rhetoric serves to justify pre-emptive military strategies in the name of protecting democracies from populist instability. The rise of radical populism may not please the United States, and some may find it offensive when these leaders blame all of their nation's ills on U.S. imperialism, but this is the price of democracy. As William M. LeoGrande points out, U.S. policymakers have found it easier to provide military aid and training to suppress radical movements than deal with the root causes of populism: "The antidote to radical populism is honest, responsive government and economic policies that improve living standards and provide opportunity to all classes. Whereas the United States has tended to see populist movements as a threat, Latin Americans identify poverty and social exclusion as the real threat."[111] General James Hill, former head of the U.S. Southern Command, sees a security threat in populism when it becomes "radicalized" and undermines the democratic process by decreasing the protection of individual rights. Those involved in Latin American policymaking in Washington and monitor security and U.S. military assistance see a greater security threat when the only solution to radical populism is through U.S. military assistance designed to contain or reverse the trend created by Hugo Chávez and Evo Morales.[112]

U.S. security planners have elevated the dangers from radical populism as a security threat in order to justify regime change, strengthen representative democracies, and contain bursts of populist turbulence. What has happened in the Andes over the past fifteen years is the growth of populist leaders, often with indigenous roots and backing, who operate within the context of representative democratic governments. The democratic legitimacy associated with Latin America's new wave of populist leadership makes it difficult for Washington to deal with them—either diplomatically or militarily—when they adopt policies that are at odds with those of the United States. So far the strategic response to "radical populism" has been to return to a Cold War national security doctrine that calls for U.S. military involvement in the internal affairs of nations willing to contain populist movements of any kind. According to Latin News' *Security and Strategic Review*, efforts to re-create a Cold War environment are evident in public and off-the-record statements in which "The core message was that Cuba, allied with Venezuela, have embarked upon a campaign to destabilize democratic governments in the region and foster anti-U.S. sentiment—and that Argentina and Brazil are suspected of tolerating, maybe even sympathizing with, their aims."[113]

To deal with Cuba and Venezuela—two challenges in Latin America—the CIA, as requested from the Bush administration, created a Mission Manager in 2006 to "pay more attention" to President Chávez because "he has spent millions and millions of dollars to support his extremist ideas in various parts of the world" and constitutes a threat to U.S. foreign policy."[114]

Why does President Chávez pose a threat to intelligence agencies and the mainstream media in the United States? By providing benefits derived from oil revenue, the Venezuelan president plans to build anti-American solidarity in a region where the U.S. companies are heavily invested in tourism and aluminum processing. Leftists throughout the region applaud him as a nationalist leader determined to provide an alternative to U.S. imperialism. In his examination of a new form of global domination, Michael Hardt points out that "[s]ome governments that defy the neoliberal order and U.S. command—Venezuela, again, is a good example—bring enormous benefits to their populations in literacy, healthcare, economic opportunity and other essential domains."[115] Chávez's creative social movement is not designed to confront U.S. imperialism, but to achieve autonomy and interdependence. If this is the case, what makes the Bolivarian Revolution a threat to Latin America and the United States?

The Bolivarian Revolution being carried out by President Chávez is not a threat to the security of the United States, whether in its domestic or international policies. The overemphasis on security/terrorism-related issues by Washington means that efforts embodied in the Bolivarian Revolution to deal with poverty, inequality, and social injustice are seen as inconsequential for U.S. national interests. When the United States talks of finding capable partners to address regional conflicts and then stresses the importance of financing the training and equipment of foreign governments with military assistance, this strategy hardly resonates as an effective measure of conflict prevention and resolution.

Are Chávez and chavismo a threat to the United States? According to former conservative scholar Mark Falcoff, "The United States would be well advised to heed the lessons of history and allow the Chavez revolution to run its course like an unpleasant fever. To pursue him as a threat that needs to be exorcised is exactly what he wants and what he has been trying to coax the United States into doing. One can hope that this time, at least, our need for oil will restrain us if we find ourselves once again incapable of learning from past mistakes."[116]

CHAPTER 4

The Southern Cone and Brazil

The Southern Cone (*Cono Sur* in Spanish) region of South America is made up of Argentina, Chile, Paraguay, and Uruguay; at times the southern and southeastern regions of Brazil are included along with parts of Bolivia, although Bolivia is typically part of Andean America. The Southern Cone region has distinct racial mixtures and linguistic groups unlike those of most of Latin America as a result of historical patterns of colonization and immigration. The indigenous population is considerably smaller than in Andean South America, and in some cases, such as Uruguay, the indigenous population is now extinct. Parts of Argentina and Paraguay have Lebanese and Syrian immigrants who speak Arabic and maintain ties to the Middle East. With over six million Muslims in Latin America, mostly in South America, there is a tendency of Pentagon policy planners to treat the region as a hot spot when in fact none exists. The populations of Argentina and Uruguay are composed mainly of people of white, European descent, with large portions living in urban areas. The Southern Cone is also distinguished by higher standards of living and quality of life. Argentina and Chile are considered developed countries as measured by the United Nations' Human Development Index. For example, Argentina and Chile are relatively rich countries, particularly in the Latin American context. However, despite the end of repressive military dictatorships and the seeming consolidation of liberal democracy, the Southern Cone region faces daunting economic and social problems. In a recent overview of the politics of Argentina, Aldo C. Vacs exposes the flaws in the political economy by arguing that "the implementation of stringent free market policies has reinforced inequitable patterns of income distribution, fostered unemployment, led to a continuous increase in poverty, and fostered the multiplication of social problems."¹ Whether these deeply rooted problems translate into security-based hot spots remains to be seen, even in the Tri-Border Area (TBA) at the intersection of Argentina, Brazil, and Paraguay, where corruption and crime mix with a large Muslim population.

The economic prosperity found in the Southern Cone (except in Paraguay) has not always translated into a stable political environment. During the second half of the twentieth century, all of the Southern Cone countries experienced rule by military dictatorships that destroyed democracy and engaged in human rights violations that involved repression, torture, and disappearances in an effort to eliminate all forms of leftist opposition, including urban guerrillas. The Cold War was particularly violent in the Southern Cone region, where networks of state-sponsored terrorism contributed to massive human rights violations and the spread of national trauma that still complicates the task of governing effectively and honestly. However, during the past two decades Southern Cone countries have replaced dictatorships with democracies and elected effective and reformist governments, many of whom have campaigned on promises to pursue economic and security policies opposed by Washington policymakers.

Brazil is the largest country in South America, occupying almost half of the South American continent and bordering on all the other South American nations except Chile and Ecuador. With the world's eighth largest economy, Brazil is a major exporter of primary products and industrial goods. The Amazon region comprises 60 percent of Brazil's national territory and is important for its biodiversity and impact on the global climate. With the exception of the dangers associated with the destruction of the Amazon rain forest and the growing problem of crime and urban gangs, Brazil is not known for having hot spots that threaten the security of the United States. The U.S. public knows little about Brazil, and Washington policymakers have only a vague, distorted awareness of Brazilian politics and society. The U.S. media tend to ignore Brazil, often referring to the country as a "sleeping giant" with enormous wealth and potential, if only it followed a development path resembling the United States'. During times of crisis—World War I, World War II, the Cold War, and the global war on terrorism—the United States shifted its indifference toward Brazil to one of cooperation and friendship, regardless of the type of political regime. However, once the security crisis passed, the United States returned to a policy of benign neglect. Despite this pattern, the United States provides substantial sums of military aid to Brazil and remains on friendly terms with the armed forces, even when they intervene in domestic politics. The United States has huge economic stakes in Brazil, a major trading partner with business investment greater than in China or Mexico. Brazil's current president,

Luis Inácio Lula da Silva, clashed with the George W. Bush administration during his first term over trade, South American integration, the Iraq war, and the resurgence of populism in the Western Hemisphere. Despite efforts of the corporate media to portray the Brazilian president as a threat because of his friendly relations with Cuba and Venezuela, relations have improved with a recognition that both countries have a mutual interest in tackling such issues as drug trafficking, terrorism, energy security, fair trade, human rights, and HIV/AIDS.

The security-based hot spots that have emerged since the return of democracy are located in the TBA, where Muslim communities engage in a variety of legal and illegal activities and maintain close ties with some Islamic groups in the Middle East. With the exception of the criminal activities in the TBA, the Southern Cone region does not have the security-based hot spots that threaten U.S. interests by having the capacity to flare up and trigger international wars or U.S. intervention on a major scale. The first hot spot in this chapter is the Amazon Basin, where environmental destruction is connected with the economic activities of multinational corporations involved in mining, logging, and many other forms of careless development. The last discussed is political volatility in the TBA. Other low-level hot spots in this chapter include the Beagle Channel dispute, the Falklands/Malvinas fracas, governance and corruption, and Mapuche power in Chile.

AMAZON POWDER KEG

Latin America has some of the richest forest and marine ecosystems on earth, and the Amazon rain forest provides an important sanctuary for thousands of rare animals as well as huge numbers of plants, which help reduce global warming by producing oxygen and absorbing carbon dioxide. Because foreign exploitation and growing demand for forest and agricultural products, oil, and minerals, the Amazon Basin is threatened by logging, mining, and energy-related development, which are taking their toll on vital ecosystems. The Amazon region covers 60 percent of Brazil; however, 20 percent of its rain forest has already been destroyed by careless development. Since 2002 an area the size of South Carolina has been stripped by loggers and farmers, who often gun down those who try to stop them. In the rugged frontier state of Rondônia, ranchers, miners, and loggers have invaded nature reserves and Indian reservations, resulting in the highest rate of deforestation in the Amazon. Unless stricter controls are imposed to protect the people, wildlife, and natural landscapes from the environmentally destructive activities of multinational corporations, the Amazon will become a powder keg. The most serious environmental threats are from illegal logging, mining, oil

Deforestation north of Macapá, Brazil. The destruction shown in the photo is the result of farmers who often destroy the forest to clear land for grazing cattle. (The Image Works)

drilling, hydroelectric development, and cattle ranching. Brazil's tropical rain forest is threatened by a severe rate of deforestation, the result of agricultural and cattle industries that are cutting and burning vast stretches of land to create giant plantations to produce soybeans for European, Asian, and North American markets. Brazil's national and state governments now have parks and protected areas, but farmers and ranchers continue to exploit these areas with impunity. In the United States, the Natural Resources Defense Council is at the forefront of mobilizing citizen activists to reduce the environmental threats in Latin America's wildlands and has achieved numerous successes, but corporate greed makes this an uphill battle.[2]

Anti-imperialist forces have aligned themselves against the militarization and exploitation of the Amazon region. Speaking at a multinational conference on the Amazon Basin, Venezuelan President Hugo Chávez criticized the "imperialist forces" for targeting Amazonia for its resources and wealth. The final document from the 2004 Pan-Amazonian Social Forum said, "We set ourselves radically against the process of militarization which Latin America is undergoing, through Plan Colombia and the dispersion of U.S. military bases in our countries."[3] In response to the violent conflicts over logging, ranching, and environmental protection, the Pará state government in Brazil announced in 2006 that it had put 58,000 square miles of the Guiana Shield region under government protection. The Washington-based environmental group Conservation International donated $1 million to facilitate the expansion, a vast preservation corridor that touches Guyana, Suriname, and French Guiana. Still, the entire Guiana Shield area is not yet protected, and those involved in the controversy are unclear how the changes will help stall deforestation.[4] Until the United States decides to confront the reality of global warming and serious international efforts to combat it, the Amazon region is likely to be ignored as a threat to security and economic interests. There is little in the way of a security threat to the United States from economic exploitation in the Amazon region, although the emergence of guerrilla groups or terrorist cells could change this in the future. In an effort to spur economic growth, President Lula da Silva has started to emphasize large public works projects, including two dam projects that have raised the ire of environmentalists concerned about permanent damage to the rain forest. With one dam close to Bolivia, there is the possibility of generating tensions over the cost of energy, future supplies, and the negative impact of illegal immigrants, who are sure to cross the border in search of employment in the public works sector.[5]

BEAGLE CHANNEL DISPUTE

Named after the exploring ship H.M.S. *Beagle*, on which Charles Darwin sailed, the Beagle Channel lies between Argentina and Chile, south of the Straits of Magellan. The dispute involves three small islands located in the middle of the channel. When the boundaries were drawn in 1881, the Beagle Channel line was left open to arbitration; this set in motion a search for some mechanism to arbitrate the dispute. The Chileans invited the British government to settle the conflict in 1967, and in 1971 the two countries named members to an arbitration board chaired by a British judge. It took six more years before Queen Elizabeth announced an Arbitral Award granting the three islands to Chile, thus denying Argentine claims. When General Pinochet of Chile met with the head of the Argentine military junta, General Ernesto Videla, in 1978, Pinochet was told the award was "void," and tension between the two dictatorships began to rise. With rumors of petroleum deposits and accusations of hegemonic pretensions leveled at Chile, by the end of 1978 it appeared as if the two countries were headed toward war. There were also reports that Peru would move into northern Chile if the Argentines attacked Chile. In a search for some mechanism to prevent war, the United States called for a meeting of the Permanent Council of the Organization of American States to take action, and the Chilean foreign minister urged the Vatican to take an interest in the matter. Papal intervention led to lengthy consultations, and the two governments eventually agreed to a proposal awarding the islands to Chile, but granted Argentina territorial waters to the east of the islands. However, it took nearly six years, and the return of civilian government in Argentina, before a formal agreement was finally signed at the Vatican in May 1985.

Since the discovery of oil in the early 1990s, both countries have confronted each other again to position themselves to take advantage of the meager petroleum reserves there. It is hard to imagine a war over oil in this remote territory, but nationalist impulses sometimes get out of hand. It is important to note that although both countries had military governments, they chose bargaining as a means of conflict resolution instead of war. Optimists who have studied the issue see little danger of a serious security threat from this distant location.

FALKLANDS/MALVINAS FRACAS

The 1982 war that developed between Argentina and Great Britain over a chain of seemingly worthless islands in the South Atlantic had a major impact on U.S.–Latin American relations at the time and eventually led to the demise of Argentina's military government, the source of the invasion. Argentina's military junta did not expect the British to launch a counterinvasion or the United States to oppose the Argentine position for resolving the dispute. There are conflicting claims as to which party—Argentina or Great Britain—is the sovereign when it comes to the Falklands/Malvinas Islands, and efforts to understand the junta's decision to fight a war have been inconclusive. The dispute also rests on how each country refers to the islands: for the British, their possessions are called the Falklands Islands; whereas Argentina insists on the name Islas Malvinas (Malvinas Islands).

What the Falklands/Malvinas fracas demonstrates is how little the international system understands about the value nations attach to their overseas possessions. This means that there is a strong potential for future conflict over the islands, and therefore it remains a potential hot spot in the Southern Cone. "There are three perennial [national] passions in Argentina: football [soccer], the tango[,] and the country's claim to Britain's South Atlantic outpost, the Falklands Islands."[6] There is certainly no guarantee that the democratic nature of the regimes involved in the simmering dispute will avert another war to settle the issue, which has existed for more than a century.

The basis of the war involved a number of factors that coalesced in the early 1980s to prompt the invasion. First, Argentina has always maintained

Falklands War victory parade in London, England, shortly after the end of the war with Argentina over the disputed Falklands/Malvinas Islands, October 13, 1982. (The Image Works)

it has a legal and historical claim to sovereign title since gaining independence in 1816. Second, the years of failure of negotiations to achieve Argentine control over the islands has produced perennial frustration. Third, Argentina's strong perception of greatness in South America fostered a sense of ardent nationalism that reduced the need for major gains from a failed effort. Fourth, Argentina's military government decided to encourage a heightened sense of nationalism by invading the Malvinas Islands to turn attention away from a disastrous economic situation in April 1982. Fifth, the military government ordered the invasion assuming that the United States would remain neutral, the British would not come to the defense of the islands, and the Latin American states would be sympathetic to Buenos Aires's claim of sovereignty, regardless of the chosen methods to achieve these ends. Sixth, although the invasion was a desperate and risky gamble, the regime faced no formal political opposition at home and possessed the capacity to propagandize in favor of winning the battle without a nagging and critical press.[7]

Although the war lasted only 45 days, 255 British troops were killed and 777 seriously wounded in the struggle to regain the Falklands. The cost to Argentina was considerably greater: 746 troops were killed and 1,336 wounded in defending their effort to regain sovereignty over the Islas Malvinas. The financial costs were substantial: both countries paid between $2 billion and $3 billion to prosecute the six-week war. The fact that the Reagan administration sided with Britain generated widespread Latin American criticism of the United States, but the anti-Americanism did not linger. Of greater significance was the fact that the war put an end to the human rights violations associated with Argentina's "Dirty War" against dissidents by discrediting the Argentine junta and contributing to its replacement by a freely elected government, an outcome that would have taken much longer without the folly of war and destruction. The conflict over the Falklands/Malvinas Islands in 1982 helped Cuba rally Latin American nations on a nationalistic basis against the United States, and this was instrumental in reversing Cuba's isolation from Latin America at the time.

Néstor Kirchner, Argentina's Peronist president, started a series of provocative moves in 2006 to win control of the Malvinas and has inlisted the support of other left-leaning leaders in Latin America, including Cuba's Fidel Castro and Venezuela's Hugo Chávez. Using the sovereignty issues as a rallying point, President Kirchner wants to create an "anti-colonial bloc" that will help him recover the Malvinas for the homeland. Although he is not advocating another war with Great Britain, he wants a more aggressive diplomacy that will resume negotiations with Britain. The Falklands have prospered economically since 1982, in large part as a result of the success of commercial fishing, but there is little interest in negotiations leading to Argentine sovereignty. The islanders, nicknamed Kelpers, claim a right to decide their own future and have no interest in bowing to Argentina's claims, particularly when they enjoy the highest per capita income in South America. Nevertheless, the cost of maintaining control over the Falklands is extremely high: Britain deploys 1,200 military personnel to protect 2,600 islanders at a cost of almost $1 million for each inhabitant.

Argentina's renewed interest in the islands is a result of (1) the president's drive for re-election in 2007, toward which this would seem to be a good campaign issue, (2) 2007 marks the twenty-fifth anniversary of the 1982 invasion, and (3) the rise of left-leaning governments in South America has stirred demands for a united front against colonialism and imperialism. The new mood in Argentina represents a marked change in the conciliatory, passive approach that Argentine presidents have pursued since the fall of the military dictatorship in 1982. In the end, the cost of maintaining neighborly relations may be too high for Argentina to settle for the status quo when opportunities to recover lost territory/sovereignty arise.

The Falklands/Malvinas issue is not an international hot spot; however, it carries the potential for greater conflict between Britain, Argentina, and South America. Hugo Chávez, president of Venezuela, has joined the struggle by siding with Argentina. He met with President Kirchner in July 2006 and signed a document urging Argentina and the United Kingdom to renew talks over the Falklands Islands, urging a "peaceful, fair and definitive solution to the sovereignty dispute, including the principle of territorial integrity." There is a moral imperative here, but the history of control and ownership of the islands does not augur well for either a quick, a fair, or a definitive solution to the international problem. There is a threat as a security hot spot, but the level is quite low.

GOVERNANCE AND CORRUPTION

Problems of governance have plagued the Southern Cone region for the past century, known for enduring dictatorships and military rule. Dictators friendly to U.S. interests, with the backing of anti-Communist politicians in the United States, were established to uproot almost any political opposition no matter how inspired by stirrings for democracy, social justice, or human rights. The increasing use of the term "state failure" in the Southern Cone region is often associated with institutional flaws, lack of legitimacy and accountability, social inequality, and chronic violence. However, of the Southern Cone countries, only Paraguay is listed by the Fund for Peace in Washington as a failed state.[8] A failing state is fragile because it has lost its monopoly on the use of force, can no longer uphold its internal legal order, and is unable to deliver public services to its population. Once a state has failed in one or several of the areas, new forms of violence tend to emerge associated with narco-trafficking, paramilitary organizations, violent youth gangs, and guerrilla groups that mix ideology with economic gain. Brazil, for example, has been plagued with death and destruction from violent gangs operating in São Paulo and Rio de Janeiro. Unable to control attacks on police headquarters, buses, and public buildings, Brazil's government has refused to negotiate with gangs because of the magnitude of the violence and the success of the prison uprisings and the fear that federal intervention would only highlight the failure of São Paulo State's security policies. In a burst of gang violence in May 2006, leaders operating behind bars managed to coordinate more than 250 attacks, executions, and chaos in about seventy prisons in São Paulo State.[9] Southern Cone governments have had to contend with demands for justice from victims of human rights violations during the dirty wars of the 1970s and 1980s. In Paraguay, Martín Almada, a schoolteacher imprisoned and tortured during the 1970s as an "intellectual terrorist," discovered a cache of government documents that later came to be known as the Archives of Terror, which detailed the political arrests and fate of thousands suspected of terrorist/Communist activity under Stroessner's repressive rule.

The economic scene has changed dramatically in the Southern Cone region in the past twenty years. Major stock exchanges exist in Santiago, São Paulo, and Buenos Aires. More and more manufactured goods are being made in the region, and modern aspects of Western consumption such as mass retail stores, cell phones, cable TV, computers, and automobiles inundate the countries of the region. Globalization and neoliberal economic reforms have had some positive results, with increased consumption, greater production, and lower inflation; however, neoliberal reforms have also added to the highly inequitable distribution of wealth and income that have plagued the region. Austerity measures have been unpopular and have led to antigovernment rioting and other forms of political violence. National political leaders have had a tough time and at times have been forced from office after chaos erupted while they were trying to implement economic reforms. Growing inequality that has marginalized the masses has spawned major leftist gains in national elections throughout the Southern Cone area.

Chile's foreign-dominated economy is the result of demand for minerals—copper, gold, and nitrate—that, in times of war, heightened security concerns. During the Cold War the United States and Chile clashed over Washington's demands for an anti-Communist foreign policy that would make the United States more secure in its relations with South American governments. The Pinochet years (1973–1990) produced more conflict between the United States and Chile, first over the issue of human rights and later over the question of democratization. U.S.–Chilean relations have improved with the end of the Cold War and the return of Chilean democracy. There is now more emphasis on free trade and investment instead of the prior battles over political ideology, human rights abuses, and the ownership of vital economic resources. Chile is strongly committed to free trade with the United States, and its investment laws welcome foreign investment. It has signed free trade agreements with several important economies, including the United States.

Neoliberal beliefs have guided public policymaking in Chile since the military coup that ended the activist government programs that shaped economic policy under previous governments, including Christian Democrats and Socialists. Once in power following the military takeover from Salvador Allende, General Pinochet introduced the first, most comprehensive neoliberal policies in Latin America, and these continued after the center-left Concertación Democrática—a coalition of Christian Democrats, Socialists, and radicals—gained power in 1990. Neoliberalism represented a reaction against Keynesians, state socialists, and import-substitution industrialists, who were held responsible for economic stagnation, government deficits, foreign debt, nepotism, corruption, bureaucratic bottlenecks, and trade deficits. Soon, according to Charles F. Andrain and James T. Smith, neoliberal assumptions began to "diverge from the activist, egalitarian policies promoted by Keynesians, state socialists, and import-substitution industrialists. Individualism, self-interest, personal responsibility, and competition take priority over collectivism, social responsibility, cooperation, and concern for the public good that transcends the pursuit of economic self-interest."[10] The outcome of this shift in economic models had its effect on income distribution: after 1973 deflationary neoliberal economic policies produced greater income inequality than had prevailed under previous regimes, all the result of regressive taxes, decreased government expenditures for social services, privatization, and deregulation of labor and capital markets. Among the four Latin American countries in the Andrain and Smith study, Chile has managed to evade widespread corruption: "Despite its wide gap between rich and poor, Chile's high growth rate and relatively honest government have produced greater support for democracy than in Mexico, Brazil, as well as stronger institutional trust than in the other three Latin American societies."[11] During her first year in office, Michelle Bachelet struggled to maintain a balance between change and continuity, clearly aware of the major obstacles to significant reform of Chilean society. This means that Concertación governments choose to govern by shifting ideologically to the middle of the political spectrum and making only minor reforms to the free-market economy imposed during the Pinochet era.[12]

Chile's system of governance continues to struggle with its authoritarian past and demilitarization. Running as a Socialist with a political campaign that offered "change with continuity," Michelle Bachelet was elected president with more than 53 percent of the vote in January 2006. She is the first woman to be elected head of state in South America and has been able to maintain approval ratings above 50 percent. Her campaign promises focused on doing a better job than her predecessors of meeting the needs of the poor and women, improving the ailing pension system, improving education, preserving Chile's economy, and maintaining close ties with the United States. Chile has experienced sustained economic growth since the end of the Pinochet dictatorship, thanks to record prices for copper, prudent fiscal management, and low levels of corruption. By emphasizing the country's social agenda as a priority, each successive government to follow Pinochet has made a significant reduction in overall and extreme poverty. According to Vinay Jawahar, "None of this has been accomplished at the expense of democracy; in fact, there has been notable progress towards dismantling the remaining vestiges of Pinochet's authoritarian rule."[13] Pinochet's legacy of authoritarianism and free-market capitalism that reversed decades of social welfare reforms continue to influence those in Chile who argue that his economic policies—privatization of national health care and social security programs—contributed to the creation of unnecessary social and economic inequalities. Chile's copper windfall beginning in 2003 has not reduced the great inequalities enough to satisfy those Chileans who resent the large amount of revenue the armed forces are guaranteed from yearly copper revenues. According to recent estimates, the Chilean armed forces will receive nearly an additional $1 billion in 2007 while investment in housing, education, and pensions lags behind promises and expectations.[14]

Pinochet's legacy also includes the so-called "Pinochet Precedent" that grew out of the aging dictator's arrest in 1998 while visiting London. British authorities arrested him on a Spanish extradition warrant for the alleged murder and torture of Spanish citizens during his dictatorship. Pinochet's arrest was a turning point in international human rights law that dismissed "sovereign immunity" so that those who carry out repressive measures to eliminate large segments of the population can be brought to justice. After 16 months in British detention, he was allowed to return to Chile in 1999, but continued to face more legal actions by those who insisted he stand trial in Chile for human rights abuses and other violations during the dark years of his brutal military regime. According to the *Economist*, "General Pinochet liked to portray himself as the selfless defender of God and country against atheist communism."[15] Pinochet's legacy is still being examined and investigated by those in Chile, and in Washington, D.C., who feel that the Pinochet

Precedent needs to be applied to the deeds of Donald Rumsfeld, Alberto Gonzalez, and other American officials who adopted Pinochet's methods of torture in U.S. military detention centers. According to Marc Cooper, "At the time of Pinochet's death, more than 200 criminal accusations were still pending against him."[16] Shortly after Pinochet's death, President Bachelet decided to push for the invalidation of an amnesty law that has protected Pinochet's subordinates from prosecution on murder and torture charges for nearly 30 years. The Bachelet administration maintains that Pinochet's 1978 amnesty was an illegitimate decision that should have never been applied and should never be used again.[17]

The ability of Augusto Pinochet to escape prosecution and incarceration for more than thirty years was also helped by the Bush family's role in the cover-up of the Chilean dictator's notorious deeds, including a sense of impunity because of powerful friends in Washington. As Robert Parry points out, "In the 1980s, when George H. W. Bush was Vice President, Pinochet's regime helped funnel weapons to the Nicaraguan contra rebels and to Saddam Hussein's Iraq, an operation that also implicated then-CIA official Robert M. Gates, who replaced Donald Rumsfeld as U.S. Secretary of State."[18] In a letter published after his death, Pinochet expressed regret at having to carry out the bloody 1973 coup against Allende. However, because "Marxist-Leninist ideology" had "entered the fatherland," the coup and its aftermath were necessary in order to eliminate ideological and armed fanaticism.[19]

For many Chileans who voted for President Bachelet, she is someone who personalizes the recent history of Chile. As Larry Rohter points out, "She is a toughened survivor of the Pinochet dictatorship, which was responsible for her father's death and her imprisonment, torture and exile, and she embodies for many Chile's painful reconciliation with those dark years."[20] During her victory speech she declared, "I was the victim of hatred, and I have dedicated my life to reversing that hatred." Nevertheless, Chileans have struggled with the politics of punishing Pinochet for human rights abuses. In October 2005 General Pinochet lost his immunity from prosecution in connection with an estimated $27 million that he and his family are alleged to have obtained and deposited in overseas bank accounts. As a result, prosecutors moved to charge the 89-year-old former dictator with tax fraud, perjury, and use of falsified documents. Previous charges involving murder and human rights abuses were eventually overturned on grounds that the dictator was not mentally or physically fit to stand trial. Shortly thereafter, Pinochet was arrested on tax fraud and passport forgery charges stemming from secret bank accounts that he maintained under false names outside of Chile. Chilean legal authorities estimate that Pinochet's personal fortune is far greater than the former dictator was willing to admit before he died on December 10, 2006.

During the September 11, 1973, anniversary in 2006, President Bachelet delivered a speech to the nation that emphasized the importance to healing the wounds from the past while split television screens showed a part of La Moneda burning after attacks on the palace by anarchists adorned with black hoods. After more than 30 years since the overthrow of Allende, Chileans are still divided between the politics of authoritarianism popularized by General Pinochet and the more open and conflictive model of pluralist democracy. President Bachelet's relationship with the Chilean military is surprisingly good, and she considers the United States a "strategy ally" in solving hemispheric problems. If Bachelet manages to transform Chile in terms of empowering women, pension reform, and expanding preschool education, she will have made important strides in addressing the needs of those who have experienced little benefit from globalization and economic integration. "However," according to Pascale Bonnefoy, "by tapping into state coffers only to fill in the social gaps where neoliberal policies have failed, without structural reforms required to reverse inequality, her administration will probably be remembered more for continuity than for change."[21]

The demands for reforms in Chile's education system began in 2005 with complaints against school bus fares and university entrance exam fees. By the following year it had grown into a nationwide movement demanding quality education for all Chileans. Chilean students who were also angry at how much was being spent on military hardware at the expense of educational needs were at the forefront of street protests calling for major educational reforms in 2006. After months of protests they forced the government to increase educational spending and overhaul an educational system flawed by vast inequalities between the rich and the poor. President Bachelet pledged grants for university entrance exams, free school meals, funds to repair dilapidated buildings, and free bus passes for the poorest 20 percent of municipal school pupils. The student uprising clearly showed the growing influence of students in Chile as significant political actors who operate without fear of the national government. Still, Chile has to confront high rates of economic inequality and sharp class differences within its education system.[22] The legitimate authority of the current regime is bolstered by very little corruption and expanding revenues from copper exports.

MAPUCHE POWER?

The Mapuche are an indigenous people who lived in Chile long before the Spanish conquistadors arrived in the sixteenth century. The Mapuches are now involved in a struggle to take back the lush forests of southern Chile, which once belonged to this indigenous group. Today, the Mapuches constitute approximately one million of Chile's 15 million people. This means the Mapuches account for approximately 86 percent of Chile's indigenous population. The verdant forests they once inhabited are now the property of timber companies that supply lumber to the United States, Japan, and Europe, but the Mapuches complain of false land titles, environmental damage, and threats to their traditional way of life. In an effort to take back lands they claim belong to them, Mapuche leaders are frequently accused of burning forests and farmhouses and destruction of forestry equipment and trucks. The Chilean government has responded by using a modified version of an antiterrorist law that prohibits "generating fear among sectors of the population"—a statute that dates from the Pinochet dictatorship from 1973 to 1990.

The Mapuches, concentrated in the southern region of Araucania, have become more militant in recent years in their efforts to recover ancestral lands and their repeated calls for territorial autonomy. The Council of the all the Lands (*Consejo de Todas las Tierras,* CTT) is working on legislation that would grant special-territory status for the Mapuche lands south of the Bío Bío river. If the Mapuches are successful in their efforts to achieve territorial autonomy, their communities will be run under traditional Mapuche authorities and customary law. An indigenous parliament would mediate between the Mapuche people and the national government. The fact that the Mapuches are not recognized for their distinctiveness as indigenous people in the Chilean constitution means that the political struggle is far more difficult than it would be if Chile were a signatory of the International Labor Organization (ILO) Convention 169. As a standard for recognizing the fundamental human rights of indigenous and tribal peoples in independent countries, the General Conference of the ILO adopted the convention in 1989, and it went into force in 1991. The new standards found in Convention 169 remove the assimilationist orientation of earlier standards and put greater stress on the rights of indigenous people to maintain and develop their own identities, languages, and religions within the independent states in which they live. Efforts to shift more political power to the Mapuches worry many Chilean politicians who fear the consequences of losing absolute control over Chilean territory. If this were to happen, it would weaken Chile's territorial claim over lands it obtained from Bolivia as a result of the War of the Pacific. There is little in the way of a security threat from the Mapuches, but they are making demands on the national government that could raise questions of security if they form alliances with other indigenous groups—a growing trend in the Americas—in South America.

TRI-BORDER AREA TERRORISM

One of South America's current hot spots is the region that straddles Argentina, Brazil, and Paraguay, a haven for all kinds of nefarious activities, from weapon smugglers and drug traffickers to Islamic extremists who have used the profits from criminal activities in this area to fund terrorist operations. With Brazil in the lead, the United States and South American nations have created an international intelligence center in the TBA to combat varieties of crime and terrorist threats. U.S. military involvement in the TBA is constrained by a lack of troop infrastructure for dealing with terrorism and "U.S. law that bans many military-to-military relationships with signers of a treaty establishing an international criminal court."[23] Brazil, Argentina, and Paraguay are signers to the Rome Statute, which established the International Criminal Court (ICC). Congress passed the American Service-members' Protection Act (ASPA) to prevent U.S. troops from having to face a trial before the ICC. ASPA places restrictions on providing military assistance to governments that are part of the Rome Statute. The problem with the ASPA

Children of Lebanese descent protesting against war in the Middle East in Ciudad del Este, the center of the Tri-Border Area in South America. The Tri-Border Area is home to thousands of Arabs and Muslims who live and work in the area and maintain connections to virtually all parts of the Middle East. (Photograph by Luis Leon, Archivolatino. Courtesy of Redux Pictures.)

safeguards is that they restrict U.S. military cooperation with almost a dozen Latin American governments. However, Latin American countries that are designated "major non-NATO allies" such as Argentina receive waivers to ASPA and can receive international military education and training (IMET) funds. To circumvent the ASPA restrictions, the U.S. Southern Command conducts joint military exercises to coordinate approaches to security, including a multinational simulation defending the Panama Canal against maritime threats. According to State Department officials and international security experts, the fight in the TBA is less important than the one in Colombia, where the United States has invested billions of dollars to help the Colombian government combat rebel forces that control large parcels of national territory. However, recent efforts to link Iran with terrorist activities in the TBA could quickly change the threat level and security concerns in the Southern Cone region.

In March 2005 the State Department's office of counter-terrorism claimed that Middle East terrorist connections in Latin America have visited the TBA.[24] While the South American region is on the Pentagon's "watch list" for terrorists, and alleged operatives of Islamic Fundamentalist Groups have been observed in the TBA, the entrenched nature of indigenous crime groups and nonindigenous mafias from more than a dozen foreign countries, including China, Ivory Coast, Japan, Korea, Lebanon, Nigeria, Russia, and Taiwan, pose serious problems for locating and eliminating organized crime and terrorist groups, regardless of their international connections and networks. However, to date the United States has invested little in the region.

The several free-trade areas in Latin America with large Middle Eastern populations are infested with Islamic terrorist groups, organized crime mafias, and corrupt officials. These include Colombia's Maicao, Venezuela's Margarita Island, Guyana, the TBA, and Chile's port Iquique. With huge profits from drug trafficking, arms dealing, money laundering, contraband, and product piracy, Islamic fundamentalist groups in the TBA send between $300 million and $500 million to radical Islamic groups in the Middle East.[25] The Muslim population—mostly Sunni—in Latin America is estimated to number 6 million, 1.2 percent of Latin America's total population. Only four Latin American countries—Argentina, Trinidad and Tobago, Guyana, and Suriname—have Muslim populations that exceed 1 percent of the population.

The Lebanese radical, Iran-backed, Shi'ite Hezbollah is considered the major international terrorist threat in Latin America. It has a significant influence in the TBA but has small cells operating in Colombia, Venezuela, Guyana, and Ecuador. It has been rated as the best organized and most competent Islamist terrorist organization in the world, with an annual budget of over $100 million. Most of its funding and guidance comes from Iran and Syria, along with criminal organizations in the Western Hemisphere. Its major activities include narcotics, smuggling, terrorism, fundraising, and recruitment. Much of what it does is guided by Iranian intelligence operatives working inside of Iranian embassies. In retaliation for Israel's assassination of Hezbollah leader Sheikh Abbas al-Musawi and his family in the early 1990s, Hezbollah is alleged to have bombed the Israeli Embassy in Buenos Aires, Argentina, and attacked the Argentine-Israeli Mutual Association (AIMA).[26] Hezbollah officially denies any responsibility for attacks in Argentina, claiming it operates only in the Israel-Lebanon area to defend Lebanese sovereignty against Israeli threats. It is hard to confirm responsibility for these events and to establish a clear connection between terrorism and organized criminal groups. The pursuit of Iran for its alleged involvement in the 1994 bombing of the Jewish community center is part of a renewed effort by President Néstor Kirchner to counter Iran's influence in the region by issuing arrest warrants for nine former Iranian officials accused of involvement in the 1994 attacks. Kirchner's attempt to prosecute Iranian officials was carried out prior to President Ahmadinejad's visit to Latin America to build alliances with Venezuela, Bolivia, Ecuador, and Nicaragua—strong anti-American actors with leftist governments. Kirchner's rebuke of Iran has raised questions about the possibility that Argentina is being manipulated by the United States in an effort to use the court rulings to stir international outrage against Iran over its involvement in Iraq and its nuclear policy.[27]

Latin American countries have attempted to curry favor with Washington by linking narcotics traffickers to some form of terrorism. For example, the attention paid to the alleged threat emanating from the Arab Muslim community on Margarita Island, Venezuela, has more to do with the ongoing tensions between the Bush administration and that of President Chávez than the dangers posed by counterfeiting, piracy, drug trafficking, and weapons smuggling.[28] It seems clear that the Bush administration would like to find some way to collaborate with a South American government in order to increase international outrage against the current Iranian government.

In order to give the military a more active intelligence role in counter-terrorism, the Pentagon is using small teams of special operations troops inside American embassies in hot spots or unstable parts of the world. Their placement is not in traditional hot spots, namely the Middle East, but in areas like the TBA, where terrorists are thought to be operating, planning attacks, raising funds, laundering money, or seeking safe haven. In planning counter-terrorism missions, the goal of these Military Liaison Elements (MLEs) is to enhance military, interagency, and host nation coordination and planning against terrorism networks that are linked with the trafficking of arms, drugs, and uranium. Under Special Operations Command in Florida, the MLEs operate in regions where the U.S. military is not based in large numbers and, in particular, where the United States is not at war. This new defense approach presents a number of difficulties, not the least of which is bureaucratic rivalries embedded in the national intelligence agencies. The Special Operations Command now operate according to the Pentagon's new "4-F" catchphrase: "find, fix, finish, and follow-up." This new approach is described as a kind of "shorthand for locating terrorist leaders, tracking them precisely, capturing or killing them, and then using the information gathered to plan another operation."[29] In addition to bureaucratic rivalries and the perils of covert operations, this new approach is hampered by the lack of a clear definition of terrorism and a poor record of finding individuals who fit the military's profile and constitute a serious threat to the security of the United States. While it may be acceptable to U.S. ambassadors to assist with covert operations of this nature, host country governments are likely to be less receptive to U.S. involvement in counter-terrorism activities when sovereignty is an issue and innocent civilians are killed when plans go awry.

Until he was arrested in Foz do Iguaçu in June 2002, Assad Mohamed Barakat was generally identified as Hezbollah's military (i.e., terrorist) operations chief in the TBA and the organizations chief fund-raising official in the Southern Cone. After the 9/11 attacks, an international arrest warrant was issued for Barakat's arrest. He fled the TBA in October 2001 and was indicted in Paraguay on charges of tax evasion and assorted criminal activities. After his arrest in Foz do Iguaçu, he was imprisoned in Brasilia. Barakat was born in Lebanon, but he left the civil-war torn country at age 17 and emigrated to Paraguay with his father. Over the years in Ciudad del Este, he accumulated numerous companies, including an engineering and construction company with offices in Ciudad del Este and Beirut. Barakat has acknowledged owning businesses in Chile and the United States (Miami and New York), but his visa was revoked after September 11, 2001, after his name appeared on the U.S. Department of State's "suspected terrorists" list. Most of those associated with Hezbollah in the TBA have connections to Lebanon and remit large sums of money to banks there almost daily. Efforts to eliminate the TBA underworld have been difficult, particularly when large campaign contributions to corrupt members of Paraguay's ruling Colorado Party have paved the way for arrested members of Hezbollah to escape from prison.[30] The financial connection between corrupt government officials in Latin America and Islamic terrorist groups highlights the importance of good governance in countering criminal and terrorist groups. Unfortunately, corruption and poor governance act as major obstacles to political stability and policy effectiveness in the region. The hot spots that form in this region are likely to be rooted in high levels of corruption, disgust with democracy, and overall poor governance, things over which the United States has little control.

CHAPTER 5

The Caribbean: Cuba and Haiti

The Caribbean is a region of the Americas consisting mainly of the Caribbean Sea, located southeast of North America and north and west of South America. The Caribbean is made up of thousands of islands, reefs, and cays. It is also known as the West Indies, consisting of the Greater and Lesser Antilles. The name "Caribbean" stems from the dominant Amerindian groups that occupied the region at the time of European contact and colonization at the end of the fifteenth century. The analogous "West Indies" originated with Christopher Columbus, who believed he had landed in the Indies (south and east Asia) when he first arrived in the Americas. Geopolitically, the Caribbean includes sovereign states, overseas departments, and dependencies, all reflecting different historical connections to Europe (mainly French, English, Dutch, and Spanish) and the United States. Since there are no hot spots in the Caribbean outside of Cuba and Haiti, only these two sovereign states will be included in the hot spot histories in this volume. The English-speaking Caribbean consists of fourteen small independent nations that rely heavily on tourism and are rarely discussed as security threats to the United States, Canada, Europe, or the rest of Latin America. Nearly all the Caribbean nations are involved in narco-trafficking and, in the case of Jamaica, large-scale production and export of marijuana.

The Caribbean states play an important role in the Organization of American States (OAS), representing a voting bloc of fourteen out of thirty-four members of this regional body. During the Cold War some of the Caribbean states achieved some attention when they opposed U.S. foreign policy and joined hands with revolutionaries in other parts of Latin America. In some cases, such as Grenada, the United States invaded the island of 100,000 people in order to prevent a "second Cuba" and reassert U.S. hegemony over the region, the first instance of "pre-emptive" war in American foreign policy. The following hot spots are discussed in this chapter: Cuba's long-distance civil war; drug trafficking and terrorism; governance: instability and corruption; and Haiti as a failed state.

CUBA'S LONG-DISTANCE CIVIL WAR

Cuba is a constant thorn in the side of American presidents who are stuck in a Cold War mindset and influenced by powerful domestic political interests. In its global assessment of terrorism, the U.S. Department of State lists Cuba as a state sponsor of terrorism, despite evidence to the contrary. The United States stands alone in its efforts to bring about regime change on the island, and most Latin American governments fear that the U.S. approach—isolation and hostility—only increase the prospects for violence in Cuba when political change does occur, rather than advancing the chances of a peaceful, democratic transition after Fidel Castro dies.[1] However, experts on Cuba and high-level government officials in Washington were surprised when there was calm and nor-

Fidel Castro, Cuba's aging leader, speaking before the Communist Party Central Committee, 1989. After falling ill in July 2006, Fidel Castro turned over the reins of power to his younger brother, Raúl, and has not appeared in public while he is recovering from a severe intestinal disorder. (The Image Works)

The long-distance civil war between the United States and Cuba is captured during an immigrants' rights protest in Little Havana in Miami, Florida, 2006. The anti-Castro sign is designed to connect Fidel Castro with terrorism, a common strategy used by Cuban exiles in the United States. (The Image Works)

malcy, not chaos and hysteria, when Fidel Castro turned over power to his brother Raúl before undergoing intestinal surgery on July 31, 2006. With Raúl in charge, it appears that the political system—once thought by Washington policymakers to rest solely on the power of one man—is much stronger and may not change much at all after Fidel dies. The whole notion that Cuba is a hot spot because of the tenuous nature of Fidel's grip on politics and society is in need of serious reconsideration in the aftermath of the country's first permanent transition in recent history.[2] At the time Castro's illness was announced, President Bush said on Miami's Radio Mambi that the United States has a plan in place to help the Cuban people adopt a new system more acceptable to the United States. It is obvious that Washington plans to change Cuba in the name of freedom and democracy when Fidel Castro dies; however, the entire $80 million plan indicates that there will be more American meddling in the internal affairs on the island. It is quite possible that Venezuela's Hugo Chávez, the most influential leader in Latin America, will try to keep Cuba's power structure intact and keep the United States out in order to preserve the remnants of Cuban socialism and anti-imperialism. As far as

Washington is concerned, Cuba will remain a Caribbean hot spot, with or without Fidel Castro and his brother Raúl.

After decades of efforts to depose Fidel Castro, the Bush administration's blueprint for a democratic transition—with a Cuban transition coordinator and a new CIA mission manager to oversee intelligence gathering—has faded as many Western nations with substantial economic investments on the island have little enthusiasm for risking Cuba's destabilization in the name of greater political freedom and democracy. According to Erikson, "many in the US military, schooled in the harsh lessons of nation-building in Iraq, are anxious to avoid a Cuban adventure that could lead to a refugee crisis or involve peacekeeping responsibilities. Stability, not democracy, is the watchword in the Pentagon and the Miami-based US Southern Command."[3] Apparently, strategic thinking in Washington is now based on the view that the difficulties of implanting democracy in Cuba make it a less important foreign policy goal than *stability* in a post-Castro Cuba designed to avoid a mass exodus of refugees from the island or the unsuccessful, and costly, tasks of democratizing Cuba. It is quite possible that the future of a post-Castro Cuba will have more to do with powerful foreign actors such as President Chávez and Chinese President Hu Jintao, both heavily invested in the island, than with either the exile community in the United States or reformist segments among the next generation of Cubans on the island. It seems clear that the absence of new ideas in Washington and Miami has paralyzed any serious efforts by the United States to facilitate meaningful change in Cuba, thus allowing Raúl Castro's ascendance to occur with little opposition. If Cuba remains a security-based hot spot after Fidel Castro dies, the United States will carry some of the blame for that outcome.

The politics of hostility that separates Cuba from the United States is based on many factors; however, the long-distance civil war between those who won in 1959 and those who lost and fled to the United States, and Washington's obsession with punishing Cuba for the transgressions of Castro, help explain current policy. According to Jatar-Hausman, "The early years of the revolution put an end to a hot, local civil war, but ushered in a more distant, colder confrontation between those who left their assets and social positions and those who took them over. Each side in this confrontation joined forces with one of the two superpowers then engaged in the Cold War, and the Cuban issue became an East-West fault line. The winners took over real estate and productive assets. The losers joined forces with the United States and attempted military action before settling on the trade embargo as the weapon of choice."[4] There have been many opportunities over the past 45 years to settle the differences between the winners, the losers, and the United States; however, a failed policy has been passed from one presidential administration to another, through eleven successive administrations—Republicans and Democrats, liberals and conservatives, generation after generation, with minimum public debate. A majority of Cuban Americans are in favor of a policy change in Washington, as measured by a Florida International University Poll that found 65 percent of Cuban Americans polled supported a dialogue with the Cuban government and 55 percent favor allowing unrestricted travel to Cuba for all Americans.

After the 9/11 terrorist attacks on the United States, Cuba expressed solidarity with the American people, called for a dialogue over differences, and offered to sign bilateral agreements for joint efforts against terrorism. Later, in the wake of the devastation wrought by Hurricane Katrina in 2005, Cuba offered to send medics, field hospitals, and 83 tons of medical supplies to ease the humanitarian disaster in the United States. The Bush administration rebuffed these efforts and continued its call for Castro's downfall. When asked about the president's response to Castro's offer, press secretary Scott McClellan told journalists that Castro needs to offer the Cuban people their freedom. Although his health is failing and his age is finally catching up to him, Fidel Castro remains steadfast in his commitment to the Revolution and his defiance of the United States. The price of appearing "soft on Fidel" is too high for most American politicians, who worry about being pilloried for ignoring the dangers posed by the evil nature of Castro's regime, as portrayed by the media in the United States, and his current ties to Venezuela's Hugo Chávez.

In what has become a foreign policy by obituary, the United States refuses to negotiate with either Fidel Castro or his heir apparent, Raúl Castro. The fact that the recent creation of a Commission for Assistance to a Free Cuba and a 500-page "action plan" have failed to bring an end to Castro's regime and have had a negative affect on U.S. credibility has not stopped the White House from pursuing a costly and counterproductive policy of confrontation instead of negotiation. The Helms-Burton Law, passed in 1996, had all the earmarks of punitive legislation designed to destroy Fidel Castro by adopting measures to assist in winning the long-distance civil war. Many of the provisions of the Helms-Burton Law are devoted to property claims, additional economic sanctions, and a transition government without Fidel Castro or Raúl Castro. This would mean that even if Fidel Castro dies and his brother Raúl succeeds him, the Helms-Burton Law forbids any negotiated settlement of claims between the two countries. All these punitive measures have had predictable results: known as the "Law of Slavery" and by many Cubans "the Platt Amendment revisited,"[5] Helms-Burton turned much of the animosity directed at their government into support based on Cuban nationalism and U.S. hostility.

The Cuban community in Florida is well organized and has learned to play the electoral game very well beginning in the late 1970s. Paradoxically the Helms-Burton Law had little to do with Senator Jesse Helms and Congressman Dan Burton. Although staffers from these two members of Congress played a role in formulating the law, Cuban American members of Congress—Ileana Ros Lehtinen, Lincoln Díaz Balart, and Robert Menéndez—and the Cuban American National Foundation (CANF) helped formulate the legislation. The importance of Florida as a heavyweight Electoral College state and the power of the Cuba lobby centered on the Cuban American National Foundation were important in pushing through the legislation. Lawyers working for the prerevolution Cuban property owners were key players in drafting the Helms-Burton Law. At first, President Clinton refused to sign Helms-Burton into law, claiming it had questionable legality with its extraterritorial provisions. However, after several Cuban American pilots were killed after flying over Cuban air space, the uproar left President Clinton little choice but to sign the legislation, in an election year where the Cuban community has been able to deliver a swing vote in a populous state such as Florida.

The exiled Cubans in the United States and their supporters in the U.S. government have tried to demonize Fidel Castro (and Ché Guevara) in an effort to drive him from power. Unfortunately, the twisted relationship is full of examples in which the United States has created a subjective threat to provoke Castro into doing something foolish so that he could be attacked and his revolution could be destroyed. Until 1998, when 10,000 pages of documents were declassified, the full history of U.S. attempts to remove Castro were not well known. In 1962, in what became known as Operation North Woods, the U.S. Joint Chiefs of Staff wrote a document titled "Pretexts to Justify U.S. Military Intervention in Cuba." Among the options included a variety of U.S. terrorist campaigns (real or simulated) that could be used to justify a U.S. military invasion of the island after the failed Bay of Pigs invasion in 1961. Although the schemes were never implemented, it was clear that the Pentagon believed that only a full-scale invasion would get rid of Fidel Castro. If the Cubans could be blamed for downing a passenger plane with American civilians on board, and the threat hyped to a level that would justify military intervention, then a purported national security threat posed by a Communist regime so close to the United States could be solved.

The Cuban "problem" contains none of the security threats used by the U.S. military to explain why a hot spot exists, jeopardizes U.S. security, and deserves close attention. For example, Cuba is not involved in Caribbean drug trafficking or money laundering, or a major source of Caribbean migration to the United States. It is not beset with insurgencies, urban gangs, and ungoverned spaces, and after the 9/11 attacks it offered to assist the United States in its battles against terrorism. Cuba has never attacked the United States, either on the mainland or at Guantánamo Bay. The converse cannot be said for the United States. None of this matters when the United States declares it will not deal with the existing government. It is painfully obvious that the Bush administration's call for a democratic transition on the island has few listeners and even fewer interested in responding to what Washington means by "Cuba's transition to democracy."

At the root of this remarkable policy, which continues despite its clear failure to fulfill its objectives, is the sheer effrontery and humiliation of the challenge presented by Fidel Castro in his constant rhetorical assaults on the United States. The anti-U.S. venom spewing from Castro's mouth is full of defiance, arrogance, and accusations against Washington for more than 60 years of deeds and misdeeds in Cuba before 1959. Never in the history of U.S.-Latin American relations has a Latin American government mounted such a strident attack on the past policies and practices of the United States. Despite the accuracy of Fidel's language, Washington policymakers have described him as insane, psychotic, or mentally unbalanced. This was particularly true in the early years of the Revolution when hostile books were written by exiled Cubans and other enemies of the new regime in hopes of sparking a counter-revolution and ultimately the removal of Castro. President Eisenhower concluded Castro was a "madman"; to President Nixon he was "that bastard."[6] For almost 50 years, Fidel Castro has produced an attitude in the United States determined to punish him by making his governing life miserable. Much of what Washington has done to punish Castro—assassination attempts, economic siege, repeated violations of Cuban airspace—have failed, and some would clearly be called state-sponsored terrorism today. Fidel Castro has refused to submit to U.S. demands formulated as laws to wreak havoc in Cuba. As a result, internal security has become an absolute necessity for regime survival. In an assessment that is rarely mentioned in the mainstream media in the United States, historian Louis Pérez, Jr., argues, "It is the height of cynicism and hypocrisy for the United States to condemn Cuba for the absence of civil liberties and political freedoms, on the one hand, and on the other, to have pursued policies variously employing assassination, subversion, sabotage, and threatened invasions as a means to topple the government of Fidel Castro."[7]

As the United States prepares for a post-Castro Cuba, it would be wise to contemplate how Castro came to power and how Washington policymakers mishandled Cuba and in doing so helped Castro to survive for almost 50 years. With close to a million Cuban Americans in South Florida devoted to maintaining the Republican Party in a policy of confrontation rather than dialogue, Florida remains a key state for winning presidential elections for both political parties.

In analyzing the roots of counter-insurgencies, Ian F. W. Beckett finds that the urban insurgencies in the late 1960s and 1970s had much in common with international terrorism. What happened in Cuba to bring Fidel Castro to power had more to do with the failures of the Batista dictatorship and the withdrawal of U.S. aid in 1958 than the strategies and tactics of Castro's small number of guerrillas. As Beckett points out:

> It was a remarkable victory, but those who attempted to emulate Castro tended to ignore the special circumstances in which he had succeeded, not least Che Guevara and his collaborator, Régis Debray, who constructed *foco* in the belief that revolution on the Cuban model could be reproduced as a matter of course throughout Latin America, if not the third world as a whole.[8]

The United States has had trouble in the past understanding Latin American countries, leaders, and cultural values. This faulty understanding contributed to the use of misplaced analogies and flawed metaphors used to comprehend Latin American hot spots. For example, Washington policymakers frequently used false analogies to understand Fidel Castro's rhetoric and motivations and the problems of development in Latin America and the Caribbean. During the Cold War all revolutionary agitation and ferment was attributed to Soviet meddling or Cuban-inspired Marxist guerrillas; the recent global war on terrorism has used the same discourse, although this time the purported threats are viewed through the prism of a more generic form of violence, mostly centered on groups and organizations in the Middle East. The United States has not grasped the fact that for many Cubans the real appeal of the Cuban Revolution is its nationalistic orientation and that the more attempts are made to destroy it, the stronger and more legitimate it gets. As the present author has stated elsewhere, "Failing to recognize that the Cuban Revolution was a fundamentally nationalist movement, the Bay of Pigs invasion [1961] was a 'gift of the gods' for Castro in his effort to consolidate power and pursue his radical reforms."[9] The continuing hostilities with the United States have played into Castro's hands and helped keep him in power, an embattled nationalist leader of a small Caribbean island, standing firm against an aggressive world superpower. Castro has survived for 50 years because of other factors as well: strategic relationships with the Soviet Union and, more recently, with Venezuela's President Chávez and with the Chinese; the continuing growth of the tourist industry; billions of dollars of remittances that Cubans in the United States send to family in Cuba every year; the export of dissidents and counterrevolutionaries to the United States and elsewhere; and Castro's clever ploy of conflating the arguments of the dissidents with the machinations of a historically hostile superpower.[10]

DRUG TRAFFICKING AND TERRORISM

Drug trafficking—often connected with gangs and criminal organizations—is the major threat to the United States from the Caribbean, not terrorism or immigration. Since President Richard Nixon declared a war on drugs in 1971, the strategy of eradicating drugs has been flawed in its conception and execution, made worse by a refusal of each presidency to change course in the face of failure.[11] Instead of a strategy of preventative programs and rehabilitation of addicts in the United States, the United States strongly emphasizes Andean eradication programs, military bases, interdiction of traffic, and punishment of offenders. Without an emphasis on demand-side programs, the war on drugs is a failure with devastating results. According to Patterson, "Political corruption and payment in arms threatens the sovereignty and stability of many states" by increasing violence, criminality, and the chances of state failure.[12] The United States may be unwilling to recognize the true nature of the drug crisis at home and abroad, and how it threatens its security.

The Caribbean serves as a corridor for the transshipment of cocaine from the Andes region of South America. The drug-related money laundering in many Caribbean countries is facilitated by the many well-developed offshore banking systems and bank secrecy laws that dot the region. Although international law enforcement activity has increased since 2000 and has contributed to a decline in the documented flow of cocaine from South America, the flow of drugs continues. Most of the cocaine flow originates in Colombia and arrives in one of the Caribbean countries via go-fast boats or small aircraft. In 2001, illicit drug shipments in the Caribbean were the source of more money than the top five legitimate exports combined.

The Caribbean countries closest to the United States are the most active in the transshipment of illicit drugs. The Bahamas' location and its large territorial area almost guarantee that it will continue to be one of the preferred routes for drug transshipment and other criminal activity. The Caribbean is also an attractive transshipment corridor for illicit drugs because of government corruption and the large number of sport fishing vessels and pleasure craft in the area. According to the U.S. Department of State, "The Government of Cuba (GOC) intercepts and destroys drug contraband, but Cuba's geographical position and the GOC's refusal to implement an effective use-of-force policy encourages drug traffickers to risk transiting through the island's territorial water and airspace."[13] Cuba's effectiveness in drug prevention and interdiction stems "primarily from its tyrannical and coercive policing methods," according to the State Department report. The fact that Cuba is not a major drug-producing country and its level of internal consumption is considered low means that it not seen as a threat or hot spot because of drug trafficking; however, the U.S. government does not believe that the Cubans are serious about bilateral agreements to combat drug trafficking, terrorism, and the trafficking in migrants. There is little chance of a dialogue and agreements until the Cuban regime abandons its party and state institutions, Fidel Castro and his brother depart, and it puts an end to its role as a state sponsor of terrorism. Cuba is now importing Bolivian coca leaves for "legal consumption" on the island, the result of the People's Trade Agreement signed in Havana among Cuba, Bolivia, and Venezuela on April 29, 2006. There is no evidence that Cuba is attempting to process the raw coca leaves into cocaine or other illegal substances.

The Dominican Republic serves as a major drug transit country from South America for cocaine and heroin en route to Europe and the United States. Although there have been increased numbers of seizures and extraditions, and some progress in bank fraud linked to drug trafficking, the Dominican Republic is plagued by corruption and weak governmental institutions to deal with illegal narcotics and terrorism. Coca and opium poppy are not cultivated in the Dominican Republic, although marijuana is grown on a small scale for local consumption. Judicial reform and good governance would go a long way toward developing the infrastructure to handle narcotics trafficking organizations and other security threats, including arms trafficking and human smuggling.

The Dutch Caribbean and the Eastern Caribbean countries serve as transshipment points for cocaine, heroin, and marijuana coming from Colombia and Venezuela, but there is not a sufficient amount to have a major effect on the security of the United States. Nevertheless, there is a drug abuse problem in Aruba that is a cause of concern for those on the island and its reliance on tourism, particularly cruise ships that stop there. South American traffickers transport drugs mostly by sea using go-fast vessels, larger fishing boats, and freight carriers. Cocaine trafficked to Europe is transported primarily in commercial containerized cargo. According to the U.S. Department of State, "Drug trafficking and related crimes such as money laundering, drug use, arms trafficking, official corruption, violent crime, and intimidation have the potential to threaten the stability of the small, democratic countries of the Eastern Caribbean and, to varying degrees, have damaged civil society in some of these countries."[14] With the exception of Grenada, Haiti, Suriname, and Guyana, the Caribbean is a low-risk hot spot that Washington tends to ignore. Even Jamaica, the largest Caribbean producer and exporter of marijuana, is not considered a security threat to the United States. As a result, the U.S. government invests little in stopping the flow of drugs or in dealing with the core problems—lack of resources, limited law enforcement capabilities, drug-related corruption, and an inefficient bureaucracy—that create the political risks in the first place.

GOVERNANCE: POLITICAL INSTABILITY AND CORRUPTION

Official U.S. policy toward Latin America under the George W. Bush administration makes a point of stressing the importance of democracy, good governance, and anti-corruption policies. Yet, in its March 2006 National Security Strategy report, it refers to Cuba as one of the "regional challenges" that demand the world's attention: "In Cuba, an anti-American dictator continues to oppress his people and seeks to subvert freedom in the region." Despite the end of the Cold War, Cuba remains a pariah in Washington and shows no signs of being treated in a way that would respect Cuba's sovereignty and put an end to over 45 years of political and economic hostility. Preaching the importance of democracy and good governance is easy for Washington policymakers; however, creating a democratic culture is not easy and may well be an impossible challenge for Latin American elites. Certainly Washington displayed little interest in Cuban democracy during the sixty-year period that the Cuban government was a protectorate of the United States. Yet Washington continues to believe that "The most effective long-term measure for conflict resolution is the promotion of democracy." Current Cuban policy is based more on conflict promotion and regime change directed at Fidel Castro than a serious effort to convert Cuba from a regional "hot spot" to an island of stability and prosperity and democratic rule.

The World Bank believes that corruption is a major obstacle to economic and social development and has emphasized the connection between responsible leadership and economic progress. The Bush administration's policy of promoting prosperity is to encourage free trade and a more efficient foreign aid that will promote good governance and reduce poverty. In what is called the Millennium Challenge Account, Latin American countries "that govern justly and honestly, uphold the rule of law, fight corruption, invest in the health and education of their people, and promote economic freedom" will see increases in core development assistance from the United States.[15]

GUANTÁNAMO BAY: IS THE U.S. NAVAL BASE AT RISK?

Since the end of the Spanish-Cuban-American War, the United States has held an indefinite lease on Guantánamo Bay, a prime piece of coastal real estate in southeast Cuba. The existence of a U.S. military base within

Guantánamo Bay ("Gitmo"), Cuba, January 2002. U.S. Marine security teams in a rehearsal for incoming detainees at Camp X-Ray, one of the main holding facilities for Taliban and al Qaeda suspects placed there as "enemy combatants." (The Image Works)

Communist territory is one of the anomalous aspects of U.S.-Cuban relations under Fidel Castro. It is the oldest U.S. overseas military base and one of two old-style military bases in Latin America. The other is Soto Cano (better known during the Contra war as Palmerola), located in Honduras, where 600-plus members of Joint Task Force Bravo are located. Guantánamo houses about 3,000 troops, about half the total military presence in Latin America. It has a dual function: to interrogate suspected terrorists from around the world and as a detention center for would-be illegal immigrants from Latin America. No doubt it would be a key part of any future discussions over the normalization of relations between the United States and Cuba. Although the base has been a source of contention between the United States and Cuba, its occupation by U.S. military forces has not produced a major conflict between the two countries. After the selection of Guantánamo Bay as a site for Islamic militants captured in Afghanistan and elsewhere, the BBC emphasized the ongoing tensions at the naval base, calling Guantánamo "one of the world's most dangerous military flashpoints" where political strain and mutual suspicion are a way of life.[16] If Cuba is considered a hot spot by Washington policymakers, it is not because Guantánamo Bay is in danger of being eliminated from the hundreds of military bases that make up the U.S. empire; even with the current status it would hardly qualify as a "military flashpoint" or "Caribbean hot spot." The United States faces little prospect of being forced out of its military base at Guantánamo as long as there is no dialogue with the government in Havana.

After three Muslim captors committed suicide in June 2006, U.S. officials called the deaths at Guantánamo "asymmetric warfare" and nothing more than a publicity stunt. The state of desperation for most of the prisoners and the ignoring of basic human rights by Washington officials has undermined U.S. legitimacy and allied support in the war on terrorism.[17] After the Supreme Court rejected Bush administration policies that have imprisoned hundreds for years without trials, U.S. officials agreed to apply the Geneva Conventions to all terrorism suspects in U.S. custody. Nevertheless, the Bush administration, after reaching a compromise with Republican senators on detention and interrogation in September 2006, signaled that it will continue to use the CIA to secretly detain certain terrorist suspects and those being held at Guantánamo Bay, claiming that what the United States is doing there clearly conforms with international law. By letting President Bush issue his own interpretation of the Geneva Conventions in an executive order, senators have tried to walk a tightrope between allowing and preventing torture now at the center of the war on terrorism. In a critical editorial of the executive-legislative agreement, the *Washington Post* declared, "In effect, the agreement means that U.S. violations of international human rights law can continue as long as Mr. Bush is president, with Congress's tacit assent. If they do, America's standing in the world will continue to suffer, as will the fight against terrorism."[18]

Fidel Castro has always referred to the U.S. occupation of the western side of Guantánamo Bay as "illegal" and insists that the status of the base be part of an agenda devoted to the normalization of relations between the two countries. There have been very few flare ups over Guantánamo that would suggest a security-based hot spot, even with the controversy over the use of the naval base to detain over 600 suspected "enemy combatants" in the war on terrorism. Since 2001, Guantánamo Bay has served as a secret overseas facility for prisoners suspected of committing terrorist acts. The Defense Department chose the Cuban facility because it was remote and in a foreign country, where they hoped prisoners would be outside the reach of U.S. legal protections. The number of detainees—some as young as 12 years of age—has decreased since 2001, but there are constant calls in the media, and in Congress, to close the detention center for good.

Beginning in 2002, the Bush administration claimed the Geneva Conventions did not apply by law to terrorism suspects held at Guantánamo because the conventions were too vague and could expose the U.S. military to adverse treatment. In June 2006 the Supreme Court rejected the special military commissions established by the Bush administration to circumvent U.S. law and the Geneva Conventions. The court ruling represents a defeat for the Bush administration's efforts to define detainees at Guantánamo as terrorist threats regardless of international legal procedures. According to David Remes, a lawyer who represents detainees at Guantánamo Bay, "The legal architecture of the war on terror was built on a foundation of unlimited and unaccountable presidential power, including the power to decide unilaterally whether, when and to whom to apply the Geneva Conventions."[19]

Despite the Supreme Court ruling in 2006, Guantánamo Bay will continue as an overseas facility for prisoners suspected of committing terrorist acts. As long as the U.S. Naval Base is used as a detention camp, negotiating a new relationship with Cuba is likely to be far more difficult than when Guantánamo was being considered for base closing to save U.S. taxpayers money. Although there are planned changes in policy as a result of the Supreme Court decision, there is a resistance to the idea of bringing the prisoners into public scrutiny.

The furor over the rights of prisoners at the detention camps is not likely to make Guantánamo Bay a security-based hot spot; however, with over 8,000 U.S. servicemen and women and their dependents living on the island, and the lingering hostility between the U.S. government and the Castro regime, a clash between Cuban and American forces would constitute a major provocation for any U.S. president. Guantánamo Bay remains a strange remnant from the imperialist urge after the Cuban-Spanish-American War and the Cold War. It has symbolic value for the United States because it represents a thorn in the side of Castro and constitutes one of the last vestiges of U.S. military power in the Caribbean. In the meantime, the Guantánamo lease agreement remains in effect until both parties agree to modify it, and Washington enjoys one of its best real estate bargains for an overseas military base. Guantánamo Bay at the same time enables the Cubans to denounce the military base as a form of U.S. occupation and opposition to Cuba's nationalist revolution.

HAITI AS A FAILED STATE

Haiti shares the island of Hispaniola with the Dominican Republic and lies six hundred miles off the coast of Florida. More than 80 percent of Haiti's approximately 8.5 million people live below the poverty line, which means that it is the poorest country in the Western Hemisphere, with extremely high rates of illiteracy along with staggering health and environmental problems. Close to six percent of the population has HIV/AIDS, and Haitian life expectancy is 52 years. In its Country Profile of Haiti, BBC News gives a snapshot of the country's troubled political, economic, and social life: "The world's first black-led republic and the first Caribbean state to achieve independence, Haiti's pride has been dented by decades of poverty, environmental degradation, violence, instability and dictatorship which have left it as the poorest nation in the Americas."[20] After René Préval, a 63-year-old agronomist who had served as president from 1996 to 2000, won the February 2006 elections, an unexpected peace has descended on Haiti, despite a limited mandate of the UN's multinational peacekeeping mission and a perception that the UN mission has been a gross failure because it has taken sides with the government and refused to give any legitimacy to the backers of former President Jean-Bertrand Aristide. Many in Haiti give more credit to the poor, who voted in large numbers for Préval to make sure that a second round of voting would be averted, potentially sparing the country from renewed violence and political strife.[21]

Haiti is a troubled country that is close to ungovernable, plagued by serious economic, social, political, environmental and health problems, and closely watched by various international actors: bilateral donors (France, Canada, and the United States) and international organizations (United Nations, Organization of American States, and Caricom), and Latin American drug cartels. The United States is most concerned with drug cartels, corruption, and the role of exiled President Aristide in

Haiti's political affairs. The current conflict centers on the supporters of former President Aristide against the wealthy business community, now-alienated former supporters of Aristide, and former elements of Haiti's now-disbanded military. Despite having representation in government and through a variety of civil society organizations, low-intensity conflict between pro- and anti-Aristide factions continues while the Haitian National Police (PNH) and the UN Stabilization Mission in Haiti (MINUSTAH) struggle to secure the country. There have been international efforts to convert the PNH into an effective, impartial, and professional law enforcement body, but it is still considered a highly politicized and corrupt organization. In a study published in the British medical journal *The Lancet* in August 2006, Haiti has experienced a pattern of widespread human rights abuses by an assortment of political actors since the overthrow of President Aristide in February 2004. The level of political violence revealed in the study found that an estimated 8,000 people were murdered during this period, nearly half by governmental or anti-Lavalas (anti-Aristide) forces. The study also found an extremely high level of sexual violence committed since the coup against Aristide. Until this failure in state power is changed, Haiti will remain a weak and failing state in the Caribbean and of considerable concern to the United States, Canada, and the rest of Latin America. This sad political situation in Haiti is compounded by the fact that Canadian, French, and U.S. government officials participated in the campaign to overthrow the elected government and install Prime Minister Gerard Latortue as part of the interim government.

Democracy building is mentioned frequently in Washington, but despite aid for electoral assistance and civilian police training, Haiti is far from a stable, democratic state. The State Department believes that Haiti would be better off without Aristide and stands accused of facilitating his removal from power in February 2004. Haiti's new president, René Préval, has indicated he may allow Aristide to return to Haiti from his exile in South Africa, but this would jeopardize economic assistance from the United States and could undermine the fragile political situation in Haiti. Préval's win is discomforting for Washington because it continues a trend in Latin America where voters have consistently opted for leftist candidates opposed to U.S. policies. Nevertheless, the Bush administration has promised to work with the incoming government regardless of its political ideology, although it is often considered the final arbiter of Haiti's domestic situation.[22] Préval claims his top priority in office will be to provide relief to the two-thirds of the population living in extreme poverty; he also wants to recruit Haitian professionals from abroad to help rebuild the government, attract more investment from the United States, and reconcile differences that exist between his lower-class supporters and opponents from the middle and upper classes. He claims that people appreciate him and his style of leadership because he is honest, eschews violence, respects freedom, and is not corrupt.[23]

Haiti ranks first among the ten Latin American countries on the 2005 Failed State Index. The two most important indicators of a failed state—uneven development and criminalization of the state—are particularly pronounced in Haiti as its governmental authority and effectiveness continues to erode. As a result, Haiti has come under the domination of local gangs, private militias, and international drug cartels. The perennial instability of the country ensures a high degree of lawlessness, poor law enforcement, and chronic civil unrest that is unlikely to improve without significant and prolonged international involvement in the country. Even with economic assistance from the United States and other foreign donors, Haiti's prospects are grim. Haiti is currently rated among the most corrupt countries in the world and first in Latin America; corruption contaminates all levels of government, and a large majority of Haitians believe corruption to have increased in the last few years. In Transparency International's 2004 corruption index, Haiti ranked dead last: 145th out of a total of 145 countries in the world. The problem of corruption is so endemic that it affects all public institutions. It is interesting that Haitians perceive the office of the president as being the least corrupt among all institutions studied. There is very little democratic culture in Haiti, even though it manages to go through the ritual of periodic elections; the last for president in February 2006 was postponed four times. Haiti is clearly the least democratic country in Latin America as measured by the World Democracy Audit, and Haiti ranks last among the Latin American countries in the Human Development Index for 2003.

Inside the Bush administration, Secretary of State Colin Powell played a role in bringing an end to President Aristide's constitutional rule in February 2004.[24] Powell's role in the Haitian affair emerged from, first, his willingness to rely on the right-wing ideologues led by Assistant Secretary of State Roger Noriega and former White House aide Otto Reich, both hardliners who view Latin America almost exclusively through the prism of anti-Castroism. Second, Powell's relatively few speeches on Latin America emphasized trade, market reforms, and a simplified view of democracy promotion. Third, Powell displayed little interest in the expansion of poverty and the increasing concentration of wealth, but reserved his indignation for left-of-center regimes that opposed U.S. foreign policy. Angry at the region's reaction to the Iraq war, Powell tried without success to dragoon a few Latin American governments into joining the "Coalition of the Willing." Powell's successor, Secretary of State Condoleezza Rice, continued the policy of neglect fostered by Powell combined with the lack of any real understanding of the political trends in Latin America. Like Powell and those in charge of Latin American policy, Rice attacked Cuba and Venezuela as troublesome threats to U.S. security and displayed little tolerance for the new generation of populist leaders in Argentina, Bolivia, Brazil, and Uruguay.

The U.S. media's role in demonizing Aristide served to back the views of the Republican right wing in the United States and Haiti's conservative elite. While the mainstream media portrayed Aristide as a psychopathic mass murderer who resigned and left Haiti willingly for a destination of his own choosing, independent media outlets reported, on the basis of first-hand observation, that Aristide was kidnapped through a well-orchestrated coup d'état. According to Goodman and Goodman, "The story that most American media overlooked was how the United States has had a nearly unbroken record of sabotaging Haitian democracy. From backing Haitian death squads that overthrew Aristide in the 1990s, to blocking lifesaving development aid when Aristide was reelected in 2001, the United States has been obsessed with keeping Haiti in virtual serfdom."[25] Since the removal of Aristide in 2004, Haiti still suffers from the lack of democracy, poverty, and political instability. Poverty drives a great deal of the frustration: 55% of Haitians live on less than one dollar per day. Kidnappings have reached 14 per day, and street gangs (flush with weapons) proliferate.[26]

U.S.–Caribbean Community (Caricom) relations have been strained since 2004, largely because of opposition to the Iraq War and the role of the United States in the removal of President Aristide. The United States wants the Caribbean Community to soften its position on the Iraq war and to recognize the new government in Haiti in hopes of preventing it from falling into chaos again. Apparently, United Nations peacekeepers are not the solution to Haiti's political ills; the mission, led by soldiers, police officers, and civilian experts, was sent to Haiti in June 2004 to restore order and help with new elections after a violent uprising and the U.S.-backed coup that forced President Aristide from power. Haiti has managed to pull off a vote that brought Préval back to the presidency. No matter who is president of Haiti, the task of bringing together the political splits that haunt Haiti is daunting, if not impossible.

CHAPTER 6

Non-Iberian South America: Guyana and Suriname

Non-Iberian South America consists of two independent states (Guyana and Suriname) and one French colony, Guyane. Guyana (British Guiana until independence in 1966) is the third smallest country on the mainland of South America and the only South American country whose official language is English. Guyana has cultural similarities to parts of the West Indies; it is an ethnically diverse society with a population made up primarily of East Indian (Asian Indian), African, and Amerindian groups with East Indians and Afro-Guyanese in the majority. Colonized by the Dutch and British, it has a history marked by economic dependency, racial and radical politics, and considerable instability. More than a third of Guyanese are descendants of African slaves brought to pick sugar cane and cotton, and nearly half of those of Indian descent were imported as contract laborers in the nineteenth century.

After World War II Guyana became embroiled in the intense ideological aspects of the Cold War, setting off alarm bells in Washington over who would control Guyana's new government. Because of perceived ideological and security threats posed by its two dominant leaders, Cheddi Jagan and Forbes Burnham, the Central Intelligence Agency (CIA) became covertly involved to prevent a Communist or Castro-type regime in South America. Although Presidents Eisenhower, Kennedy, and Johnson considered Guyana a security-based hot spot based on Cheddi Jagan's leftist connections, Washington never intervened militarily or invoked the Monroe Doctrine to rid Guyana of socialism or chronic misrule and corruption.

Guyana has border disputes with both Suriname and Venezuela, although the multiple claims on the land have not resulted in open warfare. Guyana is plagued with corruption and electoral violence, often the result of ethnic and class differences. One of the poorest countries in the Western Hemisphere, Guyana—site of the notorious Jonestown massacre in 1978—suffers from extremely high rates of murder and other crimes. Sugar, gold, and bauxite dominate the economy, in which many industries have large foreign investments. Because of poor health care, many Guyanese seek medical treatment in the United Kingdom, the United States, or Cuba. Moreover, the flight of managerial, technical, and professional talent to the United States and Europe does not bode well for the future of Guyana.

Suriname is located between French Guiana (Guyane) and Guyana and shares a border with Brazil. Suriname is the smallest sovereign state in South America as measured by area and population. Formerly a Dutch colony, Suriname did not become independent until 1975. Suriname continues to suffer from poverty, military coups, and erratic economic growth, particularly in the dominant bauxite industry. There are a great number of ethnic groups in Suriname that in turn makes it difficult to govern effectively. Although Suriname and Guyana are often in a state of heightened political tension, they are not considered hot spots in terms of security for the United States, Brazil, Venezuela, or the United Kingdom. In 1992, President Jimmy Carter, along with 100 international election observers, traveled to oversee what were judged Guyana's first free and fair elections in its history.

In this chapter three potential hot spots in non-Iberian South America will be briefly examined: border disputes, political instability and corruption, and Caribbean–South American terrorism.

BORDER CONFLICTS

Guyana is currently in border disputes with both Suriname and Venezuela because of conflicting claims over land east of the Corentyne River (Suriname) and land west of the Essequibo River (Venezuela). Although negotiations concerning the disputed geographical areas have failed and most maps still display the borders incorrectly, the border conflicts have not sparked either a foreign invasion or economic sanctions. Today, the discovery of vast offshore oil reserves in the contested territorial waters may push the centuries-old conflict to the point of open warfare if the border issue is not resolved. The social and economic problems of the two nations are being exacerbated by the risks and promises of oil wealth and corporate rivalry over concessions to drill for oil in coastal areas with conflicting claims of jurisdiction. Peaceful options may be running out as each side charges that it is the other country that is frustrating the bilateral negotiations. Guyana, the poorer of the two countries and the one with the fewest options, has accused Suriname of violating international law of the sea and demanded it stop developing the disputed sea area. The danger, or threat, now is that the dispute has increased tensions down to the community level, where increasingly Guyanese and Surinamese are seeing the other as enemy, competitor, or scapegoat. The border conundrum lingers without a diplomatic solution while the international oil companies jockey for control of these valuable resources.[1] A project where joint development and profit prevails seems unlikely given the history of the dispute among the three parties. Over the past ten years the border dispute has been complicated by drug trafficking, oil discoveries, Hugo Chávez's South American foreign policy, military expansion, and the lack of political will for a peaceful settlement.

GOVERNANCE: POLITICAL INSTABILITY AND CORRUPTION

Race and political ideology have been the dominant characteristics of Guyanese politics. Today, politics is based more on ethnicity than political ideology or religion. Two political parties have dominated the political scene since independence: People's Progressive Party (PPP) and the People's National Congress (PNC). Historically, the PPP has represented Guyanese of East Indian extraction, mostly rice farmers and sugar workers in the rural areas. The PNC draws its support mainly from urban blacks, and for many years its purpose was to make Guyana a non-aligned socialist state. Past efforts by governments to build a socialist state caused a massive emigration of skilled workers that led to a significant decline in the overall quality of life. Although Guyana maintains a commitment to democracy and has moderated its political economy to reflect free markets and foreign investment, its government is faced with public demonstrations and violence, major crime problems, high unemployment and indebtedness, and rampant corruption. With a per capita gross domestic product of $950, Guyana is one of the poorest countries in the hemisphere; however, with increased foreign investment in the export sector (mainly sugar, bauxite, gold, and rice), Guyana has made some progress in improving economic and social conditions. The United States and Guyana have maintained positive relations since the 1992 elections as Guyana has pursued policies of support for economic growth, sustainable democratic institutions, and the promotion of stability and security. In January 2003, President George W. Bush named Guyana as one of only two countries in the Western Hemisphere to be included in his Emergency Plan for AIDS Relief, a five-year multimillion-dollar program of education, treatment, and prevention of the disease. The U.S. military operates small medical and engineering teams that conduct training exercises and a mixture of nation-building activities.

Suriname faces some of the same political problems as Guyana with military coups, fraudulent elections, and a weak economy. In the fall of 2006, Suriname's army was sent to Nickerie in anticipation of the possible illegal immigration of Guyanese trying to escape potential violence during Guyana's August 2006 election. The election turned out to be peaceful, and the anticipated immigration crisis never materialized. With the ability of some Guyanese to emigrate to the United States or the United Kingdom, Guyana's political system currently has a safety valve that moderates security-based hot spots.

CARIBBEAN-SOUTH AMERICAN TERRORISM

After four suspects from Guyana and Trinidad and Tobago were named in a June 2007 plot to blow up Kennedy Airport in New York City, U.S. authorities worried about the possibility that radical Muslim groups could transform the Caribbean into a terrorist breeding ground. The concerns center on increasing economic and political ties between Iran, Venezuela, Guyana, and Trinidad; the growing influence of Trinidad's radical Islamic organization Jamaat al-Muslimeen, a group heavily involved in drug trafficking and money laundering; and Iranian and Venezuelan involvement in the growing Muslim community. Iranian influence, although small, is growing in Guyana, where 10 to 15 percent of the population is Muslim. According to *Newsday*, "The Caribbean also has been visited by suspected al-Qaida member Adnan Gulshair Muhammed el Shukrijumah, who has lived mostly in Saudi Arabia and Florida but is part Guyanese and carried a Guyana passport."[2] Those who have studied Jamaat al-Muslimeen say it is more of a local criminal gang than a serious global terrorist group with links to al-Qaeda and is clearly not representative of the Trinidadian Muslim community. Most of the 1,000 members of Jamaat al-Muslimeen are Trinidadians of African descent who converted to Islam in the 1980s after the rise of the Nation of Islam in the United States. Despite the racial divide found in political parties and the religious community—with most of the country's churches, mosques, and temples either black or Indian—Jamaat claims that its primary focus is domestic, assisting the poor and protecting the faithful from the excesses of the annual Carnival celebration.[3] Abdel Nur, who surrendered to authorities in Trinidad because of his alleged involvement in the JFK plot, was known to have close ties with Jamaat al-Muslimeen leader Yasin Abu Bakr, best known for his involvement in a failed bloody coup in Trinidad in 1990. Nevertheless, after Abdel Nur turned himself in to authorities in Trinidad shortly after the plot was discovered, the leader of Jamaat al-Muslimeen told the press that his group had no connection to the JFK plot, but he would not say whether he knew any of the suspects. FBI and police investigators called the failed plan a "terrorist plot" with the potential damage far exceeding the devastation from the September 11, 2001, attacks on New York and Washington, D.C. U.S. military intelligence has identified Islamic radicals in several South American cities, indicating that a possible threat exists, albeit at a low security threat level. According to a U.S. military intelligence official, "there are Islamic radical groups throughout Latin America and the Caribbean and not just in the tri-border area."[4] Others disagree with this assessment of the Caribbean terrorist threat, arguing that the threat level is low and the linkages between the so-called radicals is nonexistent or tenuous at best.

Despite these developments, counter-terrorism officials in the United States are not ready to declare a serious threat to the homeland as a result of the way the plot at JFK was planned. Furthermore, the Caribbean region is not known for serious religious and racial tensions; Guyanese Muslims have resoundingly condemned the JFK plot despite many who deeply resent the U.S. treatment of Muslims, whether in Guantánamo Bay (Cuba), Gaza, or Iraq. Many Guyanese also blame the United States for the drug trafficking, violent crime, and poverty because of U.S. demand for illicit drugs. Russell Defreitas, one of the three Guyanese arrested in the JFK plot, was known for his hatred of the United States for its support of Israel, the ongoing war in Iraq, and the overall plight of Muslims worldwide. Although Defreitas's plans may not have been as catastrophic as he envisioned, he had the determination to seek foreign terrorist assistance to carry out his attack on the United States.[5] The success in thwarting the Kennedy Airport attack plot may lead to further efforts to investigate hot spots within areas of South America and the Eastern Caribbean not previously afforded serious scrutiny by counter-terrorism investigations focused on the Tri-Border Area to the south (see Chapter 4). The Guyana connection may increase the importance of Islamist terrorist operations in northern South America, particularly if a connection can be established to Venezuelan President Chávez, a lightning rod for those in search of security-based hot spots, regardless of whether there is an actual connection or not. Nevertheless, U.S. concerns continue to grow as Latin America witnesses an expanding Iranian presence in the region and parts of South America become transit points for terrorists moving in and out of the area.[6]

Among the Guyanese in New York, the JFK plot is nothing more than a peculiar aberration and an embarrassment for the immigrants who do not care about the Middle East and are unlikely to be involved in religious-based terrorism. Instead of being alarmed of a growing Caribbean terrorist network, Guyanese immigrants worry about a backlash aimed at both Indo-Guyanese and Afro-Guyanese who fled violence and political turmoil at home, lured to the United States by calmness and economic opportunity. According to the *New York Times*, "In 2005, 143,476 Guyanese lived in New York City, 73,316 of them black and 31,342 of them of Indian descent."[7] Most Guyanese are content with life in the United States, with newer arrivals rarely speaking favorably of the country they left behind, in large part because of crime, violence, racism, and unemployment. Many Guyanese think the JFK plot was foolish and silly; according to one female immigrant living in New York, "This is like the Three Stooges. . . Everybody is laughing" when they hear about the plotters.[8]

The link between Guyana and Trinidad and Tobago in the JFK Airport plot may indeed be an aberration; however, the Iranian-backed Hezbollah has taken root in South America, where it finances a training campus, propaganda operations, and bomb attacks by Islamic radicals who hate the United States for its policies in the Middle East, including support for Israel, Saudi Arabia, the underreported death and destruction in Iraq, and continual threats to attack Iran. If current security trends continue, South America may become a source of a growing number of security-based hot spots with clear roots in the aftermath of the global war on terrorism that is central to the Bush doctrine and American foreign policy.

CHAPTER 7

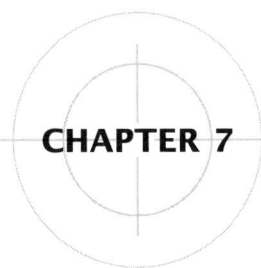

Conclusion

The 2007 Failed States Index published by *Foreign Policy* magazine and the Carnegie Endowment for International Peace finds most of the Western Hemisphere relatively free of conditions that produce failed states. Only Haiti and Colombia rank high on the Failed State Index, while the rest of Latin America ranks much lower. When U.S. foreign policy experts—government, military, and intelligence—were asked to name a single country that has produced the largest number of global terrorists, the most selected countries were located in the Middle East, Africa, and South Asia, with Saudi Arabia, Egypt, and Pakistan named as responsible for producing over 85 percent of the world's terrorists.[1] These perceptions point to one of the strange paradoxes in the global war on terrorism: the top three producers of terrorists are some of America's key allies in the Muslim world and have cooperated with the United States in fighting drug trafficking, money laundering, and terrorism. Latin America is not among the top ranks of failed states and is not considered an incubator of terrorist groups with a global reach to threaten the security of the United States. Only Colombia, the third largest recipient of U.S. military and economic assistance, is considered a major threat to the United States because of insurgencies, narco-terrorism, and the failure of civilian governments to put an end to these activities. After spending over $5 billion on military and economic assistance to Colombia, House Democrats want to shift a majority of the funding toward economic and humanitarian aid. However, Plan Colombia is a failure and will not succeed without a negotiated settlement of some kind.

Nevertheless, when those in Washington scan the globe for hot spots with the capacity to threaten the security of the United States, Latin America is often on the hot spot radar screen. For example, although

Cuba and Venezuela rank low on the Failed State Index and are not considered terrorist threats, those in the U.S. intelligence community often inflate the risk of threats from these countries because they do not accept the legitimacy of the regimes in power. Each of the democratic elections that has brought to power leaders who oppose American foreign policy and the prescriptions of international lending agencies has been defined as a security threat to the United States. It is unfortunate that members of both political parties in the U.S. Congress often overreact and perceive populist and left-wing governments in Latin America as threatening to U.S. interests. U.S. policymakers—both in the executive and legislative branches of government—need to be reminded of the diverse nature of these governments and to respect the decisions of Latin American electorates in fair elections.

Part of the problem in the use of hot spot terminology stems from the lack of understanding of Latin America's style of democratic rule combined with the inability to understand Latin America's chronic problems of development. Latin America's view of democratic rule is that for it to function properly it requires a strong president, a political philosophy that stretches back to the nineteenth century. In his study of *Dilemmas of Democracy in Latin America*, Howard J. Wiarda points out that President Hugo Chávez, one of the Pentagon's major security threats in South America, "may not be our kind of democrat, but he is very much a Venezuelan and Latin American one."[2] As a "Bolivarian democrat," Chávez is no more a threat to the United States than other Latin American leaders such as Daniel Ortega, Rafael Correa, Evo Morales, Felipe Calderón, and Álvaro Uribe. In order to deal with Latin America in a fair and respectful way, Washington needs to understand the reality of Latin American democracy by reassessing their concept of democracy, how best to promote it, and the true level of threats from democracies that produce strong leaders who seek to extend their rule beyond the limits imposed by constitutions, elections, and the media.

One of the key findings in this study is that hot spot metaphors for threats from Latin America are often misused in responding to security concerns. For example, using terror as a metaphor in political discourse serves the primary purpose of creating confusion and this in turn leads individuals to seek order, stability, and predictability. If people do not find this, then they start to believe in the "ghosts of threats or ghosts of solutions."[3] The use of security threats for political gain also exists in Latin America. President Chávez canceled a planned trip to New York in 2003 on the grounds of security threats, including reports that former Venezuelan military personnel were training in Florida for a future invasion of Venezuela. In the aftermath of September 11, 2001, *U.S. News and World Report* claimed in an alarming report—"Terrorism

Close to Home"—that Venezuela was becoming a hub of terrorism in the Americas by providing assistance to Islamic fundamentalists. The Venezuelan government denies the allegations made in the report, and its ambassador has provided counter-information to refute the charges that Venezuela is a terrorist threat to the United States.

Another problem with the concept of security-based hot spots is the tendency to emphasize security as a solution to a particular conflict. In most cases there is no military solution to dealing with hot spots, whether in Latin America or other parts of the globe. Peace will take more than just efforts to eliminate trouble spots through the use of U.S. military personnel, private military contractors, and large amounts of military aid from the United States. In his 2005 testimony before the Subcommittee on the Western Hemisphere dealing with hot spots in Latin America, Marc Chernick highlights the flaws in ways the United States and Colombia have treated the civil strife in Colombia:

> To conclude, the war in Colombia has endured, in one form or another, for 58 years. The war antedates the drug boom. It is not simply a terrorist or narco-terrorist conflict. The situation can be characterized as an escalating military stalemate—both sides have escalated their capacities and neither side is likely to defeat the other. Under these conditions, I am convinced that there is no military solution to the conflict. This does not mean the Colombian government does not have the legitimate right to defend itself. Yet peace will take more than battling the FARC or pushing coca cultivation into different corners of the country. It will ultimately require a negotiated settlement and the construction [of] a legitimate state presence that provides services, administers justice, promotes economic development and provides security. Current policy prioritizes security. It is a necessary but insufficient formula. Progress in confronting political violence, terrorism, and drug trafficking will only be made when the broader concerns are addressed and the illegal armed actors are re-incorporated into the political system after more than a half century.

If Chernick is correct in his assessment, and I believe he is, it means that current approaches to many of Latin America's hot spots need to change if threats emanating from current conflicts are going to be either reduced or eliminated. The problem of how best to respond to Latin American hot spots is not only illustrated by what the United States is doing (or not doing) in Colombia. Those in the Pentagon involved in dealing with global hot spots seem to be convinced that insurgencies run out of steam and disappear after ten years or so and the best thing the United States can do is to improve its counterinsurgence/terrorism doctrine, establish enough military bases or forward operations locations in the theater of conflict, and then run out the clock without having to negotiate a peaceful settlement or assist in the creation of a legitimate state apparatus with respect for government institutions before they completely fail. Security alone is not a winning strategy, no matter how many U.S. forces and dollars are injected into the particular conflict.

The U.S. military is in the process of "rethinking" the connection between insurgencies, security threats, and security-based hot spots. In "Rethinking Insurgency," Steven Metz, a civilian analyst at the Army War College, argues in a recent paper that since 9/11 the U.S. military has revived the idea that insurgency is a significant threat to the United States, but has failed to correct the mindset that still views contemporary insurgencies as closely related to past insurgencies rather than the more complex conflicts that characterize the post–Cold War era. "At the strategic level," according to Metz, "the risk to the United States is not that insurgents will 'win' in the traditional sense, take over the country, and shift it from a partner to an enemy. It is that complex internal conflicts, especially one involving insurgency, will generate other adverse affects: the destabilization of regions, resource flows and markets; the blossoming of transnational crime; humanitarian disasters; transnational terrorism; and so forth. Protracted conflict, not insurgent victory, is the threat."[4] Either way, protracted conflict or insurgent victory, the United States faces a range of security-based hot spots in Latin America. However, most of these have more to do with poor governance—corruption, bureaucratic inefficiencies, poor leadership, and perverted social priorities—than with the few conflicts on the Pentagon "watch list" with the capacity to slide or revert to war.

Unfortunately, Washington policymaking is often counterproductive in dealing with the threats from hot spots and keeping democracy on track to achieve some measure of stability that will not threaten U.S. hegemony in the region. Some journals point out that the U.S. strategic approach is characterized by a "Tri-Border Syndrome," in which a threat is manufactured when there is no evidence that one exists.[5] For example, the three Tri-Border Area (TBA) countries say that they have never detected terrorist activity or cells in the region. Although it is possible that terrorist groups once in the TBA have moved to less scrutinized locations in Latin America in an effort to continue their activities without detection, many Latin American governments—preoccupied with such pressing social issues as poverty, gangs, crime, and unemployment—do not consider the global war on terror their war, and therefore they want to avoid what they consider a politically unpopular cause. For example, only the small, poor, and dependent countries in Latin America—the Dominican Republic, El Salvador, Honduras, and Nicaragua—provided troops for Operation Iraqi Freedom's international stabilization force, and by 2006 most of these small contingent of troops had left the chaos connected with the U.S. occupation of Iraq. The United States insists that the Latin American governments must use their military and intelligence-gathering agencies to stop terrorism; however, most countries in the region do not have the means to control their borders, deny terrorists safe haven in ungoverned territories, eliminate money laundering, or restrict the abilities of potential terrorists and guerrilla insurgencies.

With large numbers of economically marginalized and disenfranchised groups—Muslim and non-Muslim—for terrorists to exploit, the potential for terrorism in the TBA and elsewhere clearly exists. There are target-rich environments for financial support, safe haven, and recruitment of terrorists in Latin America, primarily in the Amazon regions of Suriname, Guyana, Venezuela, Colombia, Ecuador, Peru, Bolivia, and Brazil and the free trade zones of Iquique, Chile; Maicao, Colombia; and Colón, Panama. In the Andes Colombia, Bolivia, and Peru offer cocaine as a lucrative source of income for guerrillas. The fact that Cuba and Venezuela have cooperative agreements of various sorts with Syria, Libya, and Iran make these two countries suspect in the eyes of those who search the world for security-based hot spots.

There is no doubt that Latin America has some of the characteristics that serve as a breeding ground for terrorist groups; however, the only way to put a halt to this is for countries to make changes in their judicial systems, improve their law enforcement and military capabilities, reduce corruption, and learn to cooperate in ways that promote peace and stability. Until this happens, current policies that emphasize security alone will fail and hot spots will continue to flourish in the Americas.

The Latin American policy of the United States has contributed to the worsening image of the United States in Latin America, particularly in the way hot spots are handled in the Americas. The abuses committed in the name of the war on terror; the real and symbolic damage from the detention of "enemy combatants" without access to justice at Guantánamo Bay, Cuba; U.S. reliance on military power above diplomacy; and the lack of emphasis on generous, poverty-alleviating aid and fair trade have done little to eliminate hot spots or remove security threats as perceived by the United States. There is much to be done to improve the image of the United States in Latin America, but it will take a more determined effort by internationally minded lawmakers who are willing to stand up for different strategies in dealing with Latin American hot spots, from changing U.S. policy toward Cuba, immigration reform and border security, incorporating labor and environmental concerns to reshape trade policy, and greater respect for the sovereignty of the Latin American governments themselves.

Notes

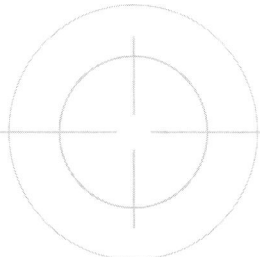

Introduction

1. General Hill's remarks are quoted in Tom Barry, "Mission Creep in Latin America—U.S. Southern Command's New Security Strategy" (Silver City, NM: International Relations Center, July 11, 2005: 10).

2. David W. Dent, *Historical Dictionary of U.S.-Latin American Relations* (Westport, CT: Greenwood Press, 2005: 372).

3. Edward S. Herman, "Threat Inflation: Going after Hapless Countries," *Z Magazine* (March 2003: 1).

4. For example, Chalmers Johnson, author of *Blowback* (New York: Henry Holt, 2004), argues that few people in the United States made the connection between the clandestine arming of the mujahadeen by the Reagan administration to drive the Soviets out of Afghanistan and the 9/11 terrorist attacks that hit New York and Washington, D.C.

5. See, for example, John Bailey and Lucía Dammert, eds. *Public Security and Police Reform in the Americas* (Pittsburgh, PA: University of Pittsburgh Press, 2006).

6. One of the common forms of military response to hot spots in Latin America is gunboat diplomacy. By dispatching naval gunboats to hostile ports or coastlines, Washington hopes to quell threats to U.S. strategic or economic interests. According to Dent, "The display of force and military resolve was designed to bolster pro-U.S. governments, coerce obedience among warring factions, and help restore order." See David W. Dent, *Historical Dictionary of U.S.-Latin American Relations* (Westport, CT: Greenwood Press, 2005: 212–213).

7. Daphne Eviatar, "Latin Left Turn," *The Nation* (December 25, 2006: 5–6).

8. Glenn Kessler and Bradley Graham, "Diplomats Will Be Shifted to Hot Spots," *Washington Post* (January 19, 2006).

9. Andrew Higgins, "Anti-Americans on the March," *Wall Street Journal* (December 9–10, 2006).

10. Vice President Cheney's interview preceded the change in intelligence gathering and communication recommended by the 9/11 Commission.

11. Elisabeth Bumiller, "'Cheney in the Morning,' Or Something Like That," *New York Times* (January 24, 2005).

12. In February 2001 the Bush administration created the National Security Presidential Directives (NSPD) to replace the Presidential Decision Directives that had been used by previous administrations, and it created the first of a new series of Homeland Security Presidential Directives (HSPDs) governing homeland security policy. See Federation of American Scientists, "National Security Presidential Directives [NSPD], George W. Bush Administration" (http://www.fas.org/irp/offdocs/nspd/).

13. Scott Shane, "In New Job, Spymaster Draws Bipartisan Criticism," *New York Times* (April 20, 2006: A1).

14. Daniel Smith, "World at War," Special Issue of the *The Defense Monitor*, Vol. 35, No. 3 (May/June 2006).

15. John Mueller, *Overblown: How Politicians and the Terrorism Industry Inflate National Security Threats, and Why We Believe Them* (New York: Free Press, 2007). For another critique of threat inflation, see Edward S. Herman, "Threat Inflation: Going After Hapless Countries," *Z Magazine* (March 2003).

16. Eldon Kenworthy, *America/Américas: Myth in the Making of U.S. Policy Toward Latin America* (University Park, PA: Pennsylvania State University Press, 1995: 121).

17. After Congress ordered a halt to the Contra rebels operating on behalf of the Reagan administration in 1984, Robert Gates, then second in command at the Central Intelligence Agency, worried—in a memo to CIA Director William Casey—that Nicaragua's close alliance with the Soviet Union and Cuba made it "unacceptable to the United States and that the United States will do everything in its power short of invasion to put that regime out." Gates's recommendations—air strikes, withdrawal of U.S. recognition of Nicaragua, economic sanctions, and recognition of a Nicaraguan government in exile—were never adopted, but the desire for regime change continued and eventually led to the Iran-Contra affair. See George Gedda, "Memo: Gates Pushed Nicaragua Airstrikes in '84,'" *Arizona Republic* (November 25, 2006).

18. See Testimony of William LeoGrande before the House Armed Services Committee, 109th Congress, 1st Session, September 21, 2005. The reconceptualization of security is also discussed in Paul W. Drake and Eric Hershberg, eds., *State and Society in Conflict: Comparative Perspectives on Andean Crises* (Pittsburgh, PA: University of Pittsburgh Press, 2006: 76–78).

19. Chris Hawley, "China Hurting Mexico," *Arizona Republic* (September 28, 2005).

20. Media Matters for America, "Robertson Called for Assassination of Venezuela's President" (August 22, 2005).

21. David W. Dent, *Historical Dictionary of U.S.-Latin American Relations* (Westport, CT: Greenwood Press, 2005: 160).

22. Murray Edelman, *The Symbolic Uses of Politics* (Urbana: University of Illinois Press, 1964; 1972: 70).

23. For example, in the wake of the foiled airline plot in Britain in August 2006, President Bush claimed that "the country is safer than it was before 9/11" and that his administration has "taken a lot of measures to protect the American people. But obviously, we're not completely safe, because there are people that still plot and people who want to harm us for what we believe in." See Sheryl Gay Stolberg, "Bush, on a Quick Trip from His Texas Ranch, Says Americans Are Safer Than Before Sept. 11," *New York Times* (August 11, 2006). To heighten the sense of fear over this issue the president portrayed the threat as originating with "Islamic fascists."

24. Editorial, "Wanted: Scarier Intelligence," *New York Times* (August 25, 2006). In a congressional report issued in August 2006, top Republican lawmakers accused U.S. intelligence agencies of producing intelligence that lacked what they considered to be needed ominous warnings about the threats that Iran presents to the United States. Republicans angry about the mild security assessments wanted scarier reports in order to confront Iran directly over its nuclear program and ties to terrorism. See Mark Mazzetti, "Some in G.O.P. Say Iran Threat Is Played Down," *New York Times* (August 24, 2006).

25. Steven Holmes, *The Matador's Cape: America's Reckless Response to Terror* (Cambridge, UK: University of Cambridge Press, 2007).

26. See for example, Lars Schoultz, *Beneath the United States: A History of U.S. Policy Toward Latin America* (Cambridge, MA: Harvard University Press, 1998) and David W. Dent, *Historical Dictionary of U.S.-Latin American Relations* (Westport, CT: Greenwood Press, 2005).

27. Latin American Newsletters, Latin American Special Report, "Institutional Vulnerability in Latin America" (November 2004: 14).

28. In a 2006 *New York Times*–CBS Poll, 42 percent of Americans said they believed the Republicans were more likely than Democrats to make the right decision about the war on terror, while the same percent said they thought Democrats were more likely to make the right decision about the war in Iraq. Republicans have been successful since September 11, 2001, in spotlighting terrorist threats in election seasons to convince the American voter that they are the party to trust when it comes to keeping the nation safe and free of threats from foreign terrorists. See Adam Nagourney, "Arrests Bolster G.O.P. Bid to Claim Security as Issue," *New York Times* (August 11, 2006). However, the Republican losses of both the U.S. Senate and House of Representatives in the November 2006 elections were interpreted by many as a repudiation of the perception that the Republican Party is stronger on national security and dealing with threats from abroad.

29. Robert A. Pastor, *Not Condemned to Revolution: The United States and Nicaragua* (Boulder, CO: Westview Press, 1987: 277).

30. William F. Jasper, "Communism's Resurgence," *The New American* (January 24, 2005). See also Latin News, Security and Strategic Review, "Reviving a Cold War Atmosphere" (January 2004). At the 2004 Summit of the Americas in Monterrey, Mexico, the United States gave the impression that it was trying to recreate a Cold War atmosphere by claiming that Cuba and Venezuela are destabilizing democratic governments in the region while other governments in the region are not doing enough to counter their anti-American activities.

31. Tom Tancredo, *In Mortal Danger: The Battle for America's Border and Security* (Nashville, TN: WND Books, 2006).

32. Patrick J. Buchanan, *State of Emergency: The Third World Invasion and Conquest of America* (New York: Thomas Dunne, 2006).

33. Quoted in Margaret O'Brien Steinfels, "Death and Lies in El Salvador: The Ambassador's Tale," *Commonweal Magazine* (October 26, 2001).

34. Walt Bogdanich and Jenny Nordberg, "Mixed U.S. Signals Helped Tilt Haiti Toward Chaos," *New York Times* (January 29, 2006). According to Otto J. Reich, head of Latin American policy at the time, Ambassador Curran was removed because "we did not think the ambassador was carrying out the new policy in the way we wanted it carried out."

35. Koonings and Kruijt argue that the Latin American states do not fit the failed state scenarios in which there is near-total disintegration of state institutions and the proliferation of intrastate armed conflict. Instead, they find that phenomenon of state failure in Latin America is only "partial," meaning that "The formal institutions of the state endure, albeit with varying legitimacy and effectiveness." See Kees Koonings and Dirk Kruijt, eds., *Armed Actors: Organised Violence and State Failure in Latin America* (London: Zed Books, 2004: 2).

36. Simon Romero, "Death-Squad Scandal Circles Closer to Colombia's President," *New York Times* (May 14, 2007: A6).

37. "Rebuilding Failed States: From Chaos, Order," *The Economist* (March 3, 2005).

38. Justin Logan and Christopher Preble, "Failed States and Flawed Logic: The Case Against a Standing Nation-Building Office," *Policy Analysis*, No. 560 (January 11, 2006).

39. In *Failed States: The Abuse of Power and the Assault on American Democracy*, foreign policy critic Noam Chomsky goes so far as to argue that the *United States* is a failed state, based on the abuse of power associated with the Iraq War and the destruction of democratic principles at home.

40. See Country Indicators for Foreign Policy (CIFP), "CIFP Country Risk Assessment: Medium Term 'Watch List'" (Ottawa, Canada: Carleton University, Spring/Summer 2004). In an effort to understand what causes civil war, James D. Fearon and David D. Laitin found in a 2003 study that a greater degree of ethnic or religious diversity does not make a country more prone to civil war. Instead of focusing on ethnic demography, the debate needs to focus on the need for good government, economic development, and adequate policing. See Gary J. Bass, "What Really Causes Civil War?" *New York Times Magazine* (August 13, 2006: 18–19).

41. Country Indicators for Foreign Policy (CIFP), "CIFP Country Risk Assessment: Medium Term 'Watch List'" (Ottawa, Canada: Carleton University, Spring/Summer 2004: 11).

42. Ron Suskind, *The One Percent Doctrine: Deep Inside America's Pursuit of Its Enemies Since 9/11* (New York: Simon and Schuster, 2006: 62). Suskind notes that the "one percent solution" divided analysis and action, something that had never been done in the annals of American foreign policy. Furthermore, the one percent rule or solution freed Vice President Cheney from the years of

frustration with analysts who offered balanced assessments of hot spots or risks with caveats and disclaimers. This form of decision making also dovetailed with President Bush's penchant for "gut" decisions without the burden of detailed evidence, study, and solid investigation. It also conformed to the negative view of Congress by Cheney and other top officials in the Bush administration.

43. Jeffrey Kluger, "Why We Worry About the Things We Shouldn't . . . and Ignore the Things We Should," *Time* (December 4, 2006: 71). Psychologists argue that people, and countries, with vast amounts of political power are more likely to inflate risks in order to demonstrate resolve and domination than to analyze more nuanced options that require more time, honesty, and accurate data. A more secure nation also depends on a citizenry that takes the time to evaluate the accuracy of what political leaders are telling them, something that has been lacking in the United States since the end of the Cold War.

44. David Rose, "Neo Culpa," *Vanity Fair* (January 2007). In the wake of President Bush's "surge in troops" speech on January 10, 2007, the mainstream media reported that neoconservatives such as William Kristol and Robert Kagan were major forces in helping the president craft his "new" Iraq policy.

45. Moisés Naím, "The Lost Continent," *Foreign Policy* (November/December 2006).

46. In a May 2006 CBS Poll, just 3 percent of the nationwide sample named terrorism as the country's most important problem, behind Iraq, gas/oil prices, jobs and the economy, and immigration. Nevertheless, terrorism remains the number one foreign policy priority for the U.S. government, and the "war on terror" is now the primary mission of the U.S. military. The fact that the military must confront an ill-defined enemy and now views Latin America through the lens of terrorism often leads to a grossly distorted diagnosis of the region's problems and encourages a potential military solution for dealing with "hot spots" when none is possible or likely to succeed.

47. Chicago Council on Foreign Relations, "Global Views 2004" (www.ccfr.org/globalviews2004).

48. In *Trouble Spots: The World Atlas of Strategic Information* (Sparkford, England: Sutton Publishing Limited, 2000), Andrew Duncan and Michel Opatowski consider Latin America as a region with few conflicts: "Most of these troubles [over the past 20 years] are now thankfully over and democracy has been restored more or less throughout the continent." Although they consider Latin America "outside the mainstream," they do devote brief attention to (1) Panama's takeover of the canal, (2) the Falklands/Malvinas controversy, (3) civil war and drug trafficking in Colombia, (4) the terrorism of the Shining Path in Peru, and (5) the Zapatista rebellion in southern Mexico. Overall, the authors believe that the world's strategic agenda needs to face the fact that today's world is not going to be particularly peaceful.

49. Peter H. Smith, *Democracy in Latin America: Political Change in Comparative Perspective* (New York: Oxford University Press, 2005: 354–55).

50. For a recent examination of civil-military relations in the Andean region, see Carlos Basombrío Iglesias, "The Military and Politics in the Andean Region," *Inter-American Dialogue Working Paper* (April 2006). According to

Basombrío, "One obstacle to much-needed reforms is the recurrent tendency to involve the armed forces in tasks [fighting drug traffickers, maintaining citizen security, and public order] other than those directly related to defense."

51. Quoted in Kelly Hearn, "Exclusive: Selling the Amazon for a Handful of Beads," *AlterNet* (January 18, 2006). Hearn's exposé documents how foreign oil companies have penetrated the Ecuadoran armed forces to the point that petroleum companies have established their authority over the military. This relatively new relationship is connected with the cross-border involvement of Colombian guerrilla forces operating in Ecuador's *Oriente*.

52. "Strains of Sleaze," *The Economist* (November 11, 2006: 69).

53. Robert I. Rotberg, "Nation-State Failure: A Recurring Phenomenon," Paper written for the National Intelligence Council (NIC) 2020 Project (November 6, 2003: 1).

54. Charles F. Andrain and James T. Smith, *Political Democracy, Trust, and Social Justice: A Comparative Overview* (Boston: Northeastern University Press, 2006: 56). The large gap between the rich and poor in Latin America stems from the failure of public schools to provide a high-quality education. Public spending per pupil on primary education ranges from $190 in Nicaragua to $1,400 in Chile; far below what is spent in the United States, Canada, and Europe. The problems of inequality, inefficiency, and low levels of academic learning have a direct bearing on corruption, good governance, and state failure in Latin America. See, for example, *2006, Quantity Without Quality: A Report Card on Education in Latin America* (Washington, D.C.: Partnership for Educational Revitalization in the Americas, 2005).

55. Charles F. Andrain and James T. Smith, *Political Democracy, Trust, and Social Justice: A Comparative Overview* (Boston: Northeastern University Press, 2006: 56).

56. Ibid., p. 152.

57. William M. LeoGrande, "U.S. Insecurity in Latin America: 'Radical Populism,'" *CrossCurrents* (March 2006).

58. David Rieff, "A Nation of Pre-emptors?" *New York Times Magazine* (January 15, 2006).

59. The names of the "unstable nations" on the "watch list" are classified; however, it is not difficult to connect the threat-based thinking in Washington to specific Latin American nations that fit the instability profile.

60. After the fourth year in Iraq, the global image of the United States continues to decline. In a poll carried out by the Pew Research Center in fifteen nations in June 2006, strong majorities in thirteen of fifteen countries said the war in Iraq posed more of a danger to world peace than Iran's nuclear intentions. According to Andrew Kohut, "when you get many more people saying that the U.S. presence in Iraq is a threat to world peace as say that about Iran, it's a measure of how much Iraq is sapping good will to the United States." See Brian Knowlton, "Global Image of the U.S. is Worsening, Survey Finds," *New York Times* (June 14, 2006: A9). According to Lisa Haugaard, "The Bush administration's choice to abandon international human rights standards, particularly in the detention and treatment of prisoners, has eroded U.S. moral authority in Latin

America as well in other parts of the world." See Lisa Haugaard, "Tarnished Image: Latin America Perceives the United States" (Washington, D.C.: Latin American Working Group, March 2006: 1).

61. David W. Dent, *Historical Dictionary of U.S.-Latin American Relations* (Westport, CT: Greenwood Press, 2005: 147). See also Cole Blasier, "Democracy: Dilemmas in Promoting Democracy: Lessons from Grenada, Panama, and Haiti," *North-South Issues*, Vol. 4, No. 4 (1995).

62. Economist.com, The Americas, "The Democracy Dividend" (December 7, 2006). For an assessment of the recent electoral trends in Latin America, see Michael Shifter, "A New Politics for Latin America?" *America*, Vol. 195, No. 20 (December 18, 2006).

63. For a brief examination of these changes, including the humiliation of the United States at the OAS General Assembly meetings in 2005, see Isabel Hilton, "Latin America Rises Up," *New Statesman* (June 20, 2005). Hilton also discusses Latin America's growing trade with Asia and the expansion of internal economic integration in the Americas.

64. These differences are discussed in the Worldviews 2002 Survey of American and European Attitudes and Public Opinion on Foreign Affairs (http://www.worldviews.org/detailreports/europeanreport/html/intro.html, accessed April 15, 2006).

65. Steven Kull and Doug Miller, "Global Public Opinion on the U.S. Presidential Election and U.S. Foreign Policy," *Program on International Policy Attitudes (PIPA)* (September 8, 2004).

66. In contrast to the United States, most Latin American governments are reluctant to label illegal armed groups as international terrorist organizations. In response to the tendency of past military dictatorships to apply the terrorist label unfairly to dissidents, Latin Americans are more careful to distinguish being a "terrorist" from engaging in acts of terrorism. Some in Colombia, for example, are not bothered by the ideas espoused by armed groups such as the FARC or the ELN but are bothered by their use of violence to impose those ideas. For others it makes no sense to quibble about definitions when only a total defeat or elimination of all terrorist organizations is the solution for national salvation.

67. Matthew Davis, "New Name for 'War on Terror,'" BBC News (July 27, 2005).

68. Associated Press, "U.K. Ends Use of Phrase 'War on Terror,'" (MSNBC.com accessed April 16, 2007).

69. Francis Fukuyama, "After Neoconservatism," *New York Times Magazine* (February 19, 2006).

70. SIPRI. *SIPRI Yearbook 2003, Armaments, Disarmament and International Security* (Oxford: Oxford University Press, 2003: 7)

71. Ibid.

72. William Langewiesche, *The Atomic Bazaar: The Rise of the Nuclear Poor* (New York: Farrar, Straus and Giroux, 2007). According to Langewiesche, "The spread of nuclear weapons . . . may not be as catastrophic as is generally believed and certainly does not meet the category of threat than can justify the suppression of civil liberties or the pursuit of pre-emptive wars."

73. Thomas Homer-Dixon, "Terror in the Weather Forecast," *New York Times* (April 24, 2007: A25). Homer-Dixon argues that many of the world's hot spots are associated with climate change where frail governments must face a plethora of conditions—cropland degradation, deforestation, soil erosion, and scarcity of fresh water—that lead to failed states where extremism and terrorism flourish.

74. Juan Forero and Larry Rohter, "Bolivia Leader Tilting Region to Left," *New York Times* (January 22, 2006: A1).

75. Gaston Chillier and Laurie Freeman, "Potential Threat: The New OAS Concept of Hemispheric Security," *Washington Office on Latin America* (July 2005).

76. "Blurring the Lines: Trends in U.S. Military Programs with Latin America," Latin American Working Group Education Fund, Center for International Policy and WOLA (Washington, D.C., September 2004).

77. Henry A. Kissinger, *White House Years* (Boston: Little, Brown, 1979: 654).

78. Charles F. Andrain and James T. Smith, *Political Democracy, Trust, and Social Justice: A Comparative Overview* (Boston: Northeastern University Press, 2006:128).

79. Shana A. Kushner, "Threat, Media and Foreign Policy Opinion," Paper prepared for delivery at 2005 APSA Political Communication on International Communication and Conflict (2005).

80. For a sobering study of America's century of intervention and regime change, see Stephen Kinzer, *Overthrow: America's Century of Regime Change from Hawaii to Iraq* (New York: Times Books/Henry Holt & Company, 2006).

81. Adam Isaacson, "Closing the 'Seams': U.S. Security Policy in the Americas," *NACLA Report on the Americas* (May June 2005: 13–17).

82. Ibid., p. 13.

83. Thom Shanker, "A New Enemy Gains on the U.S." *New York Times* (July 30, 2006). In what he calls a "significant modernization of classic guerrilla warfare," Shanker calls Hezbollah a new kind of threat: "Hezbollah still possesses the most dangerous aspects of a shadowy terror network. It abides by no laws of war as it attacks civilians indiscriminately. Attacks on its positions carry a high risk of killing innocents. At the same time, it has attained military capabilities and other significant attributes of a nation-state. It holds territory and seats in the Lebanese government. It fields high-tech weapons and possesses the firepower to threaten the entire population of a regional superpower, or at least those in the northern half of Israel." Hezbollah's influence in Latin America is nowhere near what it is in Lebanon. Nevertheless, it has attached itself to small pieces of territory and has the capacity to carry out network warfare with relative impunity.

84. For a discussion of these categories, see William I. Robinson, "Democracy or Polyarchy?" *NACLA Report on the Americas* (January/February 2007: 34–35).

85. See, for example, Chalmers Johnson, "Republic or Empire: A National Intelligence Estimate on the United States," *Harper's Magazine* (January 2007: 63–69). Johnson argues that the expense of the U.S. empire is based on "military Keynesianism" that places its emphasis on the available supply of money in the

United States, not on the demand for defense. He believes that one of the consequences of military Keynesianism is bankruptcy and collapse and a loss of control over international affairs.

86. Cole Blasier, *The Hovering Giant: U.S. Responses to Revolutionary Change in Latin America, 1910–1985*, Revised Edition (Pittsburgh, PA: University of Pittsburgh Press, 1985: 297).

87. Jorge I. Domínguez, et al., "Boundary Disputes in Latin America," *Peaceworks* (Washington, D.C.: U.S. Institute for Peace, 2003).

88. Félix E. Martín, "Hegemonic Peace in South America: Fact or Fiction?" *Delaware Review of Latin American Studies*, Vol. 6, No. 2 (January 15, 2006). Martín argues that most of the U.S. military interventions since 1945 took place outside of Latin America and most of the interventions were not aimed at preserving intraregional, interstate peace.

89. Ibid., p. 297.

90. Chalmers Johnson, "Republic or Empire: A National Intelligence Estimate on the United States," *Harper's Magazine* (January 2007: 64).

91. Nadia Martínez, "Political Upheaval: Latin America Challenges the Washington Consensus," *In These Times* (April 5, 2006; http://inthesetimes.com/site/main/print/2564/, accessed May 23, 2006).

92. Bruce Finley, "High Noon in Latin America: U.S. Targets 'Lawless' Areas," *Denver Post* (December 5, 2004). In 2004 the United States provided Latin American with $937.8 million in economic and social aid and $866.6 million in military and police aid. This is a dramatic change from previous eras when economic aid was 8 times the amount given for military/police aid.

93. Juan Forero, "U.S. Aid Can't Win Bolivia's Love as New Suitors Emerge," *New York Times* (May 14, 2006).

94. Democracy promotion, beginning with President Ronald Reagan, included economic assistance to several government agencies, the creation of the NED, with an emphasis on human rights, elections assistance, judicial systems assistance, and democratic participation. For a critical discussion of political development assistance, see Thomas Carothers, *In the Name of Democracy: U.S. Policy Toward Latin America in the Reagan Years* (Berkeley, CA: University of California Press, 1991). According to Carothers, the Reagan administration's policies did not contribute significantly to democratic development in Latin America in the 1980s. According to Reagan, the main threat to democracy in Latin America was Communism. Therefore, "fighting communism was equivalent to promoting democracy." Carothers (pp. 257–258) argues that "the main obstacles to democracy in Latin America have historically been a variety of structural domestic factors such as the extreme concentration of economic and political power in the hands of undemocratic elites, sociopolitical marginalization of whole classes of citizens, and the lack of any underlying national consensus on basic democratic values."

95. Thomas Carothers, "The Backlash Against Democracy Promotion," *Foreign Affairs* (March/April 2006).

96. Louis A. Perez, Jr., "Fear and Loathing of Fidel Castro: Sources of U.S. Policy Toward Cuba," *Journal of Latin American Studies*, Vol. 34 (2002).

97. For an explanation of the relative inefficiency and failure of economic sanctions, see David W. Dent, *Historical Dictionary of U.S.-Latin American Relations* (Westport, CT: Greenwood Press, 2005: 170-72).

98. For a discussion of the role of Blackwater as a mercenary force, see Jeremy Scahill, *Blackwater: The Rise of the World's Most Powerful Mercenary Army* (New York: Nation Books, 2007).

99. David W. Dent, *Historical Dictionary of U.S.-Latin American Relations* (Westport, CT: Greenwood Press, 2005: 358).

100. For the merits of mercenary armies in dealing with global hot spots, see Ted Koppel, "These Guns for Hire," *New York Times* (May 22, 2006: A25). According to Koppel, "The underlying theory [of using private forces] seems to be that where a host government is unable to protect American business interests overseas and where the American government may be reluctant or unable to intervene, there is another option conveniently available."

101. Charles F. Andrain and James T. Smith, *Political Democracy, Trust, and Social Justice: A Comparative Overview* (Boston: Northeastern University Press, 2006: 13–14).

102. Greg Grandin, "Democracy, Diplomacy and Intervention in the Americas," *NACLA Report on the Americas* (January/February 2007: 22–25)

103. Some historians have found, while researching foreign archives, that the perils of foreign designs on the Western Hemisphere were often exaggerated to expand American power abroad and justify presidential action in foreign affairs. See, for example, Nancy Mitchell, *The Danger of Dreams: German and American Imperialism in Latin America* (Chapel Hill: University of North Carolina Press, 1999).

104. Inter-American Dialogue, "Responding to the Hemisphere's Political Challenges," Report of The Inter-American Dialogue Task Force on the Organization of American States (June 2006: 6).

105. See remarks by Otto J. Reich to the Heritage Foundation, "The Administration's Four Goals in the Western Hemisphere" (Washington, D.C., October 31, 2002). According to Reich, "Security is a *sine qua non*" because the other three goals are dependent on the government's ability to provide a safe environment, both at home and in "our neighborhood."

106. Michael Coppedge, Statement before the Subcommittee on the Western Hemisphere, House Committee on International Relations, United States Congress, hearings on "Keeping Democracy on Track: Hotspots in Latin America" (September 28, 2005: 5). For a similar set of prescriptions to improve U.S.-Latin American relations, see David W. Dent, *Historical Dictionary of U.S.-Latin American Relations* (Westport, CT: Greenwood Press, 2005).

107. Thomas Carothers, "The Backlash Against Democracy Promotion," *Foreign Affairs* (March/April 2006).

108. Simon Romero, "Venezuela, Tired of U.S. Influence, Strengthens Its Relationship in the Middle East," *New York Times* (August 21, 2006).

109. For an example of anti-immigration arguments that conflate illegal immigration with terrorism, see J. D. Hayworth, *Whatever It Takes: Illegal Immigration, Border Security and the War on Terror* (Washington, DC: Regnery, 2006).

Hayworth is a conservative Republican former congressman from Scottsdale, Arizona, who was critical of President Bush's immigration plan to establish a limited guest-worker program and often stirs up fear among his supporters of the possibility of Al Qaeda shipping a nuclear weapon across the U.S. southern border.

110. Tom Barry, "Anti-Immigrant Backlash on the 'Home Front,'" *NACLA Report on the Americas* (May/June 2005: 29).

111. Raymond Tanter, *Classifying Evil: Bush Administration Rhetoric and Policy Toward Rogue Regimes*, Foreign Policy Focus No. 44 (Washington, D.C.: Washington Institute for Near East Policy, February 2003).

112. Michael Shifter, "In Search of Hugo Chávez," *Foreign Affairs*, Vol. 85, No. 3 (May/June 2006).

113. Robin Anderson, "Invading Grenada," *Extra!* (January/February 2007). Anderson's article argues that the U.S. invasion of Grenada in 1983 "was the first time that 'pre-emption' for security reasons was posed as a justification for military intervention," and the parallels between the invasion of Grenada (Reagan) and Iraq (George W. Bush) in that both relied on flawed intelligence that exaggerated the type and amount of weapons in each case.

114. Michael Cooper, "In Speech, McCain Intends to Push for Cap on Emissions," *New York Times* (April 23, 2007: A16).

115. Eva Golinger, "CIA Classified Venezuela as Top 'Potentially Unstable Country'" (*Venezuulanalysis.com* accessed February 16, 2005).

116. Tim Padgett, "Why Pat Robertson's Statements Help Hugo Chavez," *Time* (August 23, 2005).

117. Juan Forero, "Chávez Ousts U.S. Diplomat on Spying Charge," *New York Times* (February 3, 2006: A8). In testimony before the Senate Intelligence Committee, John D. Negroponte, director of national intelligence, postulated that Chávez was meddling in the internal affairs of his neighbors and in the process of establishing closer economic and military ties with Iran and North Korea. Chávez's accusations of embassy spying and assassination attempts orchestrated in Washington, and the Bush administration's threat-based rhetoric, helps him solidify his anti-American credentials at home and abroad while contributing to media reports that hype the Venezuelan danger as a Latin American hot spot. In his effort to heighten the threat from Venezuela, Defense Secretary Donald Rumsfeld told reporters in early 2006 "We've got Chávez in Venezuela with a lot of oil money. He's a person who was elected legally, just as Adolf Hitler was elected legally, and then consolidated power." In a move to salvage his failures in Iraq, President Bush appointed Negroponte to be Condoleezza Rice's deputy in the State Department in January 2007.

118. Mary Anastasia O'Grady, "Don't Count on Argentina to Help Fight Terror," *Wall Street Journal* (July 8, 2005: A11). After Evo Morales received a landslide victory in the December 2005 presidential election in Bolivia, O'Grady wrote an opinion piece called "Axis of Evo" in which she accused him of assembling a cabinet of "radical and Marxist militants" and letting Cuba and Venezuela annex his country while he neutralizes the Bolivian military. If Bolivia is not a threat-based hot spot after a free and fair election, O'Grady's reporting will no doubt contribute to the ideological fears and hatred so important to the right-wing

media in the United States. See O'Grady, "Axis of Evo," *Wall Street Journal* (January 27, 2006).

119. See Peter Kornbluh, "A Safe Harbor for Luis Posada Carriles," *NACLA Report on the Americas*, Vol. 39, No. 4 (January/February 2006).

120. The long exchange between President Bush and Tim Russert can be found in Thomas E. Ricks, *Fiasco: The American Military Adventure in Iraq* (New York: Penguin Press, 2006: 375–376).

Chapter 1: Mexico

1. Solana Larsen, "The Anti-Immigration Movement: From Shovels to Suits," *NACLA Report on the Americas*, Vol. 40, No. 3 (May/June 2007: 16).

2. David W. Dent, *Encyclopedia of Modern Mexico* (Lanham, MD: Scarecrow Press, 2002).

3. The White House, September 17, 2002.

4. Carlos Lozada, "Does Poverty Cause Terrorism?" *National Bureau of Economic Research* (May 2005; http://www.nber.org/digest/may05/w10859.html, accessed on July 15, 2006).

5. While the porous nature of the U.S.-Mexican border has the potential for allowing terrorists to move into the United States from Mexico, since September 11, 2001, not one case of a terrorist crossing into the United States from Mexico has been documented.

6. Katherine McIntire Peters, "Security vs. Bureaucracy," *Government Executive* (April 1, 2002; http://www.goverexec.com/features/0402/0402s1.htm, accessed May 12, 2006).

7. John Pomfret, "Bribery at Border Worries Officials," *Washington Post* (July 15, 2006). "The massive buildup of Border Patrol agents in recent years has led to worries that hiring standards have been lowered; and, as smugglers demand higher and higher fees to bring illegal immigrants into the United States, their efforts to bribe those guarding the border have intensified."

8. "Harper's Index," *Harper's Magazine* (February 2006: 11).

9. The private prison industry in the United States is the key beneficiary of the policy of jailing undocumented immigrants. Private prison companies controlled 20 percent of federal detention beds in 2007, up from 3 percent in 2001. Detainees–over 230,000 yearly–are of all ages, nationalities, and backgrounds, suggesting a far more complicated process of handling Mexicans once they cross into the United States and are then subsequently arrested by immigration and border authorities. See, for example, Forrest Wilder, "Detention Archipelago: Jailing Immigrants for Profit," *NACLA Report on the Americas*, Vol. 40, No. 3 (May/June 2007).

10. Rod Ai Camp, "The Media and Democracy in Mexico and the United States—The Role of the Press," Keynote Address, Woodrow Wilson Center (June 2006).

11. Faye Bowers, "Why Mexico Helps U.S. Fight Terror," *Christian Science Monitor* (January 26, 2006).

12. John Pomfret, "Bribery at Borders Worries Officials," *Washington Post* (July 15, 2006).

13. See, for example, Solana Larsen, "The Anti-Immigration Movement: From Shovels to Suits," *NACLA Report on the Americas* (May/June 2007).

14. "The War on the Border Streets," *The Economist* (June 30, 2005).

15. PINR, Power and Interest News Report, "Central American Street Gangs are Drawn into the World of Geopolitics," PINR (August 26, 2005).

16. Michael T. Klare, "The Growing Traffic in Arms," *NACLA Report on the Americas*, Vol. 31, No. 2 (September/October 1987). See also Howard LaFranchi, "Mexicans Too Have a Border Problem: Awash in Guns," *Christian Science Monitor* (April 11, 1997).

17. Committee on International Relations, House of Representatives, "U.S. Annual Drug Certification" (April 29, 1998).

18. Michael Shifter, "United States-Latin American Relations: Shunted to the Slow Track," *Current History* (February 1998).

19. Sam Enriquez, "Fox Decides Not to Sign Drug Legalization Bill," *Los Angeles Times* (May 4, 2006).

20. Ibid.

21. David W. Dent, *Encyclopedia of Modern Mexico* (Lanham, MD: Scarecrow Press, 2002: 98–102).

22. Latin American Working Group Education Fund, "Erasing the Lines: Trends in U.S. Military Programs with Latin America" (Washington, D.C.: Center for International Policy, Latin American Working Group Education Fund, and the Washington Office on Latin America, December 2005).

23. David Rieff, "The Populist at the Border," *New York Times* (June 4, 2006: 38).

24. James C. McKinley, Jr., "In Race for Mexico's Presidency, Populist Tilts at a Privileged Elite," *New York Times* (June 17, 2006: A8).

25. Dick Morris, "Menace in Mexico," *New York Post* (April 3, 2006, Online Edition).

26. Sam Enriquez, "Leftist Comes Out Swinging, Regains Lead in Polls," *Los Angeles Times* (June 15, 2006).

27. David W. Dent, *Encyclopedia of Modern Mexico* (Lanham, MD: Scarecrow Press, 2002: 92).

28. Joseph Klesner, "Fitzgibbon Survey of Scholarly Images of Democracy in Latin America, 2005" (Kenyon College, 2005; http://www2.kenyon.edu/)

29. James C. McKinley Jr., "Mexico's Enforcers Take On Election-Year Mudslingers," *New York Times* (June 12, 2006).

30. James C. McKinley, Jr., "Amid Fights and Catcalls, Mexico's President is Sworn In," *New York Times* (December 2, 2006).

31. Ginger Thompson, "Report on Mexican 'Dirty War' Details Abuse by Military," *New York Times* (February 27, 2006: A3).

32. Nathan Thornburgh, "Inside America's Secret Workforce," *Time* (February 6, 2006).

33. Ibid. p. 42.

34. "State of the Union: The President's Speech," *New York Times* (February 1, 2006).
35. Rachel L. Swarns, "Rift on Immigration Widens for Conservatives and Cardinals," *New York Times* (March 19, 2006).
36. See Allan Wall, "The Mexican Presidential Race and Immigration" (NewsMax, May 2, 2006, http://www.newsmax.com).
37. David Rieff, "The Populist at the Border," *New York Times* (June 4, 2006: 40).
38. Roberto Lovato, "Voices of a New Movimiento," *The Nation* (June 19, 2006).
39. Edward E. Telles, "Incorporating Race and Ethnicity into the UN Millennium Development Goals," *Inter-American Dialogue* (January 2007: 3).
40. George Colman, "Teachers and APPO in Oaxaca and Mexico," Znet (November 9, 2006; http://www.zmag.org/content/print_article.cfm, accessed December 6, 2006).
41. Laura Carlsen, "Oaxaca Fights Back," Znet (November 12, 2006; http://www.zmag.org/content/print_article.cfm, accessed December 6, 2006).
42. Marc Lacey, "Painting Over Signs of Strife to Tidy Up for the Tourists," *New York Times* (December 28, 2006).
43. Lynn Stephen, "Election Day in Chiapas: A Low-Intensity War," *NACLA Report on the Americas*, Vol. 131, No. 2 (September/October, 1997: 11).
44. Quoted in James C. McKinley, Jr., "Marcos Back in Public Eye in Mexico," *New York Times* (May 10, 2006: A12).

Chapter 2: Central America

1. "The Americas" is a term that (although in common parlance simply means North and South America) is here used interchangeably with "Latin America" to refer to these two continents exclusive of the United States and Canada—a world region that stretches from Mexico to the tip of South America, a distance of 7,000 miles. This enormous and extremely diverse region, when taken as a whole, is larger than Europe and is approximately as large as the United States and Canada combined. Latin America, strictly speaking, consists of those countries in the Americas that speak the Romance languages of Spanish, Portuguese, and French; however, in a more general sense the region also encompasses the English- and Dutch-speaking countries located in the Caribbean and South America.
2. Ralph Lee Woodward, Jr., *Central America: A Nation Divided*. Second Edition (New York: Oxford University Press, 1985: 3).
3. Thomas W. Walker and Ariel C. Armony, eds., *Repression, Resistance, and Democratic Transition in Central America* (Wilmington, DE: Scholarly Resources, 2000).
4. David W. Dent, *Historical Dictionary of U.S.-Latin American Relations* (Westport, CT: Greenwood Press, 2005: 1–2).

Notes

5. Pascal O. Girot, "The Darien Gap Region Between Colombia and Panama: Gap or Seal?" (Berkeley, CA: Nautilus Institute for Security and Sustainable Development, March 1998: 30).

6. United States Agency for International Development, "Central America and Mexico Gang Assessment" (Washington, D.C.: USAID, April 2006).

7. WOLA, "Gang Violence in Central America," Washington Office on Latin America (March 4, 2006).

8. "Central America's Street Gangs Are Drawn into the World of Geopolitics," *Power and Interest News Report* (July 12, 2005).

9. Geoff Thale, "Conference Tackles Youth Gang Violence in Central America," *Cross Currents* (July 2005).

10. Rubén Castañeda, "Gang Members Describe Life Inside MS-13," *Washington Post* (October 18, 2006).

11. Jim Garamone, "Rumsfeld Meets with Six Central American Presidents," *Armed Forces Information Service* (May 12, 2005).

12. Indira A. R. Lakshmanan, "Gangs Roil Central America: Troubles Linked to U.S. Deportees, *Boston Globe* (April 17, 2006).

13. Sara Burnett, "Special Report: Gangs in Colorado," *Rocky Mountain News* (January 20, 2007).

14. *Ibid.*, p. 22A.

15. National Alliance of Gang Investigators Associations, *2005 National Gang Threat Assessment* (Washington, D.C.: U.S. Department of Justice, 2006).

16. Arian Campo-Flores, "The Most Dangerous Gang in America," *Newsweek* (March 28, 2005).

17. Latin News, Security and Strategic Review, "U.S.-Central America: Street Gang's Status Raised to Major Security Threat" (May 2005).

18. Clare Ribando, "Gangs in Central America," *Congressional Research Service* (January 9, 2005).

19. Simon Romero, "Touched by Oil, and Hope," *New York Times* (February 21, 2006).

20. Max Manwaring, *Street Gangs: The New Urban Insurgency* (Carlisle Barracks, PA: Strategic Studies Institute (SSI) Monographs, March 2005; www.carlisle.army.mil/ssi/).

21. Latin American News, Security and Strategic Review, "From an Imagined U.S. Base to the Real Ones," *Security and Strategic Review* (July 2005; http://www.latinnews.com/lss/LSS6888).

22. Michael Radu, "The Other Side of Democratic Transition," *Democracy at Large*, Vol. 2, No. 3 (2006).

23. Fairness and Accuracy in Reporting, "Reviving Cold War Reporting on Nicaragua," *Action Alert* (April 5, 2005).

24. James C. McKinley, Jr., "Ortega Redux: A History Smolders on Cold War Embers," *New York Times* (November 11, 2006).

25. N.C. Aizenman, "Former Contras Bemoan Ortega's Return to Power in Nicaragua," *Washington Post* (November 12, 2006).

26. "Guatemala's Murdered Women," *New York Times* (October 21, 2005).

27. Donald E. Shulz, "The Growing Threat to Democracy in Latin America," *Parameters* (Spring, 2001: 59–71).

28. Mitchell A. Seligson, "The Measurement and Impact of Corruption Victimization: Survey Evidence from Latin America," *World Development*, Vol. 34, No. 2 (2005).

29. David W. Dent, *Historical Dictionary of U.S.-Latin American Relations* (Westport, CT: Greenwood Press, 2005: 333).

30. Marifeli Pérez Stable, "Latin America: China Offers Opportunities, Poses Threats," *Inter-American Dialogue* (February 17, 2005).

31. Claudio M. Loser, "The Growing Economic Presence of China in Latin America" (Center for Hemispheric Policy, University of Miami, December 15, 2006). This paper is the result of a paper presented as part of the China–Latin America Task Force at the University of Miami in March–June 2006.

32. Peter T. R. Brookes, "China's Influence in the Western Hemisphere," testimony before the Subcommittee on the Western Hemisphere Committee on International Relations, United States House of Representatives (April 6, 2005).

33. Michael T. Klare, "Revving Up the China Threat," *The Nation* (October 24, 2005).

34. Roger F. Noriega, "China's Influence in the Western Hemisphere," statement before the House Subcommittee on the Western Hemisphere (Washington, D.C., April 6, 2005).

35. Julie Watson, "Nicaraguans Dream of Canal Like Panama's," *Denver Post* (October 19, 2006).

Chapter 3: Andean South America

1. Jo-Marie Burt and Philip Mauceri, eds., *Politics in the Andes: Identity, Conflict, Reform* (Pittsburgh, PA: University of Pittsburgh Press, 2004: 1).

2. See David Mares, *Violent Peace: Militarized Interstate Bargaining in Latin America* (New York: Columbia University Press, 2001).

3. Simon Romero, "Bolivia Reaches for a Slice of the Coast That Got Away," *New York Times* (September 24, 2006).

4. Latin News, Security and Strategic Review, "Chile-Bolivia-Peru: Determined Bid to Lower Tensions," *Security and Strategic Review* (February 2004).

5. Latin News, Security and Strategic Review, "Proliferation of Provocative Incidents Strains Determination to Maintain Peace" (January 2004).

6. Bruce Finley, "High Noon in Latin America: U.S. Targets 'Lawless' Areas," *Denver Post* (December 5, 2004).

7. James Painter, "Colombia War Colours Regional Ties," *BBC News* (July 14, 2005).

8. For a discussion of various kinds of violence in Colombia, see Diane E. Davis, "The Age of Insecurity: Violence and Social Disorder in the New Latin America," *Latin American Research Review*, Vol. 41, No. 1 (February 2006).

9. Robert I. Rotberg, "Failed States, Collapsed States, Weak States: Causes and Indicators," in Robert I. Rotberg, *When States Fail: Causes and Consequences* (Princeton, NJ: Princeton University Press, 2004: 15).

10. Juan Forero, "In Colombia, A Dubious Disarmament," *Washington Post* (October 17, 2006).

11. Antonio Navarro Wolff, "Ending the Conflict with FARC: Time for a New Course," *Inter-American Dialogue* (January 2007).

12. Mario A. Murillo, "Colombia's Indigenous Caught in the Conflict," *NACLA Report on the Americas* (January/February 2006).

13. Dan Eggen, "With Guilty Pleas, Cali Cartel Finished, U.S. Says," *Washington Post* (September 27, 2006).

14. Juan Forero, "U.S. Indicts 50 leaders of Colombian Rebels in Cocaine Trafficking," *New York Times* (March 23, 2006).

15. Rodrigo Pardo, "A New Uribe? Álvaro Uribe's Second-Term Challenges," *Inter-American Dialogue* (November 2006: 11).

16. John Tierney, "Reading the Coca Leaves," *New York Times* (September 23, 2006).

17. "Chavez, Ecuador Oppose U.S. Drug War," (http://www.msnbc.com/id/16302074/, accessed December 24, 2006).

18. Álvaro Vargas Llosa, *Liberty for Latin America: How to Undo Five Hundred Years of State Oppression* (New York: Farrar, Straus and Giroux, 2005: 76).

19. "Institutional Vulnerability in Latin America," *Latin American Newsletters*, Latin American Special Report (November 2004).

20. "Bolivia: Friends Not Clones," *Economist.com* (June 7, 2007).

21. Simon Romero, "Link to Chavez May Have Hurt Ecuadorean Candidate," *New York Times* (October 17, 2006).

22. Mary Anastasia O'Grady, "Will Ecuador Join the Axis of Outcasts?," *Wall Street Journal* (October 6, 2006).

23. Marifeli Pérez-Stable, "New Leaders' Challenges: Institutions, Social Fabric," *Miami Herald* (December 7, 2006).

24. For a discussion of pre-Chávez Venezuela, see Barry C. Lynn, "Chaos and Constitution," *Mother Jones* (January/February, 2003).

25. Corruption can be found in all nations, rich or poor, and many times corruption is an integral part of the way a government works. There is no doubt that money distorts America's political system, and because the process is largely legal, does not make it less corrupt.

26. Tina Rosenberg, "The Taint of the Greased Palm," *New York Times Magazine* (August 10, 2003).

27. Angel Paz, "CIA Gave $10 Million to Peru's Ex-Spymaster," *AlterNet* (July 3, 2001; http://www.alternet.org/story/11131/, accessed January 25, 2006). Fujimori was born to Japanese immigrants to Lima, Peru; directed the National Agrarian University; hosted a television show; and ran for president of Peru as the head of a new political party, *Cambio 90* (Change 90). With a campaign that focused on poorer neighborhoods and rejected market-oriented reforms, Fujimori won the 1990 election with 57 percent of the vote. He won three terms in office,

but his last victory was marred by corruption and fraud in 2000. After being condemned by Peruvians and the Organization of American States, Fujimori faxed his resignation while traveling in Japan. Peru's legislature rejected his resignation and voted him out of office as "morally unfit." His success in pursuing Shining Path guerrillas and reducing inflation made him popular during his first term, despite human rights violations, corruption, manipulation of the media, and the erosion of democratic rule. Fujimori spent five years in self-imposed exile before deciding to return to Peru to run for another term as president. However, he was arrested after arriving in Chile and was never able to enter the race. He remained under house arrest in Santiago, Chile until he was extradited to Peru in 2007. Peru's case against Fujimori is based on corruption and human rights abuses, including the authorization of death squads.

28. Jeanneath Valdivieso, "Ecuador Declares State of Emergency," *Denver Post* (March 23, 2006).

29. Juan Forero, "Ecuador: Government Clamps Down on Protests," *New York Times* (March 23, 2006).

30. "At the Double, Ollanta the Outsider," *The Economist* (March 25, 2006).

31. BBC News, "Peru Minister Quits Over Lynching" (May 6, 2004; http://newsvote.bbc.co.uk/mpapps/pagetools/print/news.bbc.co.uk/1/hi/world/americas/368, accessed August 8, 2006).

32. Brian Walsh, "Resolving the Human Rights Violations of a Previous Regime," *World Affairs* 158, no. 3 (1996). For a brief discussion of the International Criminal Court, see David W. Dent, *Historical Dictionary of U.S.-Latin American Relations* (Westport, CT: Greenwood Press, 2005).

33. For a discussion of the complexities of truth commissions, see Sam Logan and Stephen A. Garrett, "Truth Commissions in Latin America: An Analysis of Truth Commissions in Argentina, Brazil, and Chile" (http://sand.miis.edu/research/documents/logan_truth.pdf, accessed April 26, 2006); P. B. Hayner, "Fifteen Truth Commissions—1974–1994: A Comparative Study," *Human Rights Quarterly* 16, no. 4 (1994).

34. "Bolivia: Morales the Bountiful," *The Economist* (December 13, 2006).

35. Barbara Slavin, "U.S. to Resume Training Militaries in Latin America," *Arizona Republic* (October 10, 2006).

36. World Bank, "Colombia: Development and Peace in the Magdalena Medio Region" *En Breve* (July 2002).

37. Jeffrey Vogt, "MAS Victory in Bolivia Signifies Mandate for Change," *Cross Currents* (March 2006).

38. Daphne Eviatar, "Evo's Challenge in Bolivia," *The Nation* (January 23, 2006).

39. Marcella Sanchez, "Fear of Evo," *Washington Post* (December 22, 2005).

40. Pamela Constable, "For Bolivian Victor: A Powerful Mandate," *Washington Post* (December 20, 2005).

41. Michael Shifter and Vinay Jawahar, "Latin America's Populist Turn," *Current History* (February 2005: 57).

42. Christian Parenti, "Morales Moves," *The Nation* (June 19, 2006).

43. Monte Reel, "6 Bolivian Leaders Cut Ties With Morales," *Washington Post* (November 21, 2006).

44. Juan Forero, "Bolivia Elects a President Who Supports Coca Farming," *New York Times* (September 19, 2005: A).

45. Carter Dougherty, "Oil Companies Not Entitled to Payment, Bolivian Says," *New York Times* (May 12, 2006). See also Juan Forero, "Step 1 in Bolivian Takeover: Audit of Foreign Companies," *New York Times* (May 4, 2006). Although the announcement of the nationalization was intended to reassure the multinationals of a fair and dignified process, it had the opposite effect, particularly with the use of auditors from Petróleos de Venezuela, S.A. (PDVSA), and concern for a large increase in gas prices.

46. William Finnegan, "The Economics of Empire: Notes on the Washington Consensus," *Harper's Magazine* (May 2003: 49).

47. Ibid., p. 41.

48. Juan Forero, "Who Will Bring Water to the Bolivian Poor?" *New York Times* (December 15, 2005: C1).

49. David Rieff, "Che's Second Coming?" *The New York Times Magazine* (November 20, 2005).

50. Juan Forero, "Advocate for Coca Legalization Leads in Bolivian Race," *New York Times* (November 26, 2005: A3).

51. Genaro Arriagada, "Petropolitics in Latin America: A Review of Energy Policy and Regional Relations" *Inter-American Dialogue* (December 2006: 1).

52. Daphne Eviatar, "Bolivia Steps on the Gas," *The Nation* (May 29, 2006).

53. "Ecuador Cancels Deal With Occidental Petroleum," *New York Times* (May 17, 2006: C10).

54. Bruce Finley, "High Noon in Latin America: U.S. Targets 'Lawless'- Areas," *Denver Post* (December 5, 2004).

55. Genaro Arriagada, "Petropolitics in Latin America: A Review of Energy Policy and Regional Relations," *Inter-American Dialogue* (December 2006).

56. Simon Romero and Brian Ellsworth, "New Venezuela Tensions Worrying Oil Executives," *New York Times* (January 24, 2005).

57. Noam Chomsky, "Latin America and Asia Are at Last Breaking Free of Washington's Grip," *The Guardian* (March 18, 2006).

58. Simon Romero, "Venezuela, Tired of U.S. Influence, Strengthens Its Relationships in the Middle East," *New York Times* (August 21, 2006).

59. Jens Erik Gould, "Plan for South American Pipeline Has Ambitions Beyond Gas," *New York Times* (December 2, 2006).

60. Ibid.

61. Paulo Prada, "Brazil's Oil Giant Is Drilling Far From Home Waters," *New York Times* (July 7, 2006).

62. Quoted in David Scott Palmer, "Peru: Democratic Forms, Authoritarian Practices," in Howard J. Wiarda and Harvey F. Kline, eds. *Latin American Politics and Development* (Boulder, CO: Westview Press, 2000).

63. J. Patrice McSherry, *Predatory States: Operation Condor and Covert War in Latin America* (Lanham, MD: Rowman and Littlefield, 2005: 1). Operation Condor involved the military regimes of Argentina, Chile, Uruguay, Paraguay, Bolivia, and Brazil. Peru and Ecuador joined later but played less central roles to the overall operation. The United States acted as a secret partner and sponsor by

providing organizational, intelligence, financial, and technical support for the counterinsurgency effort.

64. Those who have studied Sendero in Peru point to three factions within the guerrilla organization. The largest has about 600 members within the prisons and about 1,200 on the outside and acknowledges Abimael Guzmán as its leader. There are two other armed factions with an estimated 200 members. One operates in the upper Huallaga Valley and the other along the left bank of the Ene River.

65. A proclamation of Túpac Amaru and his death sentence are reproduced in Orin Starn, Carlos Iván Degregori, and Robin Kirk, eds., *The Peru Reader* (Durham, NC: Duke University Press, 1995: 157–161; http://www.eureka.edu/emp/jrodrig/webpage/tupac.htm, accessed October 3, 2007). A descendant of the Inca emperors who rose on behalf of all Peruvian-born, both those of Spanish ancestry ("creoles") and indigenous people, he has been claimed by Peruvian patriots of all stripes.

66. In an interview with Michael Schifter of the Inter-American Dialogue, President-elect García says he will be more successful in his second term (2006–2011), claiming he should have used more repression against the Sendero guerrillas instead of offering small loans to farmers that drained the national treasury.

67. Jo-Marie Burt, "Plotting Fear: The Uses of Terror in Peru," *NACLA Report on the Americas* (May/June 2005).

68. W. T. Whitney, Jr., "U.S. Threats to Venezuela's Revolution Escalate," *People's Weekly World Newspaper* (February 7, 2006; http://www.pww.org/article/8534, accessed August 28, 2006). The Army publication "Doctrine for Asymmetric Warfare Against Venezuela," suggests that the both defense and intelligence agencies in the United States are preparing to wage war against Venezuela because of its ties to countries considered enemies of the United States.

69. Michael Shifter, "A New Politics for Latin America," *America*, Vol. 195, No. 20 (December 18, 2006).

70. Michael Shifter and Vinjay Jawahar, "Latin America's Populist Turn," *Current History* (February 2005). See also "Is Latin America Shifting to the Left?" *Latin American Newsletters,* Special Report (July 2003).

71. Juan Forero, "Chávez Condemns U.S., Citing Efforts to End His Rule," *New York Times* (March 11, 2004).

72. Joel Wendland, "Hugo Chavez and the Bolivarian Revolution in Venezuela" (http://politicalaffairs.net/article/view/1707/1/115/, accessed April 4, 2006).

73. Juan Forero, "Venezuela: Official Horse Takes a Turn Left," *New York Times* (March 9, 2006).

74. *The Economist*, "The Democracy Dividend" (December 9, 2006: 46).

75. David W. Dent, *The Legacy of the Monroe Doctrine: A Reference Guide to U.S. Involvement in Latin America and the Caribbean* (Westport, CT: Greenwood Press, 1999: 369–370).

76. See Greg Palast, "Hugo Chávez," *The Progressive* (July 2006) for a feisty interview in which the Venezuelan leader criticizes the United States for destabilizing the region and interfering in the elections in other Latin American countries.

Chávez predicts that by the end of the century "We will see the burial of the empire of the eagle." The use of "burial" is reminiscent of a pledge made by Nikita Khrushchev at the United Nations in which he declared Communism would eventually bury the capitalist United States. In his visit to the United Nations in September 2006 President Chávez attacked President Bush in his UN speech, calling him "the devil," and later, during a presentation at a Harlem church, referred to Bush as "an alcoholic and a sick man."

77. Simon Romero, "In Venezuela, Chavismo is Dissected by Fans and Foes," *New York Times* (January 24, 2007)

78. U.S. Department of State, "The State of Democracy in Venezuela" (December 1, 2005).

79. Juan Forero, "Chavez, Seeking Foreign Allies, Spends Billions," *New York Times* (April 4, 2006).

80. Ibid.

81. *Latin American Newsletters,* Special Report, "Is Latin America Shifting to the Left?" (July 2003).

82. Juan Forero, "Chavez, Seeking Foreign Allies, Spends Billions," *New York Times* (April 4, 2006).

83. Jack Chang, "Chávez Urging Trade Bloc to Reject Private Enterprise," *Arizona Republic* (January 19, 2007).

84. Steve Rendall, "Imperial Mythology: Venezuela, Hugo Chavez and the U.S. Media," *Extra!* (November/December 2006).

85. Renwick McLean, "Spain Scraps Venezuela Plane Deal," *Denver Post* (October 19, 2006).

86. For an excellent history of WOLA and its activities in Washington, see Coletta A. Youngers, *Thirty Years of Advocacy for Human Rights, Democracy and Social Justice* (Washington, DC: WOLA, 2006).

87. For a discussion of the backlash against democracy promotion, see Thomas Carothers, "The Backlash Against Democracy Promotion," *Foreign Affairs* (March/April 2006).

88. Iran contends that its nuclear program is for peaceful energy development, not for the purpose of building nuclear weapons. In August 2006 it tested ten short-range missiles and indicated it did not intend to stop its uranium enrichment program. In a radio broadcast, one of Iran's senior clerics warned the United States of the dangers of insecurity in the region if it decided to start a war with Iran. See Nazila Fathi, "Iran Fires Practice Missiles and Affirms Nuclear Stance," *New York Times* (August 21, 2006).

89. Sam Logan and Julio Cirino, "Venezuelan Nuclear Technology Is a Long Shot," *ISN Security Watch* (October 26, 2005). Logan and Cirino raise doubts about the seriousness of President Chavez's nuclear ambitions, but they also recognize that his intentions are part of an effort to create an anti-U.S. alliance in the region and cause headaches for Washington in its efforts to deal with nuclear threats brewing in North Korea and Iran. "If Chavez is serious about bringing nuclear power to Venezuela, he would need at least ten years, if not closer to 20, to realize the first kilowatt of nuclear power output. There is currently little guarantee that he can stay in power that long." Whatever intentions President

Chávez has in developing nuclear technology, his contacts with Argentina, Brazil, Iran, and North Korea are enough for Washington policymakers to worry about Venezuela as an international hot spot.

90. Bill Weinberg, "Muslims in the Americas Face Scrutiny," *NACLA Report on the Americas*, Vol. 38, No. 6 (May/June 2005: 25–27).

91. Steve Rendall, "Imperial Mythology: Venezuela, Hugo Chávez, and the U.S. Media," *Extra!* (November/December 2006).

92. Thom Shanker, "A New Enemy Gains on the U.S.," *New York Times* (July 30, 2006).

93. Michael Shifter, "In Search of Hugo Chávez," *Foreign Affairs*, Vol. 85, No. 3 (May/June 2006: 51). Shifter offers a critique of Chávez's political project and blames oil and Washington's neglect of the region and its counterproductive Cold War mindset.

94. "The Latinobarómetro Poll: The Democracy Dividend," *The Economist* (December 7, 2006; http://www.economist.com/world/la/displaystory.cfm?story_id=8381789, accessed October 26, 2007).

95. Simon Romero, "Chávez Unscathed as Crime Soars in Venezuela," *New York Times* (December 2, 2006).

96. Michael Shifter, "Don't Count Chavez Out," *New York Daily News* (July 13, 2006).

97. Greg Grandin, "Countervailing Powers," *LASA Forum*, Vol. 37, No. 1 (Winter 2007:16).

98. Justin Delacour, "The Op-Ed Assassination of Hugo Chavez," *Extra!* (November/December 2005).

99. Mary Anastasio O'Grady, "Defining Democracy Down," *Wall Street Journal* (December 15, 2006).

100. Antonio Maira, "U.S. Warnings and Threats to Telesur," *Resource Center of the Americas* (June 27, 2005; http://www.americas.org/item, accessed July 27, 2005).

101. Since the media-backed coup against Chávez in 2002, government-media relations have been strained in Venezuela. In an effort to strengthen his control over the broadcast industry, President Chávez decided to not renew the broadcast license of RCTV because of its editorial policies and its role in the brief removal of Chávez as president in 2002.

102. Mary Anastasia O'Grady, "Terror's Apologist in Caracas," *Wall Street Journal* (April 7, 2006).

103. Steve Rendall, "Imperial Mythology," *Extra!* (November/December 2006).

104. "Venezuela, Hugo Chávez & the Press," *Extra!* Vol. 19, No. 6 (November/December 2006).

105. Joel Wendland, "Hugo Chavez and the Bolivarian Revolution in Venezuela" (http://politicalaffairs.net/article/view/1707/1/115/).

106. For an assessment of the war of words between Caracas and Washington, see Michael Shifter, "In Search of Hugo Chavez," *Foreign Affairs*, Vol. 85, No 3 (May/June 2006).

107. News Release, Pew Research Center, April 10, 2003.

Notes

108. Jonah Gindin and Gregory Wilpert, "At OAS Venezuela Says U.S. Intervention is Prelude to Aggression," *Venezuelanalysis.com* (February 25, 2005).

109. Quoted in William M. LeoGrande, "U.S. Insecurity in Latin America: Radical Populism," *Crosscurrents* (March 2006: 10).

110. Simon Romero, "U.S. Officials Say Venezuela Knew Military Equipment Was in Seized Cargo," *New York Times* (August 28, 2006: A7). U.S. diplomatic and military personnel deny this and claim a manifest was sent to airport officials before the shipment—ordered before the ban on military equipment—was brought to Venezuela aboard a C-17 military transport plane.

111. William M. LeoGrande, "U.S. Insecurity in Latin America: Radical Populism," *Crosscurrents* (March 2006: 10).

112. "U.S.-Region: 'Radical Populism': What Kind of Threat?" *Security and Strategic Review* (June 2005).

113. "Reviving a Cold War Atmosphere," *Latin News, Security and Strategic Review* (January 2004).

114. Eva Golinger, "Bush Orders More CIA Activity in Venezuela," *Venezuelanalysis.com* (January 19, 2007). According to Golinger, "The recent elections in Ecuador, Nicaragua and Bolivia indicate a growing trend towards a more socialist-cooperative oriented foreign and national policy in Latin America that follows Venezuela's lead and a clear rejection of U.S. domination in the hemisphere."

115. Michael Hardt, "From Imperialism to Empire," *The Nation* (July 31/August 7, 2006).

116. Mark Falcoff, "The Chavez Revolution," in Damian Fernandez and Daniel Erikson, eds., *Cuba, Venezuela and the Americas: A Changing Landscape* (Washington, DC: Inter-American Dialogue, 2005: 13).

Chapter 4: The Southern Cone and Brazil

1. Aldo C. Vacs, "Argentina," in Harry E. Vanden and Gary Prevost, eds. *Politics of Latin America: The Power Game* (New York: Oxford University Press, 2002: 400).

2. Natural Resources Defense Council, "Latin American Wildlands in Danger" (http://www.nrdc.org/international/flamerica.asp, accessed December 12, 2005).

3. "Venezuela: Chávez: the 'Imperialist Threat,'" *Latin American Security and Strategic Review* (February 2004).

4. Peter Muello, "Lawless Region of Amazon Rain Forest Put Under Protection," *Denver Post* (December 5, 2006).

5. Larry Rohter, "Both Sides Say Dam Project is Pivotal Issue for Brazil," *New York Times* (June 11, 2007).

6. Ewen MacAskill, Uki Goni, and Oliver Bach, "Argentina Ups the Ante in New Battle Over Falklands," *The Guardian* (July 1, 2006).

7. Jason McClure, "The Falklands War: Causes and Lessons," *Strategic Insights*, Vol. 3, No. 11 (November 2004). Using prospect theory, McClure argues that in assessing gains and losses the Argentine junta calculated that gains would outweigh losses if it was possible to "recover" the islands in a quick and successful attack.

8. Paraguay's long history of dictatorship left a legacy of terror, corruption, and fear as the mainstays of political life. For most of the Cold War, General Alfredo Stroessner ruled through a continual state of siege that placed the president above the law; security forces that arrested, killed, and intimidated the political opposition; an economy administered so corruptly that it was often explained as the cost of maintaining peace; and a United Nations voting record that backed the United States on virtually every important issue. Backed by the United States, Stroessner and other military rulers seized power in South America and worked together to undercut Marxist or terrorist threats to the dictatorships. After thirty-five years in power, a military faction removed Stroessner from power in 1989. He spent the final years in exile in Brazil, where he died of a stroke at the age of 93. See Diana Jean Shemo, "Gen. Alfredo Stroessner, Colorful Dictator of Paraguay for 35 Years, Dies in Exile at 93," *New York Times* (August 17, 2006).

9. Paulo Prada, "5 Days of Violence by Gangs in Sao Paulo Leaves 115 Dead Before Subsiding," *New York Times* (May 17, 2006).

10. Charles F. Andrain and James T. Smith, *Political Democracy, Trust, and Social Justice: A Comparative Overview* (Boston: Northeastern University Press, 2006: 28–29) Andrain and Smith offer a lengthy critique of neoliberalism, offering a more positive view of government than that of free-market capitalists.

11. Ibid., p. 57.

12. Pascale Bonnefoy, "Chile Looks (Slightly) Left," *The Nation* (March 20, 2006).

13. Vinay Jawahar, "Latin America: Looking Left?" *The Internationalist*, Vol. 3, No. 1 (Spring 2006). For an alternate view of Chile's poverty reduction, see Andrain and Smith (2006).

14. Larry Rohter, "Chile Copper Windfall Forces Hard Choices on Spending," *New York Times* (January 7, 2007). Thanks to the copper law's largesse, Chile spends more per capita on the military than any other country in Latin America. The recent purchases—F-16 aircraft, frigates, submarines, and tanks—have caused expressions of alarm in Peru and Bolivia and brought condemnation of the United States for supplying the weapons.

15. "Augusto Pinochet: The Passing of a Tyrant," *Economist.com* (December 13, 2006).

16. Marc Cooper, "Pinochet's Legacy," *The Nation* (January 1, 2007)

17. Larry Rohter, "Chile's Leader Attacks Amnesty for Pinochet-Era Crimes," *New York Times* (December 24, 2006).

18. Robert Parry, "Pinochet's Death Spares the Bush Family," *Consortium-news.com* (December 12, 2006; http://www.consortiumnews.com/, accessed December 12, 2006). Parry claims, on the basis of declassified government documents, that the Bush family cover-up of Pinochet's guilt began in 1976, when George H. W. Bush was director of the CIA and diverted investigators away from Pinochet's guilt in a Washington car bombing, and continue under George W. Bush, when he sidetracked an FBI recommendation to indict Pinochet in the car bomb murders.

19. Eduardo Gallardo, "In Letter, Pinochet Called Abuses in Chile 'Necessary,'" *Washington Post* (December 25, 2006).

Notes

20. Larry Rohter, "A Leader Making Peace with Chile's Past," *New York Times* (January 16, 2006).
21. Pascale Bonnefoy, "Chile Looks (Slightly) Left," *The Nation* (March 20, 2006: 6).
22. Justin Vogler, "The Rise of the Penguins," *NACLA Report on the Americas* (January/February, 2007).
23. Joe Pappalardo, "South American Hotspot Garners U.S. Attention," *National Defense Magazine* (June 2005; http://www.nationaldefensemagazine.org/issues/2005/Jun/uf-south_america.htm, accessed March 7, 2006).
24. See also Rex Hudson, "Terrorist and Organized Crime Groups in the Tri-Border Area (TBA) of South America" (Washington, D.C.: Federal Research Division, Library of Congress, July 2003).
25. Ibid., p. 4.
26. Chris Zambelis, "Radical Islam in Latin America," *Terrorism Monitor*, Vol. 3, No. 23 (December 2, 2005).
27. Monte Reel, "Argentina Pursues Iran in '94 Blast as Neighbors Court Ahmadinejad," *Washington Post* (January 14, 2007).
28. See, for example, James Dao, "Threats and Responses: South America; U.S. Expanding Effort to Block Terrorist Funds in Latin Region," *New York Times* (December 21, 2002), and Timothy L. O'Brien, "South America Area is Cited as Haven for Terrorist Training," *New York Times* (October 10, 2003).
29. Thom Shanker and Scott Shane, "Elite Groups Get Expanded Role on Intelligence," *New York Times* (March 8, 2006).
30. Rex Hudson, "Terrorist and Organized Crime Groups in the Tri-Border Area (TBA) of South America," report prepared by the Federal Research Division, Library of Congress (July 2003). See also Blanca Madani, "Hezbollah's Global Finance Network: The Triple Frontier," *Middle East Intelligence Bulletin*, Vol. 4, No. 1 (January 2002); Monte Reel, "Paraguayan Smuggling Crossroads Scrutinized," *Washington Post* (August 3, 2006). In an effort to uncover money laundering by groups linked to terrorism, the United States has launched a series of new measures, including more banking sector involvement in regional efforts against money laundering as well as training courses for investigators and prosecutors in charge of combating possible terrorism links.

Chapter 5: The Caribbean: Cuba and Haiti

1. For a brief discussion of the failure of the Bush administration's efforts to transform a post-Castro Cuba, see Wayne S. Smith, "A Bankrupt Cuba Policy," *The Nation* (August 28/September 4, 2006: 8). "What we have here, " according to Smith, "is a totally bankrupt policy. The [Bush] Administration will not deal with the existing government, whether led by Fidel or Raúl. It calls for a democratic transitional government but has no means of bringing one into being."
2. Ginger Thompson, "Surprising Experts, Cuba Stays Calm With Castro on Sidelines," *New York Times* (August 14, 2006).
3. Daniel P. Erikson, "After Fidel: Oh, Brother ... " *Current History* (February 2007: 91).

4. Julia Jatar-Hausmann, *The Cuban Way: Capitalism, Communism and Confrontation* (West Hartford, CT: Kumarian Press, 1999: 132)

5. The Platt Amendment was a clause in the 1902 Cuban constitution that gave the United States the right to intervene for the preservation of Cuban independence, political stability and the protection of U.S. investments on the island. It was the brainchild of Elihu Root, although it was named after Republican senator Orville Platt of Connecticut.

6. Louis A. Pérez, Jr., "Fear and Loathing of Fidel Castro: Sources of U.S. Policy Toward Cuba," *Journal of Latin American* Studies, Vol. 34 (2002).

7. Ibid.

8. Ian F.W. Beckett, *Modern Insurgencies and Counter-Insurgencies: Guerrillas and Their Opponents since 1750* (New York: Routledge, 2001: 169).

9. David W. Dent, *Historical Dictionary of U.S.-Latin American Relations* (Westport, CT: Greenwood Press, 2005: 393).

10. Bella Thomas, "A Cuban Death Rehearsal," *Prospect Magazine* (June 2007).

11. Orlando Patterson, "The Other Losing War," *New York Times* (January 13, 2007).

12. Ibid.

13. U.S. Department of State, "International Narcotics Control Strategy Report: The Caribbean" (Washington, D.C.: Bureau of International Narcotics and Law Enforcement Affairs, March 2006).

14. Ibid.

15. Otto J. Reich, "The Administration's Four Goals in the Western Hemisphere," Remarks to the Heritage Foundation, Washington, DC, October 31, 2002.

16. BBC News, "Destination Guantánamo Bay" (December 28, 2001).

17. In what he calls the Guantánamo syndrome, David Ignatius argues that it's time to close the Guantánamo prison because of what it doing to American captors and the image of the United States abroad. See David Ignatius, "A Prison We Need to Escape," *Washington Post* (June 14, 2006).

18. Editorial, "The Abuse Can Continue," *Washington Post* (September 22, 2006).

19. Charles Babington and Michael Abramowitz, "U.S. Shifts Policy on Geneva Conventions," *Washington Post* (July 12, 2006).

20. BBC News, "Country Profile: Haiti" (http://newsvote.bbc.co.uk/mpapps/pagetools/, accessed December 3, 2006).

21. Reed Lindsay, "Peace Despite the Peacekeepers in Haiti,"*NACLA Report on the Americas* (May/June 2006).

22. Saul Hudson, "U.S. Prods Likely Haiti Victor to Shun Aristide," *Reuters AlertNet* (February 10, 2006; http://www.alertnet.org/thenews/newsdesk, accessed February 10, 2006).

23. Ginger Thompson, "Candidate of Haiti's Poor Leads In Early Tally with 61% of Vote," *New York Times* (February 10, 2006).

24. For a first-hand examination of the removal of Aristide in February-March 2004 and the role of the State Department and U.S. media in the rebellion, see Amy Goodman and David Goodman, *Static: Government Liars, Media*

Cheerleaders, and the People Who Fight Back (New York: Hyperion, 2006: Chapter 7).

25. Ibid., p. 125.

26. Ginger Thompson, "Fear and Death Ensnare U.N.'s Soldiers in Haiti," *New York Times* (January 24, 2006). For an extremely detailed account of U.S. policymaking toward Haiti, including the role of the U.S. ambassador, the National Endowment for Democracy, and the role of the neoconservatives in getting rid of Aristide, see Walt Bogdanich and Jenny Norberg, "Mixed Signals Helped Tilt Haiti Toward Chaos," *New York Times* (January 29, 2006). They also discuss the role of the anti-Castro Fanjul brothers in the Dominican Republic, working with the Haitian opposition to undermine democracy when it did not suit Washington.

Chapter 6: Non-Iberian South America: Guyana and Suriname

1. Anton Foek, "Oil Fuels Suriname-Guyana Border Clash," *Corpwatch.org* (July 5, 2005).

2. Letta Taylor, "Caribbean Terror Fears," *Newsday.com* (June 6, 2007).

3. Marc Lacey, "Trinidad Group Denies Link to New York Bomb Plot," *New York Times* (June 10, 2007).

4. Joseph Contreras, "Iran's Foray Into Latin America," *MSNBC.com/ Newsweek* (February 5, 2007).

5. Steve Schippert and Kyle Dabruzzi, "Coming to America: Guyana and the JFK Plot," *ThreatsWatch.org* (June 2007).

6. Pablo Gato and Robert Windrem, "Hezbollah Builds a Western Base," *MSNBC.com* (May 9, 2007).

7. Ellen Barry and Ethan Wilensky-Lanford, "Many Guyanese in New York Are Puzzled by Terror Arrests," *New York Times* (June 5, 2007).

8. Ibid.

Chapter 7: Conclusion

1. "The Terrorism Index," *Center for American Progress* (June 14, 2006).

2. Howard J. Wiarda with the assistance of Esther M. Skelly, *Dilemmas of Democracy in Latin America: Crises and Opportunity* (Lanham, MD: Rowman and Littlefield, 2005).

3. See, for example, Paul Wilkinson, *Terrorism Versus Democracy: The Liberal State Response* (London: Frank Cass, 2002: Chapter 9).

4. Steven Metz, "Rethinking Insurgency," report published by the Strategic Studies Institute of the Army War College (June 2007).

5. See, for example, David Adams, "'Narcoterrorism' Needs Attention," *St. Petersburg Times* (March 10, 2003); April Howard and Benjamin Dangl, "City of Terror: Painting Paraguay's 'Casbah' as Terror Central," *Extra!* (September/October 2007); Joe Pappalardo, "South America Hotspot Garners U.S. Attention," *National Defense* (June 2005); and Mark P. Sullivan, "Latin America: Terrorism Issues," *CRS Report for Congress* (January 22, 2007).

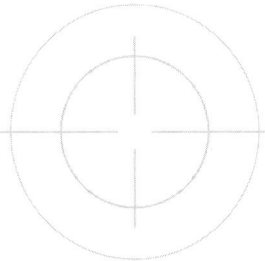

Select Bibliography

Print Sources

Andrain, Charles F., and James T. Smith. *Political Democracy, Trust, and Social Justice: A Comparative Overview* (Boston: Northeastern University Press, 2006). A valuable comparative study of the importance of trust, distrust, and tolerance in the democratic process. Using a political exchange framework, the authors find that public officials gain support and legitimacy when they can demonstrate they are taking prudent measures against a threatening group. The importance of a trust-based reciprocal relationship between the governed and public officials is demonstrated in an age in which those in power can easily manipulate information about dangerous groups in order to gain support for a range of domestic and foreign policies.

Arnson, Cynthia J., ed. *Comparative Peace Processes in Latin America* (Washington, DC/Stanford, CA: Woodrow Wilson Center Press/Stanford University, 1999).

Bailey, John, and Lucía Dammert, eds. *Public Security and Police Reform in the Americas* (Pittsburgh, PA: University of Pittsburgh Press, 2006). A comparative study of public security, police reform, crime, and threats to democratic rule in five Latin American countries and the United States. Analysis suggests that attempts to address problems of public security by applying methods that have been tried in the United States to crime/violence problems in Latin America may be inappropriate and that public security and police reform are far more complex than is frequently assumed. Whether insecurity is rooted in criminal violence or in terrorism, it provides one of the pillars for understanding hot spots in the Americas. Terrorism was defeated in Peru through careful police work, not repression or U.S. military involvement—an important note for those who claim to be involved in eliminating hot spots worldwide.

Bjørgo, Tore, ed. *Root Causes of Terrorism: Myths, Reality, and Ways Forward* (New York: Routledge, 2005). A succinct examination of the root causes of terrorism that should be taken into account by those in the security community with responsibility for tracking and responding to hot spots around the globe.

Blum, William. *Rogue State: A Guide to the World's Only Superpower* (Monroe, Maine: Common Courage Press, 2000). A powerful critique of the dangerous consequences of U.S. global intervention in order to maintain American hegemony. Written before the terrorist attacks of September 11, 2001, Blum argues that the search for enemies and exaggerated threats have been part of American foreign policy for at least a century. His chapters on Washington's love/hate relationship with terrorists and human-rights violators and a history of global intervention that negates official rhetoric that America stands for freedom, social justice, and democracy should awaken everyone to the hypocrisy involved in dealing with global hot spots.

Bouvier, Virginia M., ed. *The Globalization of U.S.-Latin American Relations: Democracy, Intervention and Human Rights* (New York: Praeger, 2002). Edited volume with essays that focus on the key issues that confront the governments of the Americas from a historical perspective. Important topics such as human rights and U.S. military intervention provide context to understanding the foreign policy rationale for dealing with security-based hot spots, particularly when foreign influence is involved.

Burt, Jo-Marie, and Philip Mauceri, eds. *Politics in the Andes: Identity, Conflict, Reform* (Pittsburgh, PA: University of Pittsburgh Press, 2004). An important work on Andean politics with an emphasis on ethnic identity, drug trafficking, violence, human rights, poverty, and state building and dismantling. Despite its contemporary focus on political instability, there is not enough discussion of the role the United States has played in economic reform efforts, the impact of counterinsurgency on democracy, and different modes of conflict resolution.

Buxton, Julia. *The Failure of Political Reform in Venezuela* (Aldershot, England: Ashgate, 2001).

Carothers, Thomas. *In the Name of Democracy: U.S. Policy Toward Latin America in the Reagan Years* (Berkeley: University of California Press, 1991). Critical assessment of President Reagan's democracy promotion efforts in Latin America, in which the author claims that Reagan's Latin American policies did not contribute significantly to democratic development in Latin America because of "structural domestic factors such as the extreme concentration of economic and political power in the hands of undemocratic elites, sociopolitical marginalization of whole classes of citizens, and the lack of any underlying national consensus on basic democratic values." Important work for understanding why neoconservatives in the United States often fail to succeed in bringing democracy and freedom to countries and regions where hot spots exist.

Chillier, Gastón, and Laurie Freeman. "Potential Threat: The New OAS Concept of Hemispheric Security," WOLA Special Report (Washington, D.C.: Washington Office on Latin America, July 2005). A threat-based report on the expansion of the concept of security in the Americas.

Chomsky, Noam. *Failed States: The Abuse of Power and the Assault on American Democracy* (New York: Metropolitan Books/Henry Holt, 2006). A powerful critique of American foreign policy by a long-time critic who argues that the United States is a failed state because of the abuse of power associated with the Iraq war and the destruction of democratic principles at home.

Chua, Amy. *World on Fire: How Exporting Free Market Democracy Breeds Ethnic Hatred and Global Instability* (New York: Doubleday, 2003). Professor at Yale Law School finds that those who believe that free markets and democracy are essential to curing the world's ills are naive and misguided. Chua says that all too often bringing free markets and elections to developing nations leads to hate-mongering, discrimination and genocidal violence of major proportions.

Crandall, Russell. *Gunboat Democracy: The United States Interventions in the Dominican Republic, Grenada, and Panama* (Lanham, MD: Rowman and Littlefield, 2006). A careful examination of the motives for intervention and occupation in Latin America with lessons for dealing with Latin American hot spots deemed important to U.S. security by those in decision-making positions.

Crandall, Russell, Guadalupe Paz, and Riordan Roett, eds. *The Andes in Focus: Security, Democracy, and Economic Reform* (Boulder, CO: Lynne Rienner, 2005). Edited volume devoted to major problems in the Andes, often connected to security-based hot spots in the region.

Crotty, William, ed. *Democratic Development and Political Terrorism: The Global Perspective* (Boston: Northeastern University Press, 2005). A collection of useful essays on the connection between democratic development and political terrorism. The difficulties of defining and responding to terrorist threats illustrated in this volume should be read by those involved in the global war on terrorism.

Delacour, Justin. "The Op-Ed Assassination of Hugo Chavez," *Extra!* (November/December 2005).

Demmers, Jolle, Alex Fernández Jilbert, and Barbara Hogenboom, eds. *Good Governance in the Era of Global Neoliberalism: Conflict and Depolitization in Latin America* (New York: Routledge, 2004). An important book on the concept of good governance—a political regime based on the liberal democratic polity model. The in-depth case studies provide insights for understanding the causes and effects of neoliberalism, one of the primary sources of discontent driving Latin American voters to choose leaders who oppose neoliberal restructuring and development.

Dent, David W. *The Legacy of the Monroe Doctrine: A Reference Guide to U.S. Involvement in Latin America and the Caribbean* (Westport, CT: Greenwood Press, 1999). Major reference work devoted to the history of U.S. involvement in twenty-four Latin American and Caribbean nations since President James Monroe's message to Congress in 1823. As a founding myth of the United States, the Monroe Doctrine tried to ban extracontinental interventions in the Americas but ignored U.S. interventions in Latin America. As a justification for intervention, the Monroe Doctrine was a source of anti-Americanism in Latin America.

———. *Historical Dictionary of U.S.-Latin American Relations* (Westport, CT: Greenwood Press, 2005). An exhaustive compilation of more than 260 entries detailing the key events, people, treaties, wars and interventions, and key concepts that have gone into the making of the often contentious relations between the United States and the Latin American and Caribbean region. The topics in the dictionary that are important to understanding security-based hot spots include: anti-Americanism, backyard metaphor, banana wars, Contras, death squads, democracy and democracy promotion, domino theory, guerrilla warfare, imperialism, Monroe Doctrine, Operation Condor, Operation Northwoods, Plan Colombia, Reagan Doctrine, regime change, revolutions, scandals and blunders, terrorism, and threat perception/assessment.

Drake, Paul W., and Eric Hershberg, eds. *State and Society in Conflict: Comparative Perspectives on Andean Crises* (Pittsburgh, PA: University of Pittsburgh Press, 2006). Edited volume with essays in search of the common elements of crisis in the Andes region. Where strains between state and society have produced political breakdown and endangered Latin American democracies, the domestic stress can be observed in poor economic growth, inequalities in wealth distribution, social unrest, and political instability. These crises have aroused international concern to the point that Washington policymakers have often referred to these events as security-based hot spots requiring police or military training to put out the fires of resentment. Valuable for its examination of how the United States has taken issues traditionally conceived as political and social problems and turned them into "security threats" when they in fact may pose no danger to the vital interests of the United States.

Duncan, Andrew, and Michel Opatowski. *Trouble Spots: The World Atlas of Strategic Information* (Phoenix Mill, UK: Sutton, 2000). British scholars examine the content of "trouble spots" around the globe but consider Latin America a region with few conflicts because democracy has been restored to the region after the Cold War. After considering Latin America to be "outside the mainstream," authors devote brief attention to five hot spots, all of which are included in this book. In conclusion, the authors feel that the world's strategic agenda needs to face the reality that the current global situation is not going to be peaceful.

Ellner, Steve, and Daniel Hellinger, eds. *Venezuelan Politics in the Chavez Era: Class, Polarization, and Conflict* (Boulder, CO: Lynne Rienner, 2003). One of the best studies of Venezuelan president Hugo Chávez, often considered a threat to U.S. interests in Latin America because of his foreign policy based on use of petroleum power to offset U.S. influence, his rhetoric critical of U.S. policy in the region, his association with "enemies" of the United States, and the "dictatorial" policies connected with his Bolivarian Revolution.

Fruhling, Hugo, Joseph S. Tulchin, and Heather A. Golding, eds. *Crime and Violence in Latin America: Citizen Security, Democracy, and the States* (Baltimore, MD: Woodrow Wilson Center Press and the Johns Hopkins University Press, 2003). An examination of citizen security in Latin America, where violence and crime pose serious threats to fragile democracies and weak states. A valuable collection of case studies by regional experts with specific policy recommendations/lessons for handling current and future threats.

Gill, Lesley. *The School of the Americas: Military Training and Political Violence* (Durham, NC: Duke University Press, 2004). A first-hand examination of the U.S. Army School of the Americas, a Cold War institution designed to stop Communism through counterinsurgency training of Latin American military officers at Ft. Benning, Georgia. With a new name—Western Hemisphere Institute for Security Cooperation—in 2001, the training school reformulated its course offerings to respond to the exposure of the use of manuals that included assassination and torture. Gill's book is highly critical of the School of the Americas, wants it closed permanently, and worries that the Bush administration's war on terrorism may justify the proclivity of Latin American militaries to violate human rights in the same way that anti-communism justified human rights violations during the Cold War. A useful critique for understanding how the United States responds to security-based hot spots in Latin America and the Caribbean.

Goodman, Amy, and David Goodman. *Static: Government Liars, Media Cheerleaders, and the People Who Fight Back* (New York: Hyperion, 2006). A valuable critique of how the Bush administration has manipulated and fabricated news events concerned with "security threats" and how the corporate media have served as cheerleaders for war, torture, and the violation of civil liberties at home. In a first-hand account, the Goodmans detail how the United States secretly supported armed rebels determined to overthrow the democratically elected government of Haitian President Jean-Bertrand Aristide in 2004.

Gott, Richard. *Hugo Chávez and the Bolivarian Revolution* (New York: Verso, 2005). Solid account of Hugo Chávez's rise to power, the essence of his Bolivarian Revolution, the infamous U.S.-backed coup attempt in 2002, and continuing efforts to bring about regime change in Venezuela. A revealing account of one of Washington's major hot spot headaches in South America.

Gross, Liza. *Handbook of Leftist Guerrilla Groups in Latin America and the Caribbean* (Boulder, CO: Westview, 1995). Well-crafted reference book on Latin American revolutionaries from nineteen countries. Each of these groups is characterized by a political ideology that is Marxist-Leninist, Trotskyist, Maoist, Guevarist, or Castrist; professes goals that seek the subversion of the established sociopolitical structure and its replacement by a Marxist or Marxism-inspired state; displays a commitment to armed struggle and the use of violence; and operates in a clandestine manner rather than as open organizations. Author concludes that guerrilla groups in only three countries have been successful—Cuba, Nicaragua, and Grenada—with the rest failing to achieve their basic goals of political and social change.

Hakim, Peter. "Is Washington Losing Latin America?" *Foreign Affairs*, Vol. 85, No. 1 (January/February 2006). After more than five years in power, Hakim faults the Bush administration for ignoring Latin America and the tremendous costs in security for doing so.

Hayworth, J. D. *Whatever It Takes: Illegal Immigration, Border Security and the War on Terror* (Washington, DC: Regnery, 2006). Former Arizona congressman's fear-based volume that argues that Latin American immigration should be halted because of the connection between illegal immigration and terrorism. Hayworth's alarmist rhetoric, including the certainty that al-Qaeda has the capacity to ship a nuke across the border, contributed to his defeat in the 2006 election.

Herman, Edward S., "Threat Inflation: Going After Hapless Countries," *Z Magazine* (March 2003).

Holmes, Steven. *The Matador's Cape: America's Reckless Response to Terror* (Cambridge, UK: Cambridge University Press, 2007). Important work that suggests that security threats and hot spots are ideologically malleable in the hands of politicians who are more interested in intelligence that suits their political ideology than more accurate assessments of threats around the globe. Holmes argues that the purpose of U.S. military intervention around the globe, whether to remove a dictator, eliminate dangerous weapons or guerrilla groups, or douse the fires of hot spots, is often designed to advertise the folly of defying the power of the United States.

Homer-Dixon, Thomas, "Terror in the Weather Forecast," *New York Times* (April 24, 2007). Journalistic account of the relationship between the world's hot spots and climate change. Author argues that many security-based hot spots are associated with climatic alterations where frail governments must face a plethora of conditions—cropland degradation, deforestation, soil erosion, and scarcity of fresh water—that lead to failed states where extremism and terrorism flourish.

Johnson, Chalmers A. *Nemesis: The Last Days of the American Republic* (New York: Metropolitan Books, 2007). Final volume of a series of books on the failures of American foreign policy and the consequences for the American political system. Johnson makes a convincing case that imperial overstretch is undermining the republic itself, both economically and politically. The current leaders in Washington have furthered U.S. dependence on a permanent war economy, which means that threat perceptions often drive the need to respond to hot spots, no matter what the evidence that a danger lurks beyond the seas or borders.

———. "Republic or Empire: A National Intelligence Estimate of the United States," *Harper's Magazine* (January 2007). A brief article in which Johnson argues that the expense of the U.S. empire is based on "military Keynesianism," which places its emphasis on the available supply of money in the United States, not on the need or demand for defense. Among his conclusions is that the consequences of this form of government spending are eventually bankruptcy, collapse, and a loss of control over international affairs.

Kagan, Robert, and William Kristol, eds. *Present Dangers: Crisis and Opportunity in American and Defense Policy* (San Francisco: Encounter Books, 2000).

Kampwirth, Karen. *Women and Guerrilla Movements: Nicaragua, El Salvador, Chiapas, Cuba* (University Park: Pennsylvania State University Press, 2002). Using in-depth interviews, Kampwirth examines the political, structural, ideological, and personal factors that motivated Latin American women to join guerrilla forces in Nicaragua, El Salvador, and Mexico. A useful study for understanding the complexities of Latin American revolutionary movements and the need for better understanding of such movements in Washington.

Karl, Terry. *The Paradox of Plenty: Oil Booms and Petro-States* (Berkeley: University of California Press, 1997).

Kelly de Escobar, Janet, and Carlos Romero. *The United States and Venezuela: Rethinking a Relationship* (New York: Routledge, 2002).

Kinzer, Stephen. *Overthrow: America's Century of Regime Change from Hawaii to Iraq* (New York: Time Books/Henry Holt & Company, 2006). A sobering historical study of America's intervention and regime change in which the author argues that not only were many of the U.S. interventions in Latin America and around the world ruthless and costly—the majority were utterly unnecessary. A must read for neoconservatives committed to regime change wherever a hot spot is located and placed on the military intervention radar screen.

Kluger, Jeffrey. "Why We Worry About the Things We Shouldn't . . . and Ignore the Things We Should," *Time* (December 4, 2006). A brief but valuable article that shows that psychologists have found that people, and countries, with vast amounts of power, are far more likely to inflate security risks in order to demonstrate resolve and domination instead of following a decisionmaking path that involves more nuanced options that require more time, honesty, and accurate (unmanipulated) data. On the other hand, national security also depends on a responsible citizenry and national media that takes the time to understand the accuracy of what political leaders are telling them, particularly during times of war, intervention, and occupation.

Koonings, Kees, and Dirk Kruijt, eds. *Armed Actors: Organised Violence and State Failure in Latin America* (London: Zed Books, 2004). An informative examination of partial state failure in five Latin American countries with an emphasis on "new types of organized violence." The presence of social actors (drug mafias and urban gangs) and state-related actors (police, military, intelligence agencies, and paramilitary forces) have contributed to severe challenges to the legitimate state apparatus with the possibility of the reinstallation of authoritarian regimes. Of importance in this book is the observation that partial state failure is rooted in the failure of neoliberal economic policies and the inability of weakened state structures to deliver jobs, social services, and an improved quality of life.

Kushner, Shana A. "Threat, Media, and Foreign Policy Opinion," paper prepared for delivery at the 2005 APSA Political Communication on International Communication and Conflict (2005). Interesting paper devoted to an understanding of how leaders and the media manipulate threats in the conduct of American foreign policy. Kushner's results show that the media generate threat perceptions, general fears of other countries and groups, and the emergence of hot spots with security implications that over time can create negative predispositions among the American public that make it easier to use military force against a foreign power or nonstate actor. While showing that American attitudes shifted from 2000 to 2002 to a more "hawkish" foreign policy, Kushner points out that a heightened security threat frequently promotes increased in-group solidarity, intolerance, ethnocentrism, negative stereotyping of foreign leaders, and support for curtailing civil liberties. This study provides important implications for the so-called global war on terrorism.

Latin American Newsletters, Special Report. "Is Latin America Shifting to the Left?" (July 2003). Brief examination of political trends in Latin American elections that shows that the shift to the left in Latin America is real; however, to understand this trend means that prior threat assessments need to be reevaluated in light of this trend. The report's conclusion is that there is a noticeable shift to the left, but not one that should signal a danger to the United States or the member states of the Americas.

Logan, Justin, and Christopher Preble. "Failed States and Flawed Logic: The Case Against a Standing Nation-Building Office," *Policy Analysis*, No. 560 (January 11, 2006).

Loveman, Brian. *Addicted to Failure: U.S. Security Policy in Latin America and the Andean Region* (Lanham, MD: Rowman and Littlefield, 2006).

Mallon, Florencia E. *Courage Tastes of Blood: The Mapuche Community of Nicolás Ailío and the Chilean State, 1906-2001* (Durham, NC: Duke University Press, 2005). Using oral histories and archival documents, author contributes to an understanding of the history of ethnic conflict in southern Chile.

Manwaring, Max G. "Venezuela's Hugo Chávez, Bolivarian Socialism, and Asymmetric Warfare" (Carlyle Barracks, PA: Strategic Studies Institute, October 2005). Major military think tank assesses the possible threats from what is happening in Venezuela during the Chávez revolution.

Mares, David R. *Violent Peace: Militarized Interstate Bargaining in Latin America* (New York: Columbia University Press, 2001). Theoretical analysis of inter-American security in which the author attempts to explain the use of force in Latin American democracies. Emphasis is placed on the management of conflict, not necessarily its resolution. By inference, hot spots tend to escalate when political leaders ignore the positive effects of deterrence.

———. *The Political Economy of the International Drug Trade* (Washington, DC: CQ Press, 2006).

McCaughan, Michael. *Venezuela: Polarising Politics* (London: Latin American Bureau, 2003).

———. *The Battle of Venezuela* (New York: Seven Stories Press, 2005). Leftist account of the rise of Hugo Chávez, the nature of his political legitimacy, and the current development of Venezuela under his "Bolivarian" experiment in socialism.

McCoy, Jennifer, and David Myers, eds. *The Unraveling of Venezuelan Democracy* (Baltimore, MD: Johns Hopkins University, 2004).

McSherry, J. Patrice. *Predatory States: Operation Condor and Covert War in Latin America* (Lanham, MD: Rowman and Littlefield, 2005). Ground-breaking study of Operation Condor, a covert Latin American military network created during the Cold War to capture and eliminate political opponents considered dangerous. McSherry points out that the current war against terrorism has important parallels to the Cold War anti-Communist crusade in which ruthless militaries in Latin America, aided and abetted by Washington, used methods of terror—torture and murder—to wage their anti-Communist wars in secrecy. The tremendous power of Henry Kissinger in defining threats and mobilizing secret counterinsurgency efforts is carefully documented in this important study. Unfortunately, as McSherry points out, "The legacy of Operation Condor still casts a long shadow over Latin America, the United States and the world."

Menjívar, Cecilia, and Néstor Rodríguez. *When States Kill: The U.S. and Technologies of Terror* (Austin: University of Texas Press, 2005). Sobering analysis of state repression allowed to operate for decades with the apparent support of the United States.

Mitchell, Nancy. *The Danger of Dreams: German and American Imperialism in Latin America* (Chapel Hill: University of North Carolina Press, 1999). Historical analysis of the purported "German threat" in the late nineteenth century in which the perils of foreign designs on the Western Hemisphere were often exaggerated to expand American power abroad and justify presidential action and authority in foreign affairs. A valuable multi-archival study with implications for understanding threat perceptions, hot spot determination and response, and the negative consequences of regime change.

Mueller, John. *Overblown: How Politicians and the Terrorism Industry Inflate National Security Threats, and Why We Believe Them* (New York: Free Press, 2007). A path-breaking work on threat inflation with emphasis on a tradition in American history of overreaction to overblown domestic and international threats.

Myers, David J., ed. *Regional Hegemons: Threat Perception and Strategic Responses* (Boulder, CO: Westview Press, 1991).

North American Congress on Latin America. "The Wars Within: Counterinsurgency in Chiapas and Colombia," *NACLA Report on the Americas*, Vol. 31, No. 5 (March/April 1998). Valuable assessment of the internal wars in Mexico and Colombia where poverty, civil war, and government neglect drive opposition movements to conservative governments.

———. "Bolivia Fights Back," *NACLA Report on the Americas*, Vol. 38, No. 3 (November/December 2004). Important investigative reporting on Bolivia's battle against multinational corporations with control over key commodities and resources.

———. "War on Terror, Target: America," *NACLA Report on the Americas*, Vol 38, No 6 (May/June 2005). Excellent issue devoted to demonstrating that what President Bush calls a "new war on terror" has been practiced in Latin America for decades. In an effort to expand the definition of a terrorist group, Bush's war on terror now considers radical populists, porous borders, and ungoverned spaces that lack effective sovereignty as security threats. In many unintended ways, the global war on terror has exacerbated many of the hot spots in Latin America, particularly the Colombian civil conflict, hostility toward Hugo Chávez's Venezuela, and the growth of militant Islamic groups in South America.

———. "In the Name of Democracy: U.S. Intervention in the Americas Today," *NACLA Report on the Americas*, Vol. 40, No. 1 (January/February, 2007). Valuable report on the use of democracy promotion by the United States to deal with threats from within through electoral intervention and propaganda, pressure on the Organization of American States, and other forms of intervention when democracy, as defined by the United States, fails. The problem for the United States is that Latin Americans see democracy as something quite different from the way policymakers in the United States define it.

Peeler, John. *Building Democracy in Latin America*, 2nd edition (Boulder, CO: Lynne Rienner, 2004). A new edition of a popular book on the causes and dynamics of democratization in Latin America with an emphasis on the need to deepen democracy for it to survive under conditions of globalization. Peeler argues that the low quality of democracy in Latin America provides the core of much of the pessimism surrounding the ability of liberal democracy to survive. The connection between democratic failure and security-based hot spots is implied, not specifically stated in this important book.

Peruzzotti, Enrique, and Catalina Smulovitz, eds. *Enforcing the Rule of Law: Social Accountability in the New Latin American Democracies* (Pittsburgh, PA: University of Pittsburgh Press, 2006). Cogent examination of how legal claims, media interventions, civic organizations, citizen committees, electoral observation panels, and other watchdog groups have become effective tools of political accountability. Authors claim that these social mechanisms of accountability in Latin America have been successful in combating corruption and improving the process of making policy decisions. With mechanisms for making democracies more accountable and representative, some scholars believe that the chances for the emergence of security-based hot spots is considerably reduced.

Rabe, Stephen G. *U.S. Intervention in British Guiana: A Cold War Story* (Chapel Hill: University of North Carolina Press, 2005).

Rochlin, James F. *Vanguard Revolutionaries in Latin America: Peru, Colombia, Mexico* (Boulder, CO: Lynne Rienner, 2003). Excellent treatment of the four most powerful guerrilla movements to operate in Latin America in the past several decades. Analysis assesses their strengths and successes and their weaknesses and failures. Author claims that these rebel groups "enjoyed success and suffered failure largely in accordance with how well they interpreted classic security themes within a shifting epistemological context." Valuable for understanding long-time guerrilla insurgencies such as the FARC in Colombia.

Rotberg, Robert I., ed. *When States Fail: Causes and Consequences* (Princeton, NJ: Princeton University Press, 2004).

Rotker, Susana, ed. *Citizens of Fear: Urban Violence in Latin America* (New Brunswick, NJ: Rutgers University Press, 2002).

Scahill, Jeremy. *Blackwater: The Rise of the World's Most Powerful Mercenary Army* (New York: Nation Books, 2007). In what he calls America's "Praetorian

Guard," Scahill shows how private military contractors operate at home and abroad, at tremendous cost and often without accountability and legal restraints. Although most of the book focuses on Iraq, there are chapters that show how Blackwater draws recruits from Latin America to participate in the global war on terror. An important source for understanding how guerrilla insurgencies are defined and treated in Latin America, particularly the Salvador-type operations that involved death-squad operations against leftist guerrilla insurgencies.

Scheuer, Michael. *Imperial Hubris: Why the West Is Losing the War on Terror* (Washington, DC: Brassey's, 2004). Serious critique of how little Washington understands al-Qaeda, Osama bin Laden, and the global war on terrorism. Scheurer argues that the United States would have far more security and less fear of Islamic groups if it moved to energy efficiency, ceased propping up corrupt regimes like Saudi Arabia and Pakistan, and worked to reduce the propaganda value provided to insurgents worldwide who attack the United States for what it does abroad in the name of democracy and freedom. Author's assessment of U.S. intelligence failures is more valuable than his prescriptions for dealing with security-based hot spots.

Schoultz, Lars. *Beneath the United States: A History of U.S. Policy Toward Latin America* (Cambridge, MA: Harvard University Press, 1998). Excellent historical-political treatment of how the United States responds to security threats in Latin America based on a deeply rooted set of beliefs among Washington policymakers that Latin Americans are inferior or immature and their governments—corrupt, inefficient, autocratic, and lacking sufficient resources—cannot deal forcefully and adequately with threats and attacks by hostile states or nonstate actors. Valuable for understanding threat-based rhetoric used for dealing with enemy foreign powers, Communists, terrorists, drug lords, and other nefarious criminal types. Analysis precedes the Bush Doctrine of pre-emptive war and counter-terrorist policies at home and abroad, but the beliefs that Schoultz finds among Washington policymakers have not changed.

Scott, Peter Dale. *Drugs, Oil and War: The United States in Afghanistan, Colombia, and Indochina* (Lanham, MD: Rowman and Littlefield, 2005). Critical examination of the underlying forces that drive U.S. global policy, particularly the intertwined patterns of drugs, petroleum politics, and intelligence. Useful for understanding how Washington uses commodity-based threat perceptions to search for Third World hot spots.

Sluka, Jeffrey A., ed. *Death Squad. The Anthropology of State Terror* (Philadelphia, PA: University of Pennsylvania Press, 2000).

Smith, Gaddis. *The Last Years of the Monroe Doctrine, 1945–1993* (New York: Hill and Wang, 1994). An important historical study of one of the most important foreign policy tools of the United States in dealing with past security-based hot spots in Latin America. In the years after World War II Smith argues that the U.S. government's policy of supporting repressive regimes in Central and South America hastened the death of Monroe's message. Neoconservatives in Washington have given rebirth to the Monroe Doctrine by asserting that it should be invoked again to deal with Iranian-backed Islamist groups in South America.

Suskind, Ron. *The One Percent Doctrine: Deep Inside America's Pursuit of its Enemies Since 9/11* (New York: Simon and Schuster, 2006). A recent theory of threat perception based on the way Vice President Richard Cheney has defined security threats appears in this well-researched and written book. In Cheney's view, if the risk of a terrorist attack on the United States is "one percent," it would be treated as if it were a 100 percent certainty. In this form of threat inflation, only a 1 percent chance of a threat to U.S. security—regardless of supporting evidence—means that the United States should respond with force to handle the threat.

Tanter, Raymond. *Rogue Regimes: Terror and Proliferation* (New York: St. Martin's Press, 1998).

U.S. Southern Command Joint Intelligence Center. "Panama: People's Republic of China Interest and Activities Intelligence Assessment" (1999). Previously classified secret (declassified in 2002), this intelligence assessment points to a growing danger in Panama due to China's involvement in the waterway. Report highlights the process of how threats are hyped to maintain military missions throughout the region.

Vellinga, Menno, ed. *The Political Economy of the Drug Industry: Latin America and the International System* (Gainesville: University Press of Florida, 2004).

Wilkinson, Daniel. *Silence on the Mountain: Stories of Terror, Betrayal, and Forgetting in Guatemala* (Durham, NC: Duke University Press, 2004). A history of Guatemala's 36-year internal war through personal interviews with plantation owners, military officials, guerrillas, and poverty-stricken peasants. Author highlights the role of the U.S. CIA in the Guatemala tragedy.

Wise, Carol, and Riordan Roett, eds. *Post-Stabilization Politics in Latin America* (Washington, DC: Brookings Institution, 2003). Comparative study of the effects of market reforms on domestic politics in Argentina, Brazil, Chile, Mexico, Peru and Venezuela. In this edited volume neo-liberal reforms are shown to produce mixed results, an argument that runs counter to recent election results in which populist candidates who ran opposed to market reforms have won handily.

Wright, Thomas C. *State Terrorism in Latin America: Chile, Argentina and International Human Rights* (Lanham, MD: Rowman and Littlefield, 2007).

Youngers, Colletta A. *Deconstructing Democracy: Peru Under President Alberto Fujimori* (Washington, D.C.: Washington Office on Latin America, 2000).

Youngers, Colletta, and Eileen Rosin. *Drugs and Democracy in Latin America: The Impact of U.S. Policy* (Boulder, CO: Lynne Rienner, 2005). Comprehensive study of U.S. international drug policy that argues that current drug policy has failed to stop the drug trade and increased the chances of spreading hot spots such as armed insurgents who rely on the drug trade and continue to fight one government after another. Policymakers who scan the region for trouble spots would be wise to use the recommendations in this book to rethink drug policy that are now being carried out in the name of narco-terrorism.

Zartman, I. W., ed. *Collapsed States: The Disintegration and Restoration of Legitimate Authority* (Boulder, CO: Lynne Rienner, 1995).

Online Resources

Alternet (http://alternet.com).
Online service that features material from the alternative press, including news stories from alternative weeklies, magazines, and web publications. Particularly useful stories on the war in Iraq, terrorism, security threats, and U.S. foreign policy.

Amnesty International (AI) (http://www.amnesty.org/).
Worldwide research organization devoted to the protection of internationally recognized human rights. With more than 2.2 million members, AI attempts to mobilize supporters in every region of the world, working independently and impartially to promote the respect for human rights.

BBC News/Americas (http://www.news.bbc.co.uk/2/hi/americas).
Highly respected news and analysis from around the world, including country profiles of the Americas. Services on the Web include alerts, news feeds, and podcasts.

Center for Defense Information (http://www.cdi.org/).
Now part of the World Security Institute (WSI)—a Washington-based international think tank and media organization—the Center for Defense Information (CDI) does research on defense-related issues. Website offers independent research and analysis on world "hot spots" categorized as arms trade, children and armed conflict, global warming and international security, the Middle East, nuclear proliferation, small arms and light weapons, and terrorism. Excellent sources for monitoring the U.S. military by civilian analysts and retired military officers.

Center for Hemispheric Defense Studies (CHDS) (http: //www.ndu.edu/chds/).
CHDS is a research and educational center located at the National Defense University in Washington, D.C. Its primary objective is to foster partnerships and promote effective civil-military relations in democratic societies. Defense and international security policy issues are central to its mission. It is closely tied to the U.S. Southern Command with its interest in counter-narco-terrorism, human rights, and humanitarian assistance in Latin America.

Center for International Policy (http://www.ciponline.org).
Washington-based think tank devoted to promoting a U.S. foreign policy based on international cooperation, demilitarization, and respect for basic human rights. Primary policy interests include U.S.-Cuba relations, Colombia, terrorism, and media coverage of major hot spots.

Central Intelligence Agency (CIA) World Factbook (http://www.cia.gov/library/publications).
Annual publication with basic information on security matters throughout the world, including Latin America and the Caribbean. Although "hot spot"

terminology is not mentioned, or defined, in the *World Factbook*, security-based analysis is often designed to heighten awareness of regional conflicts with the potential to jeopardize U.S. security interests.

Conflict 21/Center for Terrorism Studies (http://c21.maxwell.af.mil/cts-home.htm).

Research center located at Maxwell Air Force Base (Air War College) devoted to the study of security, proliferation of weapons of mass destruction, and future conflict scenarios. Website provides a long list of valuable links dealing with threats, adversaries, insurgents, and terrorists worldwide. Valuable for understanding the military mind and threat perceptions.

Council of the Americas (http//www.americas-society.org/).

Major interest group for large, multinational corporations in Latin America. Focus is on expanding free trade agreements and the consolidation of market-oriented reforms in the Americas.

Council on Hemispheric Affairs (COHA) (http//www.coha.org).

Washington-based liberal think tank whose goal is the promotion of good relations and sound policies with Latin America and the Caribbean. Issues of concern include diplomacy, human rights, and fair trade.

Cuban American National Foundation (www. Canfnet.org).

Hard-line Miami-based organization devoted to the removal of Fidel Castro and the eventual creation of a "free" Cuba. Its publications and lobbying efforts rely heavily on proclaiming the evils of the Castro regime and its threat to the United States and the Cuban people. As the largest Cuban organization in exile, CANF plays a major role in lobbying Congress to maintain a non-diplomatic solution to the Cuban "hot spot," and making sure presidential candidates reflect CANF's views toward normalization of relations.

Department of State (http:// www.state.gov/www/regions/wha).

State Department website with information on individual countries, hemispheric security, travel advisories and the activities of the Organization of American States (OAS). The Bureau of Western Hemispheric Affairs claims its objectives are to promote friendly relations and help the secure the region against terrorism and illegal drugs. The Website for the U.S. Embassy in Bogotá, Colombia lists 13 "Hot Bilateral Topics" of concern to the Embassy.

Fairness and Accuracy in Reporting (FAIR) (http://www.fair.org).

FAIR is a national media watch group that offers well-documented criticism of media bias and censorship in the United States. It publishes *Extra!* and produces a popular weekly radio program called *CounterSpin*. FAIR's analysis often runs counter to the propaganda used by right-wing media sources to raise the fear of security threats emanating from Latin America.

Foreign and Commonwealth Office Country Profiles (http://www.fco.gov.uk/).

Country profiles by the FCO with important information on twenty-one Latin American and Caribbean countries. UK security is the primary focus with an emphasis on terrorism, illegal immigration, weapons of mass destruction, and sustainable development.

Select Bibliography 249

Guide to Country Analysis Resources on the Web (http://www.countryrisk.com/guide/archives/).
Lengthy list of web-based resources on countries in Latin America, including background information, data and statistics, rankings, research and analysis, risk newsletters, and ratings. Includes Air Security International's Hot Spots and Failed States Index.

Handbook of Latin American Studies, HLAS Online (http://lcweb2.loc.gov/hlas/).
Annotated bibliography of scholarly resources published about Latin American studies. Its Basic Search tool is useful for tracking down a wide variety of publications, including those that deal with conflict, terrorism, and national security.

Havana Home Page (http://www.usembassy.state.gov/posts/cu1/).
Website for the United States Interest Section in Havana, Cuba. Electronic publications include mainly remarks and statements by government officials on human rights violations (by the Castro regime, not those under U.S. jurisdiction at Guantánamo Bay), political prisoners, women, and dissidents.

Human Rights Watch (http://www.hrw.org/).
International human rights organization devoted to the protection of human rights around the globe. Its principal strategy is to shame offenders by generating press attention, diplomatic and economic pressure on violators, enlisting influential governments and institutions. It also reports on basic human rights violations in the United States.

Infoplease (http://www.infoplease.com/ipa/).
Authoritative and respected online reference source with a comprehensive encyclopedia, almanac, atlas, and dictionary. Claims to be the world's largest free reference site; however, it is weak on security-based hot spot information.

Institute for Policy Studies (http://www.ips-dc.org).
Progressive research and advocacy group located in Washington, D.C. Research emphasizes strategies for creating a more responsible society built around the values of justice, nonviolence, and sustainable energy and development.

Inter-American Development Bank (http://www.iadb.org/).
International financial institution that provides funds for economic and social development in Latin America and the Caribbean. Website offers information on countries, various topics, and projects.

Inter-American Dialogue (http://www.iadialog.org/).
Moderately liberal think tank devoted to policy analysis and inter-American communication on key issues. Philosophy emphasizes engagement between public and private leaders from across the Americas.

International Monetary Fund (http://www.imf.org/).
International financial institution devoted to global monetary cooperation, security, stability, poverty reduction, and sustainable economic growth.

ISN Security Watch (http://www.isn.ethz.ch).
Security Watch provides a platform for a diversity of views and constructive debate on the course and process of international relations that go unreported

in the mainstream press. In its "Global News Headlines," readers are directed to news reports on armaments, security issues, terrorism and other topics of security interest.

Latin American Data Base (LADB) (http://www.ladb.unm.edu/).
A news and educational service devoted to articles on politics, economics, human rights, the environment, drugs, insurgencies, military issues and other topics. Archive search engine matches current articles with Latin American hot spots.

Latin American Network Information Center (LANIC) (http://lanic.utexas.edu/).
Key Latin American information resource based on a country-by-country or subject-by-subject search. Search categories are weak on national security matters, political conflict, and terrorism. Part of the Institute of Latin American Studies at the University of Texas, Austin.

Latin American Newsletters (http://latinnews.com/).
Leading source of information on politics and security in Latin America. One of its services—"Latin American Security and Strategic Review"—is particularly useful for researching hot spots in the Americas with a non-U.S. perspective. Paid registration is required.

Latin American Working Group (LAWG) (http://www.lawg.org/).
Washington-based advocacy coalition of sixty-five U.S. organizations concerned with human rights, peace and justice, and progressive diplomacy.

Latin Petroleum Analytics (http://www.latinpetroleum.com/).
Independent research organization devoted to analyzing economies, companies, finances, and economic and political markets for Latin America's petroleum industry.

Library of Congress, Country Studies (http://lcweb2.loc.gov/frd/cs/profiles/htm).
Website provides key profiles of the Latin American countries with important information on historical setting and the social, economic, political and national security systems. At present 101 countries and regions are covered.

Marshall, Monte G. "Major Episodes of Political Violence, 1946–2004" (http://members.aol.com/espmgm/warlist.htm, accessed December 30, 2005).
A chronological compilation of political violence from the early Cold War to the beginnings of the global war on terrorism. The episodes of political violence in Latin America flourished during the Cold War but have declined since the global war on terrorism.

MIPT Terrorism Knowledge Base (http://www.tkb.org/).
Research and educational organization devoted to research and analysis on global terrorist incidents, groups and leaders. Website is designed to search by groups, cases, countries/areas, incidents, leaders and members, and reference sources.

National Security Archive (http://www.gwu.edu/).
Important digital archive of government documents located at The George Washington University. Website includes search options and a list of "Hot Documents." Readers can search by "subject areas" such as "Latin America" and "government secrecy." An excellent source of declassified records of national security and intelligence policy.

Select Bibliography

National Security Strategy of the United States of America (http://www.whitehouse.gov/nsc/nss).
White House Website devoted to the contents of the president's policies for achieving international security, the defeat of global terrorism, and threat reduction.

New York Times. **Americas Directory** (http://www.nytimes.com/library/world/americas/).
Important sources of news on Latin America. Website allows for searches by country and topic.

Organization of American States (OAS) (http://www.oas.org).
Inter-American organization located in Washington, D.C. whose aim is to provide cooperative approaches to social, economic and political development in the Americas. It is also concerned with good governance, human rights, and a commitment to democracy and anti-terrorism.

Pew Global Attitudes Project (http://pewglobal.org).
Website aimed a publishing worldwide public opinion surveys on a wide variety of subjects, including U.S. foreign policy, anti-U.S. sentiment, and fear of terrorism.

Public Broadcasting System Online News Service (http://www.pbs.org).
News service provided by PBS that allows searches on issues and topics related to conflict, security and terrorism in hot spots around the globe, including Latin America.

Rotberg, Robert I. "Future Regional Crises: Failing States" (http://www.ndu.edu/inns/symposia/pacific2004/rotberg.htm, accessed January 26, 2006).

The Fund for Peace. "Failed State Index" (http://www.fundforpeace.org/programs/fsi/fsindex).
Website for the annual failed states index provided by analysts at the Fund for Peace. The FSI assesses violent internal conflicts and measures the impact of mitigating strategies over 150 countries. Digital map divides the world into states that require "alerts," "warnings," "monitoring," or "sustainability." Only Haiti and Colombia warrant "alert" status for failed states.

Threats Watch (http://www.ThreatsWatch.Org).
Conservative website devoted to threats, categorized by types and locations. Threat topics include civil war, genocide, terrorism, weapons of mass destruction, among others.

Transparency International (TI) (http://www.transparency.org/).
Global civil society organization devoted to fighting corruption by offering tools to carry out anticorruption campaigns. TI publishes an annual Corruption Perceptions Index and a Bribe Payer's Index of value in assessing security threats and hot spots.

United Nations-Economic Commission for Latin America and the Caribbean (ECLAC) (http://www.eclac.org/).
One of five regional commissions of the United Nations, headquartered in Santiago, Chile, to promote economic development in Latin America and the Caribbean. Provides useful analysis and research along with detailed publications.

U.S. Agency for International Development (USAID) (http://www.info.usaid.gov/countries/).

U.S. government agency that provides economic and humanitarian assistance worldwide. Democracy and good governance—both related to Latin American hot spots—are also part of the USAID mission.

Washington Office on Latin America (WOLA) (http://wola.org/).

Key nongovernmental organization working for human rights, democracy, and social justice in Latin America. WOLA works through several advocacy coalitions to engage policymakers in such a way as to improve U.S. policy toward the region. Frequent publications provide critical assessments of failed U.S. policy in the region.

Washington Post (http://washingtonpost.com).

Important source of news and analysis of Washington policies, both domestic and foreign. Website offers news from Central America and South America, including *Post* reporting from correspondents in Mexico City, Bogotá, and Buenos Aires.

World Audit List of Country Profiles (http://www.worldaudit.org/countries/htm).

Profiles of democratic countries featuring country links, maps, and statistics on corruption, press freedom, rule of law, human rights, civil liberties, and political rights.

World Bank (http://www.worldbank.org).

International financial and technical institution that offers assistance to developing countries in an effort to reduce poverty and improve living standards. Website tools include index on countries, projects, and publications.

World Health Organization (WHO) (http://www.who.int/whr/).

United Nations public health arm that monitors disease outbreaks, performance of health systems and provides data bases of health statistics. Contains a useful index devoted to health topics.

Index

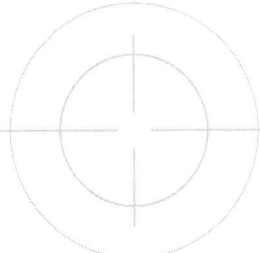

Note: Page numbers followed by an *f* refer to a figure on the indicated page. Those followed by a *t* refer to a table.

Accords on Indigenous Rights and Culture, 1996, 78
Afghanistan, 35*f*, 41, 49
Afro-Guyanese, 195, 200
AIDS, 18, 159, 191, 197–198
ALBA (Bolivarian Alternative for the Americas), 133, 144, 145
Al Jazeera, 151
Allende, Salvador, 31, 146, 153, 167, 169, 170
Al-Qaeda, 88, 198
Amazon Basin, 7, 101, 134, 159–161, 205
American Service-members' Protection Act (ASPA), 3–4, 172–173
Amnesty for human rights violators, 110, 121, 169
Andean region
  conflict, potential in, 7
  democracy, obstacles in, 101, 102, 103
  drug production in, 90, 101
  economic reforms in, 45
  government institutions in, 22
  hot spots in, 101, 102, 103–104, 106, 115, 205
  overview of, 101–104, 157
  politics in, 7
  U.S. involvement in, 107–108
Andrain, Charles F., 22, 23, 31, 167
Anti-Americanism
  coalitions, formation of, 4–5
  factors contributing to, 28, 140
  populism and, 153
  rhetoric, 32, 146, 148, 152, 153, 183
  rise of, 125, 145
  risk of, 130
Anti-imperialism, 115, 139*f*, 143, 148, 152, 154, 155, 160, 165, 179
Antiterrorism, bases involved in, 36, 37*t*
Arab Muslim communities, South American, 4, 174
Argentina
  bilateral investment treaties with, 44
  Bush, G.W., attitudes toward, 30
  Chile relations with, 161–162
  economy of, 128–129
  ethnic composition of, 157
  Iran relations with, 174
  nuclear programs in, 27, 147
  as Southern Cone nation, 157
  as stable state, 15
  territorial claims of, 162, 164–165
Argentine-Israeli Mutual Association (AIMA), 174
Aristide, Jean-Bertrand, 14, 41, 191–192, 193, 194
Armed conflicts
  in Bolivia, Guyana, and Venezuela, 16
  overview of, 8*t*–9*t*
  terrorism threat level of, 34
Armed mercenaries, 36, 43, 90
Arms trafficking
  gang activity connection to, 87, 89
  terrorism, linked to, 90, 173
  trans-border, 62, 64
Aruba, 37*t*, 186

Asamblea Popular de los Pueblos de
    Oaxaca (APPO), 75, 76
ASPA (American Service-members'
    Protection Act), 3–4, 172–173
AUC (United Self-Defense Forces of
    Colombia), 90, 110, 111
Authoritarian governments
    in Chile, 168, 170
    Organization of American States (OAS)
        dealings with, 46
    in Venezuela, 150

Bachelet, Michelle, 126, 167, 168, 169, 170
Baghdad, Iraq, prisoner treatment in, 35*f*
Bahamas, 185
Bauxite, 196, 197
Bay of Pigs invasion, 1961, 182, 184
Beagle Channel dispute, 159, 161–162
Belize (formerly British Honduras), 81, 89
Biological weapons
    assessment of, 26–27
    post-9/11 attitude toward, 18, 19, 53
    U.S. *versus* Mexican views on, 28
Blackwater Worldwide (firm), 42, 43
Bolivarian Alternative for the Americas
    (ALBA), 133, 144, 145
Bolivarian Revolution, 3, 104, 138–155, 142
Bolívar, Simón, 139, 142
Bolivia
    aid to, 40
    Chile relations with, 105
    corruption in, 21
    drug production in, 205
    ethnic composition of, 102
    as failed state, 15
    government of, 116
    hot spot potential of, 125
    military in, 121, 122
    money borrowing practices of, 145
    natural resources in, 103, 125–126, 132,
        135
    People's Trade Agreement signed by, 186
    political and economic conditions in,
        103
    poverty in, 124, 125, 127
    territorial struggles of, 102–103, 104–106
    terrorism, potential in, 205
    U.S. hostility toward, 18
    U.S. relations with, 121–122
    Venezuela, relations with, 104
Bolivia-Chile relations, 102–103, 104–106,
    126

Border conflicts (Andean region)
    Beagle Channel dispute, 161–162
    overview of, 101
    Salida al Mar controversy, 104–106
    and ungoverned spaces, 106–108, 110
Border conflicts in non-Iberian South
    America, 196–197
Border crime, 58, 60–64
Border security
    achieving, obstacles to, 58
    and immigration fears, 51
    Mexico problems with, 60
    Republican efforts toward, 72–73
    strategies for, 205
    and terrorism fears, 11, 70–71
    threat perception role in attitudes
        toward, 32
Brazil
    Bush, G. W., and relations with, 30, 159
    Colombia conflict impact on, 107
    crime in, 88, 158, 166
    nuclear programs terminated by, 27
    overview of, 158–159
    petroleum companies in, 134
    Southern Cone regions of, 157
    U.S. relations with, 158–159
Bush, George H. W., 169
Bush, George W.
    appointments of, 5–6
    border security efforts of, 59
    Brazil, relations with, 30, 159
    Colombia policy of, 107, 113–114
    critics of, 17–18
    Cuban American relations under, 34
    Cuba policy of, 179
    democracy building emphasized by, 14,
        187
    foreign policy of, 25
    free trade promotion, 128
    Guyana policy, 197–198
    Hitler, A., compared to, 53
    immigration policy of, 51, 70–71, 74
    International Criminal Court (ICC) not
        recognized by, 122
    Iraq war justified by, 53
    Latin American policies of, 29, 31,
        39–46, 44*f*
    Latin Americans' opinion of, 25, 30, 73
    Morales, E., attitude toward, 125
    Panama Canal modernization advocated
        by, 97
    on poverty-terrorism link, 57

Index

preemption doctrine of, 23
terminology of, 26
terrorism policies of, 26, 36, 38, 52, 88, 189–190
Venezuela policy toward, 52, 139f (*see also* Chávez, Hugo; Bush, G. W., relations with)

Calderón, Felipe
  anti-corruption campaign of, 59, 65
  challenges faced by, 64–65
  election of, 38, 55, 66, 67, 149
  goals of, 57, 65, 79
  Oaxaca conflict, response to, 75–76
  U.S. relations with, 73–74
Caribbean
  China involvement in, 95, 96
  economic aid to, 132–133
  regional overview, 177–178
  U.S. military bases in, 37t
Caricom, 191, 194
Carter Center, 118
Carter, Jimmy, 13, 38, 92–93
Castro, Fidel
  anti-U.S. statements by, 183
  Chávez, H., ties to, 52, 142, 146
  China ties with, 93
  Correa, R., ties with, 117
  death, scenarios following, 24, 50, 178, 180, 183, 186
  illness of, 178f, 179, 181
  López Obrador, A.M., compared to, 65
  Morales, E., ties to, 125
  removal, attempts at, 34, 42, 187
  revolutions sponsored by, 13
  rise of, 184
  threat posed by, assessment of, 27
  U.S. relations with, 181, 182, 183, 184–185, 190, 191
Castro, Raúl, 178f, 179, 180, 181, 186
Caudillo (strongman) (term), 142–143, 150
Cayman Islands, 119
Central America
  armed conflicts in, 83, 87, 97, 98, 99
  democracy in, 98
  hot spots in, 83, 100
  overview of, 81, 83
  threat assessment for, 97–98
  trade agreements with, 44
Central American Free Trade Agreement (CAFTA), 87
Central Intelligence Agency (CIA)

Cold-War role of, 195
drug war role of, 118–119
information gathering by, 5
post-Cold War role of, 6
Venezuela watch by, 51, 154–155
in war on terrorism, 189
Chávez, Hugo
  Ahmadinejad, M., alliance with, 3
  Argentina relations of, 164, 165
  assassination of, calls for, 10, 52, 152, 153
  authoritarianism promoted by, 46
  Bolivia sea access supported by, 104, 106
  Bush, G. W., relations with, 3, 29, 30, 31, 139f, 152, 174
  and Castro, F., 52, 129, 142, 143, 144, 146
  China ties with, 93, 96
  Colombia policy of, 107
  Correa, R., ties with, 116, 132
  Cuban ties of, 133, 179, 180, 181, 184
  drug wars criticized by, 114, 115, 144
  free trade opposed by, 45
  Latin American opinion of, 25
  López Obrador, A.M., association with, 65–66
  Middle East dealings, 134
  and Morales, E., 124, 126, 127, 130, 132
  opposition to, 149–150
  and Organization of Petroleum Exporting Countries (OPEC), 101
  and Peruvian elections, 120
  removal of, attempts at, 41, 47, 49, 118, 140, 153
  security threats perceived by, 202
  spending policies of, 143–144
  as successor to F. Castro, 52, 143, 144
  support and approval ratings for, 118, 140, 143, 150
  terrorist ties, suspected, 142, 147–148, 199
  trading policies of, 144–145
  U.S. attitudes toward, 51–52, 103, 129, 138, 140–141, 142–143, 144, 145, 146, 147–148, 150–152, 153, 154–155, 202
  U.S. criticized by, 139–140
Chavismo, 142, 150–152, 155
Chemical weapons, 18, 19, 26, 53
Cheney, Richard, (Dick), 5, 17
Chiapas
  racial and ethnic disparities in, 75
  rebellion in, 59, 60, 67, 76–79, 77f
  youth gangs in, 85
Chicago Council on Foreign Relations, 18, 57, 71

Chile
  Argentina relations with, 161–162
  Bolivia relations with, 105
  corruption in, 135, 167, 170
  democracy in, 168, 170
  economy of, 166, 167, 168
  government of, 167–170
  Iraq and Afghanistan, forces deployed to, 42
  military coup in, 153, 167
  military in, 122, 168
  natural resources in, 96
  poverty in, 168
  U.S. relations with, 2, 31, 166–167
China
  Caribbean involvement of, 95, 96, 180, 184
  exports to Latin America by, 10
  Latin American involvement of, 30, 93–96, 94f, 124
  Latin American trade by, 10
  Panama involvement of, 10, 50, 92, 93, 93f, 94f
  U.S. relations with, 96
  Venezuela alliance with, 51, 93, 96
  Venezuelan petroleum for, 133, 134, 141–142, 146
Citizen-government gaps
  in foreign policy goals, 28, 29t
  in ideology, 23
  on immigration, 71–72
Clinton, William (Bill) J., 27, 182
Coca
  anti-coca policies, 123, 203
  crop eradication program, 114–115, 121, 185
  Cuban import of, 186
  decriminalization, calls for, 126, 129
  production of, 107–108
Cocaine
  decriminalization, calls for, 63
  demand for, 101
  gangs, 64
  guerrillas funded through, 205
  shipment corridor for, 185, 186
  terrorist groups funded through, 112
  U.S. entry of, 61, 101, 113, 121, 186
Cold War
  Andean region in, 102
  Central America as security focus during, 81, 91
  disease metaphors during, 16
  internal enemies, emphasis on, 34
  national security doctrine of, 154
  non-Iberian South America in, 195
  policymaking during, 13, 31
  revolution, perceptions during, 184
  Southern Cone in, 158
  state failures during, 21–22
  terminology of, 50, 51
  threat assessments during, 14, 34, 40
  U.S.-Chile relations during, 166–167
  U.S.-Cuba relations, impact on, 178, 180–181
  U.S. hegemony during, 38
  war on terrorism strategies compared to, 46
Colombia
  civil war in, 103, 107, 108–112, 109f, 148, 203
  crime in, 110, 111
  democracy in, 5, 16
  drug production in, 185, 205
  drug war aid for, 63
  Ecuador relations with, 106–107
  ethnic composition of, 102
  as failed state, 14, 15, 16, 108, 201
  as hot spot, 109, 111
  instability in, 110
  Iraq and Afghanistan, forces deployed to, 42
  military coups in, 108
  military in, 109, 110
  peace efforts in, 110
  post-September 11 attitudes toward, 19
  poverty in, 122
  terrorism in, 34, 54, 90, 205
  threat assessment for, 201
  U.S. relations with, 51, 102, 107, 109–110, 111, 112, 113–114, 173
  Venezuela relations with, 107
Communism
  Andean interpretation of, 137
  in Central America, 81, 91
  disease metaphors describing, 16
  fear of, 13, 16
  hot spots and, 36
  post-Cold War threats compared to, 138
  post-Cold War views on, 13, 34
  state failures attributed to, 21–22
  threat assessment of, 34
  "total war" against, 135
Confederation of Indigenous Nationalities of Ecuador, 119

Index

Cooperative Security Locations (CSLs), 39, 90
Coppedge, Michael, 46–47, 57
Copper, 95, 101, 166, 168, 170
Correa, Rafael, 114, 115, 116, 117, 132, 202
Corruption
    in Andean region, 101, 102, 103, 135
    attitudes, impact on, 22
    in Border Patrol, 59
    in Caribbean, 185, 186, 187
    in Central America, 21, 83, 89, 90–91, 99, 100
    in Colombia, 16, 111
    defined, 22
    factors contributing to, 135
    failing state, link to, 20
    as hot spot feature, 46, 204
    of institutions, 7
    in Mexico, 57, 59, 60, 61, 64, 65, 67, 74, 75, 76
    national ranking of, 21t
    opposition to, 23
    terrorism associated with, 57
    as threat factor, 22
    in Tri-Border Area (TBA), 158
    weak state manifestation of, 16
Corruption Perceptions Index, 20–21
Costa Rica
    as Central American nation, 81
    crime in, 89
    human development in, 98
    as stable state, 15
    Taiwan, relations with, 95
Counter-drug operations
    in Andean region, 109, 115, 116
    bases involved in, 36, 39, 90, 115, 185
Counterinsurgency doctrine, 203
Counterinsurgency warfare, 135, 136
Covert operations, 32, 45, 195
Crime
    in Andean region, 107, 109
    border, 58, 60–64
    in Central America, 87, 88–89, 99, 100
    internal conflict role in, 204
    organized, 7, 64, 99, 111, 114, 173
    rise in, 92
    as social issue, 204
    in Tri-Border Area (TBA), 158
    U.S. blamed for, 199
    war crimes, 121
    wars on, 30
Criminal justice systems, 61, 86

Crop eradication program (coca) in the Andes, 114–115, 121, 185
Cuba
    Bush-Hitler comparisons by, 53
    China involvement in, 180, 184
    civil war, long-distance in, 178–185
    democracy prospects in, 5, 180, 183, 187
    drug policy of, 185–186
    economic sanctions against, 42
    export of dissidents, 184–185
    as hot spot, 177, 179, 180, 182–183, 189
    Hurricane Katrina, assistance offered after, 181
    Middle East ties of, 184, 205
    People's Trade Agreement signed by, 186
    terrorist ties, suspected of, 178
    threat assessments for, 11, 38, 45, 182–183, 202
    U.S. influence undermined by, 40
    U.S. relations with, 2, 34, 50, 178, 179–185, 187, 190–191, 205
    Venezuela alliance with, 50, 51, 133, 144, 149, 151
    weapons possession and export by, 27
Cuba lobby, 182
Cuban American National Foundation (CANF), 181
Cuban Americans, 34, 179f, 180, 181, 183–184
Cuban Revolution, 1959, 130, 135, 137, 181, 182, 183, 184, 191
Cuban-Spanish-American War, 187, 191

Darién Gap, 83–85, 84f, 108, 109
Deforestation, 85, 160, 160f, 161
Democracy
    Central American views on, 90
    corruption impact on attitudes toward, 22
    cycles of, 91
    and human rights, 120–121
    Latin American views on, 41, 47, 49–50, 176, 202
    military relationship to, 20
    national ranking of, 21t, 66
    obstacles to, 22, 23, 24, 91–92, 101, 180
    promotion of, 24, 41, 43, 46, 47, 49–50, 146
    threat, potential to, 47
    trends toward, 38–39
    U.S. security interests, conflict with, 23

Democracy building
  cycles of, 91
  Republican emphasis on/policies inconsistent with, 14, 187
  and spreading, 16, 23, 28, 39
Democratic Party, 12–13, 31–32
Democratization, 34, 50, 88
Deportations to Central America, 87, 90
Dictators and dictatorships
  Cold War era support for, 14, 52, 102, 141, 158, 165
  friendly, 12, 52, 141
  nuclear weapons programs under, 147
  public opinion on, 36, 152–153
  removal of, 41 (attempts at), 152–153
Diplomacy
  Mexican *versus* U.S. views on, 57
  military power *versus*, 205
"Dirty wars," 52, 135, 164, 166
Diseases
  Foreign Service position shifting in battle against, 4
  metaphors of, 16
  spread, prevention of, 23
  threats posed by, 28
Dominican Republic
  corruption in, 21
  drug involvement of, 186
  as failed state, 15
  geography of, 191
  Iraq war involvement of, 204–205
  trade agreements with, 44
Domino effect
  hot spot terminology assuming, 10
  Soviet Union linked to, 1, 22, 50
Drug cartels
  in Colombia, 64, 110, 112
  in Haiti, 191, 193
  in Mexico, 61, 62, 63, 87, 112
Drug certification, 42, 62–63
Drug Enforcement Agency (DEA), 58, 115
Drug legalization debate, 63–64, 126, 129
Drug lords and drug mafias, 12, 26, 64
Drug money
  guerrillas funded through, 205
  terrorist groups funded through, 2, 112
Drugs. *See also* Counter-drug operations; Narcoterrorism
  military role in fighting, 64
  narcoguerrillas, 42, 83, 85
  U.S. demand and consumption of, 62, 114, 199
  U.S. entry of, blocking, 28, 57, 61, 64
  U.S. military aid in fighting, 108
  war on (*see* War on drugs)
  youth gang involvement with, 85
Drug trade and smuggling, 16, 59, 87, 112, 115
Drug trafficking
  in Andean region, 7, 101, 103, 107, 108, 114
  in Bolivia, 125
  Brazilian addressing of, 159
  in Caribbean, 177, 182, 185, 186
  in Central America, 90, 98, 99
  in Colombia, 110, 111
  combating, 39, 90
  confronting, progress in, 203
  failed state connection to, 14, 166
  Foreign Service role in combating, 4
  gang activity connected to, 88, 89
  Islamic organization involvement in, 173, 198
  in Mexico, 56, 57
  paramilitary involvement in, 111
  poverty reduction as strategy in dealing with, 58
  and terrorism (*see* Narcoterrorism)
  trans-border, 60, 83, 85
  U.S. blamed for, 199
  weak states associated with, 58

Economic competition
  international, perceived threat of, 19t
  neoliberal promotion of, 43
Economic development, Latin American
  China impact on, 93, 95
  uneven, state failure, role in, 16
  Venezuela aid for, 133
Economic inequality
  in Andean region, 102
  in Central America, 90, 98–99
  in Mexico, 74–75, 78
  security-based threats linked to, 20
  in Southern Cone, 157, 167, 168, 170
  as threat factor, 22, 45
  wealth distribution, unequal, 7, 166
Economic sanctions, 41–42
Economic "shock therapy," 124
Ecuador
  Colombia relations with, 106–107
  corruption in, 21
  elections in, 102, 116–117, 119
  ethnic composition of, 102

Index

as failed state, 14
government of, 116, 119
international companies in, 20
military in, 110, 122
natural resources in, 95, 132
protests in, 119
terrorism, potential in, 205
as unstable nation, 24
Egypt
   as terrorist source, 201
   Venezuela alliance with, 148
Ejército de Liberación Nacional (ELN) (National Liberation Army), 103, 110, 111
Ejército Revolucionario Popular (ERP) (Zapatista Army of National Liberation), 52, 67, 68
Ejército Zapatista de Liberación Nacional (EZLN), 67, 68, 77f, 78
Electoral trends, Latin American, 192, 193–194, 202. *See also* Leftist shift
El Salvador
   corruption in, 100
   crime in, 87, 89, 90
   deportation of criminals to, 87
   Iraq war involvement of, 204–205
   pacification in, 16
   peace accords in, 98
   poverty in, 98, 100
   war in, 13–14
Enemy combatants, 40, 205
Enemy nations, 31, 34–35
Energy contracts, renegotiation of, 124, 134–135
Energy sector
   nationalization of, 124, 125–126, 127, 129–130, 135, 141
   production, 129, 131t, 135
   in South America, 131t
Environmental problems and protection
   in Amazon Basin, 159–161, 160f
   in Chile, 171
   damage, results of, 28
   and Darién Gap, 83, 84–85
   in Mexico, 75
   oil drilling as cause of, 130f, 159–160
   oil pipelines, 134
   trade policy provisions and, 56, 205
   as security threat factors, 28, 30
ERP (Ejército Revolucionario Popular) (Zapatista Army of National Liberation), 52, 67, 68

Ethnic conflict, 28, 78
EZLN (Ejército Zapatista de Liberación Nacional), 67, 68, 77f, 78

Failed State Index, 14–17, 15t, 59, 108, 193, 201, 202
Failing or failed states
   characteristics of, 16, 20, 165–166
   consequences of, 28, 39
   factors contributing to, 7, 21–22, 185
Falklands/Malvinas fracas, 159, 162–165, 163f
FARC (Fuerzas Armadas Revolucionarias de Colombia) (Revolutionary Armed Forces of Colombia), 84f, 103, 106, 107, 108, 109f, 110, 111, 113, 203
Federal Bureau of Investigation (FBI), 58, 88, 199
Foreign investment
   in Guyana, 197
   Latin American markets for, 30
   in petroleum sector, 140
   poverty as consequence of, 127–128
Forward Operation Locations (FOLs), 39, 90, 203
Fox, Vicente, 57, 61, 63, 64, 65, 66–67, 68, 71, 73
France, petroleum companies in, 134
Free trade
   agreements, 43–44, 44f, 47, 97, 112, 132, 205
   in Andean region, 102, 112, 119
   areas, 173, 205
   in Chile, 167
   Latin American views on, 127–128
   Mexican views on, 43–44, 65
   poverty eradication and, 128
   promotion of, 43–44
   protests in Ecuador against, 119
   Republican promotion of, 12, 187
Free Trade Area of the Americas (FTAA), 44, 45, 128, 144, 145, 152
French Guiana (Guyane), 161, 195, 196
Fujimori, Alberto, 114, 120, 138

Gangs. *See also* Youth gangs
   in Brazil, 88, 166
   in Caribbean, 183, 193
   in Central America, 62, 89–90
   drug trafficking and, 185
   failed states as source of, 14
   members, rehabilitation of, 86f

Gangs. *See also* Youth gangs (*continued*)
    in Mexico, 57, 61, 62, 85, 86
    military role in dealing with, 64
    as pressing social issue, 204
    terrorist organizations, links to, 26
    in United States, 85, 86–88
    U.S. *versus* H. Chávez approach to, 144
García, Alan, 114, 119, 120, 137
Gaza, 199
Geneva Conventions, 189, 190
Genocide, 23, 28
Globalization
    assumptions of, 128
    benefits, unequal of, 170
    consequences of, 143
    and Darién Gap, 83
    and immigration, 74
    Mexican views on, 65, 78
    positive results of, 166
    problems, inherent of, 75, 78
    regime change altered by, 24
    as state failure factor, 17
    threat perception, impact on, 50
"Global war on terrorism" (term), 26. *See also* War on terrorism
Gold, 166, 196, 197
Governance
    challenges to, 98, 101
    counterterrorism, role in, 176
    erosion of, 16
    good, promotion of, 7
    poor as hot spot factor, 7, 204
    poor, consequences of, 23
    responsible, encouraging, 46
Governance and corruption
    in Andean region, 116–122
    in Caribbean, 187
    in Central America, 83, 89, 90–92
    in Mexico, 59, 60, 64–67
    in non-Iberian South America, 197–198
    in Southern Cone, 159, 165–170
Government institutions, attitudes toward, 22, 23
Government legitimization
    authority, legitimization of, 20
    in Colombia, 103, 110–111
    in Ecuador, 117
    state failure associated with lack of, 165–166
    U.S. perceptions of, 202
Grenada
    armed forces in, 36
    as hot spot, 186
    U.S. invasion of, 177
Guantánamo Bay
    Muslims, treatment at, 199
    overview of, 187, 189
    prisoners at, 35*f*, 37*t*, 40, 49, 188*f*, 189–191, 205
    security of, 183, 189
Guatemala
    authoritarian government support in, 24
    corruption in, 21, 99
    crime in, 89, 91
    democracy in, 92, 99
    deportation of criminals to, 87
    as failed state, 15
    governance, poor in, 91
    pacification in and U.N. peacekeepers, 16
    peace accords in, 98, 99
    poverty in, 98, 99–100
    U.S. military in, 36
Guerrero, guerrilla conflict in, 60, 67–68
Guerrillas. *See also name of guerrilla organization, e.g.*: Hezbollah
    in Andean region, 102, 108
    attacks and uprisings, climate change as factor in, 28
    in Colombia, 16, 103, 106–107, 109, 109*f*, 110, 111, 112, 114, 122, 148
    combating, obstacles to, 205
    funding of, 205
    in Mexico, 57, 60, 67–68
    in Peru, 103, 135, 138
    poverty reduction as strategy in dealing with, 58
Guest worker program, 70, 71
Guevara, Che, 142, 182, 184
Guns, illicit trade in, 62, 88, 108
Guyana
    corruption in, 197
    environmental protection in, 161
    as hot spot, 186, 195–196
    as intervention candidate, 17
    Iranian influence in, 198
    Muslims in, 173
    politics and government in, 197–198
    terrorism, potential in, 173, 198, 200, 205
Guyane (French Guiana), 161, 195, 196
Guzmán, Abimael, 136–137, 138

Haiti
    corruption in, 21, 192, 193, 194
    democracy in, 192, 193

as failed state, 14, 15, 108, 178, 191–194, 201
as hot spot, 177, 186
Health aspects of security threats, 28, 30, 84
Hegemonic state, U.S. as, 35–39, 47
Helms-Burton Law, 181, 182
Hemispheric security doctrine, 38, 136
Heroin, 63, 112, 186
Hezbollah, 4, 34, 51, 52, 147, 148, 173–174, 175, 200
Hitler, Adolf, 52, 53, 151, 152
HIV/AIDS, 18, 159, 191, 197–198
Homeland Security Department, 19, 58, 59, 74
Honduras
  bilateral investment treaties with, 44
  crime and corruption in, 21, 89, 90
  deportation of criminals to, 87
  Iraq war involvement of, 42–43, 204–205
  poverty in, 98
Hot spot (defined), 6, 35–36, 46–47, 48t–49t, 50, 53
Hot spots. *See terms beginning with* Threat
Hot spot terminology, 1–54, 202–203
Human development
  in Central America, 83, 97–100
  index, 98, 99t, 157, 193
Human rights organizations and activists, 35f, 78, 110, 146
Human rights violations
  by anti-Communists, 52
  in Argentina, 164
  in Bolivia, 16
  in Chile, 167, 168–169
  in Colombia, 16, 110
  dealing with, 120–121
  economic sanctions as tool against, 41–42
  at Guantánamo Bay, 189, 190
  in Haiti, 192
  immigration-related, 68
  military interventions followed by, 33
  in Paraguay, 166
  in Peru, 137
  Pinochet, Augusto, amnesty for, 169
  prosecution for, 121
  in Southern Cone, 158, 166
  trans-boundary, 58
  in Venezuela, 16, 151
Human smuggling, 60, 70, 85, 186
Hurricane Mitch and economic setback, 1998, 74, 98

Hussein, Saddam, 18, 32, 34, 38, 53, 57, 128, 141
Ideology and threats, 11, 31
Illegal immigrants and immigration
  in Andean region, 105
  Border Patrol expansion to stop, 59
  into Brazil, 161
  from Caribbean, 182
  from Central America, 83, 88, 100
  conservative views on, 13
  debate over, 51, 60–61
  detention centers for, 40
  economic aspects of, 70
  and employment in U.S., 70, 71–72, 74
  factors in, 56
  gangs and, 87, 88
  government *versus* public views on, 28
  from Guyana, 199–200
  Latin American views on, 30
  from Mexico, 56, 70
  into Mexico, 60
  Mexican views on, 73–74, 79
  overview of, 68, 70–74
  post-9/11 attitudes toward, 11, 18, 19
  poverty reduction as strategy in dealing with, 58
  public opinion on, 59, 70, 71–73
  reducing, 57
  reform, 70–71, 205
  smuggling of, 60, 70
  status of, 57, 74
  workplace arrests related to, 59
IMF (International Monetary Fund), 124, 128, 129, 145
India, state oil companies in, 126
Indigenous populations
  alliances between, 171
  in Andean region, 101, 102, 116, 124
  in Bolivia, 122, 127
  in Chile, 159, 170–171
  in Colombia, 112
  in Ecuador, 119, 122, 130f
  in Mexico, 74–75, 76, 79
  in Peru, 137
  transboundary, 83, 84, 85, 89
Indigenous presidents, 44f, 103, 123, 123f
Insurgencies
  in Colombia, 108, 109, 201
  combating, difficulties in, 34, 203–204, 205
  in Mexico, 57

Insurgencies (*continued*)
  U.S. military and counterinsurgency operations, 39
Inter-American Development Bank, 68, 93, 145
Interamerican Highway, 83, 84–85
International companies
  Corruption Perceptions Index used by, 21
  and private armed forces in Ecuador, 20
International Criminal Court (ICC), 3–4, 30, 39, 121–122, 124, 172
International Monetary Fund (IMF), 124, 128, 129, 145
Iran
  Argentina relations with, 172–174
  Latin American ties of, 198, 199
  terrorist ties, suspected, 173
  threat assessments for, 11
  Venezuela alliance with, 50, 51, 134, 141, 142, 146–147, 149, 151, 205
  Venezuelan petroleum, agreements with, 133
Iraq
  democratization failure in, 50
  prisoner treatment in, 35*f*, 49
  U.S. treatment of Muslims in, 199
  Venezuela alliance with, 141
Iraq war
  Caricom opposition to, 194
  critics of, 17–18, 199
  Latin American support, lack of, 30, 42–43, 124
  Latin American troop deployment in, 42, 204–205
  overseeing, 5–6
  public opinion on, 26, 31–32, 43
  rationale for, 49, 53
  security threats in wake of, 60
  U.S.-Haiti relations in wake of, 193–194
  U.S.-Mexico relations in wake of, 57
Islamic fundamentalists, 173, 176, 203
Islamic radicals
  bomb attacks by, 200
  fundamentalist, 19*t*
  Latin American left, alignment with, 4–5
  threat, overestimation of, 26, 199
Islamists
  Chávez's suspected sympathies with, 142, 148
  forceful dealings with, rationale for, 12
  South American Muslim ties to, 159
  terminology referring to, 53
Israel, 19*t*, 24, 134, 174, 199, 200
Israeli embassy, Buenos Aires bombing of, 52, 174
Ivory Coast, crime groups and mafias from, 173

Jamaat al-Muslimeen, 198–199
Jamaica, drug production in, 177, 186
Japan, crime groups and mafias from, 173
Jawahar, Vinay, 126–127, 140, 168
Job creation in Latin America, 57, 65, 73, 79, 100
Joint Task Force Bravo, 40, 189
Judiciary, politicized, 46, 47

Kennedy Airport bombing plot (2007), 198, 199, 200
Kirchner, Néstor, 52, 164, 165, 174
Korea, crime groups and mafias from, 173

Land disputes
  in Chile, 170–171
  in Mexico, 76
Land reform
  in Bolivia, 124, 127
  in Venezuela, 140, 149
La Paz, Bolivia, 105, 123*f*, 127
Latin American
  armed forces, 20, 30
  democracy ranking, 21*t*, 66
  left, radical Islam alignment with, 4–5
  media, 151, 153
  sovereignty, 23, 40, 48, 63, 102, 185, 205
Latin Americans, Washington perception of, 11, 47
Latinobarómetro studies, 12, 24, 140, 149, 116
Lebanon
  crime groups and mafias from, 173
  terrorist connections of, 174, 175
  Venezuela alliance with, 148
Leftist shift, 23, 31, 76, 79, 91, 102, 123–124, 125, 126–127, 166, 192
  democracy promotion, backlash in wake of, 47
  elections' role in, 38, 45
  factors contributing to, 129
  and Islamic alliances, 4–5
  U.S. hegemony reassertion in face of, 33
  U.S. influence undermined by, 3, 30, 38, 122

Index

Libya, Venezuela alliance with, 141, 205
Logging, 159, 160, 171
López Obrador, Andrés Manuel, 38, 55, 65–66, 73, 149

M-19 (guerrilla organization), 111
Magdalena Medio, Colombia, 103, 122
Malaysia, state oil companies in, 126
Manta Air Base (Ecuador), 37t, 115
Mapuche people of Chile, 159, 170–171
Mara Salvatrucha (MS-13), 62, 88
Margarita Island, Venezuela, 147, 173, 174
Marginalization, 10, 26, 205
Marijuana, 63, 112, 177, 186
Marxist-Leninist ideology, 137, 169
Medellín drug cartel, 64, 112
Media
    impact of immigration debate and the, 51
    portrayal of H. Chávez in, 150–152
    threat perceptions, influence on, 2, 32, 33–34, 53, 151–152
Mercenaries, 36, 43, 90
Mercosur trade bloc, 144, 145
Metaphors, 16, 50, 202–203
Mexico
    Chinese imports into, 10
    corruption in, 135
    crime in, 74
    Cuban influence on, 63
    democracy in, 24, 66, 73, 79
    economy of, 55–56, 57, 79
    elections in, 38, 55, 65–67, 73, 79, 149
    environment of, 56
    government administration in, 66
    hot spots in, 57, 75–76, 78
    natural resources in, 95
    post-9/11 attitudes toward, 19
    private investment in, 55–56
    public opinion, Mexican *versus* U.S., 28
    U.S. relations with, 56–57, 59, 62, 66, 73–74
Middle East
    Cuba ties, suspected of, 184, 205
    Guyanese immigrant attitudes toward, 199
    Tri-Border Area (TBA) connections to, 159, 173
    Venezuelan alliances in, 50
Militarization, 16, 30, 31, 92
Military coups, 41, 116. *See also under country*
Military
    education and training (IMET) funds, 173
    exchange programs, 96, 122
    and police action. (*see* U.S. military intervention)
    relationship to democracy, 20
    resources, transactions in, 145–146
Military-to-military relationships, 39, 96, 172
Minerals, 36, 95, 101, 105, 166
Money laundering, 108, 116, 125, 173, 174, 182, 185, 186, 198, 205
Monroe Doctrine, 10, 33, 34, 46, 195
Morales, Evo, 115, 116, 123f, 132
    Bolivian attitudes toward, 103, 121
    drug policies of, 114, 116, 129
    energy policies of, 103, 134, 135
    and multinationals, 122–129
    and other Latin American leaders and, 52, 120, 146, 202
    Salida al Mar controversy, involvement in, 104, 106
    U.S. attitude toward, 29, 31, 124–125, 126, 129, 130, 153–154
MRTA (Tupac Amaru Revolutionary Movement), 104, 137, 138
Multinationals (corporations), 122–129, 132, 159
Muslim(s)
    in Latin America, 157, 159, 173, 199
    nations, Chávez's support for, 134
    terrorist connections, suspected of, 4, 147, 174, 198
    in Tri-Border Area (TBA), 157, 172f

NAFTA. *See* North American Free Trade Agreement (NAFTA)
Narcoterrorism
    in Andean region, 50, 101, 103, 201
    in Caribbean, 178, 185–187
    Chávez's suspected sympathies with, 142
Narco-trafficking. *See* Drug trafficking
National Counterterrorism Center, 6
National Endowment for Democracy (NED), 41, 49
Nationalization, economic, Latin American energy sector, 124, 125–126, 127, 129–130, 135, 141
National Liberation Army (Ejército de Liberación Nacional, ELN), 103, 110, 111
National security "doctrine," 154

National security "non-traditional" sources of, 20, 42–43
National Security Strategy report, 2006, 142, 187
Nation building, failures in, 16, 50, 180
Natural gas, 10, 43, 103, 105, 123, 124, 126, 132, 133, 134
Natural resources, 95, 96, 101, 103, 125–126. *See also* Copper; Minerals; Petroleum; Natural Nazi fugitives, harboring of, 52
Negroponte, John, 42, 138, 144
Neoliberalism
 in Chile, 167
 consequences of, 35, 44–45, 95, 127, 166
 and drug wars, 115
 economic policies of, 43, 75, 92, 117
 indigenous populations and, 78
 opposition to, 24, 123, 125, 145, 155
Nicaragua, 15t, 92t, 97, 98
 Iraq war involvement of, 204–205
 U.S. foreign policy in, 2, 13, 45, 83, 130 (*see also* Reagan, Ronald: Nicaragua policy of)
 U.S. military in, 36
Nigeria, 95, 135, 173
Nixon, Richard M., 1–2, 31, 185
Noboa, Álvaro, 116, 117
Non-Iberian South America, 195–200
Noriega, Manuel Antonio, 82f
Noriega, Roger, 146, 193
North American Free Trade Agreement (NAFTA), 44, 56, 59, 66, 73, 75, 76, 77f, 78, 128
North Korea, 11, 18
Nuclear energy and programs, 142, 147
Nuclear free zone, 27, 147
Nuclear weapons, assessment of, 26, 27

Oaxaca, 59, 56,67, 74–76, 79
O'Grady, Mary Anastasia, 52, 117, 150, 151
Oil. *See* Petroleum
OPEC (Organization of Petroleum Exporting Countries), 56, 101
Operation Condor, 136
Organization of American States (OAS), 28, 30, 57, 104, 106, 140, 141, 148, 153, 177
 exports through, 134
 Haiti watched by, 191
 members, relations among, 25, 45, 46, 118, 161

Organization of Petroleum Exporting Countries (OPEC), 56, 101
Organized crime, 7, 64, 99, 111, 114, 173
Ortega, Daniel, 91, 149, 202

Pakistan, 148, 201
Panama, 82f, 84, 84f, 92, 97, 98
 Chinese presence in, 10, 50, 92, 93, 93f, 94f
 Colombian civil war and, 108
 trade agreements with, 44
 treaties with, 38
 U.S. foreign policy in, 2, 3, 36, 50, 92, 97
Panama Canal, 50, 83, 84, 90, 93f, 97, 173
 alternatives to, 85, 97
 Chinese control of port facilities, 93f, 94f, 96
 treaties, 92–93
Paraguay
 authoritarian government support in, 24
 corruption in, 21, 165, 166
 ethnic composition of, 157
Paramilitary groups, 166
 in Colombia, 90, 108, 110–111, 114, 122
 in Mexico, 78, 79
Partisanship and threat perception, 12–14
Peace, 30, 31, 205
Peru, 138
 civil wars in, 135–138
 drug production in, 205
 elections in, 119–120, 149
 ethnic composition of, 102
 low-level conflict in, 6–7
 military in, 110
 natural resources in, 96
 poverty in, 137
 terrorism in, 34, 54, 137, 138, 205
 trade agreements with, 44
 U.S. relations with, 102
PetroCaribe, 132–133, 144
Petroleum
 in Andean region, 101, 102, 105, 123, 126, 127, 130f, 132, 135
 in Beagle Channel, 162
 in Belize, 89
 China as consumer of, 10, 95–96
 concessions cancellation in Ecuador, 119
 industry, 55–56, 95, 117
 in non-Iberian South America, 196, 197
 pipeline controversies, 103–104, 105, 126, 134
 politics of, 103–104, 105, 129–135

sale of, 89, 133, 134, 142
security concerns tied to, 107
U.S. access to, 36
Petropolitics and pipeline wars, 103–104, 105, 126, 134
Pinochet, Augusto, 105, 161, 166–167, 168–169, 171
Pinochet Precedent, 168–169
PIPA/Knowledge Network, 31–32
Plan Colombia, 113–114, 160, 201
Police, 7, 61, 86
  in Darién Gap, 84f
  and military roles, blurring of, 31, 78
Policymaking, 13, 30, 31, 204
Political ideology, 12, 53–54, 167, 197
Political instability, 50, 53, 60, 196
Populism, 12, 23, 117, 123f, 129, 153–155, 159, 194
Poverty, 7, 16, 10, 20, 100
  democracy undermined by, 92
  in free trade aftermath, 45
  in Latin America, 57, 58, 65, 75, 76, 81, 83, 91, 97–100, 103, 157
  as pressing social issue, 204
  as security issue, 10, 57
  terrorism link to, 57, 76
  as threat, 57, 154
  U.S. blamed for, 199
Preemption, doctrine of, 23, 53, 178
Préval, René, 191, 192–193, 194
Prisoners, 35f, 40, 49, 188f, 198–191, 205
Private military contractors, 39, 42–43, 90, 203
Privatization
  consequences of, 124
  of health care and social security programs, 168
  Latin America-initiated, 129
  as neoliberalism component, 43
  opposition to, 128

Radical populism, 12, 23, 153–155
Reagan, Ronald W.
  Communism threat assessment by, 1, 34
  Falklands War British support by, 164
  hegemony revival attempts of, 38
  Nicaragua policy of, 2, 9, 13, 83 (see also Iran-Contra scandal)
  Panama Canal treaties opposed by, 92–93
Reagan Doctrine, 38, 83

Refugees
  in Bolivia, Guyana, and Venezuela, 16
  from Colombia, 108
  from Cuba, 50, 180
  post-9/11 attitudes toward, 18, 19, 71
Regime change
  Cold War *versus* post-Cold War, 24, 31
  in Cuba, U.S. attempts at, 34, 178, 183, 187
  enemy nations targeted for, 34–35
  intervention for, 41
  negative consequences of, 33, 39
  in Panama, 82f
  populism as justification for, 154
  in Venezuela, attempted, 118, 146, 151, 152–153
Republican Party, 12–13, 31–32, 51, 72–73, 183–184
Resources. *See also* Copper; Minerals; Petroleum
  access to, 36
  bauxite, 196, 197
  conflicts over, 161–162, 196, 197
  Latin America as source of, 10
  natural, 95, 96, 101, 103, 125–126
Rice, Condoleezza, 4, 152, 193–194
Risk assessment theory, 14–18
Ruíz, Ulises, 67, 74, 75, 76
Rumsfeld, Donald H., 52, 53, 87, 138, 151, 152, 153, 169
Russia. *See also* Union of Soviet Socialist Republics (USSR)
  crime groups and mafias from, 173
  military equipment from, 145
  Venezuelan petroleum for, 133
  Venezuelan ties with, 141, 142

Salida al Mar controversy, 103, 104–106, 126
Sandinista revolution, 13, 83, 91
Saudi Arabia
  petroleum reserves in, 95, 142
  as terrorist source, 201
  U.S. support for, 200
School of the Americas (*renamed* Western Hemisphere Institute of Security Cooperation, WHINSEC), 39, 121, 122, 146
Second-Cuba policy, 177–178
Security
  collective systems of, 45
  economic inequality impact on, 45
  enhancement of, 46

Security (*continued*)
  overemphasis on, 155, 203, 204, 205
  post-Cold War issues of, 9–10
Security threats, 12, 47, 204
  in Caribbean, 186
  in Central America, 89
  and Darién Gap controversy, 85
  immigration and, 61
  Islamic radicals as, 199
  in Mexico, 54, 76
  new ways of dealing with, 23–24, 34, 204
  nontraditional, 10, 28
  perceived in Latin America, 201–202, 205
  populism and, 153–154
  response to, 23–25, 45
  terminology associated with, 50
  in Venezuela, 146
September 11 attacks
  factors contributing to, 5
  immigration following, 70
  Latin America ignored in aftermath of, 18
  terrorist plots, others compared to, 199
  U.S.-Cuba relations following, 181, 183
  U.S. hegemony efforts following, 38
  U.S.-Mexico relations following, 57
Shifter, Michael, 63, 126–127, 129, 140, 149
Shining Path (Sendero Luminoso, SL), 7, 34, 103, 104, 136–137, 136*f*, 138
Silva, Luiz Inácio Lula da, 126, 159, 161
Smith, James T., 22, 23, 31, 167
Social exclusion, 10, 98, 154
Socialism
  in Andean region, 102
  communal, 126
  in Cuba, 179
  of democratically elected leaders, 31, 102, 152
  perceptions of, 3
  terminology of, 53
Social services
  expenditures, decreased for, 43, 45
  for illegal immigrants, 70
  providing, 22
  unequal distribution of, 7
Socioeconomic inequality, 92, 139
Soto Cano base, Honduras, 37*t*, 40, 189
South Asia, 177, 201
SOUTHCOM (U.S. Southern Command), 27, 132, 147, 154, 173, 180
Southern Cone
  Chávez support in, 141
  economic conditions in, 166
  hot spots, potential in, 138, 159, 162, 165
  nuclear weapons programs shelved in, 27
  overview of, 157–158
Sovereignty, national, 47, 68. *See also* Latin American sovereignty
Spain
  military equipment from, 145–146
  petroleum companies in, 134
  Venezuela ties with, 142
State
  downsizing role of, 20
  weak, 46, 57, 58
State Department, 52, 58, 142–143, 173, 178, 185–186, 192
Strong-man rule, 7, 12, 101, 103
Suriname
  environmental protection in, 161
  as hot spot, 186
  military coups in, 198
  Muslims in, 173
  overview of, 195, 196
  politics and government in, 198
  terrorism potential in, 205
Syria, Venezuela alliance with, 51, 148, 151, 205

Taiwan, 93, 95, 173
Terrorism
  aid against, 76
  in Amazon Basin, 161
  in Andean region, 7, 108, 109, 111, 114, 115, 135, 136*f*, 137, 142
  border security and, 11, 64
  Brazilian addressing of, 159
  Caribbean-South American, 196, 198–200
  in Central America, 83, 85, 87, 90, 98, 100
  Chávez, H., suspected of ties to, 142, 147–148, 150
  in Colombia, 16, 54, 113*t*
  combating, goal of, 28, 36, 148
  conditions breeding, 28, 100
  confronting, progress in, 203
  counter-terrorism strategy, 25–26, 174–175
  diplomacy and, 26
  drug wars and, 103 (*see also* Narcoterrorism)
  economic sanctions as tool against, 41

Index

eliminating, 39
exaggeration of threats from, 32, 34
factors contributing to, 205
fear of, playing on, 9
and gang activity, 88, 89
immigration debates, impact on, 11, 64
insurgencies compared to, 184
internal conflict role in, 204
in Mexico, 57, 68
military expansion and intervention as factor in, 33
Morales, E., suspected of, 125, 129
overemphasis on, 155
in Peru, 54, 103
as post-Cold War security issue, 10, 50, 53
post-9/11 attitude toward, 18, 19
poverty link to, 57, 76
Republican emphasis on combating, 12
in Southern Cone, 158
state-sponsored, 135, 182, 183, 186
in Tri-Border Area (TBA), 172–176
U.S. *versus* H. Chávez views on, 144
U.S. *versus* Mexican views on, 28
war on (*see* War on terrorism)
weak states associated with, 58
weed analogy, 1–2
Terrorists
disenfranchised groups, exploitation by, 205
as elected leaders, 23, 25
failed states as source of, 14
forceful dealings with, rationale for, 12
harboring of, 52
infiltration from Mexico, 58, 59, 60, 64, 68
Latin American organizations, 4, 28, 39, 46, 86, 110, 173–174, 198–211 (*see also* Gangs)
organizations and networks, 7, 39, 113*t*
origin of, 201
safe haven for, 205
smuggling of, 132
Threat assessments
credibility, 34
ideological aspects of, 31
Islamic radicals and, 4, 173–174, 198–200
left-populist politicians and, 23
pattern, long-standing, 26
pressure concerning, 11
psychological aspects of, 32

by United States *versus* Latin America, 28, 154
U.S. hegemony impact on, 36
weapons of mass destruction (*see under* Weapons of mass destruction)
Threat definition, dilemmas of, 25–31
Threat inflation and exaggeration
government role in, 32–33
by intelligence community, 202
media role in, 2
motives behind, 45–46
nature of, 204
Threat perception
in Executive Branch, 5–12
factors affecting, 53
globalization impact on, 50
hot spot terminology reflecting, 1–2, 7, 33, 202
and intervention, 33–35
media influence on, 2, 32, 33–34, 53, 151–152
partisanship and, 12–14
political attitudes and behavior, impact on, 31–33
post-9/11, 18–20, 19*t*
and response strategies, 40
Threat presentation
during Cold War, 34
psychological and political nature of, 10–11
Threat response, 23–25, 39–46, 40
Threats
causes of, 4
defined, 17
emerging, 4, 7
nontraditional, 28, 46
terminology associated with, 10
to U.S. *versus* Latin American democratic states, 47
Torture
in Cold War era, 135
Democratic emphasis on avoiding, 12
public opinion on, 36
in Southern Cone, 158
survivors, demonstrations by, 35*f*
in U.S. military detention centers, 169, 189
Trade
Brazilian addressing of, 159
embargos, 41
fair, 205
Latin America as source of, 10, 30

Trade (*continued*)
   liberalization of, 30, 78
   ties, formation and consolidation of, 144–145
Transnacionales (foreign oil companies), 124, 129
Transparency International (TI), 20–21, 193
Tri-Border Area (TBA), 109, 138
   corruption in, 176
   hot spots, potential in, 158, 159
   investigations of, 199
   protest demonstrations in, 172*f*
   terrorism in, 172–176, 204
Trinidad and Tobago
   bilateral investment treaties with, 44
   Muslims in, 173
   terrorist suspects from, 198, 199, 200
Tupac Amaru Revolutionary Movement (MRTA), 104, 137, 138

Undocumented population. *See also* Illegal immigrants and immigration
   Central American, 69*f*
   employment of, 74
   figures for, 60
   legal status of, 57, 74
Unemployment
   in Central America, 90, 99, 100
   in Colombia, 111
   in free trade aftermath, 45
   in Mexico, 56, 73, 74, 75
   in non-Iberian South America, 197
   as social issue, 204
   in Southern Cone, 157
   in Venezuela, 149
Ungoverned spaces
   in Andean region, 106–108, 110
   in Caribbean, 183
   terrorists in, 205
Union of Soviet Socialist Republics (USSR). *See also* Russia
   arms race with, 28
   Chile relations with, 31
   collapse of, 20
   conventional war, low-cost against, 2
   Cuba relations with, 184
   hot spots, role in, 1
   Latin American threat potential of, 9, 14
   materials access interruption, potential by, 50
   post-Cold War threats compared to, 138
   threat assessments for, 38, 45
United Kingdom, 165, 196
United Nations
   collective security role of, 45
   Democratic support of, 12
   economic sanctions backed by, 42
   and peacekeepers, 194
United Nations Development Program (UNDP), 100, 118
United Nations Human Development Index, 98, 99*t*, 157, 193
United Nations Security Council, 20, 95, 141, 151
United Nations Stabilization Mission in Haiti (MINUSTAH), 192
United Self-Defense Forces of Colombia (AUC), 90, 110, 111
Unstable governments, 46–47
Uribe, Álvaro, 16, 106, 107, 108, 110, 111, 112, 202
Uruguay
   populism in, 194
   as Southern Cone nation, 157
   as stable state, 15
U.S. Border Patrol, 59, 71
U.S. business interests, 28, 43, 150
U.S.-China relations, 96
U.S. Citizenship and Immigration Services (USCIS), 58
U.S. Congress, 11, 42, 46–47, 49–50, 59, 84, 202
U.S. defense spending, 19, 32, 36
U.S. drug policy, 114–116, 123, 144, 185
U.S. economic aid
   during Cold War, 43
   to Colombia, 201
   Democratic emphasis on, 12
   for drug wars, 114
   to Haiti, 193
   under Republican leadership, 39, 40, 40*t*
   and Venezuela, 132–133, 143–144
U.S. foreign policy
   China impact on, 93, 96
   evidence presented for, 32
   global views on, 25
   goals of, 2–3, 28–30, 29*t*, 38, 59, 71, 96
   Latin American views on, 29–30, 202, 205
   military intervention to prop up, 34
   and outsourcing, 43
   partisan differences in, 2–3
   post-9/11, 200
   security threats stemming from, 2–3

Index

threats, perceived to, 155
U.S. foreign policy, opposition to
   Caribbean states, 177, 192
   from elected leaders, 23, 24–25
   threat perception based on, 14, 22
U.S. hegemony, 33, 35–39, 47, 50, 52, 92, 96, 147, 178, 204
U.S. influence in Latin America
   Chinese impact on, 93, 94f
   hegemony as avenue for, 36
   Latin American views on, 28, 32
   leftist shift impact on, 3, 30, 38, 122
   undermining of, 40, 49, 50, 132–133, 143, 144, 145, 148
U.S. interests. *See also* Resources; *specific resource type, e.g.*: petroleum
   versus corporate interests, 43
   Latin American democracy, conflict with, 23
   threats to, perceived, 18–20, 19t, 126, 202
U.S.-Latin American relations, 29–30, 47, 205. *See also* term U.S. relations with *under name of country, e.g.*: Venezuela: U.S. relations with
U.S.-Mexico border
   anti-immigration fears and, 51
   closing, economic consequences of, 70
   highway from, 84
   as hot spot, 60
   overview of, 58
U.S. military aid
   to Argentina, 173
   to Bolivia, 121
   to Colombia, 114, 201
   to Ecuador, 108
   to Mexico, 76
   pitfalls of, 132, 203
   against populism, 154
   versus regime change, 41
   Republican support for, 12, 39–40, 40t
   threat perception role in attitudes toward, 32
   Venezuelan *versus* U.S., 143–144
U.S. military bases abroad
   counter-drug operations of, 36, 39, 90, 115, 185
   limitations of, 203
   network of, 3
   opposition to, 160
   in Panama, 92
   public opinion on, post-9/11, 19
   purpose of, 37t, 40
   spending on, 36
   trends, current in, 39, 90
U.S. military intervention
   in Andean region, 117
   anti-populist, 154
   in Cuba, 182
   versus diplomacy for regime change, 41
   Iraq war compared to, 9
   limitations and pitfalls of, 22, 30
   in Mexico, 56
   preemptive, 23
   public opinion on, 32, 36
   reasons for, 11, 33, 34–35, 49, 52, 100, 132
U.S. public opinion, 28. *See also* term public opinion on *under topic, e.g.*: Iraq war: public opinion on
U.S. Southern Command (SOUTHCOM), 27, 132, 147, 154, 173, 180
U.S. Supreme Court, 189, 190
U.S. trade policies, 152, 205. *See also* Free trade

Venezuela. *See also* Bolivarian Revolution; Chávez, Hugo
   alliances of, 50
   as Andean nation, 101
   authoritarianism in, 46
   Bolivia and, 104, 146
   border conflict involvement, 106
   Brazil relations with, 159
   Colombian civil war impact on, 108
   Colombia relations with, 107
   corruption in, 21, 135, 150
   coup attempts in, 47, 118, 152, 153
   crime in, 149
   Cuban relations, 50, 51, 133, 144, 149, 151
   democracy in, 117–118, 142–143, 149, 150, 151, 202
   drug production in, 185
   economy of, 142, 149
   elections in, 102
   ethnic composition of, 102
   hostility toward, 18
   as hot spot, 138, 142, 152
   as intervention candidate, 17
   Iranian influence in, 198
   Mexico, influence on, 62
   Middle East ties of, 205
   natural resources of, 95, 101, 132, 135, 141, 146

Venezuela (*continued*)
  Nicaragua relations with, 146
  Pakistan relations with, 148
  People's Trade Agreement signed by, 186
  petroleum exports by, 132–134, 141–142, 144, 153
  political turmoil in, 50
  post-9/11 attitudes toward, 19
  poverty in, 149
  regime change advocated for, 10
  regional influence of, 129
  spending by, 143–144
  Syria alliance with, 51, 148, 151, 205
  terrorism, potential in, 205
  terrorist ties, suspected of, 202–203
  threat assessments for, 11, 51–52, 147, 151, 202
  as unstable nation, 24
  U.S. influence undermined by, 40
  U.S. natural gas supplied by, 133
  U.S. press coverage of, 151–152
  U.S. relations with, 52, 88, 107, 133–134, 140, 145–146
Vietnam
  El Salvador compared to, 13
  preventing scenarios resembling, 1, 2
  U.S. foreign policy in, 2
Violence
  in Andean region, 103
  in Central America, 81, 91, 100
  conditions breeding, 100
  drug-related, 56, 67
  labor union, 110
  in Mexico, 67
  pandemic, 7
  political, 203
  in Southern Cone, 165, 166

War of the Pacific, 1879-1884, 103, 104, 105, 171
War on drugs
  in Andean region, 102, 103, 112–116, 125
  in Central America, 83
  impact of, 30–31
  in Mexico, 60, 61–64
  military involvement in, 20
  Nixon's declaration of, 185
  opposition to, 125, 151
  threat perceptions, impact on, 18
War on terrorism
  abuses in name of, 205

Bolivia-Chile relations in, 105
border security and, 60
Cold War policies compared to, 46, 184
concept of, 26
hegemony role in, 36, 38
hot spots with roots in, 200
human rights violations in, 189
immigration and, 51, 70–71
Latin America and, 18, 30–31, 204–205
military aid linked to, 39
U.S.-Brazil relations in wake of, 158
U.S.-Cuba relations in wake of, 190–191
U.S.-Mexico relations in wake of, 57
Venezuela as obstacle to, 151
Washington Consensus, 65, 122–123, 128
Washington Office on Latin America (WOLA), 4, 63, 146
Watch list, 7, 24, 173, 204
Wealth distribution, 7, 65, 124, 166
Weapons, 14, 53. *See also* Arms trafficking
Weapons of mass destruction
  fear of, 18
  preventing acquisition of, 20
  proliferation of, 10, 148
  threat assessment for, 26–27
Western Hemisphere Institute of Security Cooperation (WHINSEC) (*formerly* School of the Americas), 39, 121, 122, 146
WOLA. *See* Washington Office on Latin America
World Bank, 7, 21
  Bolivia, economic medicine impact on, 128
  leadership-economy connection emphasized by, 187
  Magdaleno Medio region aid, 122
  opposition to policies and control of, 129, 145

Youth gangs
  in Central America, 83, 85–88, 98, 99
  in Colombia, 111
  in Southern Cone, 166

Zapatista Army of National Liberation (Ejército Revolucionario Popular, ERP), 52, 67, 68
Zapatista rebellion, 59, 60, 76–79, 77*f*

About the Author

DAVID W. DENT is Professor Emeritus of Political Science at Towson University in Baltimore, Maryland. He is the author of *Historical Dictionary of U.S.-Latin American Relations* (Greenwood, 2005), *Encyclopedia of Modern Mexico* (2002), *The Legacy of the Monroe Doctrine: A Reference Guide to U.S. Involvement in Latin America and the Caribbean* (Greenwood, 1999), and the co-author of *Historical Dictionary of Inter-American Organizations* (Scarecrow Press, 1998). Dent is the author of over 100 articles, essays, and chapters on Latin American and U.S.-Latin American relations. For over 30 years he has been a contributing editor of the *Handbook of Latin American Studies*, a biannual reference book published by the Hispanic Division of the Library of Congress in Washington, D.C.